Computational Principles of Mobile Robotics

Mobile robotics is a multidisciplinary field involving computer science and engineering. Addressing the design of automated systems, it lies at the intersection of artificial intelligence, computational vision, and robotics.

Unlike the robots of Isaac Asimov and other popular writers of science fiction, actual autonomous robots must negotiate the reality of moving, sensing, and reasoning out their environment. This book approaches these three tasks and describes the way in which existing robotic systems have addressed them.

Computational Principles of Mobile Robotics emphasizes the computational methods of programming robotics rather than the methods of constructing the hardware. The book is divided into three major parts:

- Locomotion – Concentrates on wheeled and legged mobile robots with briefer discussions of aquatic robots, aerovehicles, and space-borne robots.
- Sensing – Examines vision-based and nonvisual sensor technologies with a description of algorithms for the analysis of data from a number of sensing technologies, including sonar, vision, and laser scanners.
- Reasoning – Describes common software architectures used to represent and reason about space and explores the issues related to spatial representation with an emphasis on the problems of navigation, pose estimation, and autonomous exploration.

Advanced undergraduate and graduate students and researchers in the field of mobile robotics will find this book useful as a comprehensive treatment of the range of issues in the field.

Gregory Dudek is an Associate Professor of Computer Science and the Director of the Mobile Robotics Laboratory at McGill University.

Michael Jenkin is an Associate Professor and Chair of the Computer Science Department at York University. He has coedited three books on human and machine vision.

Computational Principles of Mobile Robotics

Gregory Dudek
School of Computer Science
McGill University

Michael Jenkin
Department of Computer Science
York University

CAMBRIDGE
UNIVERSITY PRESS

PUBLISHED BY THE PRESS SYNDICATE OF THE UNIVERSITY OF CAMBRIDGE
The Pitt Building, Trumpington Street, Cambridge, United Kingdom

CAMBRIDGE UNIVERSITY PRESS
The Edinburgh Building, Cambridge CB2 2RU, UK   http://www.cup.cam.ac.uk
40 West 20th Street, New York, NY 10011-4211, USA   http://www.cup.org
10 Stamford Road, Oakleigh, Melbourne 3166, Australia
Ruiz de Alarcón 13, 28014 Madrid, Spain

First published 2000

Printed in the United States of America

Typeface Times Roman 10.5/13 pt.   *System* LaTeX 2_ε [TB]

A catalog record for this book is available from the British Library.

Library of Congress Cataloging in Publication Data
Dudek, Gregory, 1958–
    Computational principles of mobile robotics / Gregory Dudek.
   Michael Jenkin.
      p.   cm.
   Includes bibliographical references.
    1. Mobile robots.   I. Jenkin, Michael (Michael Richard MacLean).
   1959–   .   II. Title.
    TJ211.415.D83   2000
    629.8′92 – dc21   99-18285
                                                 CIP

ISBN 0 521 56021 7 hardback
ISBN 0 521 56876 5 paperback

For Krys and Heather

Contents

Acknowledgments

This book would not have been possible without the active support of our students and colleagues who suffered through early drafts, provided imagery and papers, and who put up with us while this volume was put together. The list of people who helped is much too long to include here, but some require special mention: the International Joint Conference on Artificial Intelligence (IJCAI), for letting us do a tutorial on mobile robotics that started us on the journey; students at McGill and York, including Eric Bourque, Saul Simhon and Yiannis Rekleitis, who suffered with photocopies of early drafts; Professor Milios for his helpful comments and Professor Papadopoulos for his help on space robots; Rob Sim for his figures; and Louis Dudek for his proofreading and helpful comments.

Finally, we would like to thank Lauren Cowles and Cambridge University Press for letting us do this in the first place.

1

Overview and motivation

"Let's start with the three fundamental Rules of Robotics – the three rules that are built most deeply into a robot's positronic brain." In the darkness, his gloved fingers ticked off each point.

"We have: one, a robot may not injure a human being, or through inaction, allow a human being to come to harm."

"Right!"

"Two," continued Powell, "a robot must obey the orders given it by human beings except where such orders would conflict with the First Law."

"Right!"

"And three, a robot must protect its own existence as long as such protection does not conflict with the First or Second Laws."*

(Powell and Donovan discuss the laws of robotics)

The ability to navigate purposefully is fundamental to most animals and to every intelligent organism. In this book we examine the computational issues specific to the creation of machines that move intelligently in their environment. From the earliest modern speculation regarding the creation of autonomous robots, it was recognized that, regardless of the mechanisms used to move the robot around or the methods used to sense the environment, the computational principles that govern the robot are of paramount importance. As Powell and Donovan discovered in Isaac Asimov's novel *Runaround*, subtle definitions within the programs that control a robot lead to significant changes in the robot's overall behavior or action.

Mobile robotics is a relatively new research area that deals with the control of autonomous and semiautonomous vehicles. What sets *mobile robotics* apart from other research areas such as conventional manipulator robotics, artificial intelligence, and computer vision is the emphasis on problems related to the understanding of *large-scale space*; that is, regions of space substantially larger than those that can be observed from a single vantage point. Although at first blush the distinction between sensing in large-scale space, with its requirement for mobility, and local sensing may appear obscure, it has far-reaching implications. To behave in a large-scale environment not only implies dealing with the incremental acquisition of knowledge, the estimation of positional error, the ability to

---

* Asimov [19], p. 99. Reprinted from I. Asimov's *Runaround*, which appeared in *The Asimov Chronicles: Volume One*, An Ace Book. Published by permission of the Estate of Issac Asimov c/o Ralph M. Vicinanza, Ltd.

recognize important or familiar objects or places, and real-time response, but it requires that all these functionalities be exhibited in concert. This issue of extended space influences all of mobile robotics; the tasks of moving through space, sensing about space, and reasoning about space are fundamental problems within the study of mobile robotics. The study of mobile robots in general, and this volume in particular, can be decomposed into the study of these three subproblems.

Mobile robots are not only a collection of algorithms for sensing, reasoning, and moving about space; they are also physical embodiments of these algorithms and ideas that must cope with all of the vagaries of the real world. As such, mobile robots provide a reality check for theoretical concepts and algorithms. Mobile robotics is the domain where literally the "rubber meets the road" for many algorithms in path planning, knowledge representation, sensing, and reasoning.

In the context of humanity's ongoing quest to construct more capable machines, machines that match or even surpass human capabilities, the development of systems that exhibit mobility is a key hurdle. The importance of spatial mobility can be appreciated by observing that there are very few sophisticated biological organisms that cannot move or accomplish spatially distributed tasks in their environment. Just as the development of the wheel (and hence wheeled vehicles) marked a turning point in the evolution of manually operated tools, the development of mobile robots is an important stepping stone in the development of sophisticated machines.

Many different terms have come to be applied to the field of autonomous systems or mobile robotics. The words *autonomous*, as in autonomous system, and *automaton* have their roots in the Greek for *self-willed* (*auto + matos*: $\alpha \upsilon \tau o \ \mu \alpha \tau o \varsigma$). The term *robot* itself was introduced by Karel Čapek in his 1923 play R.U.R. (R.U.R. stands for Rossum's Universal Robots). The word robot is derived from the Czech or Polish words *robota*, meaning "labor," and *robotnik*, meaning "workman." It is interesting to note that the word automaton implies a degree of self-will that is not conveyed by the term robot, and that the word *autonomous robot* might be construed as self-contradictory.

Robots manufactured following the same general structure as humans are known as *anthropomorphic robots*, and, in fiction, robots indistinguishable from humans are sometimes known as *androids*. More generally, the imitation of biological organisms in robotics is referred to as *biomimetic robotics*.

Although androids are beyond today's technology, anthropomorphic robots and robots with anthropomorphic features are quite common. There are many reasons researchers develop robots in an anthropomorphic mold. In addition to a desire to develop an agent in "one's own image," there are practical reasons for developing systems with anthropomorphic features. The operating environment for many mobile robots is the same environment that humans inhabit, and we have adapted our environment to suit our own performance specifications. By mimicking human structures, at least at an operational or functional level, a robot may be better suited to operate in our environment. Human physiology, perception, and cognitive processes have been studied extensively. Thus, by using locomotive, sensing and reasoning systems based on biological models, roboticists can exploit the extensive literature that already exists in these fields. In addition, people seem to have a fascination with human-looking robots that goes beyond the pragmatic. That being said, mobile robots are not limited to mimicking existing biological systems, and many other mechanisms exist, from infrared sensors to alternative drive mechanisms, that can be exploited in the design of a mobile robot.

The study of mobile robots is an intrinsically interdisciplinary research area involving the following:

Mechanical engineering – vehicle design and in particular locomotive mechanisms.
Computer science – representations, sensing, and planning algorithms.
Electrical engineering – system integration, sensors, and communications.
Cognitive psychology, perception, and neuroscience – insights on how biological organisms solve similar problems.

Although most of the mobile robot systems currently in operation are experimental, some mobile robot systems are beginning to be deployed in industrial settings. Real applications in which current mobile robots have been successfully installed are characterized by one of more of the following attributes: an absence of an on-site human operator, a potentially high cost, and the need to tolerate environmental conditions that might not be acceptable to a human. As such, robots are especially well suited for tasks that exhibit one or more of the following characteristics:

- An inhospitable environment into which sending a human being would be either very costly or very dangerous.
- A remote environment into which sending a human operator would be too difficult or would take too long. An extreme instance is domains completely inaccessible to humans such as microscopic environments.
- A task with a very demanding duty cycle or a very high fatigue factor.
- A task that is highly disagreeable to a human.

Successful industrial applications for mobile robots typically involve more than one of these characteristics. Consider the application of mobile robotics to underground mining as an example. The environment is dangerous in that the possibility of rock fall or environmental contamination due to the release of hazardous gas or dust is quite real. The environment is remote in that humans operating in underground mines must travel considerable distances, typically many kilometers, to reach the rock face being worked. At the rock face, the miner is confronted with an operational environment that can be cramped, poorly illuminated, hot, and dangerous. Other ideal robotic operational environments include nuclear, extraterrestrial, and underwater environments.

Mobile robots are feats of engineering. The actuators, processors, user interfaces, sensors, and communication mechanisms that permit a mobile robot to operate must be integrated so as to permit the entire system to function as a complete whole. The physical structure of a mobile robot is complex, requiring a considerable investment of human and financial resources to keep it operating. *Robot wranglers** are an essential component for the successful operation of any robotic system. Thus, one of the goals of this book, in addition, to provoking new research, is to act as a reference for mobile robot tools and techniques for those who would develop or maintain a mobile robot. Rather than concentrating strictly on the sensors required for a mobile robot [116], or on the physical design of small autonomous robots [176], or collecting the seminal papers of the field [83], this

* Graduate students and technicians.

volume considers the computational processes involved in making a robot sense, reason, and move through its environment.

1.1   From Mechanisms to Computation

Robots can be considered from several different perspectives. At a physical, hardware, or mechanistic level, robots can be decomposed into the following:

- A mechanism for making the robot move through its environment; the physical organization of motors, belts, and gears necessary to make the robot move.
- A computer or collection of computers for controlling the robot.
- A collection of sensors with which the robot gathers information concerning its environment.
- Communications hardware to enable the robot to communicate to an offboard operator and any externally based computers. Typical examples include serial or Ethernet connections (both wireless and direct).

At the device level, the hardware details can be abstracted, and a robot can be considered as

- A software level abstraction of the motors, encoders, and motor driver boards that allow the robot to move. Most mobile robot hardware manufacturers provide support for the underlying hardware at this level rather than force the user to deal with the details of actually turning the motors.
- Software level mechanisms or libraries to provide access to the robot's sensors. For example, the current image obtained by a video camera as an array of intensities.
- A standard communications mechanism such as a serial interface or one distributed across a network to the outside world.

From a still more abstract perspective, we can consider mobile robots at a purely computational level such that the sensors, communications, and locomotive systems are seen simply as software modules that enable the robot to interact with its environment. Typical components in a software architecture include the following:

- A motion control subsystem,
- A sensor control subsystem,
- A sensor interpretation subsystem.

Even higher levels of abstraction exist. The term *cognitive robotics* is used to refer to the use of artificial intelligence techniques within a mobile robot and often assumes the existence of an idealized computational abstraction of the robot.

1.2   Historical Context

1.2.1   Autonomous Robots in Fiction

Autonomous devices have a long and checkered past in legend and literature. From ancient legends to modern films and literature, many different robots and robotlike devices have been constructed to extend the will of their creator or owner. Much of the fictional literature on autonomous systems is cautionary: the robot may follow its instructions too literally, or it may grow to have a will of its own and not follow its instructions at all. For example, in Issac Asimov's story *Runaway*, a robot is told to "get lost," which of course it does, whereas *Robots of Empire* and *Robots of Dawn,* also by Issac Asimov, describe the process of robots' evolving their own rules of operation. Given their supposed infallibility, fictional robots have also been proposed as final arbitrators of judgment. For example, in the film *The Day the Earth Stood Still*, Gort is a universal policeman who enforces the law without being influenced by sentiment.

Perhaps the earliest reference to a robot in literature can be found in Greek mythology*. According to ancient Greek or Cretan mythology, Talos was an animated giant man made of bronze who guarded the island of Crete. Talos guarded the island and enforced the law. One of Talos' flaws was that he was too literal-minded in the interpretation of his directives, and thus he became a burden by refusing to permit even normal travel to and from the island. Even in this legend, problem specification and representation were issues! This notion of the robot as protector also appears in Jewish folklore. According to legend, in sixteenth-century Prague, the Jewish population turned to a Golem to protect it from the Gentiles who wanted to kill them. The rabbi fashioned the Golem out of clay and breathed life into it.

Clay and bronze are not the only potential building materials for fictional robots. In works of fiction, autonomous agents can also be constructed out of biological components. In 1818, Mary Shelley wrote *Frankenstein* which tells the well-known story of Dr. Frankenstein and his efforts to animate dead tissue. As one recent job advertisement put it, "Dr. Frankenstein was more than just a scientist – he was an electrical engineer with the creative capability for bringing extraordinary ideas to life." Nor are all fictional accounts of robots based on anthropomorphic designs. In his 1880 story, *The Demon of Cawnpore*, Jules Verne describes a steam-powered elephant, and more recently *Blade Runner (Do Androids Dream of Electric Sheep)* [96] describes a world in which animals are almost extinct and robotic pets are popular.

Issac Asimov is often regarded as the father of robotics because of his introduction of the three laws of robotics. Introduced in 1942 in *Runaround* and reprinted at the beginning of this chapter, they are as follows:

1. A robot may not injure a human being, or, through inaction, allow a human being to come to harm.
2. A robot must obey the orders given it by human beings except when such orders would conflict with the first law.
3. A robot must protect its own existence as long as such protection does not conflict with the first or second laws.

In later works, Asimov added a zeroth law that required a robot not to injure humanity. Many of Asimov's stories center around robot (and human) attempts to find new definitions or loopholes in these laws.

Since the 1940s, mobile robots have become a common feature of science fiction literature and film. Famous fictional robots include Robbie (*Forbidden Planet*), Gort (*The Day the Earth Stood Still*), Rosie (*The Jetsons*), Robot (*Lost in Space*), Floyd (*Stationfall* and *Planetfall*), R2D2 and C3PO (*Star Wars*), Data and the partly biological Borg

---

* An earlier artificial human appears in the Taost *Lieh Tzu.*

Figure 1.1. A Dalek, a half-robot and half-biological creature from the BBC television series "Doctor Who." (Appears with the kind permission of Barry Angel.)

(*Star Trek*), HAL (*2001*), and of course Marvin, the paranoid android (*The Hitch-Hiker's Guide to the Galaxy*). More details on the evolution of robots in literature can be found in [18]. (See also [142].) It is interesting to note that fictional robots usually do not suffer from the computational, sensing, power, or locomotive problems that plague real robots. How the *Daleks* (see Figure 1.1) from the BBC television show "Dr. Who" managed to conquer most of the galaxy without having to navigate a set of stairs remains an unresolved mystery. On the other hand, fiction serves not only to predict the future but also to inspire those who might create it. Stork [342] provides some insights on the differences between a specific fictional autonomous system – HAL from 2001 – and the current state of the art in terms of real systems.

1.2.2   Early Autonomous Robots

Although fictional robots have progressed by leaps and bounds, the first steps towards real robotic systems were made during the early-to-mid-1940s. Norbert Wiener is considered the inventor of *cybernetics* and hence modern robotics. A mathematician, Wiener studied regulatory systems and their application to control. During the Second World War he was involved in a project to develop a controlling device for an antiaircraft gun. The development of such a device, which integrates sensory information (radar) via processing (simple control laws executing on an analog computer) into action (directing and firing the antiaircraft gun), resulted in one of the first robotic systems. As Wiener mused in his January 1949 article in *Electronics*,

> it has long been clear to me that the modern ultra-rapid computing machine was
> in principle an ideal central nervous system to an apparatus for automatic control;
> and its input and output need not be in the form of numbers or diagrams, but might

(a)   (b)

Figure 1.2. Analog robots: (a) Tesla's robot. (Reprinted by permission from Cheney, *Tesla: Man Out of Time*, [70].), (b) Walter's robot. (Photograph appears with the kind permission of Owen Holland.)

very well be, respectively, the readings of artificial sensors such as photoelectric cells or thermometers, and the performance of motors or solenoids.*

At the same time that Wiener was developing an automatic antiaircraft gun, work in Germany on the V1 and V2 – autonomous aircraft and self-guided rocketry – was establishing the basis for autonomous vehicle design. Although Wiener may be the father of cybernetics, and the V1 and V2 weapon systems are certainly early examples of fully autonomous systems, various autonomous vehicles built by Nikola Tesla in the 1890s are probably the earliest mobile robots. In the 1890s Tesla built wireless, radio-controlled vehicles [70]. One of his remote-controlled aquatic vehicles is shown in Figure 1.2(a).

W. Grey Walter built one of the earliest fully autonomous vehicles. Described in a series of articles published in 1950 and 1951 in *Scientific American* and in his book *The Living Brain* [374], Walter's electronic turtle (see Figure 1.2[b]) had phototube eyes, microphone ears, contact-switch feelers, and capacitors used as memory devices to perform associations. Dr. Walter named the robot Tortoise after the creature in *Alice in Wonderland*. The Tortoise performed tasks such as locating the recharging hutch and wandering without mishap.

With the development of digital computers came the potential of more complex mobile robots. Between 1966 and 1972, Nils Nilssen, Charles Rosen, and other researchers at

---

* *Electronics*, January 1949. Reprinted in [229].

the Stanford Research Institute developed Shakey, the first mobile robot to be operated using artificial intelligence techniques [267]. The 5-foot-tall robot used two stepper motors in a differential drive arrangement to provide locomotion and was equipped with touch-sensitive bumpers. An optical range finder and vidicon television camera with controllable focus and iris were mounted on a tilt platform for sensing. Offboard communication was provided via two radio channels, one for video and the other for command and control. Shakey is shown in Figure 1.3(a).

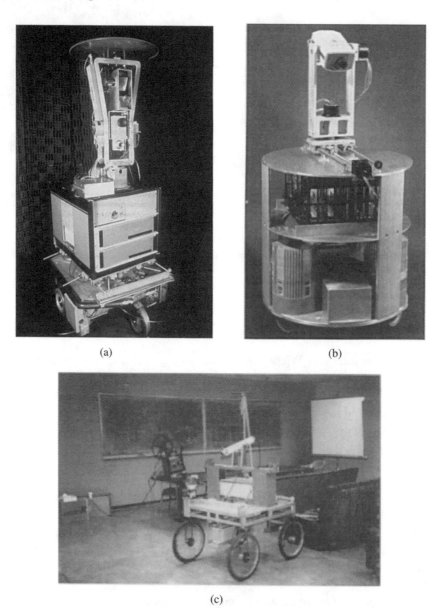

(a)   (b)

(c)

Figure 1.3. Early wheeled digital robots: (a) Shakey. (Reprinted by permission from Stork (Ed.), *Hal's Legacy* [342], 312.), (b) Carnegie Mellon University Rover and (c) Stanford cart. (Reprinted by permission from Moravec, "The Stanford Cart and the CMU Rover" [246], (c) 1983, IEEE.)

Work on Shakey concentrated on automated reasoning and planning that used logic-based problem solving based on STRIPS (the Stanford Research Institute Problem Solver). The control of movement and the interpretation of sensory data were secondary to this logic-based component. Simple video processing was used to obtain local information about empty floor space, and Shakey constructed a global map of its environment based on this information. A typical mission for Shakey was to find a box of a given size, shape, and color in one of a specified number of rooms and then to move it to a designated position. Shakey had to cope with obstacles and plan actions.

The Stanford cart [244, 245, 246] (see Figure 1.3[c]) was developed by a group including Hans Moravec at SAIL (the Stanford Artificial Intelligence Laboratory) between 1973 and 1979 and moved with Moravec to Carnegie–Mellon University in 1980. Throughout this period it underwent major modifications and served as the initial test device upon which solutions to several classic robot problems were developed. The Stanford cart relied on stereo vision to locate objects and planned paths to avoid sensed obstacles using a world model based on stereo data. The stereopsis algorithm was based on a single camera mounted on a sliding track perpendicular to the camera's optical axis. A single view of the environment was based on nine images taken at different positions along this track. A comparison of the images over time was used to determine the motion of the cart, whereas comparisons of the images from a single position were used to build an environmental model. The robot was controlled by an offboard computer program that drove the cart through cluttered spaces. The cart moved roughly 1 m every 10 to 15 minutes.

The kinematic structure of the Stanford cart introduced a number of limitations in the robot. Recognizing these limitations, the Carnegie Mellon University Rover project (started in 1980) developed a robot that relied on a synchronous drivelike assembly rather than the carlike steering of the Stanford cart. The Rover project (see Figure 1.3[b]) added infrared and sonar proximity sensors to the robot and modified the camera mount for the video sensor so that it could pan and tilt as well as slide, motions which were not possible with the Stanford cart.

Researchers working in France on another early robot system, the Hilare I project [54, 135] constructed an indoor mobile robot based on a differential drive system. Hilare's perceptual system relied on sonar units, a video camera, and a laser range finder. The laser and camera were mounted on a pan-and-tilt station to direct the sensor in different directions.

In parallel with these early wheeled mobile robots, legged robotic systems began to appear in the 1960s. The first legged or walking robots appeared in a patent for a mechanical horse in 1893, but it was not until the early 1960s that an operational walking vehicle was constructed. Perhaps the most famous of the early legged vehicles is the General Electric Quadruped [211, 249]. Each of the four legs of this vehicle had three simple joints; the knee joint was composed of a single joint, whereas the hip joint used two. The GE Quadruped was controlled by an onboard operator. In practice it was a very difficult device to control, although the vehicle did exhibit considerable mobility.

From the mid-1980s on, there was an explosion in mobile robot design. A number of companies began to manufacture and market off-the-shelf mobile robot platforms. With the availability of standard platforms, many different robotic projects emerged, but almost all can trace their underlying design to one of these early robot designs. Figure 1.4 shows a timeline of some of the earlier mobile robot systems, and a survey of mobile robot systems prior to 1986 can be found in [53].

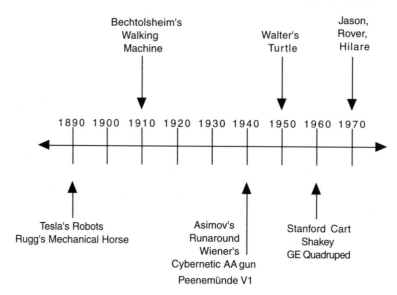

Figure 1.4. Early mobile robot timeline.

1.3   Operational Regimes

There are very few, if any, fully autonomous robots outside of highly constrained research environments. Most robots are designed to operate with some level of human guidance or control. Even autonomous systems are expected to obey their programming.

When a robotic system is described as being *fully autonomous*, the system is typically designed to operate without full-time external human control. This is to be distinguished from *semiautonomous* systems in which an operator is required full-time but where the robot is permitted to make certain decisions on its own. Within the continuum of semiautonomous systems, two different operational regimes can be identified: *teleoperated systems* in which the remote device is controlled moment by moment at a very low level, and *telerobotic systems* in which low-level operator commands are interpreted or filtered by complex software layers that may use sensors located on the robot to limit or interpret the operator's actions. Telerobotic systems include those in which an operators commands may serve as macros for more complex action sequences on the part of the robot.

1.4   Operational Modes

Simple robotic systems can be controlled by a single central processor. More sophisticated systems incorporate subsidiary processors to deal with real-time device control (such as the use of programmable microcontrollers to control and monitor sensors). As the processing needs of the robotic system increase, multiple computing units may be necessary, and the control of the robot becomes distributed over these processors. Because onboard computation is limited by weight and power consumption (not to mention economics), some of these processors may be deployed offboard at the far end of a slow

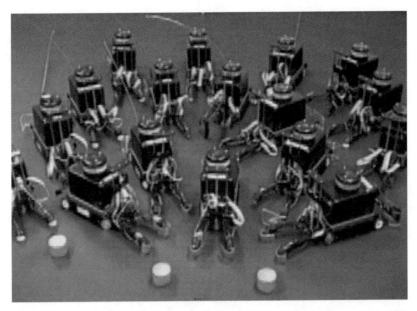

Figure 1.5. A swarm of robots, "The Nerd Herd: a family of 20 IS Robotics R1 mobile robots." (Reprinted by permission from Maja Mataric, photograph taken at the University of Southern California's Interaction Laboratory in Los Angeles.)

communications link. The effective distribution of tasks in such a heterogeneous environment can be very difficult. In addition to distributing the computation between multiple processors, some of which may be located offboard, it is also possible to distribute the robotic work over multiple robots. This *collective* or *swarm* of robots could itself be centrally controlled, or both the robotic task and the computation might be distributed. Figure 1.5 shows a sample robot collective. The design of a collective with distributed computation and task achievement is very complex.

1.5 A Guide to this Book

This book is organized along the themes of locomotion, sensing, and computation. Chapter 2 provides a brief overview of nonsensor robot hardware. It concentrates on different models of locomotion for wheeled robots but also considers other locomotive strategies. Chapters 3 and 4 cover visual and nonvisual sensors and their algorithms. Chapter 5 addresses the task of representing and reasoning about space, and Chapter 6 details how the software modules that make up a mobile robot can be constructed. Chapters 7 and 8 consider pose maintenance and maps. Finally, Chapter 9 provides a survey of practical robot tasks and the robots that have been constructed for them, and Chapter 10 looks forward to the future of mobile robots.

1.6 Problems

1. Many robot information sources are available, including the Internet and your local library. Identify which robotic journals are available locally and which robot

conference proceedings are available. Search the world wide web for the resources available there.

2. If a mobile platform is available locally, obtain a copy of the system documentation for the device. How is it powered, recharged, and controlled? Learn how to power the device on and off and how to control it via software.

3. Take a fictional robot from film or literature. What is the robot designed to do? How is the robot constructed? How does it sense its environment? How does it move about within its environment?

Part one

Locomotion

If a mobile robot is to do anything within its environment it must be able to move and it must be able to sense. The next three chapters consider exactly these issues.

Chapter 2 examines the problems involved in getting a robot to move. Although the vast majority of mobile robots are wheeled, technologies based on aquatic, limbed, and flying movement and even robots based on rocket propulsion exist. Regardless of the technology used to move the robot, two fundamental problems need to be addressed:

- Given the control inputs, how does the robot move? This is known as the forward kinematics problem.
- Given a desired motion, which control inputs should be chosen? This is known as the inverse kinematics problem.

These tasks are considered in some detail for wheeled and legged vehicles.

2

Mobile robot hardware

A mobile robot is a combination of various physical (hardware) and computational (software) components. In terms of hardware components, a mobile robot can be considered as a collection of subsystems for

Locomotion: how the robot moves through its environment;
Sensing: how the robot measures properties of itself and its environment;
Reasoning: how the robot maps these measurements into actions; and
Communication: how the robot communicates with an outside operator.

Later chapters consider the algorithms and representations that make these capabilities possible, whereas this chapter concentrates on the underlying hardware with a special emphasis on locomotion for wheeled robots.

2.1   Locomotion

locomotion *n*. Power of motion from place to place.*

Locomotion is the process of causing an autonomous robot or vehicle to move. In order to produce motion, forces must be applied to the vehicle. The study of motion in which these forces are modeled is known as *dynamics*, whereas *kinematics* is the study of the mathematics of motion without considering the forces that affect the motion. That is, kinematics deals with the geometric relationships that govern the system, whereas dynamics includes the energies and speeds associated with these motions. Here we will consider the kinematics of various locomotive strategies.

Although many different locomotion strategies have been proposed by mobile robot designers, a robot's motive system design is typically driven by the application and its domain: How fast must the robot move? Does the robot have to climb structures? Does the robot need to overfly the terrain? Is the application environment smooth or rough?

On the basis of the application domain, four broad categories of mobile robots have emerged:

Terrestrial. Terrestrial robots are those that walk on the ground. They are designed to take advantage of a solid support surface and gravity. Although the

---

* *The Concise Oxford Dictionary*, Oxford University Press, 1976.

most common terrestrial mobile robots are wheeled, robots exist that can walk, climb, roll, use tracks, or slither in order to move. Terrestrial robots are also known as ground-contact robots.

Aquatic. Aquatic robots operate in water, either at the surface or underwater. Most existing aquatic vehicles use either water jets or propellers to provide locomotion. Aquatic robotics is a potentially important application domain because not only is most of the Earth's surface covered with water, but much of the ocean is not readily accessible to humans.

Airborne. Airborne robot vehicles often mimic existing aircraft or birds. Robotic helicopters, fixed-wing aircraft, robotically controlled parachutes, and dirigibles have been developed. Flying robots share many issues with aquatic robots, including the need for energy output even to remain stationary.

Space. Space robots are designed to operate in the microgravity of outer space and are typically envisioned for space station maintenance. Various locomotive devices enable robots in these environments to move about their environment. The two main classes of robot are those that move by climbing (over a larger vehicle) and those that are independently propelled (known as free flyers).

2.1.1 Wheeled Mobile Robots

Mechanical devices such as wheels or limbs exploit friction or ground contact to enable the robot to move. Consider an idealized wheel as depicted in Figure 2.1. If the wheel is free to rotate about its axis (the x axis), the robot exhibits preferential rolling motion in one direction (in the direction of the y axis) and a certain amount of lateral slip. The actual net motion of the wheel may then be along the line z, but for low velocities rolling wheel motion is a reasonable model.

One of the most prevalent motion estimation techniques used on wheeled mobile robots is odometry; that is, the estimation of distance traveled by the measurement of how much the wheels have turned. The simplest case is a single freely rotating wheel. In the case

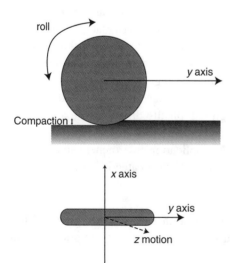

Figure 2.1. Side view and top view of an idealized rolling wheel. For a wheel rotating about the x axis, motion along the y axis is known as roll. Any component of motion in the x direction perpendicular to the direction the wheel is rolling is known as lateral slip. An ideal wheel moves only along the roll direction.

of an ideal wheel, this implies a distance $2\pi r$ has been covered for each rotation of a wheel with radius r. In practice, even the behavior of a single wheel is substantially more complicated than this. In addition to lateral slip, insufficient traction can also lead to slipping or sliding in the direction of the wheel's motion, which makes an estimate of the distance traveled imprecise. Additional factors arise owing to compaction of the terrain (see Figure 2.1) and cohesion between the surface and the wheel. Because these factors depend on variable characteristics of the terrain, it is very difficult to estimate elapsed distance *accurately* directly from wheel rotation. Because deviation from the ideal model occurs most commonly when the wheel has forces applied to it (for example to accelerate or decelerate), a light wheel that is not powered or load bearing is often employed specifically to estimate distance traveled.

Now consider a vehicle with several wheels in contact with the ground surface. For all wheels in contact with the ground to roll, the motion of each of the vehicle's wheels must be along its own y axis (Figure 2.2). Thus, for a wheeled mobile robot (WMR) to exhibit rolling motion, a point must exist around which each wheel on the vehicle follows a circular course. This point is known as the *instantaneous center of curvature* (ICC) or the *instantaneous center of rotation* (ICR). For the vehicle to change its ICC, some property of the wheels, such as individual wheel orientations with respect to their vertical axis, must be changed. In practice it is quite straightforward to identify the ICC because it must lie on a line coincident with the roll axis of each wheel in contact with the ground. Various mechanisms to change the ICC are possible, and a number of these are discussed in this chapter.

If all of the wheels in contact with the ground are to exhibit rolling contact, then not only must the ICC exist, but each wheel's velocity must be consistent with a rigid rotation of the entire vehicle about the ICC. A vehicle located on a plane has three degrees of

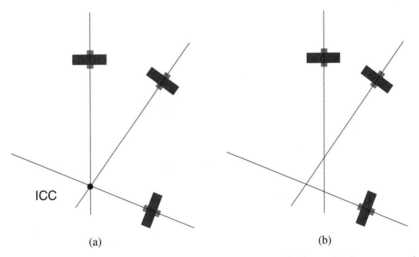

Figure 2.2. Instantaneous center of curvature (ICC). In (a) the three wheels are arranged such that the line drawn through the roll axis of each wheel intersects at a single point (the ICC). For (b) no such point exists. A robot relying on the wheels in (a) can exhibit rolling motion, whereas a robot relying on the wheel arrangement in (b) cannot.

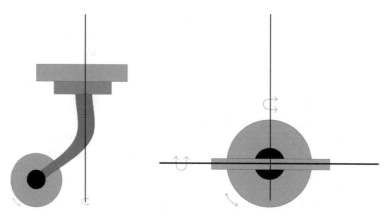

Figure 2.3. Castor wheels. (a) Castor wheel (b) Rollerball wheel.

freedom: an (x, y) position and a heading or orientation θ.* This triplet (x, y, θ) is often referred to as the *pose* of the robot on the plane.

Mobile robots usually do not have complete independent control over all three pose parameters and must undergo complex maneuvers to reach a particular pose. Consider parallel parking an automobile as an example. To park an automobile in a specific spot, the operator may have to perform a complex series of maneuvers, and the maneuvers required depend critically on the nature of the environment and the configuration of the vehicle. In a car it is not possible to change the pose of the vehicle arbitrarily, nor are changes in position independent of the vehicle orientation. This is an example of a *nonholonomic constraint*, which is discussed in some detail in Section 5.2.1.

Some lightweight vehicles are equipped with additional wheels or contact points that provide support but do not contribute to either steering or propulsion. Known generally as castor wheels (see Figure 2.3) these wheels are typically ignored in the computation of a vehicle kinematics.

Differential drive   Differential drive is perhaps the simplest possible drive mechanism for a ground-contact mobile robot. Often used on small, low-cost, indoor robots such as the TuteBot [176] or Khepera [183], larger commercial bases such as the TRC Labmate [360] and the Robuter [321] utilize this technology as well. As depicted in Figure 2.4, a differential drive robot consists of two wheels mounted on a common axis controlled by separate motors.

Kinematics deals with the relationship between control parameters and the behavior of a system in state space. Consider how the controlling wheel velocities determine the vehicle's motion. Under differential drive, for each of the two drive wheels to exhibit rolling motion, the robot must rotate about a point that lies on the common axis of the two drive wheels. By varying the relative velocity of the two wheels, the point of this rotation can be varied, and different trajectories chosen. At each instant in time, the point at which the robot rotates must have the property that the left and right wheels follow a path that

---

* In this book we will take $\theta = 0$ to imply that the robot is facing along the $+x$ axis and treat counterclockwise rotations as being positive.

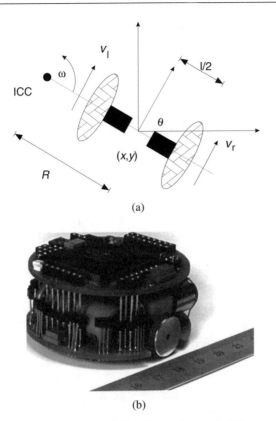

(a)

(b)

Figure 2.4. Differential drive kinematics. (a) A differential drive robot controls its pose by providing independent velocity control to the left v_l and right v_r wheels. Most differential drive robots use castor wheels for stability. (b) Khepera robot. (Reprinted by permission. Photograph by A. Herzog).

moves around the ICC at the same angular rate ω, and thus

$$\omega(R + l/2) = v_r$$
$$\omega(R - l/2) = v_l,$$

where l is the distance along the axle between the centers of the two wheels, the left wheel moves with velocity v_l along the ground and the right with velocity v_r, and R is the signed distance from the ICC to the midpoint between the two wheels. Note that v_l, v_r, ω, and R are all functions of time. At any instant in time, solving for R and ω results in

$$R = \frac{l}{2} \frac{(v_l + v_r)}{(v_r - v_l)}, \qquad \omega = \frac{v_r - v_l}{l}.$$

A number of special cases are of interest. If $v_l = v_r$, then the radius R is infinite and the robot moves in a straight line. If $v_l = -v_r$, then the radius is zero and the robot rotates about a point midway between the two wheels (i.e., it rotates in place). This makes differential drive attractive for robots that must navigate in narrow environments. For other values of v_l and v_r, the robot does not move in a straight line but rather follows a curved trajectory about a point a distance R away from the center of the robot, changing both the robot's position and orientation.

The kinematic structure of the vehicle prohibits certain vehicle motions. For example, there is no combination of v_l, v_r such that the vehicle can move directly along the wheel's common axis.

A differential drive vehicle is very sensitive to the relative velocity of the two wheels. Small errors in the velocity provided to each wheel result in different trajectories, not just a slower or faster robot. Differential drive vehicles typically have to use castor wheels for balance. Thus, differential drive vehicles are sensitive to slight variations in the ground plane. This limits their applicability in nonlaboratory environments.

Forward kinematics for differential drive robots   Suppose that the robot is at some position (x, y) and "facing" along a line making an angle θ with the x axis (Figure 2.4(a)). Through manipulation of the control parameters v_l and v_r, the robot can be made to take on different poses. Determining the pose that is reachable given the control parameters is known as the forward kinematics problem for the robot. Because v_l and v_r and hence R and ω are functions of time, it is straightforward to show (see Figure 2.5) that if the robot has pose (x, y, θ) at some time t, and if the left and right wheels have ground-contact velocities v_l and v_r during the period $t \rightarrow t + \delta t$, then the ICC is given by

$$\text{ICC} = [x - R \sin(\theta), y + R \cos(\theta)]$$

and at time $t + \delta t$ the pose of the robot is given by

$$\begin{bmatrix} x' \\ y' \\ \theta' \end{bmatrix} = \begin{bmatrix} \cos(\omega \, \delta t) & -\sin(\omega \, \delta t) & 0 \\ \sin(\omega \, \delta t) & \cos(\omega \, \delta t) & 0 \\ 0 & 0 & 1 \end{bmatrix} \begin{bmatrix} x - \text{ICC}_x \\ y - \text{ICC}_y \\ \theta \end{bmatrix} + \begin{bmatrix} \text{ICC}_x \\ \text{ICC}_y \\ \omega \, \delta t \end{bmatrix} \qquad (2.1)$$

Equation (2.1) describes the motion of a robot rotating a distance R about its ICC with an angular velocity given by ω. Different classes of robots will provide different expressions for R and ω.

By integrating Eq. (2.1) from some initial condition (x_0, y_0, θ_0), it is possible to compute where the robot will be at any time t based on the control parameters $v_l(t)$ and $v_r(t)$, that

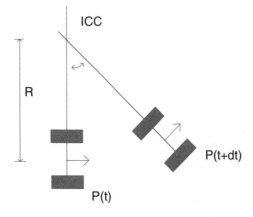

Figure 2.5. Forward kinematics geometry. The ICC is the location at $(x, y) + R[\cos(\theta + \pi/2), \sin(\theta + \pi/2)]$ that simplifies to $[x - R \sin(\theta), y + R \cos(\theta)]$. To compute the position of the robot at $t + \delta t$ the robot must be rotated about the ICC by an amount $\omega \, \delta t$. Mathematically this can be accomplished by translating the ICC to the origin, and rotating the robot about the origin by $\omega \, \delta t$ and then translating back to the ICC (see Eq. 2.1).

is, to solve the forward kinematics problem for the vehicle. In general, for a robot capable of moving in a particular direction $\theta(t)$ at a given velocity $V(t)$

$$x(t) = \int_0^t V(t) \cos[\theta(t)] \, dt$$

$$y(t) = \int_0^t V(t) \sin[\theta(t)] \, dt \qquad (2.2)$$

$$\theta(t) = \int_0^t \omega(t) \, dt,$$

and for the special case of a differential drive vehicle

$$x(t) = \frac{1}{2} \int_0^t [v_r(t) + v_l(t)] \cos[\theta(t)] \, dt$$

$$y(t) = \frac{1}{2} \int_0^t [v_r(t) + v_l(t)] \sin[\theta(t)] \, dt \qquad (2.3)$$

$$\theta(t) = \frac{1}{l} \int_0^t [v_r(t) - v_l(t)] \, dt.$$

A more interesting question, and one somewhat more difficult to answer, is, How can the control parameters be selected so as to have the robot obtain a specific global pose or follow a specific trajectory? This is known as the task of determining the vehicle's *inverse kinematics*: inverting the kinematic relationship between control inputs and behavior. It is also related to the problem of trajectory planning (see Section 5.3).

Inverse kinematics for differential drive robots Equations 2.2 and 2.3 describe a constraint on the velocity of the robot that cannot be integrated into a positional constraint. This is known as a *nonholonomic constraint* and is very difficult to solve in general, although solutions are straightforward for limited classes of the control functions $v_l(t)$ and $v_r(t)$ (see also Section 5.2.1). For example, if it is assumed that $v_l(t) = v_l$, $v_r(t) = v_r$, and $v_l \neq v_r$, then Eq. (2.3) yields

$$x(t) = \frac{l}{2} \frac{v_r + v_l}{v_r - v_l} \sin\left[\frac{t}{l}(v_r - v_l)\right]$$

$$y(t) = -\frac{l}{2} \frac{v_r + v_l}{v_r - v_l} \cos\left[\frac{t}{l}(v_r - v_l)\right] + \frac{l}{2} \frac{v_r + v_l}{v_r - v_l} \qquad (2.4)$$

$$\theta(t) = \frac{t}{l}(v_r - v_l),$$

where $(x, y, \theta)_{t=0} = (0, 0, 0)$. Given a goal time t and goal position (x, y). Equation 2.4 solves for v_r and v_l but does not provide for independent control of θ.[*]

---

[*] There are actually infinitely many solutions for v_l and v_r from Eq. (2.4), but all correspond to the robot moving about the same circle that passes through $(0, 0)$ at $t = 0$ and (x, y) at $t = t$; however, the robot goes around the circle different numbers of times and in different directions.

Rather than trying to invert (Eq. 2.3) to solve for the control parameters that lead to a specific robot pose, consider two special cases of the motion of the differential drive vehicle. If $v_l = v_r = v$, then the robot's motion simplifies to

$$\begin{pmatrix} x' \\ y' \\ \theta' \end{pmatrix} = \begin{pmatrix} x + v\cos(\theta)\,\delta t \\ y + v\sin(\theta)\,\delta t \\ \theta \end{pmatrix}$$

(i.e., the robot moves in a straight line), and if we choose $-v_l = v_r = v$, then Eq. (2.3) simplifies to

$$\begin{pmatrix} x' \\ y' \\ \theta' \end{pmatrix} = \begin{pmatrix} x \\ y \\ \theta + 2v\,\delta t/l \end{pmatrix}.$$

(i.e., the robot rotates in place). Thus, to drive the robot to some goal pose (x, y, θ), the robot can be spun in place until it is aimed at (x, y), then driven forward until it is at (x, y), and then spun in place until the required goal orientation θ is met. These are, of course, not the only possible solution to the inverse kinematics of a differential drive robot. Other solutions, such as those based on smoothly changing trajectories are also possible (cf. [329]).

Synchronous drive   In a *synchronous drive* robot (also known as *synchro drive*), each wheel is capable of being driven and steered. Typical configurations involve three steered wheels arranged at the vertices of an equilateral triangle often surmounted by a cylindrical platform. A *steered wheel* is a wheel for which the orientation of the rotational axis of the wheel can be controlled. All of the wheels turn and drive in unison. All of the wheels always point in the same direction and turn at the same rate. This is typically accomplished through the use of a complex collection of belts that physically link the wheels together (cf. [315, 270, 93]). In a synchronous drive robot, the vehicle controls the direction in which the wheels point and the rate at which they roll.

A common mechanical arrangement for a synchronous drive vehicle is to use two independent motors, one that rolls all of the wheels forward and one that rotates them (for turning). Because all the wheels remain parallel, synchronous drive robots always rotate about the center of the robot. Thus synchronous drive robots have the ability to control the orientation θ of their pose directly. The ability to control the rotation and forward speed of the robot independently simplifies overall vehicle control and allows such a robot to serve as a convenient model for the idealized point robot. Typical commercial examples are the Nomadics 200 and the IS Robotics B21.

Differential drive and synchronous drive robots are sensitive to small variations in the ground plane. In the case of differential drive, a small variation in the ground plane may give rise to loss of drive wheel contact and hence errors in robot pose, whereas in the case of synchronous drive robots, ground plane variations may give rise to wheel alignment problems because the distance each wheel travels is different.

Forward kinematics for synchronous drive   Synchronous drive robots rotate about their center at a rate ω, and the translational speed v is also under direct control. Substituting into (Eq. 2.2) obtains the forward kinematics of a synchronous drive robot

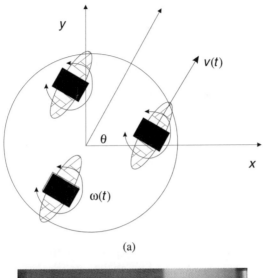

(a)

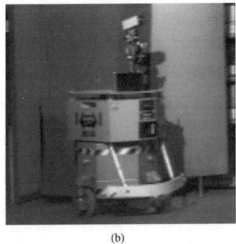

(b)

Figure 2.6. Synchronous drive kinematics. (a) Synchronous drive. A synchronous drive robot controls its pose by providing velocity and orientation control to each of its wheels. (b) ARK-1 robot. The ARK-1 robot is built around the Cybermotion Navmaster platform, which utilizes a synchronous drive.

as follows:

$$x(t) = \int_0^t v(t) \cos[\theta(t)] \, dt$$

$$y(t) = \int_0^t v(t) \sin[\theta(t)] \, dt$$

$$\theta(t) = \int_0^t \omega(t) \, dt.$$

Note that the ICC for a synchronous drive robot is always at infinity and that changing the orientation of the wheels manipulates the direction to the ICC.

Inverse kinematics for synchronous drive   Because changes in orientation can be completely decoupled from translation, the inverse kinematics of a synchronous drive vehicle are very similar to the special case of the inverse kinematics of the differential drive robot discussed earlier. We can consider two special cases of interest: (1) If $v(t)^\cdot = 0$ and $\omega(t) = \omega$ for some period δt, then the robot rotates in place by an amount $\omega\,\delta t$; and (2) if $\omega(t) = 0$ and $v(t) = v$ for some period δt, then the robot moves in the direction it is pointing a distance $v\delta t$.

Steered wheels   Robots that do not use either differential or synchronous drive technologies typically have one or more wheels that can be steered and one or more wheels whose rotational axis cannot be changed. For these robots the process of calculating the potential region of the ICC can be more complex.

Consider the problem of determining the ICC of a bicycle. The ICC must lie at the intersection of lines drawn through and perpendicular to the rotational axis of each wheel. Thus the ICC lies in the region of space drawn as a heavy line in Figure 2.7.

For a bicycle, the ICC must lie on a line passing through the rotational axis of the rear wheel that is perpendicular to the body of the bicycle. The front wheel can be steered, and thus the ICC lies on that part of the line passing through the rear wheel that intersects the line drawn along the axis of the front wheel. Given a maximum steering angle of the front wheel, a bicycle has a minimum turning radius and rotates about a point on the line passing through the rear axle.

If the front and rear wheels of a bicycle are steerable, the region of the ICC would be somewhat more complex but can be found geometrically by determining the loci of points that satisfy the perpendicular line constraint.

Tricycle, bogey, and bicycle drive   Tricycle, bogey (wagon), and bicycle drive robots have very similar kinematics. Rather than dealing with each we will deal with the tricycle case because it is the most common in mobile robots. A typical tricycle drive robot (cf. [127]) has three wheels and odometers on the two rear wheels, and steering and

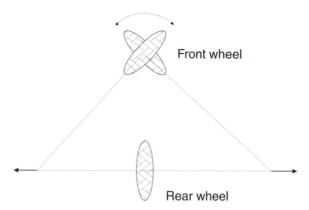

Figure 2.7. Finding the ICC for a bicycle. The ICC must lie on the line that passes through, and is perpendicular to, the fixed rear wheel. It must also lie on a line that passes through and is perpendicular to the front wheel. Given a limited turning angle of the front wheel (say 45°), the ICC must lie on the heavy part of the line in the figure.

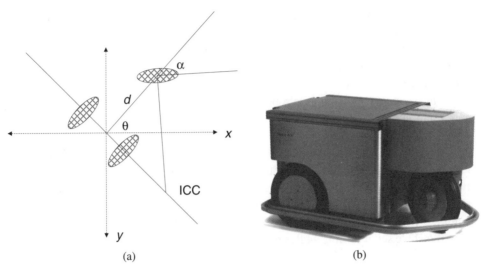

(a)   (b)

Figure 2.8. Tricycle kinematics. (a) Tricycle schematic. (b) Mecos mobile robot. (Reprinted by permission from Mecos Robotics AG.)

power are provided through the front wheel. The robot motion is controlled by the steering direction α and velocity v provided through the front wheel (see Figure 2.8).

Forward kinematics for steered vehicle   If the steered front wheel or set of bogeys is set at an angle α from the straight-ahead direction, the tricycle, bicycle, or bogey steering vehicle will rotate with angular velocity ω about a point lying a distance R along the line perpendicular to and passing through the rear wheels, where R and ω are given by

$$R = d \tan(\pi/2 - \alpha), \quad \omega = v/(d^2 + R^2)^{\frac{1}{2}},$$

v is the ground velocity of the front wheel and d is the distance from the front to the rear axle as shown in Figure 2.8. Substituting R and ω into Eq. (2.1) obtains the forward kinematics of the vehicle.

Inverse kinematics for steered vehicle   As with a differential drive vehicle, the general inverse kinematics problem is very difficult, and it is often more profitable to look at special cases. Two cases are of particular interest. If $\alpha = 0$, the robot drives straight ahead and Eq. (2.1) reduces to

$$\begin{pmatrix} x' \\ y' \\ \theta' \end{pmatrix} = \begin{pmatrix} x + v \cos(\theta)\,\delta t \\ y + v \sin(\theta)\,\delta t \\ \theta \end{pmatrix}.$$

If the vehicle is capable of turning its driving wheel through $\pm 90°$, then we can turn the vehicle in place and

$$\begin{pmatrix} x' \\ y' \\ \theta' \end{pmatrix} = \begin{pmatrix} x \\ y \\ \theta \pm v\,\delta t/d \end{pmatrix}.$$

Note that if the front wheel cannot be turned or the robot driven with a ±90° turning angle, it will be impossible to change the orientation of the robot without changing its position. A limited turning range of the wheel results in limits on the radius of curvature of the circle the vehicle can drive around. This limited radius of curvature appears in most real-world robots that utilize steered wheels. In practice, even without a limit on the attainable radius of curvature many wheeled mobile robots exhibit translation while attempting to execute a pure rotation.

The inverse kinematics problem can be solved in a manner similar to that for synchronous or differential drive vehicles if the tricycle drive robot is capable of driving with a turning angle of ±90°. If, however, the turning angle is more limited, the problem of driving the robot to a particular pose is considerably more complex. Strategies such as those used in parallel parking must then be considered to obtain certain poses, and given a complex environment with obstacles poses can exist that would be obtainable with a larger allowable set of turning angles but that are not obtainable with a more restricted set.

Car drive (Ackerman steering)   *Ackerman steering* (also known as *kingpin steering*) is the type of steering found on most automobiles. In the Ackerman steering model, the front steering wheels each rotate on separate arms so as to be able to rotate different amounts to point at the ICC, which must lie on the line passing through the rear axis of the vehicle (see Figure 2.9(a)). The inside wheel must turn through a larger angle than the outside one, and the inside wheel travels a shorter distance than the outside one.

Ackerman steering is the preferred mechanism for larger vehicles expected to operate either on existing roads or carry large payloads off-road (e.g., Navlab [355] and Oto Melara [274]). The size of the vehicle permits extensive onboard sensing and computation and allows navigation over reasonably rough terrain.

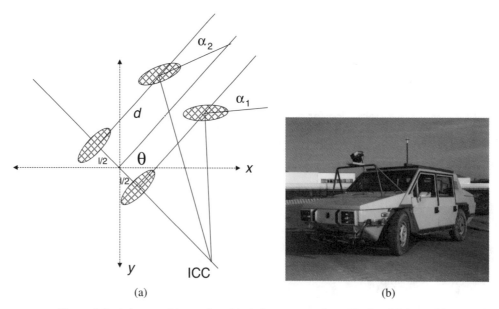

(a)   (b)

Figure 2.9. Ackerman kinematics. (a) Ackerman steering. (b) Oto Melara. (Photograph reprinted by permission from OTOBREDA.)

Forward kinematics for Ackerman drive   Under Ackerman steering, the vehicle rotates about a point lying on the line passing through the rear axle a distance R from the centerline of the vehicle, where

$$R + l/2 = d \tan(\pi/2 + \alpha_1).$$

In order for the wheels to exhibit rolling motion, the other steering wheel must be rotated through an angle α_2, where

$$R - l/2 = d \tan(\pi/2 + \alpha_2).$$

In general all four wheels travel along the ground at different speeds, and specifying the speed of one wheel specifies the velocity of them all. Ackerman steering is sophisticated and subtle, and there is insufficient space to cover it in full detail here. For example, on most cars the wheels rotate not only about a vertical axis but also about a longitudinal one in order to change the vertical orientation of the tire with respect to the road.

Inverse kinematics for Ackerman drive   The inverse kinematics of an Ackerman vehicle is a highly complex process, as can be attested by anyone who has parked a car in a congested urban area. Most Ackerman vehicles have a very large minimum turning radius owing to the limited turning range of the wheels. This implies that cars (Ackerman vehicles) must undergo complex maneuvers such as three-point turns and parallel parking in order to move to certain positions.

2.1.2   Complex Wheels

Given the kinematic limitations of simple wheels, one alternative is to construct a robot with complex or compound wheels. Complex wheels are wheels that exhibit more than one preferred rolling direction. Such wheels can result in omnidirectional robots. For example, a Mecanum wheel is essentially a simple wheel augmented with rollers mounted about the rim. If these extra rollers are locked in position, the entire wheel behaves exactly like a simple wheel. Alternatively, the main axis can be locked and the rollers placed about the rim can be rotated, causing the vehicle to move in a different direction. Combinations of these two mechanisms result in a net motion that is a combination of the preferred rolling direction of the two mechanisms. Compound or complex wheels can be found on vehicles such as Hermies [316]. Mecanum wheels suffer from limited bump height; that is, the maximum diameter of the object over which they can safely traverse is a function of the roller diameter rather than the overall wheel diameter. An alternative complex wheel approach based on a rolling ball is described in [120]. Actuators roll the ball in the three directions required in order to provide omnidirectional motion.

Omnidirectional robots are considerably easier to control than robots based on simple wheels because the motion of the robot is independent of the (x, y, θ) pose of the robot. The set of complex wheels is almost endless. As an extreme case, consider [257], which describes a robot wheel shaped like a tube tapered at both ends. An autonomous vehicle equipped with such a wheel can change direction by leaning towards one side or the other.

Figure 2.10. REMOTEC tracked vehicle. (Photograph reprinted by permission from REMOTEC.)

2.1.3 Tracked Vehicles

Tracked vehicles are similar to differential drive vehicles in terms of their kinematics but are more robust to terrain variations. The two differential wheels are extended into treads that provide a larger contact area with the ground, but rather than assuming perfect rolling contact with the ground surface, tracked vehicles rely on ground slip or skid to change direction. The large contact area of the treads in tracked vehicles permits treaded vehicles to cross small voids in the surface and climb steeper gradients than wheeled vehicles. For example, the REMOTEC Robot [317] (see Figure 2.10) is capable of climbing stairs.

The fact that tracked vehicles rely on slip between the treads and the ground surface to change orientation introduces complications in using the vehicle's kinematics to compute its pose. Although tracked vehicles can be thought of as differential drive vehicles with "extended" wheels, the large amount of slip between the treads and the ground makes it impossible to predict a tracked vehicle's motion accurately from the motion of its treads. Thus tracked vehicles must rely on some other external mechanism for determining their motion rather than just examining the motion of the treads. One option for overcoming this limitation is to add a castor or omnidirectional wheel to the treaded vehicle to measure motion with respect to the ground plane.

2.1.4 Limbed Vehicles

Given the sophistication of existing wheeled and tracked vehicles, why should robots be designed with different types of ground-contact locomotion? Perhaps the primary limitation associated with wheeled or tracked vehicles is the need for ground contact support along the entire path of motion. In rough terrains such as those found in forests, near natural or man-made disasters, or in planetary exploration, it will not always be

Figure 2.11. Ambler walking robot. (Photograph reprinted
by permission. © 1992 by Carnegie Mellon University.)

possible to guarantee physical support for the robot along a continuous path. Local terrain
modulations may be sufficiently large to make the ground impassable even for treaded
vehicles. But provided that separated footholds can be found throughout the environment,
a limbed robot may be capable of traversing the space.

We have seen that in wheeled vehicles the problem of effecting locomotion can be
described in terms of the mechanisms used to drive and steer the vehicle. Limbed vehicles
can be described in terms of the design of the legs and the way in which the legs are moved
to enable the vehicle to change its pose. Ambler, an example of a large, complex walking
robot is shown in Figure 2.11.

Vehicle stability   If a limbed robot is designed so that its balance is maintained
at all times even if all its legs were to freeze in position, then the robot is said to exhibit *static
stability*. More formally, static stability is maintained as long as the vehicle's center of
gravity remains inside the convex hull of the support polygon defined by the legs currently
in touch with the ground (see Figures 2.12 and 2.13). A major advantage of static stability
is that the vehicle will not topple as a result of delays in leg motion or vehicle power
failure. Static stability is the mechanism of choice for the vast majority of limbed robots,
including Dante I [379] and II [378] and Thing [218]. Under static stability, the *stability
margin* is a measure of the current stability of the robot and is defined as the minimum
distance from the vertical projection of the robot's center of gravity to the boundary of the
vertical projection of the convex hull of the support polygon.

If the center of gravity of the robot is allowed to move outside of the convex hull of the
support polygon and the robot moves in a controlled manner, the robot is said to exhibit

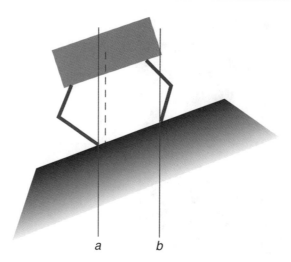

a   b

Figure 2.12. Vehicle stability. A side view of a simple 2-D legged robot. The body of the robot is shaded gray and is supported by two articulated legs above a sloped floor that meets the ground at points a and b. If the projection of the robot's center of gravity (dotted line) remains inside the segment $a - b$, the robot remains statically stable.

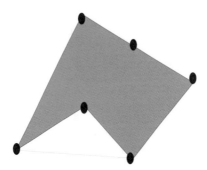

Figure 2.13. Convex hull. Top view of a 2-D six-legged robot showing the ground contact points of its legs. If the center of gravity is within its convex hull – the region of space formed by constructing the smallest convex region containing all of the vertical projection of the ground contact points – then the robot is stable.

dynamic stability. Under dynamic stability the robot maintains stability through controlled motion of the robot and the modeling and use of inertia. This implies a sophisticated model of the dynamics of the robotic system and highly developed control and locomotion processing. Raibert [311] has developed a number of dynamically stable robots, including one-, two-, and four-legged machines [311]. See also the Honda walking robot [150] (Figure 2.14). Although static stability is easier to control, it does limit the robot's gait and its upper speed.

Number of legs   Limbed robots have been built with as few as one leg [311, 312], but it is more common to see designs with four [308, 337, 218], six [194], and eight [379, 378] legs. Even 12-legged vehicles exist [359]. Because at least one leg must be free to move if a robot is to change its pose, for a statically stable robot to maintain its center of gravity over the convex hull of the support polygon, then the minimum number of legs is four: three to maintain the support polygon and one to move. If the robot is to

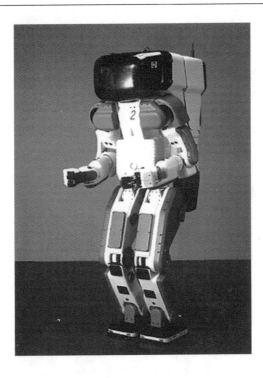

Figure 2.14. The Honda $\rho2$ walking robot. (Appears with the kind permission of Honda Canada.)

exhibit dynamic stability, the minimum number of legs is one, such as Raibert's hopping monopod [311, 312]. Here we assume that a foot's contact with the ground can be modeled as a point contact. It is also possible to construct robots with extended feet with larger foot–ground contact areas.

Although four is the minimum number of legs required for static stability, four legs may not be an ideal number for all applications. If a statically stable robot has only four legs, then its gait must be particularly simple. It may only move one leg at a time, and the robot must shift its weight as part of its gait. A robot with more legs – say six – can move more than one leg at a time and may not have to plan to move its center of mass as a separate component of its gait.

Limb design and control   Consider the design of a limb on a robot or biological system. A given limb has a fixed point at one end attached to the body, and a hand or foot known as the end-effector at the other. In a limbed robot, it is usually desirable to maximize the region over which the foot can be placed. To operate in three dimensions a minimal robot limb requires joints that provide sufficient degrees of freedom in order to be able to cover the three-dimensional leg–ground contact space. Physically, most robot joints offer a single degree of freedom. These *simple joints* can be combined to simulate more complex joints such as ball joints. Although three simple joints are the minimum required to cover three-dimensional space, the actual working space of the leg may be improved by using more than three joints, and if ground–leg contact orientation must also be controlled, then additional joints are required.

Similar to the study of robotic manipulators, a robot limb can be modeled as a collection of rigid links connected by simple joints. A base link is attached to the body of the robot, and the end of the limb (the end-effector) may or may not be in contact with the ground. Simple

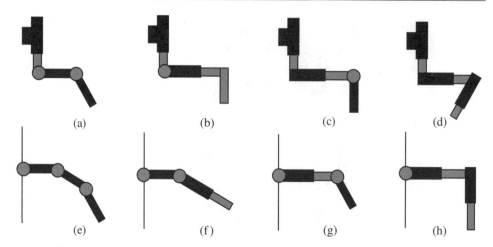

Figure 2.15. Sample limb designs. Eight three-jointed limbs based on simple prismatic and rotational joints. Rotational joints are indicated by small circles, whereas prismatic joints are indicated by two intensity-level rectangles. (a) through (d) utilize prismatic joints at the contact with the robot body, whereas (e) through (h) utilize rotational joints. The final prismatic joint of (d) is directed out of the page.

robot limb joints come in two standard flavors: rotational and prismatic. Rotational joints introduce a rotation between the two rigid links to which they are connected, whereas prismatic joints induce a translation. More complex joints can be modeled in terms of these two simple joint types. There are thus eight basic three-dimensional robot limb designs based on the various choices of simple joints. These eight designs are sketched in Figure 2.15.

Given a particular limb design, the task of moving a limb involves manipulating the joints of the limbs so as to be able to reach different locations in space. This is the forward kinematics problem for robot limbs: how to compute the location and orientation of the end-effector (or foot) given the joint angles.

The classic formulation of this problem is to use homogeneous coordinates to represent the position of each link in the limb and then to compute a homogeneous matrix that represents the transformation from a base coordinate system to a coordinate system aligned with the end-effector or foot.

Before tackling the general problem, consider the simple two-dimensional leg shown in Figure 2.16. This leg consists of two rotational joints separated by rigid limbs of lengths

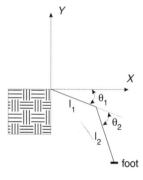

Figure 2.16. Two-dimensional leg. The leg connects to the body of the robot at an angle θ_1 from the horizontal. The second joint is at θ_2 from the straight-ahead direction of the first link.

l_1 and l_2. Placing the origin of the coordinate system at the joint of the leg with the robot body, the position of the foot as a function of θ_1 and θ_2 (the joint angles) is given by

$$\begin{bmatrix} x \\ y \end{bmatrix} = l_1 \begin{bmatrix} \cos(\theta_1) \\ \sin(\theta_1) \end{bmatrix} + l_2 \begin{bmatrix} \cos(\theta_1 + \theta_2) \\ \sin(\theta_1 + \theta_2) \end{bmatrix}.$$

This is the solution to the forward kinematics for this leg. The inverse kinematics for the leg involves determining the angles θ_1 and θ_2, which are required to place the foot at a point (x, y). A small amount of geometry results in

$$\cos(\theta_2) = \frac{x^2 + y^2 - l_1^2 - l_2^2}{2 l_1 l_2},$$

which can be then used in either the expression for x or y in the forward kinematics equation to obtain a solution for θ_1. Note that in general the inverse kinematics will not result in a unique solution and that multiple solutions may be possible.

Not all specifications of (x, y) necessarily result in a solution. Some (x, y) positions are not reachable by the limb. These points are said to be outside the limb's workspace. Suppose that the first joint is limited to the range $|\theta_1| \leq \pi/2$ and that $l_2 = l_1/2$. The resulting workspace of the limb is sketched in Figure 2.17.

Given a set of points attainable by the robot's limb, an important question to consider is, How well can the motion of the limb be controlled near these points? If $\dot{x}$ is the velocity of the end-effector in Cartesian space, and $\dot{\theta}$ is the velocity in joint space (θ_1, θ_2), then $\dot{x} = \mathcal{J}(\theta)\dot{\theta}$, where $\mathcal{J}(\theta)$ is the Jacobian matrix. That is

$$\mathcal{J}(\theta) = \begin{bmatrix} \frac{\partial x}{\partial \theta_1} & \frac{\partial x}{\partial \theta_2} \\ \frac{\partial y}{\partial \theta_1} & \frac{\partial y}{\partial \theta_2} \end{bmatrix}$$

and

$$\begin{bmatrix} \frac{dx}{dt} \\ \frac{dy}{dt} \end{bmatrix} = \mathcal{J}(\theta) \begin{bmatrix} \frac{d\theta_1}{dt} \\ \frac{d\theta_2}{dt} \end{bmatrix}.$$

The Jacobian relates the velocity of the joint angles $(d\theta_1/dt, d\theta_2/dt)$ to the velocity of the end-effector in Cartesian space. Conversely, given a desired trajectory of the limb in

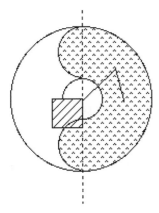

Figure 2.17. Limb workspace. The region reachable with the tip of the limb is lightly shaded.

Cartesian space, we can examine the inverse of the Jacobian $\dot{\theta} = \mathcal{J}(\theta)^{-1}\dot{x}$ to determine the appropriate velocities in joint space.

When a limb loses one or more degrees of freedom as viewed in Cartesian space, such as at the boundaries of the limb workspace, motion singularities are said to occur. The existence of a singularity in some configuration of the limb means that it is impossible to move the limb in an arbitrary direction from this point. Singularities exist at the boundary of the workspace but may also occur within its interior. Mathematically, within the robot's workspace, singularities can be identified through an examination of the Jacobian. When the determinant of the Jacobian is equal to zero, the Jacobian has lost full rank, and singularities exist. For the simple 2-D leg considered here

$$|\mathcal{J}| = \left| \begin{bmatrix} \frac{\partial F_1}{\partial \theta_1} & \frac{\partial F_1}{\partial \theta_2} \\ \frac{\partial F_2}{\partial \theta_1} & \frac{\partial F_2}{\partial \theta_2} \end{bmatrix} \right| = l_1 l_2 |\sin(\theta_2)|.$$

A singularity exists whenever $\sin(\theta_2) = 0$, that is, when $\theta_2 = 0$ or $\pm\pi$. Physically this corresponds to the foot being either stretched straight out or bent in upon itself.

Forward and inverse kinematics The two-dimensional problem considered above is relatively straightforward because the state of the limb is defined by its position (x, y) and its orientation θ. In three dimensions, six scalar parameters are required to represent the state of the limb: three positional and three rotational. Transformations such as translations and rotations that are reasonably straightforward in two dimensions become quite cumbersome in three dimensions if separate position and orientation representations are retained. A common representation that has proven to be more useful is to use homogeneous coordinates to represent points and homogeneous transforms to represent transformations between one coordinate frame and another or to represent position and orientations generally. This allows both rotations and translations to be expressed uniformly as matrix multiplication. It also allows multiple transformations to be readily computed as a matrix product.

A point $P = (x_1, x_2, x_3)$ in homogeneous coordinates can be represented as $P_h = [x_1, x_2, x_3, 1]^T$. This allows us to express rotation and translation as matrix multiplication so that the effect of transforming P to $P' = (y_1, y_2, y_3)$ through a rotation by some rotation matrix $\mathbf{R}$, where

$$\mathbf{R} = \begin{bmatrix} r_{1,1} & r_{1,2} & r_{1,3} \\ r_{2,1} & r_{2,2} & r_{2,3} \\ r_{3,1} & r_{3,2} & r_{3,3} \end{bmatrix},$$

followed by a translation $D = (t_x, t_y, t_z)$, can be written in homogeneous coordinates as

$$\begin{bmatrix} y_1 \\ y_2 \\ y_3 \\ 1 \end{bmatrix} = \begin{bmatrix} r_{1,1} & r_{1,2} & r_{1,3} & t_x \\ r_{2,1} & r_{2,2} & r_{2,3} & t_y \\ r_{3,1} & r_{3,2} & r_{3,3} & t_z \\ 0 & 0 & 0 & 1 \end{bmatrix} \begin{bmatrix} x_1 \\ x_2 \\ x_3 \\ 1 \end{bmatrix}$$

or $P' = TP$, where

$$T = \begin{bmatrix} r_{1,1} & r_{1,2} & r_{1,3} & t_x \\ r_{2,1} & r_{2,2} & r_{2,3} & t_y \\ r_{3,1} & r_{3,2} & r_{3,3} & t_z \\ 0 & 0 & 0 & 1 \end{bmatrix}.$$

Suppose that we establish one coordinate system attached to the foot or end-effector of a mobile robot and another coordinate system is attached to the body. Then there exists a homogeneous transformation T that maps points in the coordinate system attached to the foot to the coordinate system attached to the body. T will be a function of the joint angles and links that make up the leg. Determining T is in essence the process of establishing the forward kinematics for the limb. Suppose now that the coordinate system attached to the end-effector has its origin at the tip of the limb. Then solving the inverse kinematics for the limb involves solving

$$T^{-1} \begin{bmatrix} x \\ y \\ z \\ 1 \end{bmatrix} = \begin{bmatrix} 0 \\ 0 \\ 0 \\ 1 \end{bmatrix}$$

for some setting of the joint angles, where (x, y, z) is the desired position of the limb in body coordinates.

Establishing T for a given limb is often simplified by establishing a series of working coordinate systems along the limb and noting that if ^2_1T maps points in coordinate system 1 to points in coordinate system 2, and if ^3_2T maps points in coordinate system 2 to point in coordinate system 3, then $^3_1T = {}^3_2T {}^2_1T$.

Gait and body control   Gait refers to the pattern of leg placements made by a walker. Eadweard Muybridge (1830–1904), a photographer in the American West, is credited with the earliest studies of gait in biological systems. In 1872 Leland Stanford, then Governor of California, bet a friend that once every stride all four legs of a running horse are simultaneously off the ground. Muybridge was hired to settle the bet. Muybridge developed a system of cameras that were set up along the horse's path. Each camera was triggered by a wire the horse would run through along this path, and in 1877 Muybridge produced the first time sequence photographs of humans and animals and demonstrated that horses do in fact lift all four legs off of the ground when running – that they are not statically stable. Collections of these photographs and a description of the various gaits employed by quadruped [255] and biped [254] walkers show the considerable sophistication used in gaits by biological systems over flat and rough terrain.

Much of the robotic literature concerning gait has its foundations in the biological literature. As is the case with biological systems, gait plays a major role in the trade-off between speed, energy utilization, and stability.

The *stride* of a limbed robot can be decomposed into the synchronized *steps* made by each limb. In terms of providing support to the robot, two different phases can be identified: the *transfer phase*, in which the limb is not in contact with the ground, and the *support phase*, in which it is. The time taken for a complete step to be taken by a limb is known as the *cycle time*, and the *duty factor* for a leg is that fraction of the cycle time in which the leg is in the support phase.

Nonperiodic gaits are typically used in biological systems on rough terrain. Periodic gaits are preferred in biological systems over flat terrain and are the usual strategy for limbed robots in the absence of obstacles. Muybridge identified eight different periodic gaits used by quadrupeds in locomotion over flat surfaces [255]. They are as follows:

1. The *walk* (including crawl as a special case). One leg moves at a time. *Crawl is the only statically stable gait.*
2. The *amble*. Faster than a walk. Support alternates between one and two feet.
3. The *trot*. Support is provided by diagonal pairs of feet.
4. The *rack* (or *pace*). Support is provided by lateral pairs of feet rather than by diagonal pairs of feet in the trot.
5. The *canter*. Unlike earlier gaits, the canter can not be broken into a left and right part.
6. The *gallop*. The gallop is the fastest of the quadrupedal gaits. Central to the gallop is a ballistic phase in which the quadruped jumps forwards from its hind feet to catch itself with its forward ones. Two different gallops are identified in biological quadrupeds:
   (a) The transverse gallop. The pattern of foot falls moves transversely across the body.
   (b) The rotatory gallop. The pattern of foot falls moves cyclically around the body.
7. The *ricochet*. Motion as a sequence of bounds, hops, jumps, or skips. Typically found in the rapid motion of the Australian marsupials: the kangaroo and the wallaby.

To describe the pattern of leg motions that give rise to these different gaits, various graphical representations have been devised. Hildebrand's gait diagrams [149] provide a precise description of gait. They show the contribution of each leg towards the support of a robot as a function of time. A horizontal line is assigned to each leg, and the darkened regions correspond to the support phase. Legs one and two are the front legs, and three and four are the rear. Odd-numbered legs are on the left-hand side of the robot. Figure 2.18 sketches the gait diagrams for each of the eight gaits described by Muybridge.

Machine gaits for statically stable robots are usually more simple than the biological gaits studied by Muybridge. Song and Waldron [337] identify a number of different machine gaits. The wave and equal-phase gaits shown in Figure 2.19 are periodic gaits designed to be used by machines on flat open terrain. The equal-phase gait provides an optimal stability margin, and the equal wave equally distributes the placing and lifting segments of each leg throughout the entire stride.

Once the pattern of footfalls has been established, the task of scheduling body motions remains. Raising and lowering the limbs in a particular pattern does not necessarily cause the center of mass of the robot to move forward. In addition to choosing when and where to place the feet, the entire body must be moved forward at some point in the gait. Two basic strategies have emerged for scheduling body motions. The first is to minimize the number

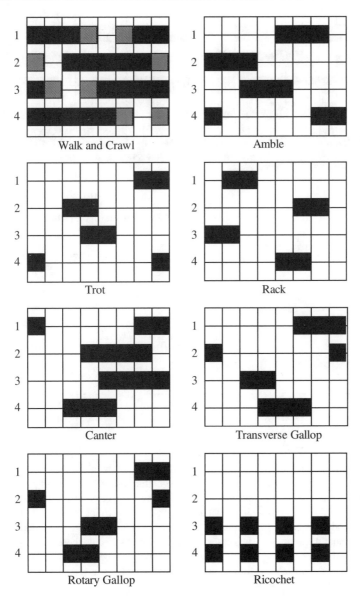

Figure 2.18. Eight quadrapedal gaits (after [255]). Each plot depicts the ground-contact phase for each leg as a function of time. The crawl gait is a slow walk gait and includes the black- and gray-colored regions. Note that only the crawl gait is statically stable. Legs 1 and 2 are the "front" legs, whereas legs 3 and 4 are the "rear." Legs 1 and 3 are on the left side of the body, whereas legs 2 and 4 are on the right.

of body motions. A second alternative is to move the center of mass so as to maximize the robot's stability margin.

A possible implementation for scheduling body motions in a quadruped crawl gait is shown in Figure 2.20. Snapshots of the motion of the robot are shown in left-to-right, top-to-bottom order. Body motions (indicated by an arrow) are scheduled at two points during the motion even though the legs move forward throughout the entire gait.

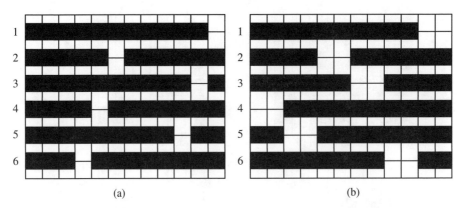

Figure 2.19. Wave (a) and equal-phase (b) gaits for a six-legged robot. (After [337].)

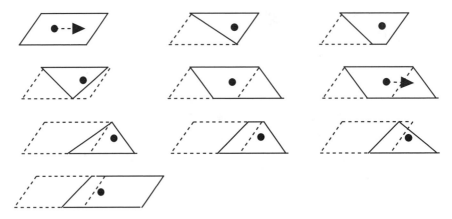

Figure 2.20. Scheduling body motions in a crawling gait. (Ten snapshots of the motion are shown. Snapshots are shown in left-to-right, top-to-bottom order. The support polygon of the robot is shown as a solid line and the dotted line shows the original position of the robot. The center of mass of the robot is shown as a black dot. The robot moves from left to right almost one body length. Body motions are scheduled at frames 1 and 6 even though the legs move throughout the entire gait. It is essential that the robot schedule these body motions. For example, had the body motion to shift the center of gravity not been scheduled at frame 1, the robot would be very unstable at frame 2 when the right rear leg was raised.

Dynamic gaits Rather than planning limb motions to maintain static stability, an alternative is to control the motion of the robot dynamically and achieve balance. Under a dynamic gait, the motion of the vehicle must consider the energy involved in each limb and actuator.

Running is a form of legged locomotion that uses ballistic flight to obtain a high speed. Perhaps the simplest possible dynamic legged device is a one-legged hopper (see Figure 2.21) [313]. This device actively models the dynamic exchange of energy between the mass of the robot, its actuators, and the ground in order to hop in three dimensions. The dynamic nature of the device results in a very high maximum speed. Raibert et al. report a maximum speed of 4.8 mph for this one-legged robot.

Multiple-legged robots can be thought of as linked one-legged robots. For example, [151] describes a bipedal robot that basically hops on alternate legs and can reach a top speed of 11.5 mph. The robot is also capable of performing forward flips and ariels.

Figure 2.21. 3-D hopping monopod. The 3-D one-legged hopper can hop in place, travel at a specific rate, or follow simple paths. (Reprinted by courtesy of MIT Leg Laboratory. Photograph by Marc Raibert. © 1984.)

Quadruped robots can also be built based on hopping on all four legs alternately, but this is difficult to achieve in practice owing to difficulties of balance [314]. An alternative is to use the legs in pairs to act as a single "virtual" leg. Gaits such as trot, rack, and ricochet are possible.

2.1.5   Aquatic Vehicles

Aquatic vehicles, such as the Twin-burger [132] and THESEUS [121] (see Figures 2.22[a] and [b]), use the surrounding water to support propulsion. Two basic designs are popular. The first is a torpedo-like structure [121, 341] (see Figure 2.22[b]). Here a single propeller or propeller assembly is used to provide forward and reverse thrust while control surfaces, are used to control the direction in which the vehicle travels. The control surfaces may provide only horizontal directional control, or they may provide vertical directional control as well by manipulating dive planes. Depth may also be controlled by manipulating the buoyancy of the vessel. These torpedo-shaped robots suffer from poor maneuverability owing to the direct coupling of turning with translational motion and the indirect nature of the rudder.

A second alternative, and the design used on vehicles such as the Twin-burger [132] and URV [71, 72] robots, is to use a collection of *thrusters* distributed over the vessel rather than just a single propeller (see Figure 2.22[a]). By controlling sets of the thrusters, a vessel such as the URV can change its orientation and position independently. This results in a considerably more maneuverable vessel at the expense of maximum operational speed.

Finally it is worth pointing out that it is possible to build aquatic systems that lack active propulsion control. For example, [347] describes an underwater glider that uses active buoyancy control to provide propulsion.

Aquatic robots provide a number of unique challenges for sensing and control. The surrounding water makes the use of sensors based on vision-based sensing problematic at long ranges. Water can contain suspended material that may make light-based sensing

(a)

(b)

Figure 2.22. Aquatic robots. (a) Twin-Burger robot. (Appears with the kind permission of Tervo Fujii.) (b) THESEUS robot. (Appears with the kind permission of International Submarine Engineering Ltd.)

impossible even at close ranges. Although water does provide buoyancy and locomotion, it is impossible to estimate odometry accurately using the rate of turn of the propeller and the position of the control surfaces.

The vast majority of aquatic robots operate in a tethered manner; they are physically connected to a support vessel by a cable that provides power and communication to the robot. This simplifies a number of problems in terms of the engineering of the robot (as discussed in Section 2.2) and also provides a mechanism for retrieving the robot should something go wrong. Power and communication pose difficult challenges for untethered aquatic autonomous vehicles.

2.1.6 Flying Vehicles

Aerial robots have grown from the autopilots found in many commercial aircraft to fully autonomous vehicles. Fixed-wing autonomous vehicles utilize control systems similar to those found in commercial autopilots. Remote commands are provided from a ground station, and sophisticated localization strategies based on systems such as the Global Positioning System (GPS) are used to localize the aircraft in the sky.

As a result of their energy efficiency, fixed-wing vehicles are desirable for long-distance travel, but they lack the maneuverability required for many robotic tasks. Designs based on automated helicopters (cf. [28, 208]) modify radio-controlled helicopters through the use of limited onboard computation coupled with sophisticated sensing and ground control (see Figure 2.23[b]).

Unfortunately helicopter control can be very difficult. In spite of considerable advances, reliable control remains an elusive goal. Helicopters are much more complex devices to control than are fixed-wing aircraft and require more powerful onboard computers in order to maintain reliable automatic control. Tail-sitter designs such as [250] (see Figure 2.23[a]) use a much simpler mechanical structure while retaining the maneuverability of the helicopter design. In a tail-sitter design, a single downward-pointing engine and propeller assembly is used to provide lift, and translation and stability are obtained by manipulating the slipstream from the propeller and its control surfaces.

Buoyant vehicles are those which float; zeppelins are a familiar example. Buoyant vehicles or *aerobots* (also known as *aerovehicles* or *blimps*) are the most readily controlled class of flying robot in part because the consequences of even a total systems failure are typically not disastrous. Potential application domains for buoyant robots include inside large buildings, outdoors, and in the atmospheres of other planets. In addition to forgiving control regimes, such vehicles have advantages in terms of energy efficiency, long potential duty cycles, vertical mobility, and a potential for long-range travel.

Unpowered autonomous flying vehicles have also been developed that are essentially computer-controlled parafoils. Steckemetz describes a system that can be used to deliver sensitive packages via parachute to a given landing site with high accuracy [340]. This "falling" robot uses various onboard sensors, including GPS, to drive the robot to its goal.

2.1.7 Space Robots

Space robotic devices are envisioned to assist in the construction, repair, and maintenance of future space stations and satellites. Space vehicles must exhibit a significant level of autonomy because communication delays and signal dropout make teleoperation unattractive [330].

To increase the mobility of space robots, *free-flying systems* in which one or more manipulators are mounted on a thruster-equipped spacecraft have been proposed and are currently in the implementation phase. Attitude rockets or thrusters mounted on the body of the vehicle are used to provide corrections or modifications to the vehicle's trajectory. Power and reaction mass (fuel) are the primary constraints on existing free-flying space vehicles. In free-flying systems, dynamic coupling between any onboard manipulators and the spacecraft exists, and therefore manipulator motions induce disturbances to the

(a)

(b)

Figure 2.23. Aerial robots. (a) UTA SDDR 94 robot (Reprinted with the kind permission of Luis Sanoja) and (b) USC AFV. (Reprinted with the kind permission of Jim Montgomery and the University of Southern California Robotics Research Laboratory.)

system's spacecraft. The modeling and control of such devices are a critical challenge. Thruster jets can compensate for these disturbances, but their extensive use severely limits a system's useful life span [98]. To increase a system's life, operation in a free-floating mode has been considered [98, 283, 376]. In this mode of operation, spacecraft thrusters are turned off, and the spacecraft is permitted to translate and rotate in response to its manipulator motions. In practice, this mode of operation can be feasible if the total system momentum is zero; if nonzero momentum develops, the system's thrusters must be used to eliminate it. Selecting the correct sequence of actions to move the manipulator itself as well as produce an appropriate motion in the spacecraft entails a sophisticated model of the dynamics and kinematics of the entire device.

Simulating free-flying space robots is straightforward. However, even a simple system with two six-degree-of-freedom manipulators requires 18 differential equations to describe it. If one is interested in choosing a description of the spacecraft orientation that is not susceptible to representational singularities, these equations can be even more complicated [284]. Real-time integration of these equations for predictive displays is not possible with today's workstations.

Free-floating systems exhibit nonholonomic behavior, which is due to the nonintegrability of the device's angular momentum [281]. In short, motion planning for free-flying space robots is complicated, and in some cases it may not be possible to get the robot to move from one feasible configuration to another simply owing to motion constraints.

One technique for planning free-flying space robot motions is to utilize joint space-planning techniques that take advantage of the nonholonomy in the system [284, 258]. Sophisticated numerical techniques have been used to achieve simultaneous control of a spacecraft's attitude and its manipulator's joint angles using the manipulator's actuators only, although convergence problems have been reported [258].

The apparent lack of gravity in space offers some interesting possibilities in recovering from actuator failures. Indeed, one can influence the motion of a link whose actuation system has failed with an appropriate motion of the remaining system or actuators [282]. By "waving around" a failed arm, one might be able to bring it into a specified configuration. Once the failed actuator–link has assumed the desired configuration, brakes can be applied, and the system may remain operational although with fewer degrees of freedom. However, the planning of such appropriate motions is a very complex issue that involves constraint equations at the acceleration level. Simplified motions can be found, provided that some design conditions are met [282].

2.2   Offboard Communication

Most mobile robots must interact with a human operator if only to report that the current task has been completed. This communication may require a physical substrate such as a cable, or it may utilize some wireless communication strategy such as a wireless Ethernet, serial-, infrared-, or audio-based communications channel.

2.2.1   Tethered

A *tether* simplifies offboard communications. Existing wireless communications mechanisms are considerably slower and provide a lower channel bandwidth than their wired counterparts. Tethered communication is also more robust than untethered, and thus use of a tether tends to reduce robot development time because the problems associated with dealing with an unreliable communication stream can be avoided.

Tethering a robot avoids a number of technical problems at the expense of mobility. Once the decision to tether a robot has been made, the tether can be used to provide not only communications and control linkages, but it can also provide power. This reduces or

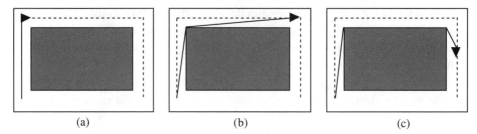

Figure 2.24. Movement of a tethered robot. (a), (b), and (c) show the motion of a tethered robot around an obstacle. As the robot follows the dotted path, the tether (drawn as a solid line) is drawn against obstacles in the environment.

eliminates concerns with respect to onboard power production and storage and the size, type, capacity, and weight of batteries as well as power consumption issues.

Given all the advantages of tethered operations, it would seem to be the ideal method for managing power and offboard communications. Unfortunately, a tether limits the robot's mobility, for the cable must have some finite length, and also introduces the task of cable management. Figure 2.24 depicts the progress of a tethered robot as it moves around an obstacle. As the robot passes the corner of the obstacle, tension in the cable will cause it to be drawn against the obstacle's corner (Figures 2.24[b] and [c]). If the cable is paid out from the ground station, then, as the robot moves farther along the obstacle, the cable will rub against the obstacle, resulting in additional strain on the cable as well as acting as a drag on the robot. For these reasons, many tethered terrestrial mobile robots are designed so that the cable is paid out from the robot rather than from the ground station. (The converse is true for aquatic robots, which typically pay out the cable from the surface station in order to be able to deal with the considerable length of tether involved.)

As a final limit on mobility, a cable interferes with the free-motion planning of the robot. Motion plans must take into account the cable trailing behind the robot. It would not be appropriate, for example, for the robot to make rotational motions without the planner's recognizing that the cable might be wrapped around the robot.

2.2.2   Untethered

If a robot is to operate in an untethered manner, the choice of the underlying wireless communications technology becomes an issue. For terrestrial mobile robots, radio- and infrared-based technologies are employed. Spread-spectrum Ethernet and serial devices, as well as infrared Appletalk and serial communications hardware are readily available. These devices attempt to emulate existing wire-based technologies without relying on the wire. Spread-spectrum communications strategies use a radio transmitter–receiver mounted on the robot and one or more base stations for communication. Multiple robots can be used within the same environment but with a reduction in effective bandwidth.

The most common problem with radio–frequency-based hardware is the existence of nulls and multipath interference within the environment. Regions may exist in the environment that either receive very poor signals and hence low bandwidth or no radio communication at all. These regions are formed by multipath signals or from the existence of barriers to the radio signal.

Infrared mechanisms hand are typically limited to a smaller operating range than are the spread-spectrum systems. Infrared systems communicate their signals through modulated

IR energy emitted from the robot and one or more ground stations. Infrared systems suffer from a number of communication problems. Either a direct line of sight or a bounced signal path must connect the sender and receiver, and this is not always possible. Sunlight and other environmental illuminants also tend to degrade performance.

2.3   Processing

The final key component of a mobile robot is the processing. Chapters 5 through 8 consider the types of computational tasks that a mobile robot must perform. Here we examine where that processing can take place.

Perhaps the most straightforward option would be to place the computational resources onboard. This choice has been followed on several systems from very simple robots to very large and complex systems such as the CMU NAVLAB. Placing the processing onboard provides the processes direct access to sensors and motor controllers, which provide locomotion for the robot. The major problem with this solution is power. Processors and their associated primary and secondary storage units consume it, and the energy budget for a robot is always a constraint in its design. A second problem arises owing to the bulk and fragile nature of computer components. In spite of advances in mobile computer technology, the significant mass and volume associated with performing the computation onboard contributes significantly towards the total vehicle payload. In addition, some processing needs cannot be met with existing laptop technology. For example, special purpose processors, which are often required for vision processes, may require more power and space than is available on an indoor robot.

The obvious alternative to providing all of the computation onboard is to perform the vast bulk of the processing offboard. Simple onboard systems provide a link between offboard processors and onboard sensors and motor controllers. This solution has a number of advantages. Power consumption for onboard processors is reduced, and more general purpose processors can be used because they do not have to be mounted onboard. This can allow more rapid prototyping for offboard environments often provide more sophisticated and standard programming environments.

Offboard processors must, however, deal with long and possibly unbounded delays between offboard computation and onboard sensors and actuators. In addition, the processor has only indirect access to the actual onboard devices, and thus certain computations involving real-time device access are difficult or impossible. The problem with offboard processing is made more severe if the communications link has a limited bandwidth or can suffer from communication delay or dropout such as those associated with wireless or infrared links.

The most typical compromise between these two alternatives is to distribute the processing between onboard and offboard components. Time-critical (real-time) processing is performed onboard, whereas less time-critical processing can safely be placed at a remote location to reduce onboard load and power consumption.

2.4   Further Reading

2.4.1   Wheeled Mobile Robots

Many different classes of wheeled mobile robots exist, and the set of combinations of steered or unsteered, driven, and idle wheels appear almost endless. The task of identifying and dealing with slippage, nonideal wheels, and many of the subtleties associated with real wheels is beyond the scope of this text. Rather than the general problem of the kinematics of wheeled mobile robots, only a few common kinematics structures are considered here. For a more abstract overview of general wheeled kinematic structures, see [6] and [64].

Only very simple kinematic models have been considered here, and many more complex strategies for specific classes of wheeled mobile robots are possible.

2.4.2   Legged Robots

A large literature exists on the forward and inverse kinematics of robotic manipulators (see [84], for example). References [337] and [312] provide indepth surveys of early legged robot designs, and [223] describes gait generation for Ambler, a more recent legged robot. Hodgins and Raibert [152] describe control using dynamic stability.

2.4.3   Space Robots

Desrochers [95] provides a collection of papers on robotic systems for deployment in space. The October 1993 issue of *IEEE Transactions on Robotics and Automation* is a special issue dedicated to space robotics.

2.5   Problems

1. Consider the two-steerable-wheeled bicycle sketched in Figure P2.1. This is a bicycle in which the front wheel (wheel 1) is powered, whereas the rear wheel just rolls on the ground. The front wheel makes an angle α_f with respect to the bike frame, and the rear wheel makes an angle α_r. The front wheel is powered with ground contact speed v_f, and the rear wheel rolls on the ground with ground contact speed v_r.
    (a) If the steering axle of the bike's rear wheel is located at (x, y) and the bike's frame points in direction θ as shown in the figure, identify the location of the instantaneous center of curvature (ICC) for this vehicle.
    (b) Under what conditions does the ICC exist?
    (c) At what speed does the rear wheel need to revolve in order for all of the wheels to roll smoothly on the ground surface?
2. Consider the robotic leg structure sketched in Figure P2.2. This leg corresponds roughly to the structure of the leg of the Honda walking robot. l_1 through l_5 are lengths of leg segments, and θ_1 through θ_5 are the angles at joints.

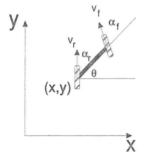

Figure P2.1. Sketch of the two-wheeled bicycle.

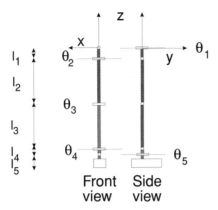

Figure P2.2. Sketch of the Honda robot leg.

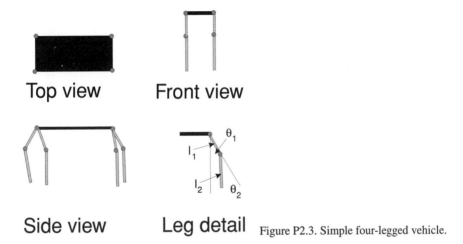

Figure P2.3. Simple four-legged vehicle.

(a) Obtain an expression for the position and orientation of the foot in the body-based coordinate system shown. The $\vec{\theta} = \vec{0}$ configuration to the leg being straight, as shown in the figure.

(b) Write a computer program that allows you to generate a view of the robot leg. That is, the program takes as input $\vec{\theta}$ and renders a view of the leg.

(c) Using the body-based coordinate system, determine if the leg can be configured such that the foot is touching the ground at (x, y, z) with orientation n and twist γ. If it can, compute the set of joint angles that makes this configuration possible.

(d) Modify the program written above to take as input the ground position, goal, orientation, and twist.

3. Consider the simple four-legged walking robot shown in Figure P2.3. The robot has eight degrees of freedom – each leg consists of two links of length l, and each leg is controlled by two joints. The legs on the robot lie in two planes, one on the left side of the robot and the other on the right.

Build a graphical simulation for this robot allowing it to be simulated on an infinite flat surface. Assume that individual legs are either in point contact with the ground surface or not. Do not do a dynamic simulation – only perform a static simulation.

(a) Assume that the legs are massless and write code to compute the center of mass of the robot and to determine if the robot is stable.

(b) Have the robot execute a crawl gait. Ensure that the robot remains statically stable.

4. Derive the kinematic equations for a two-wheeled differential-drive robot with drive wheels at diagonally opposite corners of a rectangle (assume the other corners are equipped with castor wheels for balance.)

5. Generate a graphical simulation of a round idealized wheeled robot with radius r on a plane. Your simulation should be capable of allowing the user to add polygonal obstacles to the simulation. Render the robot as a disk with a marker to indicate the front of the robot.

The robot should move like an idealized synchronous drive vehicle and should accept commands to change its orientation and move forward a given distance.

(a) Add an idealized distance sensor to the simulation. This sensor is located on top of the center of the robot and can be pointed in any direction (α) relative to the vehicle's orientation. Choose $\alpha = 0$ to correspond to the straight-ahead direction of the vehicle. Plot the location of sensor measurements.

(b) If you have access to a real vehicle, provide linkages so that the simulation talks to the real vehicle.

Part two

Sensing

Chapters 3 and 4 consider the test of enabling a robot to sense its environment. Chapter 3 examines nonvisual sensor hardwave and the algorithms used to transform the new sensor measurements into information about the robot's environment. Chapter 4 addresses the class of sensors that rely on light energy and in particular considers the problem of robot vision.

3

Nonvisual sensors and algorithms

"Nothing is in the understanding, which is not first in the senses."[*]

"Danger Will Robinson, Danger!"[†]

Sensing is a key requirement for any but the simplest mobile behavior. In order for *Robot* to be able to warn the crew of "Lost in Space" that there is danger ahead, the robot must be able to sense and reason about the sensor responses. In this chapter and the next we consider a range of sensing technologies. The sensors most fundamentally associated with mobility are those that measure the distance wheels have traveled along the ground, sensors that measure inertial changes, and those that measure external structure in the environment. For a robot to know where it is or how it got there, or to be able to reason about where it has gone, sensors and sensing algorithms are required.

Sensors and algorithms for interpreting these parameters can be highly complex. Although a wide variety of sensors exist, two different classes of sensors have emerged for mobile robots: visual sensors, which use light reflected from objects in the environment to reason about structure, and nonvisual sensors, which use various audio, inertial, and other modalities to sense the environment. Nonvisual sensing algorithms are considered in some detail here, and the class of vision-based sensors and algorithms is considered in Chapter 4.

3.1   Basic Concepts

Perhaps the most fundamental classification of sensor types is into *internal state* and *external state* sensors. Internal state sensors provide feedback on the internal parameters of a robotic system, such as the battery level, the wheel positions, or the joint angles for a robot arm or leg. The broad term for internal sensing in biological organisms is *proprioception*; this term is sometimes borrowed by the robotics community. Hunger is an example of internal sensing in humans. External state sensors deal with the observation of aspects of the world outside the robot itself: humidity, the color of objects, and so forth. External sensors that work by touching objects are *contact sensors*, whereas all other modalities, such as camera-based sensing, are *noncontact sensors*.

A specific sensor is either active (it is said to be an *active sensor*) or it is passive (it is said to be a *passive sensor*). These terms are not to be confused with the terms *active vision* and

---

passive vision to be discussed in Chapter 4. Active sensors are those that make observations by emitting energy into the environment or by modifying the environment. Passive sensors, on the other hand, are those that passively receive energy to make their observations. For example, human vision and olfaction involve the use of passive sensors, whereas touch or shouting and listening for the echo are active sensing techniques (shouting and listening for the echo is a simple way to gauge the size of a room).

Passive sensing is often preferred because it is nonintrusive and energy efficient and is similar to the preferred sensing modes of many biological organisms. Because passive sensing does not emit energy, it is especially useful when the robot should be inconspicuous (e.g., in security surveillance) as required in many military contexts, or when multiple robots occupy the same environment. Active sensing, on the other hand, because it involves direct interaction with the environment, tends to be less energy efficient but more robust in as much as it is less subject to the vagaries of the available energy sources.

This difference between active and passive sensing is illustrated by considering two alternative approaches to making a distance measurement: using passive stereo vision and using a laser-based system. Passive stereo vision works by observing the same point (e.g., the position of some mark or feature) on an object from two different cameras and thus measuring the parallax (i.e., the change in observed position). The key requirement is that the marking observed with one camera must be detected in the view observed with the second camera. If the object has a repeating pattern on it, if the object has insufficient markings on it, or if the marking is a specularity (a shiny spot) that moves with the observer's position, the required distance measurement will be difficult or impossible to make. On the other hand, if the observed marking is a laser spot projected by the robot, the high energy at a particular frequency will typically make the marking uniquely and unambiguously detectable.

The following broad but critical observations can be made regarding sensors in the context of mobile robots:

- Real sensors are noisy.
- Real sensors return an incomplete description of the environment.
- Real sensors cannot usually be modeled completely.

Underestimating the extent to which these three generalizations hold can lead to considerable difficulties when "ideal" algorithms are applied in the real world. Underestimating the real properties of sensors and environmental complexity led to the demise of many otherwise promising projects in the early years of computer vision and robotics.

The use of sensors to make inferences about the environment is often described as a problem of recovering or reconstructing the environment. This concept of environmental reconstruction has become a major theme within the sensing community. Unfortunately, this can be a surprisingly difficult problem even with a sensor that returns an apparently rich description of the environment.

A wide variety of alternative sensor technologies is available. This plethora of options can be broadly decomposed into the following four main classes based on the type of data returned:

- **Range sensors** return measurements of distance between the sensor and objects in the environment.

- **Absolute position sensors** return the position of the robot (or some elements of the position vector) in absolute terms (for example latitude and longitude).
- **Environmental sensors** return properties of the environment. These can be ambient properties, like temperature, or pointwise properties, like the color at a point in front of the robot.
- **Inertial sensors** return differential properties of the robot's position (e.g., acceleration).

A variety of additional general issues can be used to classify different sensor technologies. Although we will not go into detail, some examples of important sensor properties or criteria are given below.

- **Speed of operation.** This relates the rate at which measurements are returned when the sensor is running continuously or the time delay until a measurement is provided when one is requested intermittently.
- **Cost.** An infrared emitter-detector pair can cost as little as a few cents, whereas accurate gyroscopes can cost several thousand dollars (if not more).
- **Error rate.** Various factors can be relevant and are discussed below. These include the average error, the number of outliers (wildly incorrect measurements), and the number of missed measurements.
- **Robustness.** To what extent can the sensor tolerate various environmental deviations from the ideal operating conditions? Relevant factors may be physical disturbance, environmental noise in terms of the stimuli of interest, electrical noise, and so forth.
- **Computational requirements.** A simple contact switch may require no computation at all to transduce its result, whereas some vision algorithms require significant computational resources and perhaps special-purpose array processors to obtain a timely result.
- **Power, weight, and size requirements.** Some systems require continuous power just to remain alive so that sensor readings can be taken, whereas other sensors can be turned off and only consume power when measurements are required.

We can model the relationship between the physical properties e of interest in the environment and the sensor reading r using the sensor model $r = f(e)$. In principle, the sensor model should include a model for noise internal to the sensor itself as well as noise due to other sources. Sensor models for a number of different sensors are developed later in this chapter.

The typical sensor model includes not only a stochastic component due to noise but usually also has a range with fewer dimensions than the range of the relation. That is, the sensor model collapses a multidimensional environment into a lower-dimensional reading. The problem of recovering the environment *from* the sensor data can be described as an *inverse problem*: to recover the argument(s) to a function given the output of the function. Such problems are traditionally difficult to solve without additional information or assumptions, for the collapse of dimensions often leads to ambiguity in establishing which of several possible environmental scenarios (i.e., values of the domain) gave rise to a particular reading. Such problems are referred to as being *ill-posed*. More generally, ill-posed problems are problems with either

- A solution that is undefined,
- A solution that is not uniquely defined, or
- A solution that is not stable.

As a concrete example of an ill-posed problem, consider the task of differentiating a signal $f_0(x)$ corrupted by a small amount of high-frequency noise:

$$f(x) = f_0(x) + k \sin(\omega x).$$

The differentiated signal $f'(x)$ is given by

$$f'(x) = f_0'(x) + k\omega \cos(\omega x).$$

Now if $\omega \gg 0$ (the noise has a high frequency), rather than being corrupted by a small amplitude signal, $f'(x)$ is corrupted by much higher amplitude noise. Extracting the content of $f_0'(x)$ from within the corrupted signal $f'(x)$ is a classic example of an ill-posed problem. The derivative of $f(x)$ is unstable in the presence of high-frequency noise.

Sensors can also be unstable with respect to their input. An unstable sensor is one for which the output can vary wildly with a small variation in the input. Formally, for a sensor with output $f(e)$ instability refers to

$$\lim_{h \to 0} \frac{f(e) - f(e+h)}{h} \to \infty.$$

In practice, if the value of

$$\frac{f(e) - f(e+h)}{h}$$

is large for small values of h, the sensor may be referred to as unstable. In practice, this implies that the sensor value may vary unpredictably.

One approach to overcoming instability and other attributes of ill-posed problems is to apply techniques to overconstrain the system and to use an approach such as least-squares to make the measurement more accurate. One difficulty with least-squares systems is that the optimization cannot easily represent any smoothness or environmental constraints that are implicit in the data. Environmental assumptions can be used to resolve the ill-posedness of the problem; these assumptions can be used to select which of several possible solutions is preferred. Such assumptions come in various forms. The most general, and for that reason perhaps the most elegant, are known as regularization assumptions in the sense of Tikhonov [357]. This approach refers to formulating the inverse problem with an additional stabilizing cost term that implicitly selects some solutions over others based on their preferred cost (the cost function must also be constructed to be a seminorm (i.e., it is unambiguous)). In the case of regularization, a variational problem, the cost term is sometimes known as a *stabilizer*. The key issue with resolving the ambiguity inherent in an ill-posed problem is that the ambiguity must be resolved by selecting the correct solution, not just any solution (although this may appear self-evident, there any many examples of reconstruction problems in which the ill-posedness has been resolved without sufficient justification). Under Tikhonov's approach, the solution x to a set of linear constraints $\mathbf{M}x = y$ is given by minimizing the following quantity, sometimes referred to as an energy, with respect to x

$$\min(\|\mathbf{M}x - y\|^2 + \lambda\|Cx\|^2),$$

where

$$\|Cx\|^2 = \sum_n \int C_n(z)\left|x^{(n)}(z)\right|^2 dz.$$

Here $x^{(n)}z$ is the nth derivative of $x(z)$ and n is the order of the maximum derivative to be computed and $\mathbf{M}$ is a matrix that relates desired data x to observations and Cx is used to impose a preference biases on the solution.

Essentially Cx is a weighting term that penalizes nonsmooth solutions. Known constraints on the solution are used to choose the weighting functions $C_n(z)$ and λ. Tikhonov stabilizers have found widespread application in sensor interpretation; (cf. [300], which describes the application of regularization to low-level vision tasks.)

3.2 Contact Sensors: Bumpers

Tactile sensors are those used to create a "sense of touch." These are almost always contact sensors, although some aspects of touch may be captured with noncontact sensors that pass very close to an object's surface and exploit phenomena such as capacitance.

Touch sensors are commonly used in the bumpers of robotic vehicles. The simplest such devices are microswitches that report a binary value: open or closed. When used in bumpers, an array of switches about the circumference of the vehicle is usually enclosed in a compliant material so that pressure anywhere in the outer bumper housing will cause one or more of the switches to be depressed. Tactile sensors are also commonly used on end-effectors such as grippers.

More sophisticated approaches to tactile sensing exploit devices that return a signal over a wide range of values in proportion to the force applied to them. Approaches for such devices range from mechanical devices based on spring-loaded rods mechanically coupled to potentiometers to devices based on a compliant material that changes its resistance or capacitance in response to compression.

How bumper data are handled depends on the architecture of the particular vehicle. Bumpers are the collision avoidance sensor of last resort (even though by the time bumpers detect anything it is actually too late for avoidance). As such, they are sometimes treated as sensors and sometimes wired directly into the low-level control systems of the robot just as the nerves in our knees are coupled to muscular feedback loops that act without the intercession of our brains. On the Nomad 200 platform, for example, the bumper is just another sensor returning the position (and height) of the contact, whereas on the Cybermotion Navmaster platform, the bumper triggers the e-stop circuit, which causes the robot to halt until the circuit is released.

Although the intent of active bumpers with embedded sensors is to avoid damage in the case of a collision, if the impact velocity is high enough, the detection of the mere collision may not be sufficient to avoid damage. Many indoor robots are not equipped with active braking systems, and, even if they are, the large inertia associated with a heavy vehicle may mean that it takes a considerable distance for the vehicle to come to a full stop. In some cases, such as automobiles, bumpers are installed not so much for their sensing ability but because they provide a force-absorbing material that reduces the consequences of an undesirable impact.

3.3   Internal Sensors

Inertial sensors are the class of external sensors that make the least reference to the external world. These are sensors that measure derivatives of the robot's position variables. In particular, the term inertial sensor is commonly used to refer to accelerometers and gyroscopes, which measure the second derivatives of position (i.e., the acceleration and angular acceleration of the vehicle).

One of the earliest uses of inertial sensors for autonomous guidance over long distances can be found in the work of the German Peenemünde Group. The V1 *Vergeltungswaffe* (revenge weapon) were autonomous aircraft that relied on inertial guidance [306]. With an operational range of over 200 km, the V1 relied on multiple inertial and other sensors to guide the weapon to the target. The V1 was required to go in a particular direction, at a specific altitude, for a specific distance. Different sensors were used to address each of these requirements. For distance measurement, a windmill mounted on the nose of the fuselage was used to measure the distance the weapon had traveled. Altitude was measured using a gas capsule whose expansion and contraction were a function of height. The craft's direction was maintained using three air-driven gyroscopes and by measuring the craft's deviation from some initial setting. Because gyroscopes drift during flight, the V1 was fitted with a magnetic compass to correct for gyroscopic drift. Using multiple inertial and external sensors to deal with limitations of individual sensors while providing sufficient sensing to accomplish the overall task of the autonomous system is a common approach in autonomous systems.

3.3.1   Accelerometers

Accelerometers are essentially spring-mounted masses whose displacement under acceleration can be measured, thus exploiting Newton's law $F = ma$ and the (ideal) spring–mass relation $F = kx^2$. Solving for variable a obtains

$$a = \frac{kx^2}{m},$$

where a is the acceleration, m is the mass, and k is the spring constant. In practice, alternatives to the spring–mass system are used. Each accelerometer measures acceleration along a single direction. By mounting three accelerometers orthogonally to one another, an omnidirectional acceleration sensing device can be fabricated. Such devices are available as off-the-shelf items.

Accelerometers are sometimes viewed as sensors that need to make no reference to the external world. Although this is almost true, to correctly compute acceleration the local gravity vector must be known, both in direction and magnitude, so that it can be factored out of the accelerometer's readings. With this exception, these sensors have the versatile characteristics of being usable anywhere from undersea, to the Earth's surface, to outer space.

3.3.2 Gyroscopes

As with accelerometers, *gyroscopes* measure angular acceleration by exploiting basic Newtonian mechanics. The most familiar form of the device is the mechanical gyroscope: a rapidly spinning mass suspended in a gimbal. Because angular momentum is conserved, any attempt to change the orientation of the gyroscope results in an effective force that would, if unimpeded, lead to precession. By measuring this force, the orientation change can be determined. Thus, the gyroscope can be described as a differential compass, that is, a device for measuring differential or relative orientation.

Because it is typically used in computer-controlled navigation, the mechanical gyro involves an electrically driven rotor and an electrical readout of the precession induced and hence the orientation change. Such a device is described as a *rate gyro*. Devices that explicitly integrate the orientation changes measured by a gyroscopic system are referred to as *rate integrating*. Because the Earth itself rotates, even a system stationary with respect to the Earth's surface will observe motion.

The principal difficulty with gyroscopic orientation estimation is that small measurement errors accrue over time. In the case of gyroscopy, the gradual loss of accuracy to error accumulation is referred to as *drift*. In mechanical systems, drift results from friction and from inevitable imperfections in the gymbals. The rate that this error grows can vary from tenths of a degree to tens of degrees per second and depends on the precision of the machining, which, in turn, determines the price, which can vary by up to three orders of magnitude.

An alternative approach to the measurement of absolute orientation is to exploit an optical phenomenon discovered in the second decade of the century termed the *Sagnac effect* after its discoverer Georges Sagnac. Because the effect is a purely optical phenomenon, it permits the construction of optical gyros that involve no moving parts.

The Sagnac effect is based on the use of an optical cavity that contains a lasing medium (a medium that can be excited to emit laser light). The cavity is excited by light pulses traveling in two opposite directions (in a passive gyroscope, the laser can be outside the cavity). The light in the cavity forms a standing wave that remains stationary in an inertial frame. As the cavity rotates, the reflecting mirrors at the ends can be visualized as moving across a succession of nodes of the standing wave, leading to an observed beat frequency in the emitted light.

An alternative description of the same effect is to visualize a change dl in the length of the cavity as a result of rotational motion with angular velocity Ω [73]:

$$dl = 4\pi \frac{r^2 \Omega}{c},$$

where r is the radius of the cavity and c is the speed of light in the medium in the cavity.

For a standing wave to be produced, the light wavelength must divide the cavity length an integer number of times (i.e., with no remainder). As a result, variations in the path length lead to changes in the light wavelength. The variation in frequency induced by the variation in length is given by

$$df = \frac{2r\Omega}{\lambda}.$$

The original effect observed by Sagnac involved the phase shift $\delta\phi$ of (noncoherent) light in a ring interferometer defined by

$$\delta\phi = \frac{8\pi\Omega A}{\lambda c},$$

where A is the area of the interferometer.

This basic phenomenon has been exploited in several forms: active resonators have a cavity filled with the lasing material, whereas passive resonators use a lasing medium that is outside the resonant cavity used for the Sagnac effect. An alternative methodology allows the Sagnac effect to be observed without a laser by using interferometry, which makes this approach more suitable for mobile robots. Fiber-optic technology has recently led to dramatic and ongoing reductions in the price of optical gyroscopes and improvements in their robustness and availability. Fiber-optic implementations include those based on passive resonant cavities as well as interferometry. Typical implementations involve a coiled fiber-optical cable that leads to a very substantial cavity length.

Optical gyroscopes have drift that results from optical and electrical imperfections and noise. Without special compensation, some systems are also unable to provide measurements at low angular velocities.

Typical low-cost units can have drift rates on the order of several degrees per hour, whereas costly systems for aeronautical navigation may have accuracies of 0.001 degrees per hour.

3.3.3   Compasses and Inclinometers

An *inclinometer* is a simple device that measures the orientation of the gravity vector. Digital inclinometers are the modern-day analogue of the carpenter's plumb line. Simple (coarse) inclinometers are based on mercury switches or electrolytic-tilt switches.

Although it may seem a trivial point, the importance of integrating even a coarse-grained inclinometer within a mobile robot cannot be overstressed. A robot that lacks any internal tilt sensor cannot sense its current state of balance and hence cannot respond to unexpected ramps, bumps, or depressions in its environment, which can lead to catastrophic effects.

Although inclinometers measure deviation from the gravity frame, *compasses* measure orientation with respect to the Earth's magnetic field. Mechanical magnetic compasses use the Earth's magnetic field to orient the compass by allowing a magnet to rotate in the horizontal plane and align itself with the Earth's magnetic field. *Gyrocompasses* are gyroscopes modified so that they point towards the Earth's magnetic North Pole. Digital *flux-gate compasses* use a toroidal magnet suspended in the Earth's magnetic field.

Sensors that utilize the local magnetic field to detect north are susceptible to local variations in the ambient magnetic field. Large metal structures, such as the robot itself and its motors can have a considerable effect on the local magnetic field. It is essential to calibrate such a sensor with respect to the vehicle and the environment and to recognize that unmodeled and unexpected deviations in the local magnetic field do occur.

3.4   Infrared Sensors

Near infrared (*IR*) proximity detectors are fast and inexpensive proximity sensors. The basic concept is to emit an infrared pulse and to detect the reflected signal. The distance to the target is estimated using the strength of the recovered signal and assumptions

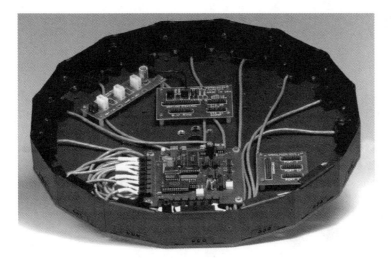

Figure 3.1. Nomadic Sensus 300 infrared proximity detector. This ring of 16 infrared sensors is connected to a small microprocessor to sequence the firing of the units and their modulation. The resulting package can easily be integrated into many mobile robot systems. (Reprinted with kind permission from Nomadic Technologies.)

concerning the reflectivity of surfaces in the environment. In order to avoid potential confusion due to other infrared sources in the environment, the emitted infrared signal is encoded, and detected signals are ignored unless the appropriate waveform is detected within them.

Simple nonencoded signals are susceptible to interference (e.g., from sunlight). Even a more complex signal can be washed out if the ambient illumination is strong. Nevertheless, given their low cost, infrared detectors are often mounted in rings about the robot. The Nomadic Technology Sensus 300 IR ring shown in Figure 3.1 is typical. The units are mounted in a ring, and a small microprocessor is used to fire the units in particular patterns so as to avoid crosstalk between the sensors.

The process of inferring accurate distance information from an infrared sonar ring is nontrivial because it is impossible to estimate the reflective properties of the surface a priori, and hence the intensity of the returned signal is a function of distance and the reflective properties of the surface. On the other hand, the mechanism is inexpensive and compact and is relatively orthogonal to other sensing mechanisms that can be mounted onboard the robot. Thus, infrared proximity sensors such as the Nomadic Sensus 300 tend to be utilized as "noncontact" extended bumpers more often than accurate distance measurement devices.

3.5   Sonar

Sonar (sound navigation and ranging) sensing refers to range sensing using acoustic (i.e., sound) signals. Sonar is an active sensing technology whereby a sound signal or pulse is emitted and its reflection is subsequently received. The time of flight, the phase shift, and the attenuation of the signal as a function of frequency are aspects of the reflected signal that have been exploited by different types of sonar sensor. Sonar has a long history

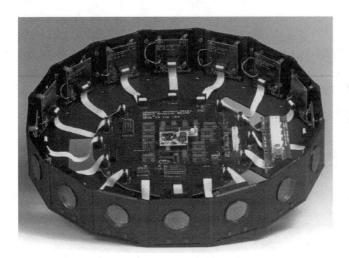

Figure 3.2. Nomadic Sensus 200 ultrasonic sonar ring. (Reprinted with
the kind permission of Nomadic Technologies.)

of use in target localization. As early as 1918, high-frequency acoustic waves were used
to determine the position, velocity, and orientation of underwater objects. Most terrestrial
sonar is based on acoustic signals in the ultrasonic range (with a frequency too high to be
heard by humans).

Sonar units are typically installed in mobile robots by mounting emitter–receiver units in
fixed positions on the base of the vehicle. One common strategy is to locate the sonar units
at uniform angular intervals around the circumference (see Figure 3.2). This is feasible
because the individual devices are comparatively inexpensive. An alternative strategy,
typically confined to research devices, is to mount the sonar emitter–receiver on a rotating
platform and thus achieve omnidirectionality.

Sonar sensing is used underwater by dolphins and other species (e.g., cetaceans and
bats). Each of these species emits chirps of various sorts to which it then attends. In the
case of some species of bat, for example, the differential reflectance of an object as a
function of wavelength allows the bat to identify many characteristics of the object; this
information is used to find and identify insects the bats hunt, for example. The particular
frequency mixes, pulse modulation strategies, and interpretation mechanisms used by bats
are extremely complex, vary by species, and are not yet fully understood.

Sonar sensors used on mobile robots tend to exploit rather simpler strategies. The simplest and most common of these is to use the same physical transducer as both the emitter
and transmitter for a short sound pulse and to measure the time delay until the echo is
received (although there are other techniques; Stanley [339], for example, uses a single transmitter and two receivers to improve the measurement process.) The standard
methodology is to send a brief high-voltage, high-frequency electrical signal through the
transducer to produce a brief acoustic pulse. The transducer then switches to a "listening"
mode and acts as a microphone. Because of residual oscillations in the transducer immediately after the acoustic pulse is generated, it is unable to detect incoming echos reliably
for a brief interval after the outgoing signal is generated; this is known as the *blanking
interval*. As a result, such sonar transducers are blind to obstacles that are very close to the

transducer surface – typically about 6 cm, although the precise value depends on various implementation details.

If the sound wave travels directly to an object, bounces off it, and returns directly to the transducer, the distance from the transducer to the object is half the total round-trip distance traveled by the sound wave and is given by

$$d = \frac{1}{2}ct \qquad\qquad\qquad (3.1)$$

Here d is the distance to the object, c is the speed of sound in air, and t is the time delay between the transmission of the outgoing signal and the received echo.

The speed of sound in air is given approximately by

$$c = c_0 + 0.6T\,\text{m/s},$$

where T is the temperature in degrees Celsius and c_0 is 331 m/s.

This expression is only an approximation. The speed of sound is also affected by the air density (and hence there is an effect of altitude and a more subtle effect of temperature) as well as other factors such as humidity or dust concentration. The speed of sound c varies as the square root of temperature (in Kelvin) and is somewhat dependent on humidity and other environmental properties. In typical office environments, a variation of roughly 2% can be expected.

Depending on the form of the sonar transducer, the spatial amplitude M profile of the emitted wave front can be shaped to a limited extent during the start of its trajectory. Once the acoustic wave front is far from the transducer, the front resembles a portion of an expanding sphere, and thus the amplitude of the signal decreases according to the inverse square law. This spherical dispersion generally dominates after well under 1 m from the transducer surface. The distribution of energy on this spherical surface is nonuniform with an oscillating amplitude within a decreasing envelope that is a function of the angle away from the normal to the transducer surface. The farther the wave travels, the more highly attenuated it becomes; thus, echos that take longer to return are likely to be weaker. This is typically compensated for, in part, by ramping up the gain of the sonar receiver as a function of time while waiting for the return signal. An additional factor that influences the amplitude of the return echo is the acoustic reflectance of the reflecting object. Typical reflectances vary from roughly 98% reflectance for concrete to only 30% reflectance for basic acoustic tile.

The acoustic frequency used in commercial sonar units is almost invariably ultrasonic – typically in the range of 40–50 kHz. Higher frequencies are attenuated more rapidly, although they provide better spatial resolution. The emitted signal has a complex amplitude profile as a function of the angle away from the transducer normal. A cross section of this multilobed shape is shown in Figure 3.3. The sonar beam itself is essentially cone shaped in three dimensions with nonuniform energy distribution over the cone. The maximum energy is in the center with multiple side lobes. In consequence, the effective cone diameter decreases as a function of distance. One implication of this broad wave front is that a returned echo may be the reflection of a portion of the wave front that leaves the transducer at an oblique angle. Thus, a single returned echo does not necessarily result in a very accurate localization of the object that reflected it using only time-of-flight methods.

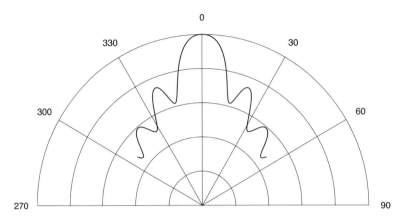

Figure 3.3. Sonar amplitude profile for the Polaroid sonar sensor showing the strength of the sonar signal as a function of orientation with respect to the center of the beam. Although most of the power is restricted to a single lobe near the center of the beam, significant side lobes exist.

The most serious impediment to inferring the location of a sonar-reflecting surface is that, at ultrasonic frequencies, most common objects are specular reflectors; that is, they exhibit mirrorlike reflection properties such that an oblique acoustic wave will be reflected away from the emitter rather than back towards it. If an echo returns to the robot at all, there is no assurance that the echo is not the result of a complex series of bounces around the environment rather than a single bounce off of the closest object in the direction the transducer is pointed. In addition, objects with a cross section much smaller than the wavelength of the acoustic wave being used will return very little energy and hence will appear almost invisible.

Although the specular reflections and difficulties of localizing the reflecting surface are often referred to as noise, they are in fact repeatable characteristics of the sensor that can be accurately modeled [195, 380]. As such, if they are considered noise it would have to be noise in the model rather than in the sensor system itself.

Acoustic signals that return to the robot after only one bounce off of a reflecting surface are often referred to as first-order reflections. Echos that result from two or more bounces are likewise known as second- or higher-order reflections. It is common to regard all second- and higher-order reflections as unusable signals to be discarded.

3.5.1 Transducer Model

Kuc and Siegel [195] constructed a widely used model of the sonar transducer impulse response. Under the assumption that the objects reflecting the sonar pulse of wavelength λ are at distances z much larger than a^2/λ from a circular transducer with radius a, oriented at an angle α away from a flat surface, the impulse response of a transducer at angle α to the sonar wave front is given by

$$h_R(t, z, a, \alpha) = \frac{2c \cos \alpha}{\pi a \sin \alpha} \sqrt{1 - \frac{c^2(t - 2z/c)^2}{a^2 \sin^2 \alpha}}$$

for c, the speed of sound in the environment, $t \epsilon [(2z - a * \sin \alpha)/c, (2z + a * \sin \alpha)/c]$,

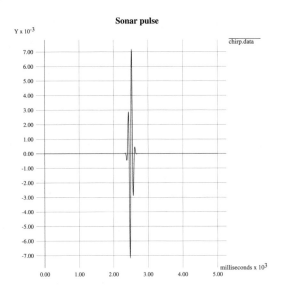

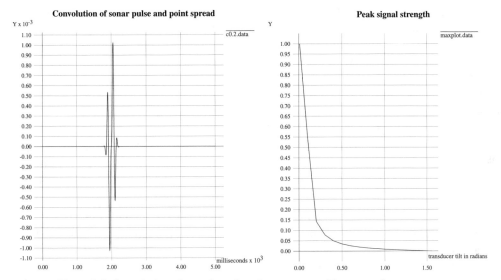

Figure 3.4. Convolution of transducer impulse response with sonar pulse.

and $0 < |\alpha| \leq \frac{\pi}{2}$. This expression is replaced with the delta function $\delta(t - 2z/c)$ when $\alpha = 0$ (the wave front leaves and hits all parts of the transducer simultaneously).

When h_R is convolved with the waveform describing the electrical signal used to excite the transducer (typically a sinusoid with a Gaussian envelope), the degree to which the sonar signal is attenuated is determined as a function of the angle α at which the resulting signal leaves (or arrives at) the transducer. Figure 3.4 shows the result of the convolution and a plot of signal attenuation as a function of transducer angle.

In addition to specular reflection, sonar signals can also be diffracted by corners and other sharp edges in the environment. Because energy is transmitted in a fan of directions, diffraction effects are usually only significant at short ranges. A simple model of this phenomenon is to assume that sharp edges such as corners give rise to uniform spherical reflectance patterns.

If only the interaction between a single sonar unit and a single obstacle in the environment is considered, the distance error associated with a given sonar response can be well modeled by a normal distribution with a slightly longer far-distance tail in the distribution than the near tail [201]. A simulation for this type of sonar error model is quite simple to design. It also suggests that a least squares or Kalman filtering type approach (see Section 3.9.2) would give rise to successful algorithms for integrating sonar measurements, for the noise associated with each measurement can be treated independently, and each can be modeled by some Gaussian process (see [221, 204] for examples of sonar measurement integration algorithms using this type of assumption). Unfortunately very few environments consist of only a single surface. For more complex environments, sonar errors are not well modeled by independent Gaussian distributions but are rather highly correlated and very complex.

To accurately model the complex interactions between the sonar pulse and multiple surfaces in the environment, a ray-tracing-like algorithm is required to follow the path taken by the pulse as it interacts with different structures in the environment [380]. In a computer graphics ray-tracing algorithm, light rays are traced from the image plane, off (and through) objects in the environment, until the ray is either lost, attenuated beyond visibility, or intersects a light source. In this sonar model, a sonar chirp is traced from its emission, through interactions with environmental structure, until the signal is either lost, attenuated beyond detectability, or is reflected back to the transducer. The simulation algorithm is described in detail in Figure 3.5.

3.5.2   Data Interpretation

In addition to the issue of multiple reflections, the interaction of the emitted sound with a single surface is also quite complex. A common but oversimplified model for the interpretation of this interaction is to model an object directly in front of the transducer at the distance measured using Eq. (3.1). It should be noted that the pattern of responses that will be observed in this case will *not* be normally distributed (although some researchers have made this convenient assumption). The repeatability of the pattern of sensor responses leads to some characteristic phenomena such as illusory walls (Figure 3.6).

In Figure 3.6 sonar measurements are overlaid on a floorplan of the robot's environment with the robot itself marked as a circle α. The measurements were taken from a number of locations in the environment as the robot moved along the indicated path. The floorplan describes some of the salient features in the robot's environment. The sonar responses often cluster into circular arcs known as *regions of constant distance* or *RCDs* [205] (see Figure 3.7). These groups of reflected measurements result because a series of wave fronts are all reflected from the same (nearest) point of a single object.

The circular arc structure resulting from walls and concave or convex corners is repeatable. In principle, the width of a reflected arc can be used to discriminate between a corner reflection and that of a planar surface. In practice, this is difficult because it depends on the surfaces in question having uniform acoustic reflection properties. An alternative is to exploit variation of the behavior of the reflected arcs under small motions of the robot to differentiate between different classes of obstacle (wall, convex corner, concave corner) (see [199]). For the same wall material, the reflections for concave corners should

```
range(θ,x,y):
   determine the range returned by a sonar measurement
   from position (x,y) of the sonar sensor facing direction θ

   initialize heap of intersections to be empty
   for each angle φ from θ − π
      to θ + π in steps of size δ
      determine: the first intersection I of a ray
      leaving (x,y) at angle φ with a model wall segment,
      the degree of attenuation of the signal as a function of
      |φ − θ|, the total distance traveled
      from the transducer, and angle
      of incidence at the intersection.
      add I to the heap (ordered by distance traveled
         from transducer)
   while the heap is nonempty
      if the intersection I at the top of the heap is at a
         distance d > maxdistance from the transducer
         return (maxdistance)
      if the intersection is within a single ray-spacing
         of the end of the model segment involved,
         generate a diffracted-ray intersection with the
         receiver also, with appropriate signal strength and
         angle of incidence
      generate the reflected ray r leaving the intersection
         based on the angle of incidence of the incoming ray
         and reduce its amplitude as a function of the
         characteristics of the segment
      if there exists an intersection of r with a model wall
         segment if the intersection is with the model segment
            representing the transducer
            compute the further attenuation of the
            incoming signal as a function of the angle
            of incidence
            if the remaining signal strength is above
               detection threshold
               return (total distance traveled/2)
      else
         add the closest intersection between r and a
         model segment to the heap
   end while
```

Figure 3.5. Ray-tracing sonar simulation algorithm.

theoretically be twice as wide as the reflected arc for planar walls, which should be larger than the RCD for convex corners. Independent of the use of RCD structure to classify the structure of obstacles in the environment, RCDs have been used successfully as a measurement primitive for navigation and environmental exploration [205].

3.6 Radar

Radar (radio detecting and ranging) is much like sonar in its principles of operation. High-frequency radio waves are transmitted, and their reflections are observed to

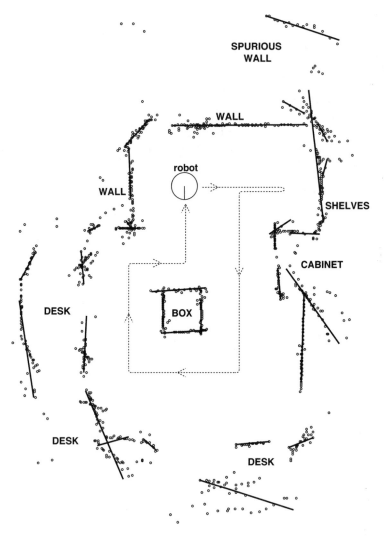

Figure 3.6. Illusory walls and other sonar artifacts. The robot is shown as a circle, and the path the robot took while taking sonar measurements is shown by a line with arrows indicating direction. Sonar measurements are grouped into line (wall) structure.

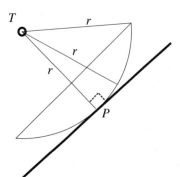

Figure 3.7. Region of constant distance. The reflection arc (*RCD*) for a planar target. A collection of sonar transducers at *T* emits a signal that strikes a planar surface at *P*. The transducer pointed directly at *P* returns a time associated with a distance *r*. Transducers slightly off-axis also return a time associated with a distance *r* owing to the wide width of the signal. A plane is not observed as a flat wall but rather as a region of constant depth or *RCD*.

obtain range measurements and other properties. Until recently this technology has been too costly and bulky for mobile robots, but recently progress has allowed it to be used on larger mobile vehicles such as the CMU NAVLAB. Radar is attractive for mobile vehicles because it is fast and also because it can provide information about surface properties as well as geometry. For example, radar can be used to discriminate between different terrain types, and this may be useful in estimating traversability. Radar can also penetrate the surface layer of an object and thus it can provide information on subsurface structures. Because it is based on radio rather than acoustic waves, radar can be used in environments lacking an atmosphere such as the surface of other planets.

Mobile robot radar systems rely on phase and frequency detection to measure distance to the target. Microwave and millimeter-wave radar systems have operational ranges and performance characteristics well suited for mobile robot applications. Like sonar systems, however, radar suffers from difficulties with specular reflections and with the relatively large footprint of the radar signal.

3.7   Laser Rangefinders

A key objective for sensing is to obtain estimates of the distance to objects in the environment. One of the preeminent sensing technologies for doing this is the laser rangefinder. Laser rangefinders are based on one of the following key alternative methodologies:

- **Triangulation.** The use of geometric relationships between the outgoing light beam, the incoming ray, and its position on the film plane.
- **Time-of-flight.** The measurement of the time delay for an outgoing light ray to hit a target whose distance is being measured and return.
- **Phase-based.** Based on the difference between the phase of the emitted and reflected signals.

The principle of triangulation-based laser rangefinders is essentially the same as those based on regular light sources, which are discussed in Section 4.7. Laser sources, however, have the advantage of being better collimated.

Laser time-of-flight and phase-based sensing, on the other hand, exploit the time delay for signal propagation rather than geometric effects. The use of a narrow collimated beam can permit high resolution and good power efficiency. This is possible with lasers in particular because they are coherent sources that can produce very brief pulses that remain collimated over substantial distances. The sensing technology is based on measurement of the delay or the phase difference between the emitted laser signal and returned reflection. The measurement process can be interferometric or direct but in either case relies on significant signal processing. The maximum range of the sensor is limited by the emitted signal strength.

Low-power systems have an operating range of a few meters, whereas higher-power systems may function over distances of a kilometer or more. This is the same technology that has been used to measure the distance from the Earth to the surface of the moon to astonishingly high accuracy. As the laser beam diverges with distance, the localization of the recovered distance becomes less accurate with more remote targets, although this is not really an issue for interplanetary targets.

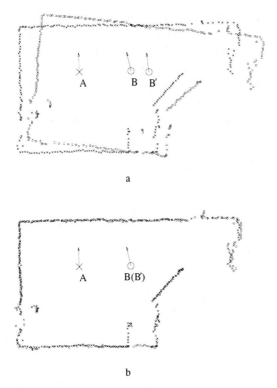

Figure 3.8. Alignment of laser scans. Appears with the
kind permission of E. Milios.

Laser systems are typically mounted on either a pan-tilt unit or as a mirror assembly to
direct the beam at different parts of the environment. Given the accuracy and repeatability
of laser systems, they are an effective alternative to other sensing technologies for robot
pose estimation. Figure 3.8(a) shows two laser scans of the same environment taken from
two different positions. In the system described in [214, 213], a nonlinear optimization
process is used to align the two scans and hence determine the robot's relative motion
between them. As can be seen from the data, laser responses from clean surfaces such as
walls provide robust measurements of environmental structure.

In indoor environments a major concern with laser-based systems is the risk of eye
damage to observers. Although the devices typically employed on an indoor mobile robot
are "eye safe" owing to low power output, it may be difficult to convince other workers in
the environment of this fact. It is also important to remember that laser light will reflect
off some surfaces (mirrors, pools of liquid, etc.), which will result in signal dropout and
may alarm others in the environment.

3.8   Satellite-Based Positioning (GPS)

In 1973 the United States Department of Defense initiated a program to develop
a position estimation system based on signals transmitted by Earth-orbiting satellites.
Beginning with launches in 1978, the first satellite of the current generation (Block II) was
launched in 1989, and by 1995 the system was declared to have satisfied the requirements

of "full operational capability." A similar system called *GLONASS* was developed under the aegis of the Soviet Union.

The U.S. system is known as the *Global Positioning System (GPS)*. It is based on a constellation of 21 orbiting satellites (there are currently 3 spares in orbit as well). The system allows an appropriately equipped receiver to compute its absolute position, velocity, and time to substantial accuracy. This has proven to be a very useful ability, and although the system was developed for and by the military, it has a plethora of civilian applications.

The system operates by allowing a user to measure the difference in time-of-flight for a radio signal to arrive from a combination of satellites. The satellites orbit the Earth in six orbital planes so that, in principle, at least five (and as many as eight) satellites are visible at any time from any point on the planet's surface. In practice, occlusion by obstacles from trees to mountains can complicate the situation.

Measuring the differences in time-of-flight for signals from these satellites allows latitude, longitude, elevation, and current time to be estimated anywhere on the Earth's surface. The satellites transmit a signal that encodes not only timing information but information on the satellite's position and atmospheric characteristics (delays due to conditions in the layer of the atmosphere known as the ionosphere) that would alter the transmission time. Obtaining an estimate of position requires a direct view of a minimum of four satellites and can be obtained at a rate of up to 2 Hz (although most low-cost systems are slower than this). The use of additional satellites permits better performance. Typical civilian receivers can be obtained at low cost and are available in portable pocket-sized form factors, including PC-CARD format. The satellite signal used by civilian receivers is referred to as the Standard Positioning System (SPS) and has an accuracy of 100 m horizontally, 156 m vertically and temporally to 167 ns. The SPS system differs from the full military-grade Precise Positioning System (PPS) signal in that some of the low-order bits are encrypted. This encryption is known as selective availibility (SA) and is based on using a low-frequency time-varying error signal that varies from satellite to satellite to corrupt the broadcast signal. The use of an error signal that varies slowly implies that the error cannot be eliminated using averaging in less that a few hours. On the basis of its rapidly increasing utility for numerous civilian applications, it appears the error intentionally embedded in the SPS signal may be eliminated over the next few years.

The GPS system uses a sophisticated model of signal error and other factors to produce a measurement. The signal from each satellite is used to compute a pseudorange, and these pseudoranges are then combined using a Kalman filter (see Section 3.9.2) to weight signals in proportion to their reliability.

One of the great advantages of the GPS system is that it does not involve any other observation of the external environment, nor does it depend on any specific form of external feature. It is also a purely passive system that involves no energy output of any kind by the receiver. One imagines that this makes it well suited to military applications.

Unfortunately, GPS does not function well in many environments of interest for mobile robotics. That is, GPS cannot be used in environments where radio signals are not receivable along direct line-of-sight pathways from the GPS satellites or where the speed of light differs from that in open air. Specifically, the system cannot be used indoors, underground, or underwater. It is also unreliable in dense forest or between tall buildings. For many applications, the accuracy level of SPS is also insufficient. Luckily, in environments where GPS itself is workable, greater accuracy is possible.

By using a combination of GPS receivers in communication with one another, substantially better position accuracy can be obtained. A variety of schemes for Differential GPS (DGPS) exist with different requirements, complexities, speeds, and accuracies. A Differential GPS system of moderate complexity can achieve accuracy in the range of 1 to 10 m, up to a hundred times better than the SPS civilian GPS and up to 20 times better than even single-receiver military PPS GPS. A still more accurate form of differential GPS called Differential Carrier GPS can achieve accuracy of 1 mm. This form of DGPS is applicable to uses such as geological surveying (e.g., the measurement of crystal deformation). Differential Carrier GPS is substantially more costly than basic DGPS.

Differential GPS is based on using one or more GPS stations to cancel the systematic bias in the GPS signal. A reference receiver is situated at a known location. Thus, it can compute the error in each satellite signal and retransmit an appropriate correction value to other receivers. This approach is based on correcting the individual pseudoranges provided by the separate satellites, and hence the DGPS reference (or base) receiver must have the ability to track and correct the values from each satellite, whereas the remote receiver to be localized must be able to apply the individual corrections – a capability beyond simple standard GPS systems.

A simpler solution is to compute a net position correction at the base and then simply apply the same correction at the remote receiver. Unfortunately, this is not effective except over very short ranges. Not only must the base and remote receiver have the same satellites in view, but they must have the same weighting matrix and geometric dilution of precision (see Section 7.2.2) that specifies how the different signals are combined. Because this latter assumption is rarely met except over very short distances, this approach leads to errors.

The corrections needed for differential GPS are often transmitted by radio. Although the high-accuracy bits of the GPS signal are encoded as a U.S. national security measure, the U.S. Coast Guard runs a system of differential GPS base stations and computes and transmits DGPS corrections over much of the U.S. coastal region. DGPS corrections are usually transmitted in Radio Technical Commission Marine (RTCM) format. The differential correction must be updated by the user at least once every 20 s to avoid falling prey to variations in the error due to signal encryption.

Although the overhead of differential GPS may be prohibitive for many applications, SPS may not prove sufficiently accurate. In the context of mobile robotics, a combination of GPS for coarse localization and an alternative sensor-based method for precise positioning within a local neighborhood may be very attractive. GPS then serves to determine or verify that the robot is in the right region of space, and then region-specific methods such as landmark-based positioning could come into play.

3.9   Data Fusion

The question of how to combine data from different sources is a major and extensively examined research issue. In the context of mobile robotics, data fusion must be accomplished in at least three distinct domains: to combine measurements from different sensors, to combine measurements from different positions, and to combine measurements from different times. We will now consider generic data fusion, just skimming a very large subject. Later in the context of localization and mapping we will revisit this topic.

Combining measurements from multiple positions, times, or sensors is closely related to interpolating, extrapolating, and fitting an analytic function to data. In addition to combining a set of measurements to obtain a combined estimate, we typically would also like an estimate of the confidence of the final estimate given the confidence of the individual input measurements.

In its simplest static form, this process of combining multiple measurements x_i, each of equal certainty, takes the form of averaging and produces a compound estimate $\hat{x}$, which is simply the unweighted mean:

$$\hat{x} = \Sigma x_i / n.$$

This can, of course, be performed with either scalar of vector measurements. Likewise, the confidence of the final average is expressed by the variance $\hat{\sigma}$ (or for a vector measurement, the covariance matrix), which can also be derived directly from the variance $\sigma_i = x_i - \hat{x}$ of the individual measurements as follows:

$$\hat{\sigma}^2 = \frac{\sigma_i^2}{n}.$$

The covariance matrix for the mean-corrected vector $[x_1, \ldots x_n]$ is given by

$$\begin{bmatrix} \sum x_1^2 & \sum x_1 x_2 & \cdots & \sum x_1 x_n \\ \sum x_2 x_1 & \sum x_2^2 & \cdots & \sum x_2 x_n \\ & & \cdots & \\ \sum x_n x_1 & \sum x_n x_2 & \cdots & \sum x_n^2 \end{bmatrix}.$$

It is often the case that measurements of different accuracies must be combined. In this case, the more accurate measurements should be weighted more heavily in computing the mean, and the compound error should also be weighted more heavily towards the more accurate data.

3.9.1 State Space Models

In general, a system may be described by a set of parameters or variables that characterize the relevant aspects of its behavior. At any time, the information of interest regarding a system can be described by a vector $\mathbf{x}$ whose components are the variables of interest. The vector $\mathbf{x}$ specifies a point in the state space description of the system (this is also referred to as the phase space in some contexts). Note that some or all of these variables of interest may not be directly measurable. Thus, the state vector must be estimated using some vector of measurements $\mathbf{z}$.

In the context of mobile robotics, and more generally in the context of control theory, it is often important to consider a dynamic version of this problem in which estimates of a set of variables of interest must be formed on an ongoing basis using observations made to date, that is, over time $t = 0 \cdots k$.

A system for which the state vector can be fully determined from a sufficient number of measurements is described as being *observable*. To describe the state estimate being computed, we use $\hat{\mathbf{x}}(k|k_1)$ to denote the estimate of $\mathbf{x}$ at time k using data from times up to *and including* time k_1. Using the observations up to, but not including, step k to form a prediction is also commonly denoted as $\tilde{\mathbf{x}}(k)$ and also, alternatively, as $\underline{\hat{\mathbf{x}}}_k(-)$. Using the observation at time k, we form an updated state *estimate* $\hat{x}(k)$, also referred to as $\dot{x}_k(+)$ in the literature.

State estimation techniques, such as the Kalman filter presented in Section 3.9.2, typically require a model of how the system of interest evolves over time as well as a model of how the sensors operate. In the context of control theory, the description of the system whose state is of interest is usually referred to as the *plant model*. A third component of the filter is a description of permitted control inputs $\mathbf{u}(t)$ and how they affect the system state.

Plant model   The plant model describes how the system state $x(k)$ changes as function of time and control input $u(k)$ and noise $v(k)$

$$x(k+1) = \Phi[x(k), u(k)] + \dot{v}(k), \tag{3.2}$$

where $\Phi()$ is the state transition function and $\mathbf{v}(k)$ is a noise function. A common and convenient form for the noise model is zero-mean Gaussian noise with covariance $\mathbf{C}_v(k)$ (this particular noise model meets the noise requirements of the Kalman filter described in Section 3.9.2).

Of particular interest is a linear plant model of the form

$$x(k+1) = \Phi x(k) + \Gamma u(k) + v(k), \tag{3.3}$$

where Φ expresses how the system evolves from one state to another in the absence of inputs (this is often an identity matrix) and Γ expresses how control inputs modify the state. A sample plant model for an omnidirectional robot can be found in Figure 3.9.

Measurement model   The measurement model describes how sensor data vary as a function of the system state. Inverting the sensor model (if possible) allows sensor data to be used to compute the state as follows:

$$z_i(k) = h[x(k), \xi] + w_i(k), \tag{3.4}$$

where $w_i(k)$ is a noise function, ξ is a model of the environment, and $h()$ is a function that describes sensor measurements as a function of the system state (e.g., the pose of the robot and its sensors). Again, a common description of the measurement noise is zero-mean Gaussian noise function with covariance $\mathbf{C}_w(k)$.

As with the plant model, a linear measurement model is of particular interest. This takes the form

$$z_i(k) = \Lambda_E x(k) + w_i(k), \tag{3.5}$$

where Λ_E is a matrix that expresses how measurements are derived as a linear transformation of the state. This simple case illustrates how an estimate of the state can be recovered from the measurements as

$$\hat{x}(k) = \Lambda_E^{-1} z_i(k) \tag{3.6}$$

if it is assumed Λ_E is invertible. A simple example of a linear measurement model is given in Figure 3.9 and a non-linear model is given in Figure 3.10.

Consider an omnidirectional robot constrained to the plane. The robot's state $\boldsymbol{x}(k)$ could be described as

$$\boldsymbol{x}(k) = \begin{bmatrix} x(k) \\ y(k) \end{bmatrix}$$

where $[x(k), y(k)]$ describes the robot's position in some global coordinate system. Suppose that robot is equipped with some sort of omnidirectional locomotive system. Then the control input $\boldsymbol{u}(k)$ could be described as an independent change in the robot's x and y location, and thus

$$\boldsymbol{u}(k) = \begin{bmatrix} \triangle x \\ \triangle y \end{bmatrix}.$$

If the error in the motion of the robot is independent in the x and y directions, and if this error can be modeled by some noise function $v_x(k)$ and $v_y(k)$, then the robot plant model is given by

$$\boldsymbol{x}(k+1) = \Phi[\boldsymbol{x}(k), \boldsymbol{u}(k)] + \boldsymbol{v}(k)$$
$$\begin{bmatrix} x(k+1) \\ y(k+1) \end{bmatrix} = \begin{bmatrix} x(k) + \triangle x(k) + v_x(k) \\ y(k) + \triangle y(k) + v_y(k) \end{bmatrix}.$$

The robot goes to where it is commanded with each motion being corrupted by the noise process. This is a linear plant model.

Now let us assume that the robot is equipped with a sensor capable of estimating the robot's displacement from the origin. Then

$$\boldsymbol{z}_1(k) = \boldsymbol{h}[\boldsymbol{x}(k), \xi] + \boldsymbol{w}_i(k)$$
$$= \begin{bmatrix} x(k) + w_x(k) \\ y(k) + w_y(k) \end{bmatrix}.$$

In this linear measurement model,

$$\Lambda_E = \begin{bmatrix} 1 & 0 \\ 0 & 1 \end{bmatrix}$$

and an estimate of the robot's position is available as

$$\hat{\boldsymbol{x}}(k) = \Lambda_E^{-1} \boldsymbol{z}_i(k) = \boldsymbol{z}_1(k)$$

because this sensor model is invertible.

Figure 3.9. Plant and measurement model for a linear omnidirectional robot.

A specific form of Eq. (3.4) is used by Leonard and Durrant-Whyte [205] for sonar data:

$$z_i(k) = \boldsymbol{h}_{st}[x(k), \mathbf{p}_t] + \boldsymbol{w}_i(k) \tag{3.7}$$

In this case, in a step known as *gating* each range measurement from sonar is either discarded or associated with a particular object model $\mathbf{p}_t$ before the Kalman filter is applied. The function $\boldsymbol{h}_{st}()$ thus associates a particular sonar range measurement with a particular geometric model.

The example plant and measurement models worked out in Figure 3.9 use simple linear models for state, input, and measurement processes. Unfortunately most WMRs cannot be modeled in this manner, and it is necessary to consider nonlinear plant, model, and estimation processes. Suppose that the robot can be modeled as a point robot and that we have independent control over the robot's orientation and velocity as we would in the case of a synchronous drive robot.

Then for this robot the control input $\mathbf{u}(k)$ can be described as

$$\mathbf{u}(k) = \begin{bmatrix} D(k) \\ \triangle \theta(k) \end{bmatrix},$$

that is, over the period k to $k+1$ the robot moves forward in the direction it is facing a distance $D(k)$ and then rotates by an amount $\triangle \theta(k)$. The system state is given by

$$\mathbf{x}(k) = \begin{bmatrix} x(k) \\ y(k) \\ \theta(k) \end{bmatrix},$$

and the nonlinear plant model is then given by

$$\Phi[\mathbf{x}(k), \mathbf{u}(k)] = \begin{bmatrix} x(k) + D(k)\cos[\theta(k)] \\ y(k) + D(k)\sin[\theta(k)] \\ \theta(k) + \triangle \theta(k) \end{bmatrix}.$$

Each motion of the robot is assumed to be combined with a noise process $\mathbf{v}(k)$, which has a known or estimatable covariance matrix $\mathbf{C_v}(k)$. This noise process is assumed to meet the requirements that assure the performance of the Kalman filter. If, in practice, the robot moves in distinct steps composed of either pure rotation or translation (i.e., only one of $D(k)$ or $\triangle \theta k$ is nonzero), then only two versions of $\mathbf{C_v}(k)$ may be required.

Now suppose that the robot is equipped with a sensor that can determine the robot's distance from a special beacon in the environment. For example, the beacon may emit a unique sound at a known time and the robot is equipped with a microphone and listens for the sound. As long as the robot and the emitter have synchronized clocks, the distance between the beacon and the robot can be estimated.

If we locate this beacon at (x_b, y_b), the measurement model for this robot is given by

$$\mathbf{h}[\mathbf{x}(k), \xi] = [(x(k) - x_b)^2 + (y(k) - y_b)^2]^{\frac{1}{2}}.$$

This measurement is assumed to be corrupted by a noise process $\mathbf{w}(k)$ with known covariance matrix $\mathbf{C_w}(k)$.

Figure 3.10. Nonlinear plant and measurement model for a simple point robot.

3.9.2 Kalman Filtering

When controlling a mobile robot, one must often combine information from multiple sources. Consider the commonsense use of information from multiple sources in the context, for example, of taking advice from friends. The advice of a trusted associate is likely to influence us strongly. A less trusted acquaintance's suggestions will be, to a large extent, ignored, and yet they might still have some small effect on our decisions. Many such less trusted acquaintances saying the same thing, however, may eventually influence us substantially. If we wish to formalize this notion, how do we decide how to weight information as a function of our confidence in it?

A general scheme for computing such weighted sums is known as a *Kalman filter* [178]. If the measurement process satisfies certain properties such as a zero mean error (these properties are itemized below), the Kalman filter provides the provably optimal method (in a least-squares sense) for fusing the data. In particular, in mobile robotics applications the Kalman filter is used to maintain an ongoing estimate of a vehicle's position and orientation, or of the parameters describing objects of interest in the environment such as another vehicle being followed. The Kalman filter allows an existing (ongoing) estimate of the robot's position (for example) to be combined with position information from one or more sensors. A critical attribute of Kalman filtering is that is permits and necessitates the ongoing estimation not only of a variety of parameters, but also the confidence in these estimates in the form of a covariance matrix. Under certain circumstances, the Kalman filter accomplishes this update in an optimal manner such that it minimizes that expected error in the estimate.

The assumptions made by the Kalman filter are as follows:

- Zero mean system noise $E[v_i] = 0$ where $E[\ ]$ is the expected value.
- Independent noise: $E[v_i v_j] = 0\ \forall i \neq j$. Otherwise, the system noise covariance is given by $E[v_i v_i] = \sigma_i(k)$.
- A linear model of system evolution over time.
- A linear relationship between the system state (i.e., pose) and the measurements being made.

Unfortunately, it is rarely the case that all of these requirements hold in any practical application. If the assumptions do not hold, the Kalman filter can still be used, but the assurances of its optimality will not be valid. If the assumptions are violated in a sufficiently severe manner, the filter may, in fact, lead to very poor results.

Combining measurements and the estimate In the case of quantitative data, and in particular state estimate data, a natural way of describing our confidence in a measurement is by using a covariance matrix. Assuming that errors are normally distributed, this allows us to describe the probability distribution for errors explicitly about the mean. The Kalman filter is a mechanism for combining information so that reliable information is more heavily weighted. The key steps involve using the Kalman gain to weigh the relative contribution of new measurements to our prior expectations. Although this derivation will not be pursued here, the Kalman gain varies in proportion to the state covariance matrix and inversely as the measurement covariance matrix.

The Kalman filter consists of the following stages at each time step (except the initial step). In the following description, we will, for the sake of convenience and expository

The simple linear robot described in Figure 3.9 can maintain an optimal estimate of its position through Kalman filtering. In order to simplify the exposition, it is assumed that $\mathbf{C_v}(k) = \mathbf{C_v}$ and $\mathbf{C_w}(k) = \mathbf{C_w}$. For each motion of the robot, the following steps are followed:

1. The robot moves and using (3.8) the known control parameters are used to estimate the robot's position at time k, as follows:

$$\hat{\mathbf{x}}(k+1|k) = \begin{bmatrix} x(k) + \triangle x(k) \\ y(k) + \triangle y(k) \end{bmatrix}.$$

2. The uncertainty of the state is generated by updating the state covariance matrix using measurements obtained up to and including time k. Because $\Phi = \mathbf{I}$,

$$\mathbf{P}(k+1|k) = \mathbf{P}(k) + \mathbf{C_v}$$

The uncertainty in the robot's position grows by $\mathbf{C_v}$ with each motion.

3. The Kalman gain is computed as

$$\mathbf{K}(k+1) = \mathbf{P}(k+1|k)((\mathbf{P}(k+1|k) + \mathbf{C_w})^{-1}.$$

4. A measurement is made with the sensor, and a revised state estimate is available from Eq. (3.13) as

$$\hat{\mathbf{x}}(k+1) = \hat{\mathbf{x}}(k+1|k) + \mathbf{K}(k+1)[\mathbf{z}(k+1) - \hat{\mathbf{x}}(k+1|k)].$$

Consider the magnitude of the Kalman gain. If $|\mathbf{C_w}|$ is large relative to $|\mathbf{P}(k+1|k)|$, then the magnitude of $\mathbf{K}(k+1)$ is small, that is, the certainty associated with the measurement is small relative to the certainty of the current state model, and hence the old state model $\hat{\mathbf{x}}(k+1|k)$ is a better estimate of $\hat{\mathbf{x}}(k+1)$ than is the measurement of the displacement $\mathbf{z}(k+1)$. On the other hand, if the magnitude of $\mathbf{P}(k+1|k)$ is large relative to the magnitude of $\mathbf{C_w}$, then the estimate $\hat{\mathbf{x}}(k+1)$ is updated to look more like the measurement $\mathbf{z}(k+1)$ than the previous estimate $\hat{\mathbf{x}}(k+1|k)$.

5. Finally the revised state covariance matrix is given by

$$\mathbf{P}(k+1) = [\mathbf{I} - \mathbf{K}(k+1)]\mathbf{P}(k+1|k).$$

Figure 3.11. Kalman filtering example.

simplicity, assume that the state transition matrix Φ and the observation function Λ_E remain constant over time, although this assumption can be trivially relaxed (Φ becomes $\Phi(k)$ and Λ_E becomes $\Lambda_E(k+1)$).

First, using the plant model Eq. (3.3) compute an estimate of the system state at time $(k+1)$ based on our knowledge of where the robot was at time k, what we did (the input $\mathbf{u}(k)$), and how the system evolves in time:

$$\hat{x}(k+1) = \Phi\hat{x}(k) + \Gamma u(k). \tag{3.8}$$

In some practical equations the input $\mathbf{u}(k)$ is not used.

We can also update our certainty of the state as expressed by the state covariance matrix $\mathbf{P}(\ )$ by "pushing it forward in time" as well:

$$\mathbf{P}(k+1|k) = \mathbf{\Phi}\mathbf{P}(k)\mathbf{\Phi}^T + \mathbf{C_v}(k). \tag{3.9}$$

This expresses the manner in which our knowledge about the system's state gradually decays as time passes (in the absence of external corrections).

The Kalman gain can be expressed as

$$\mathbf{K}(k+1) = \mathbf{P}(k+1)\mathbf{\Lambda}_E^T \mathbf{C_w}^{-1}(k+1), \tag{3.10}$$

but because we have not yet computed $P(k+1)$ it can instead be computed as

$$\mathbf{K}(k+1) = \mathbf{P}(k+1|k)\mathbf{\Lambda}_E^T \left[\mathbf{\Lambda}_E \mathbf{P}(k+1|k)\mathbf{\Lambda}_E^T + \mathbf{C_w}(k+1)\right]^{-1}. \tag{3.11}$$

Using this matrix, we can compute a revised state estimate that includes the additional information provided by the measurements. This involves comparing the actual sensor data $z(k+1)$ with the sensor data predicted using the state estimate. The difference between these two terms

$$\mathbf{r}(k+1) = z(k+1) - \boldsymbol{h}[\hat{\boldsymbol{x}}(k+1|k), \xi]$$

or in the linear case

$$\mathbf{r}(k+1) = z(k+1) - \mathbf{\Lambda}_E \hat{\boldsymbol{x}}(k+1|k) \tag{3.12}$$

is sometimes referred to as the innovation. If our state estimate were perfect, the innovation would be nonzero only owing to sensor noise. The revised state estimate is then given by

$$\hat{\boldsymbol{x}}(k+1) = \hat{\boldsymbol{x}}(k+1|k) + \mathbf{K}(k+1)\mathbf{r}(k+1), \tag{3.13}$$

and the revised state covariance matrix is given by

$$\mathbf{P}(k+1) = [\mathbf{I} - \mathbf{K}(k+1)\mathbf{\Lambda}_E]\mathbf{P}(k+1|k), \tag{3.14}$$

where $\mathbf{I}$ is the identity matrix.

When this process is used in practice, the system is initialized using the initial estimated state, and $\mathbf{P}(0) = \mathbf{C_w}(0)$. Figure 3.11 works through an example using linear Kalman filtering.

3.10   Extended Kalman Filter

In many robotics and sensing applications, the system to be modeled fails to have a white noise distribution or is not linear. So long as the errors are *roughly* Gaussian, the Kalman filter can be used, although it may not be provably optimal. To cope with nonlinearity, the *Extended Kalman Filter* (*EKF*) is used. This involves linearizing the plant (Eq. 3.2) and, if necessary, the measurement (Eq. 3.4) by deleting high-order terms from the Taylor expansion.

Linearizing the plant model involves computing the Jacobian of the plant model $\nabla\mathbf{\Phi}[\hat{\boldsymbol{x}}(k), \boldsymbol{u}(k)]$ and using this as a linear estimate of $\mathbf{\Phi}$ within the Kalman filter. Linearizing the measurement model involves computing the Jacobian of the measurement model $\nabla\boldsymbol{h}[\boldsymbol{x}(k), \xi]$ and using this as a linear estimate of $\mathbf{\Lambda}_E$. Figure 3.12 develops an EKF for the nonlinear robot and sensor considered in Figure 3.10.

The nonlinear plant and sensor model is described in Figure 3.10. In order to simplify the exposition, it is assumed that $\mathbf{C_v}(k) = \mathbf{C_v}$ and $\mathbf{C_w}(k) = \mathbf{C_w}$. For each motion of the robot, the following steps are followed:

1. The robot moves, and using Eq. (3.2) the known control parameters are used to estimate the robot's position at time $k+1$ as follows:

$$\hat{\mathbf{x}}(k+1|k) = \begin{bmatrix} x(k) + T(k)\cos[\theta(k)] \\ y(k) + T(k)\sin[\theta(k)] \\ \theta(k) + \triangle\theta(k) \end{bmatrix}.$$

2. A linearized version of the plant model is generated at the current estimate of the robot's position $\hat{\mathbf{x}}(k)$ as follows:

$$\nabla\Phi = \begin{bmatrix} 1 & 0 & -T(k)\sin[\theta(k)] \\ 0 & 1 & T(k)\cos[\theta(k)] \\ 0 & 0 & 1 \end{bmatrix}$$

3. The uncertainty of the state is generated by updating the state covariance matrix using measurements obtained up to and including time k through the equation

$$\mathbf{P}(k+1|k) = \nabla\Phi\mathbf{P}(k)\nabla\Phi^T + \mathbf{C_v}.$$

4. The sensor model is linearized around the current estimate of the robot's position $\hat{\mathbf{x}}(k)$ as follows:

$$\begin{aligned}\Lambda_{\mathbf{E}} &= \nabla\mathbf{h}[\mathbf{x}(k),\xi] \\ &= \begin{bmatrix} 2x(k)[x(k) - x_b] \\ 2y(k)[y(k) - y_b] \\ 0 \end{bmatrix}^T\end{aligned}$$

5. Using this value of Λ_E, the Kalman gain is computed as

$$\mathbf{K}(k+1) = \mathbf{P}(k+1|k)\Lambda_{\mathbf{E}}^{\mathbf{T}}[\Lambda_{\mathbf{E}}\mathbf{P}(k+1|k)\Lambda_{\mathbf{E}}^{\mathbf{T}} + \mathbf{C}_w]^{-1}.$$

6. The innovation is computed as

$$\mathbf{r}(k+1) = \mathbf{z}(k+1) - \mathbf{h}[\hat{\mathbf{x}}(k+1|k),\xi].$$

7. It is now possible to estimate the robot's position as

$$\hat{\mathbf{x}}(k+1) = \hat{\mathbf{x}}(k+1|k) + \mathbf{K}(k+1)\mathbf{r}(k+1).$$

8. Finally, the revised state covariance matrix is given by

$$\mathbf{P}(k+1) = [\mathbf{I} - \mathbf{K}(k+1)\Lambda_{\mathbf{E}}]\mathbf{P}(k+1|k).$$

Figure 3.12. EKF example.

At some interval, typically as often as possible, the derivatives used in the linearized model must be reevaluated at the current estimated state. This raises a major deficiency in the Extended Kalman Filter: If the estimated state is too far from the actual state, the linear approximation to the system's behavior will not be sufficiently accurate. This can lead to increasingly erroneous state estimates, a phenomenon known as *filter divergence*. Because of the possibility of divergence, EKF algorithms typically gait all input before processing. This involves computing the innovation, testing to see if it is unexpectedly large, and rejecting measurements that fail this test.

3.11 Biological Sensing

Because biology serves as the inspiration for most of artificial intelligence and robotics, it is appropriate to consider briefly a few of the myriad sensing mechanisms found in living creatures.

Although sensory stimuli in animals are, of course, used for diverse objectives, Pfeffer divided sensory-based behavior into two basic classes that are still used today: *tropism* and *taxis* [297]. These refer to the stimulus-driven growth of plants and sessile organisms and the oriented movements of animals, respectively. Loeb [212] described all stimulus-driven behavior, even in animals, as tropisms that were ascribed to simple, essentially reflexive mechanisms. The term *topotaxis* was developed to refer to reactions that are directed with respect to a stimulus (as opposed to undirected *phobotactic* responses such as random motions). This, in turn, led to a family of more specific behavioral categories, including *telotaxis*, which refers to a turning response that aligns an animal's direction of motion with a stimulus; *astrotaxis*, which refers to alignment to celestial objects; *polarotaxis*, which refers to orientation change provoked by polarized light; and *mnemotaxis*, which refers to a learned direction change in response to a stimulus. A related notion is that of *kineses*. These are reactions more general than orientation change, such as a change in the speed of motion (*orthokinesis*), that are triggered by a stimulus.

3.11.1 Visual Sensing

The most familiar sensing modality is based on light. The vertebrate visual system begins with the eye, whose principal attribute is a lens that focuses incoming light onto the retina. The retina, the rear surface of the eyeball, is covered in primates with cone and rod cells, each of which serve as photoreceptors and convert incoming photons to electrical energy. The cones are color sensitive (appearing in different wavelength-tuned subpopulations), whereas the rods are achromatic. In humans, the rods are associated, in particular, with peripheral and night vision.

The electrical signals from the eye lead a variety of other cells types such as bipolar cells and leave the eye via the optic nerve, which exits at the blind spot. The optic nerve then passes through the lateral geniculate nucleus and leads to the (primary) visual cortex on the rear surface of the brain. An alternate processing stream is associated with signals that move between the eye and the superior colliculus (or tectum) and the midbrain. The secondary stream is thought to be important in visual tracking and the control of eye movements.

The visual cortex can be described in terms of a set of distinct function regions that number in the dozens. Although initial processing stages appear to compute alternative descriptions of the input array that can be described in terms of simple bandpass signals (i.e., differences of Gaussian filters), the understanding of higher-level areas remains incomplete.

Insect eyes, in contrast, are composed as a large set of ommatidia. Each ommatidium is made up of a set of elongated retinula cells loosely resembling a set of closely packed telescopes. In bees, for example, there are 10 retinula cells: two sensitive to blue light, four tuned to green wavelengths, and four tuned for ultraviolet light as well as polarization.

3.11.2 Magnetic Sensing

Although the use of magnetic fields in biology is much less familiar than their use by ancient mariners, these fields appear to be exploited by organisms that range from the single-celled paramecium [191], to the termite, to the snail, and perhaps, even, the pigeon. The bacterium *aquaspirillum magnetotacticum* is equipped with a specialized organelle called the *magnetosome* that acts like a compass and appears to be useful in allowing the bacterium to decide which way is down [41]. It appears that young salmon use the Earth's magnetic field to return to their spawning grounds [309].

3.11.3 Odor Sensing

Although vision is the primary sense for humans, smell rules for most animals. More formally, the use of olfaction is one instance of chemosensory navigation. The olfactory systems of animals are often much more sensitive than those of humans and are able to detect not only smaller amounts of the chemicals that cause odors, but they are also better able to resolve different types of odors.

Various species of animals exploit olfactory marks for terrain marking, landmarks recognition, and trail marking. Olfactory markers have the advantage of being discrete and evanescent. This suggests that different agents can deposit and use their own specific markers in a given area at different times. In ants, olfactory cues are used for short-range communication (e.g., between two ants in the same place) as well as for long-range communication (e.g., to mark trails [156]). In trail following, one strategy is to lay an odor trail whose width roughly corresponds to the antenna separation. An ant following the trail then keeps one antenna on each side to the odor maximum as it walks the trail, weaving slightly to keep itself calibrated. There is also an odor variation, either in strength or type, from the source to the destination of the trail, at least with some species of ants. An ant removed from a trail and then placed at a random position will head in an arbitrary direction along the trail but after walking a short distance will turn around and head in the correct direction having, presumably, inferred the odor gradient.

3.11.4 Mapping

Mapping and exploration by animals are accomplished in various ways. It is worth noting that there appears to be evidence for techniques that include associating actions with specific landmarks as well as for maintaining full internal maps.

Bees, for example, can be intercepted en route to a group of flowers. If they are transported to a different location (deprived of sensory stimulus), when they are released they will head directly for the original target, suggesting that they maintain a complete internal map. A desert ant species *Cataglyphis fortis* has been shown to combine landmark-based position estimation with dead reckoning to accomplish navigation.

In animals, the brain structure called the hippocampus is thought to be critical to the construction of spatial maps. A specific class of pyramidal cells known as place cells appears to encode localization information. These cells show elevated electrical firing when the subject is in the spatial region to which the cell is tuned. Thus, specific locations are coded by populations of cells that fire preferentially. These cells appear to be sensitive to a variety of sensory stimuli but also fire even when the sensory cues are removed (stimulated, presumably, by dead-reckoning information). It has also been suggested that an independent neural system exists specifically for route-based navigation, driving reactions without as complete a metric representation of space.

3.12   Further Reading

3.12.1   Nonvisual Sensors

There are numerous general purpose nonvisual sensors on the market, and manufacturer's data sheets provide the best information on a specific device. An in-depth study of nonvisual sensors and their capabilities can be found in [116].

3.12.2   Kalman Filtering

A formal mathematical treatment of Kalman filtering can be found in [51]. This includes proofs of optimality and formal treatment of the operational requirements of the filter. See also [338, 133]. Leonard et al. [205] provide an in-depth treatment of the use of Kalman filtering and sonar sensors for mobile robot pose estimation.

3.13   Problems

1. Suppose that an object is dropped from some known height under the effect of gravity. Develop a Kalman filter to continually estimate the state of the object if (a) the position of the object is measured, (b) the velocity of the object is measured, and (c) the position and the velocity of the object are measured at each time instant.

2. Derive a Kalman filter that combines an a priori position estimate (with known error) with an independent translation estimate (for example from triangulation) and an orientation estimate (from a compass). Assume all errors are normally distributed with known standard deviations.

3. Assume the following slightly idealized model of sonar sensing: the sensor returns a signal whenever an object is within $\pm 15°$ of the transducer normal and is between 4 cm and 4 m distance. Plot the response of a sonar sensor located in the center of a rectangular room of size 6×3 m. Plot observed distance as a function of orientation, ignoring the effects of multiple sonar bounces.

4. Acoustic reflectance depends on a function of the surface curvature of a reflecting surface and the wavelength of the sound wave as well as the properties of the object from which the sound is being reflected. How could this be used in robotics?

5. In this question you will develop alternate versions of the sensor model used in the simulation developed above.

    (a) Add zero-mean Gaussian noise (with standard deviation σ_d) to the range returned by the idealized sensor.

    (b) Add zero-mean Gaussian noise (with standard deviation σ_α) to the direction in which the sensor points when returning the range corrupted by σ_d above.

6. Given a set of 2-D points corresponding to distance measurements, aggregate the measurements into line (wall) segments. Test your grouping algorithm on sensor measurements obtained with the sensor noise models developed in the previous problems.

4

Visual sensors and algorithms

Anyone who has had to move about in the dark recognizes the importance of vision to human navigation. Tasks that are fraught with difficulty and danger become straightforward when the lights are on. Given that *we* seem to navigate effortlessly with vision, it seems natural to consider vision as a sensor for mobile robots. Visual sensing has many desirable potential features, including its passivity, high resolution, and long range.

Human vision relies on two eyes to transform information encoded in light into electrical signals transmitted by neurons. In the biological sciences, the fields of perception and cognition investigate how this neural information is processed to build internal representations of the environment and how humans reason about their environment using these representations. From a robotics point of view, the fields of computer vision or robot vision examine the task of building computer representations of the environment from light, and the study of artificial intelligence deals in part with the task of reasoning or planning based on the resulting environmental representation. Like the previous chapter, this chapter continues the exploration of how to build descriptions of the workspace from sensor data. In this chapter, we consider the issues involved in sensing using light and related media.

Vision is strikingly powerful as a sensory medium. At the same time, it can be strikingly difficult to use for robotics, due to both the limitations of existing methods and the excessive expectations borne of our facility. Although many visual sensing problems appear trivial to naive humans, few problems in generic computational vision are fully solved. Perhaps it is easy for us to underestimate the difficulty of vision problems because so much of the human brain is devoted to solving them (current data suggest that 50 percent or more of the human brain is involved in processing visual data).

For many years, a large part of the vision community sought solutions to "shape from" problems: recovery of accurate distance measurements to points visible in an image using different visual attributes such as shading (shape from shading), motion (shape from motion), or even texture variation (shape from texture). In the last decade, it has become apparent that even complete depth information, as provided by a laser range scanner, does not alleviate the difficulty in truly interpreting arbitrary scenes. For mobile robotics, however, complete scene interpretation is not always necessary.

Vision relates measurement to scene structure. This is an important property of visual sensors that is often overlooked. Suppose that a laser range sensor is directed by a robot at different objects in an environment. The sensor returns the distance to the objects, and so (at best) the robot and any human operator associated with the robot obtain a set of distance measurements as a function of the direction in which the laser sensor is pointed. It can be very difficult to interpret this range information in terms of scene structure; for a human operator it can be extremely difficult to relate the distances to specific objects in the environment. Now suppose that a vision-based sensor is used instead. The sensor obtains a visual image of the environment, and because humans are used to dealing with visual information it is usually straightforward for an operator to determine which part of the image is associated with which structures in the environment.

It is important to recognize that many potential robotic environments were originally designed for humans to use and thus have been modified to make them easier to navigate in using vision; roads have visual lane markings, signposts have a standard visual form, and so forth. Thus, vision would seem to be an ideal sensor for the visually rich environment that we have constructed for ourselves. Unfortunately, the current state of the art in computer vision has not reached the point at which off-the-shelf solutions exist to many problems. Vision-based approaches do exist for a number of tasks, and vision-based sensors can be useful. This is especially true in constrained environments where factors that might complicate visual sensing can be eliminated, such as specular reflections (shiny spots) or ambiguous coloring.

Many robotic vision systems are based on video cameras that passively observe their environment. Alternatively *active vision* systems are systems in which the observer is active (i.e., moving) rather than static [27, 7, 145]. In an active vision paradigm, visual processing is devoted to salient components in the image and the scene rather than processing the entire image blindly. This attention can be mechanical, using robotic actuators such as pan-and-tilt units or stereo heads, for example; it can be through manipulation of intrinsic camera parameters; or it can be computational. Rather than processing snapshots, in an active vision paradigm the sensor and the environment continually interact, which explains the interest in active vision by the mobile robot community.

A fundamental difficulty with using vision as a robotic sensor is that a single image of an object does generally not determine the object's absolute distance or size. Thus, a common computational task in robot vision is the extraction of depth information from one or more images. Accomplishing this task often requires a strong model of the process of image acquisition (camera calibration) and a representation of the raw image data in some intermediate form in terms of image features. We begin with a consideration of these tasks.

4.1   Visual Sensors

Visual sensors obtain a considerable amount of data that can be very expensive to process. A standard charge-coupled device (CCD) camera obtains a grid of approximately 640×480 intensity measurements 30 times a second. A standard digitizer will convert these intensity measurements into a machine-readable quantity at this rate, resulting in 640×480 16- or 8-bit values 30 times a second. Processing this volume of data often requires either special-purpose hardware or the decision to process only a part of the incoming data stream selectively.

Visual sensors have a finite field of view. The wide field of view obtained with a wide-angle lens results in a large field of view at the cost of a lower spatial resolution and wide-angle lenses often suffer from spherical and chromatic aberrations. Telephoto lenses have a smaller field of view but a higher spatial resolution. For many robotic vision applications it is necessary to control the direction and internal camera parameters (focal length, aperture, etc.) of the video sensor(s) actively in order to have them "attend" to the portion of the world that is to be studied.

Visual sensors enforce a particular spatial and temporal sampling on the scenes they observe. Almost all video cameras are based on technology that was developed for the delivery of home video. As such, they are intended to generate video that matches one of the international video standards used for home television. In North America the NTSC standard is used, whereas in other parts of the world alternative video encoding is used, such as PAL and SECAM in Europe. These standards embody a set of compromises that minimize cost while keeping picture quality (barely) acceptable for television viewers. Unfortunately, these compromises can sometimes substantially complicate computational interpretation of the visual data. A standard CCD video camera uses a uniform spatial sampling in which each individual picture element (*pixel*) is *not* obtained at the same time. This introduces spatial and temporal sampling problems that can be difficult or impossible to overcome. A standard video signal is only available as a sequentially scanned and possibly interlaced version of the image. This scanning must be undone to access individual picture elements. That being said, the popularity of home video has resulted in a considerable decrease in the price of video sensors. Coupled with the modest cost of processing, this makes video an attractive sensor for mobile robots.

4.1.1   Calibration

Video systems for robots typically consist of two main components: an optical system that collects light from over a finite field of view and focuses this light onto an image plane, and an optoelectrical system to take this focused light and convert it into a computer-readable signal.

The process of collecting light and recording it using a computer is complex, and various models of the underlying process have been developed. Perhaps the most widely used camera model in computer vision and robotics is the pinhole camera model (see Figure 4.1). Under the pinhole camera model a point on an object is projected through a pinhole or optical center of a camera onto a planar image surface. Consider the head of the arrow viewed by the pinhole camera shown in Figure 4.1. Light from some illuminant strikes the head of the arrow and is reflected in all directions. Some of this light passes through the pinhole aperture in the camera and strikes the image plane. Because light travels in straight lines, the point to which an image feature projects on the image plane constrains the three-dimensional location of the feature to a line in space, the line consisting of the loci of points joining the tip of the arrow with its image on the image plane and the pinhole. The absolute depth of the arrowhead is lost. Pinhole cameras are often said to obtain the direction to an object rather than the distance to it.

The reduction of the three-dimensional position of a point to its two-dimensional projection within a camera is *the* fundamental problem with the use of vision in mobile robotics. This makes the recovery of a point's distance a fundamental computational challenge. Many mechanisms have been proposed to overcome this problem, including the use of

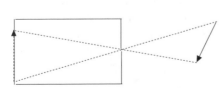

Figure 4.1. Pinhole camera model. A pinhole camera consists of a box with a pinhole through which light enters and an image plane onto which the light is projected. Because light travels in straight lines, an object (here an arrow) is projected to a unique location on the image plane.

additional assumptions that restrict the set of possible distance values, the use of multiple cameras, and the use of temporal integration. Some of these techniques will be examined shortly.

The mathematical equivalent of the pinhole camera is known as perspective projection. Given an arbitrary point in three space described in homogeneous coordinates* as $X = [X_1\ X_2\ X_3 1]^T$, under a perspective or pinhole camera model the relationship between the 2-D pixel or image coordinate $(x_1/x_3, x_2/x_3)$ and its 3-D world or scene coordinate can be described by a 3×4 matrix called the *projection matrix* $\tilde{\mathbf{P}}$ as follows:

$$
\begin{bmatrix} x_1 \\ x_2 \\ x_3 \end{bmatrix} = \tilde{\mathbf{P}} \begin{bmatrix} X_1 \\ X_2 \\ X_3 \\ 1 \end{bmatrix}.
$$

Owing to the nature of the mapping from 3-D to 2-D, $\tilde{\mathbf{P}}$ is defined only up to a scale factor. A common mechanism for specifying a unique $\tilde{\mathbf{P}}$ is to force $\tilde{\mathbf{P}}_{3,4} = 1$, although other techniques exist (e.g., [118]).

The matrix $\tilde{\mathbf{P}}$ can be interpreted in a number of different ways, but the classical interpretation (see [157] or [118]) is that $\tilde{\mathbf{P}}$ models a rigid transformation from some arbitrary 3-D world coordinate system to a 3-D coordinate system aligned with the optical center and the ideal image plane of the camera followed by a perspective projection to an ideal 2-D coordinate system on the image plane. Furthermore, $\tilde{\mathbf{P}}$ encodes an affine relationship between the real 2-D coordinate system used on the image plane and the ideal one. The parameters defining the rigid portion of the transformation are known as the *extrinsic camera parameters*, for they do not depend upon the nature of the camera itself, whereas the remaining parameters of the camera calibration are known as the *intrinsic parameters*.

Although the pinhole camera and the corresponding projective geometry are perhaps the most common models, less sophisticated mathematical models have wide applicability in restrictive imaging domains. One particular approach is to completely ignore the effects of perspective and scaling with depth. This model is known as *parallel projection* and *orthographic projection* is the special case where the light rays impinge along the normal to the film plane. Note that while parallel projection is only truly accurate for a camera that is infinitely far from the scene, it can be a good approximation whenever this distance from the camera to the scene is much larger than the extent of the scene itself. An intermediate imaging geometry known as *weak perspective* or *scaled orthographic camera* is applicable when the depth variation of an object is small compared with the average distance of the object to the camera. Under this model all of the individual points on an object are scaled by *a single* average depth value rather than by individual depth values at each point. While this model does not correspond to any physical camera system, it can be mathematically convenient. Various approximations to the perspective camera model are discussed in [8], and a vision system that takes advantage of one of these more restrictive imaging models is presented in [332].

---

* Homogeneous coordinates are a representation of an n-dimensional space in $(n + 1)$ dimensions used to express both translation scaling and other operations as matrix multiplication. See Section 2.1.4.

If necessary, the projection matrix $\tilde{\mathbf{P}}$ can be decomposed into intrinsic and extrinsic parameters by modeling the extrinsic parameters as a rigid three-dimensional transformation, a 3×3 rotation matrix, and a rigid translation vector $\mathbf{T}$ and by modeling the remaining degrees of freedom by a set of intrinsic parameters representing an affine distortion of the image plane.

In order to use vision for many mobile robotic tasks it is often necessary to obtain $\tilde{\mathbf{P}}$ for a particular camera. The process of obtaining $\tilde{\mathbf{P}}$ for a camera is known as *camera calibration*. There are many different mechanisms for calibrating a single video camera, but perhaps the simplest mechanism for camera calibration is to use a calibration object with a known 3-D pose along with its projection to solve for the calibration matrix $\tilde{\mathbf{P}}$.

One particularly simple mechanism for calibrating a camera with a calibration target is to pose the problem as a linear least-squares task [157]. Given a collection of calibration points in world coordinates X_i along with their image projections (u_i, v_i), seek a $\tilde{\mathbf{P}}$ such that the mapping $\tilde{\mathbf{P}}X_i$ results in the smallest image error, that is, seek a $\tilde{\mathbf{P}}$ with $\tilde{\mathbf{P}}_{3,4} = 1$ such that

$$\sum ((\tilde{\mathbf{P}}X_i)_1 - (\tilde{\mathbf{P}}X_i)_3 u_i)^2 + ((\tilde{\mathbf{P}}X_i)_2 - (\tilde{\mathbf{P}}X_i)_3 v_i)^2 \tag{4.1}$$

is minimized. Here we use the notation $\mathbf{A}_n$ where $\mathbf{A}$ is a matrix to indicate the nth row of $\mathbf{A}$. It is straightforward to show that $5\frac{1}{2}$ scene points, not all lying on the same plane, are sufficient to define $\tilde{\mathbf{P}}$ uniquely. Only $5\frac{1}{2}$ scene points are required as each calibration point results in two constraints and the calibration problem requires the solution of eleven linear equations. More commonly, additional scene points are available and a least-squares solution is used.

Figure 4.2 shows a simple calibration target. It consists of two planes with a collection of points located on the target in a global coordinate system. The target is imaged, and the image projection (u, v) for each point (X, Y, Z) is estimated. Equation (4.1) is then minimized using linear least-squares to obtain $\tilde{\mathbf{P}}$, which for this image is given by

$$\tilde{\mathbf{P}} = \begin{bmatrix} -4.287278 & 3.027158 & -0.396339 & 260.652618 \\ 0.716428 & 0.798423 & -6.112374 & 268.442322 \\ -0.003050 & -0.002737 & -0.001803 & 1 \end{bmatrix}.$$

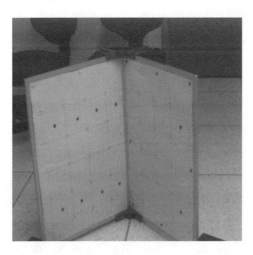

Figure 4.2. Sample calibration object.

The linear least-squares solution $\tilde{\mathbf{P}}$ is obtained by solving $AX = B$, where

$$
\mathbf{A} = \begin{bmatrix} -X_i & -Y_i & -Z_i & -1 & 0 & 0 & 0 & 0 & u_i X_i & u_i Y_i & u_i Z_i \\ 0 & 0 & 0 & 0 & -X_i & -Y_i & -Z_i & -1 & v_i X_i & v_i Y_i & v_i Z_i \\ & \cdots & & & & & & & & & \end{bmatrix},
$$

$$
X^T = \begin{bmatrix} \tilde{\mathbf{P}}_{1,1} & \tilde{\mathbf{P}}_{1,2} & \tilde{\mathbf{P}}_{1,3} & \tilde{\mathbf{P}}_{1,4} & \tilde{\mathbf{P}}_{2,1} & \tilde{\mathbf{P}}_{2,2} & \tilde{\mathbf{P}}_{3,3} & \tilde{\mathbf{P}}_{4,4} & \tilde{\mathbf{P}}_{3,1} & \tilde{\mathbf{P}}_{2,2} & \tilde{\mathbf{P}}_{3,3} \end{bmatrix}
$$

and

$$
B = \begin{bmatrix} -u_i \\ -v_i \\ \cdots \end{bmatrix}.
$$

The linear least-squares solution X is then available as $X = (\mathbf{A}^T \mathbf{A})^{-1} \mathbf{A}^T B$.

It is instructive to note that $\tilde{\mathbf{P}}$ contains considerable information concerning the camera pose. The solution of

$$
\begin{bmatrix} 0 \\ 0 \\ 0 \end{bmatrix} = \tilde{\mathbf{P}} \begin{bmatrix} C_x \\ C_y \\ C_z \\ 1 \end{bmatrix}
$$

defines the optical center (C_x, C_y, C_z) of the camera in world coordinates. In addition, each row of $\tilde{\mathbf{P}}$ defines a plane, all of which intersect at (C_x, C_y, C_z). The intersection of $\tilde{\mathbf{P}}_1$ and $\tilde{\mathbf{P}}_2$ defines the direction in which the camera points, and the intersection of $\tilde{\mathbf{P}}_2$ and $\tilde{\mathbf{P}}_3$ defines the twist of the camera with respect to that direction.

Although the pinhole camera and perspective projection model is widely used in computational vision, it is not perfect. Very few cameras are actually pinhole cameras; most utilize a finite aperture rather than a pinhole in order to admit more light onto the image plane. This blurs the resulting image, and a lens assembly is used to focus the image. Unfortunately, lenses have a finite depth of field, and objects lying outside this region will be blurred across the image plane. In addition, lenses often introduce nonuniform image distortion as well as chromatic distortions of the input. Various models exist for these more realistic lenses, but they are rarely used in robotic vision applications. One exception is their use in depth-from-focus algorithms in which a precise model of image blurring is used to estimate object depth. A common trick to make a nonideal camera behave more like a pinhole one is to use the smallest aperture setting possible and to utilize only the central portion of the image in order to reduce radial distortions.

The image plane itself complicates the imaging process. Charge-coupled device (CCD) arrays used in most robotic sensors rely on a rectangular sampling grid that is roughly aligned with the horizontal and vertical axes of the camera. Aliasing errors occur owing to the finite spatial sampling extent of the CCD arrays and to the low temporal sampling rate. The construction of nonuniformly sampled sensors (e.g., foveated sensors [370, 285]) as well as image sensors whose pixels are randomly accessible (e.g., [303]), rather than the linear access method of CCDs, is the subject of ongoing research.

4.2   Object Appearance and Shading

Before considering the application of visual sensing to robotics tasks, it is worthwhile to consider briefly the relationship between objects in the scene and their appearance. Images, be they video images or those on our retina, are composed of discrete samples of reflected intensity. In the case of standard color cameras these samples are acquired by three sets of sensors tuned to three different frequencies: typically red, green, and blue (this tuning is certainly not the only one; most cameras are also sensitive to infrared). It is not coincidental that the human eye can also be modeled as being composed of three classes of color-sensitive detector: the red, green, and blue cones. In high-quality cameras, the different color measurements associated with a given pixel come from exactly the same point in space (using colored filters). In lower-cost cameras (and the human eye), the different measurements are, in fact, acquired by different detector elements displaced from one another in space, but we will neglect this. Thus, we can consider each pixel as being the measurement of the light reflected from a single point in the scene (we will also neglect phenomena such as fog).

The light reflected from a point in the scene depends on two things: the reflectance properties of the object and the illumination that falls on the object. This relationship is formalized by the *bidirectional reflectance distribution function* (or BRDF) $R(\phi_{\text{in}}, \theta_{\text{in}}, \phi_{\text{out}}, \theta_{\text{out}})$, which expresses the fraction of received energy from a specified orientation $(\phi_{\text{in}}, \theta_{\text{in}})$ that is reflected in a given direction $(\phi_{\text{out}}, \theta_{\text{out}})$. Thus, determining the amount of light reflected along a ray back to the camera involves knowing the BRDF for the object of interest and combining the light reflected from all illumination sources (including light reflected from other objects).

A common simplification is to assume that the reflectance function of most objects is a linear combination of two types of canonical reflector: a mirror and a matte surface. Mirrorlike surfaces, known as specular reflectors, reflect almost all the incoming light energy along a ray M symmetrically opposite to the angle of incidence, and their reflectance can be approximated by

$$R_s = \rho_s (M \cdot V)^\alpha, \tag{4.2}$$

where V is the direction to the viewer, ρ_s measure the extent of specular reflectance, and α is a coefficient that determines how perfectly shiny the reflector is (perfect shininess is attained for $\alpha \to \infty$). Matte surfaces, known as *Lambertian* reflectors, reflect light equally in all directions, and the reflected intensity depends only on the relationship between the surface normal and the light source:

$$R_d = \rho_d N \cdot L, \tag{4.3}$$

where L is a unit vector pointing towards the light source, ρ_d represents the surface's reflective nature and N is the surface normal. The reflectance of an object can then be expressed with this simplified model as a sum of the two components ρ_s and ρ_d.

When these reflectance models are applied to color images, they are sometimes applied independently for each of the color channels. In practice, Lambertian reflectance tends to result from scattering of light in the surface layer of an object, and hence it takes on the object color. Specular reflectance, on the other hand, tends to be relatively unaffected by the pigment color of an object, and thus specularities often have a color akin to that of the illuminant. Although this can be useful for the detection of highlights (see [134]), it can also complicate simple color-based object recognition schemes.

4.3   Signals and Sampling

A digital image is simply a collection of samples of the visual content in the environment. In principle, we can think of a scene as a field of rays associated with all possible viewing directions from all possible vantage points. Such descriptions of a scene are known as the *lumigraph* or the *light ray manifold*. A single conventional image contains a set of samples from a single vantage point. Each individual sample is known as a *pixel* or *picture element*. The samples are typically obtained from points on a rectangular lattice and have a finite resolution such as 8, 16 or 32 bits per sample. Each pixel encodes either intensity or the intensity in each of a small number of color channels associated with this specific spatial location.

Although it is tempting to model this set of pixels as a continuous surface, it is important to recognize that the pixels are discrete samples taken in space and time. This introduces physical limits on what can be correctly viewed with a given video sensor. Figure 4.3 shows the difficulties involved in sampling a continuous function. The continuous image being sampled by the discrete image shown in the figure is a sine wave in intensity whose frequency increases linearly with vertical position, that is,

$$I(x, y) = \sin(\omega x y).$$

Each scan line in the image should appear as a sine wave, and the frequencies should increase as one moves down the image. Because the image has a finite pixel size (as does this printed page), the rate of sampling per wavelength decreases, and eventually there are insufficient samples to represent the underlying continuous structure. Signals at high frequencies can be mistaken for signals at lower frequencies, and other artifacts emerge. This phenomenon is known as *aliasing*. Although Figure 4.3 was specifically chosen to exhibit aliasing, the phenomenon occurs whenever the real world exhibits an intensity pattern that cannot be well represented within the limited sampling resolution of the video sensor.

Figure 4.3. The effects of sampling. This figure shows a sine wave with linearly increasing frequency. Because the sampling rate is constant, most of the underlying continuous image is undersampled, and aliasing results. A complex Moiré cross-like pattern should be noted.

The minimum sampling frequency that is required to represent a continuous signal completely is known as the *Nyquist frequency*. Informally, to represent a continuous signal, it is essential to sample the signal "at a rate at least twice as great as the highest frequency in the signal." Consider the one-dimensional signal $f(x) = \cos(\pi x)$. If $f(x)$ is sampled at integer points (i.e., at $0, 1, 2, 3, \ldots$), the values $1, -1, 1, -1, \ldots$ are obtained. If $f(x)$ is only sampled at even integers, then $1, 1, 1, \ldots$ is obtained. Sampling this 1-D signal at every pixel retains the information in the signal. Sampling it at every other pixel underrepresents the image, and aliasing occurs. In angular frequency, the Nyquist frequency is $\omega_{\text{Nyquist}} = \pm\pi$. When discretely sampled on an integer lattice, continuous signals with frequencies above π and below $-\pi$ cannot be well represented.

In conjunction with the Fourier transform (see [238]),

$$\hat{f}(\mathbf{k}) = \int_{-\infty}^{+\infty} f(\mathbf{x}) e^{-i\mathbf{x}\mathbf{k}} \, d\mathbf{x}$$

can be used to obtain the amplitude spectrum $|\hat{f}(\mathbf{k})|$ of a continuous signal $f(\mathbf{x})$ for $\mathbf{x}, \mathbf{k} \in \mathbb{R}^n$. Filters or image transformation operators with large values of $|\hat{f}(\mathbf{k})|$ for elements of $\mathbf{k}$ near $\pm\pi$ (the Nyquist frequency) tend to amplify unrepresentable frequencies in an image and thus perform poorly unless high frequencies are suppressed before applying the operator.

Although arbitrary operations can be applied to an image, many image operations can be expressed as linear shift invariant systems [273]. Such systems are completely characterized by their response through a convolution sum

$$y(n_1, n_2) = \sum_{k_1=-\infty}^{+\infty} \sum_{k_2=-\infty}^{+\infty} x(k_1, k_2) h(n_1 - k_1, n_2 - k_2)$$

For example, to obtain a blurred version of an image $x(k_1, k_2)$, the image could be convolved with $h(k_1, k_2)$, where

$$h(k_1, k_2) = \frac{1}{8} \begin{bmatrix} 0 & 1 & 0 \\ 1 & 4 & 1 \\ 0 & 1 & 0 \end{bmatrix}, \tag{4.4}$$

where $(k_1, k_2) = (0, 0)$ refers to the center element of h. The convolution sum is usually written as $y = x * h$.

For a linear shift invariant operator $h(k_1, k_2)$ with Fourier transform $\hat{h}(\omega_1, \omega_2)$, the 2-D Fourier transform $\hat{x}(\omega_1, \omega_2)$ of an input signal $x(n_1, n_2)$ is related to the 2-D Fourier transform $\hat{y}(\omega_1, \omega_2)$ of the output signal $y(n_1, n_2)$ via the relation

$$\hat{y}(\omega_1, \omega_2) = \hat{h}(\omega_1, \omega_2) \hat{x}(\omega_1, \omega_2).$$

In addition to providing an alternative computational mechanism for evaluating the application of a particular operator to an image, the system's transfer function $\hat{h}(\omega_1, \omega_2)$ can be used to examine the response of a linear shift operator or filter to an arbitrary input. An operator that has a large response to high frequencies (frequencies near the Nyquist rate) is likely to be a poor choice for computer vision applications because signals above this frequency cannot be represented accurately.

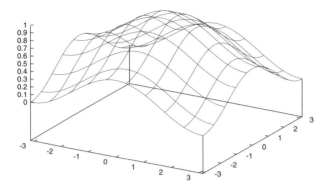

abs[4+2*cos(x)+2*cos(y)]/8 ——

Figure 4.4. Amplitude spectrum of averaging filter. This surface shows the amplitude spectrum of the transfer function of the 3×3 averaging filter given in Eq. (4.4). Note that the Nyquist rate is π in angular frequency.

For a two-dimensional operator $h(x_1, x_2)$ represented by a discrete convolution, $\hat{h}(k_1, k_2)$ is given by [273] as

$$\hat{h}(k_1, k_2) = \sum_{\alpha_1=-\infty}^{\alpha_1=+\infty} \sum_{\alpha_2=-\infty}^{\alpha_2=+\infty} h(\alpha_1, \alpha_2) e^{-(\alpha_1 k_1 + \alpha_2 k_2)}, \tag{4.5}$$

where k_1 and k_2 are continuous values of spatial frequency. References [87] and [125] use Eq. (4.5) to analyze various discrete convolution operators. For example, for the averaging operator h given in Eq. (4.4), the transfer function $\hat{h}(k_1, k_2)$ is given by

$$\begin{aligned}
\hat{h}(k_1, k_2) &= \sum_{\alpha_1=-\infty}^{\alpha_1=+\infty} \sum_{\alpha_2=-\infty}^{\alpha_2=+\infty} h(\alpha_1, \alpha_2) e^{-i(\alpha_1 k_1 + \alpha_2 k_2)} \\
&= \frac{1}{2} + e^{ik_1} + e^{-ik_1} + e^{ik_2} + e^{-ik_2} \\
&= (4 + 2 \cos(k_1) + 2 \cos(k_2))/8
\end{aligned} \tag{4.6}$$

The magnitude of $\hat{h}$, $|\hat{h}|$ is plotted in Figure 4.4. Because the averaging operator given in (Eq. 4.4) has a large nonzero response for frequencies near the Nyquist frequency, this operator can be expected to perform poorly in the presence of noise. Note that much better averaging operators exist; for example, a Gaussian – to which Eq. (4.4) is a rough approximation – is a much better averaging filter.

4.4   Image Features and Their Combination

Fundamental to many visual tasks in robot vision is the task of matching two or more views of the same object. The object may be a template. Does a particular pattern of image pixels occur in this image? Or it may be another image. Does the same object appear in two different camera views? When choosing a particular representation of visual data, it is often useful to choose a representation that simplifies the task of determining matches or *correspondences* between two or more views of a scene. Individual pixel values are only indirectly related to the intensity (or color) of objects in the underlying scene; they are the result of a complex interaction between the illumination, the placement of the camera, the presence of other structures in the environment, and the reflectance properties of the objects being observed. Thus, individual pixel values are not used directly for many robotic vision tasks. Almost all computational vision systems preprocess the pixel values in some way to highlight structures that are useful for the task at hand and are more likely to be stable over a wide range of viewing conditions than are individual pixels.

4.4.1   Color and Shading

Rather than just obtaining the intensity of structure in the image, color cameras obtain the intensity from a collection of sensors that are sensitive to different wavelengths of light. The image is then represented by a vector of values at each pixel rather than just intensity. Often these channels are called the red, green, and blue channels, but fewer (or larger) numbers of channels are possible. Color can be a very powerful tool for determining correspondences, but color sensors can also be very sensitive to illumination conditions.

One effective strategy that uses color is based on the concept of representing an object or a feature by its color histogram [346, 113]. The method describes objects by the *combination* of different colors that characterize them. As such, it is of particular value when the objects to be recognized are defined by particular *combinations of colors*.

An image is represented by a vector $(\mathbf{h}_1, \mathbf{h}_2, \ldots, \mathbf{h}_n)$ in a n-dimensional vector space, where each element $\mathbf{h}_i$ represents the number of pixels of color i in the image. This feature vector is then used to identify this feature in some other image. Given color histograms $(\mathbf{h}_1, \ldots \mathbf{h}_n)$ of image H and $(\mathbf{k}_1, \ldots, \mathbf{k}_n)$ of image K, we define the similarity or distance between them as

$$d(H, K) = \sum |h_i - k_i|.$$

In a typical application, the set of possible colors is reduced to a smaller number (256 is typical), and thus an image can be represented by 256 values. The histograms are normalized so that the similarity measure is independent of the size of the image.

4.4.2   Image Brightness Constraint

Although individual pixel values are not particularly stable over a large range of changes in the image or the imaging geometry, they can be considered stable over sufficiently small changes in imaging conditions. The image brightness constraint [158] or gradient constraint equation expresses this property that the intensity of a point remains unchanged as it moves,

$$f(x + dx, y + dy, t + dt) = f(x, y, t),$$

where $f(x, y, t)$ is the intensity of the image. A Taylor series expansion of $f(x, y, t)$ leads to

$$f(x + dx, y + dy, t + dt) = f(x, y, t) + \frac{\partial f}{\partial x} dx + \frac{\partial f}{\partial y} dy + \frac{\partial f}{\partial t} dt + \mathcal{O}(x^2)$$

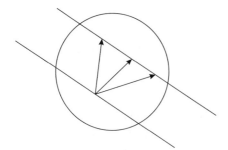

Figure 4.5. Aperture problem. Given the motion of an edge through a small aperture, only the component of motion perpendicular to the line is measurable. Motion along the direction of the line is undetectable.

Ignoring the higher-order terms and equating $f(x + dx, y + dy, t + dt) = f(x, y, t)$ results in

$$-\frac{\partial f}{\partial t} = \frac{\partial f}{\partial x}\frac{dx}{dt} + \frac{\partial f}{\partial y}\frac{dy}{dt}. \tag{4.7}$$

This provides a constraint on the image velocity $(u, v) = (dx/dt, dy/dt)$ as a function of local derivatives $(E_x, E_y, E_t) = (df/dx, df/dy, df/dt)$ of the image intensity function f. That is Eq. (4.7) relates the motion (u, v) of a patch of image intensities in the image to local changes in the intensity structure in the image E_x, E_y, and E_t. Equation (4.7) is not sufficient to compute both components (u, v) of the image velocity but rather provides a linear constraint $E_x u + E_y v + E_t = 0$. Equation (4.7) is known as the *optical flow constraint equation* [157], and the vector field (u, v) is known as the *optical flow*.

The local information contained in the optical flow constraint equation provides a linear constraint on (u, v). This constraint provides a constraint on the flow in the direction of the brightness gradient but provides no constraint on the flow perpendicular to this direction (see Figure 4.5). Thus, in order to obtain a unique optical flow field, some additional information is necessary. The unavailability of local flow information in the direction perpendicular to the direction of the brightness gradient is known as the *aperture problem* [367].

Various approaches have been proposed to overcome the aperture problem. The classic approach is based on Horn and Schunk [158]. They developed an iterative algorithm that enforces a smoothness constraint on the optical flow field and integrates measurements spatially to solve for the flow. In particular, Horn and Schunk propose the minimization of $e_s + \lambda e_c$, where

$$e_s = \iint \left(u_x^2 + u_y^2 + v_x^2 + v_y^2\right) dx\, dy$$

and

$$e_c = \iint (E_x u + E_y v + E_t)^2\, dx\, dy$$

over the image to recover (u, v) everywhere. This approach to solving the optical flow field is a classical application of regularization to solve an ill-posed problem (see Section 3.1).

Horn and Schunk's algorithm has been found to have difficulties when the underlying flow field is discontinuous. More modern algorithms exist that show considerably better performance; see [275, 35] for reviews.

4.4.3   Correlation

Although the intensity of scene structure is likely to change as the view changes, it may be the case that the local image structure near a point of interest remains constant. One popular approach is to use a patch or window as the measurement rather than a single pixel. This leads to an approach known as *correlation* in which a test pattern from one image is correlated with another to identify the location of the test pattern in the second image. This test pattern may be based on some ideal model of the pattern that will appear in the image, or it may be a region of one image that is being compared with another.

The similarity $d(\delta x, \delta y)$ between two images g and f can be defined by

$$d^2(\delta x, \delta y) = \sum \sum (f(x, y) - g(x + \delta x, y + \delta y))^2,$$

where the sum is made over the region of the two images to be compared. The place where g can be found in f will be associated with small values of d^2. Expanding d^2 results in

$$d^2(\delta x, \delta y) = \sum \sum f^2(x, y) + g^2(x + \delta x, y + \delta y)$$
$$- 2f(x, y)g(x + \delta x, y + \delta y).$$

If one assumes f and g are constant over the summation window, minimizing $d^2(\delta x, \delta y)$ is equivalent to maximizing the correlation of f and g, where the correlation is given by

$$\text{corr}(\delta x, \delta y) = \sum \sum f(x, y)g(\delta x + x, \delta y + y).$$

In a typical application, a small window in one image is correlated with windowed portions of the other.

Correlation is relatively inexpensive; the cost is related to the window size and the region to be searched, and the simple correlation function given above is sensitive to the local mean intensities of f and g. It can also be sensitive to noise in the input and to distortions between the two images that are not the result of simple shifting (i.e., "nonshift" distortions such as rotation and shear).

Normalized cross-correlation addresses a number of these problems, although it does not deal with nonshift distortions. Under normalized cross-correlation, the correlation function is computed as

$$\frac{\sum \sum W(x, y) f'(x + \delta x, y + \delta y) g'(x + \delta x, y + \delta y)}{|v_f(\delta x, \delta y) v_g(\delta x, \delta y)|^{\frac{1}{2}}},$$

where f' and g' are zero-mean corrected versions of the input, and v_f and v_g are the local variances of f and g computed within the window function W. (See [382] for an application of this approach.)

4.4.4   Fourier Methods

In 1963, Bogert et al. [43] introduced the *Cepstrum* and Cepstral analysis as a tool for detecting echos in signals. The Cepstrum of a signal $g(x)$ with Fourier transform $\hat{g}(f)$ is given by

$$g_{\text{cep}}(x) = \int_{-\infty}^{+\infty} \log|\hat{g}(f)|e^{i\pi f x}\, df.$$

Peaks in the Cepstrum $g_{\text{cep}}(x)$ is associated with the delay at which an echo occurs in the signal g.

Although initially used for echo detection, the Cepstrum can be used to compare any two signals. The basic approach is to concatenate the two signals and then to apply the Cepstrum and seek the maximum value of g_{cep}. If the two signals are simply shifted versions of each other, the determination of the echo location is equivalent to determining the unknown shift.

Cepstral techniques are popular owing to their efficiency and their ability to deal with a wide range of shifts and signal amplitude variations. Unfortunately these techniques are sensitive to the presence of energy in one signal that is not in the other and to signals with a high autocorrelation – the Cepstrum is sensitive to any echo that exists in the original signal as well as the shift between them.

4.4.5 Feature Detectors

Rather than considering the entire image, an alternative approach is to apply a simple heuristic to identify image points important to the task at hand and to use these points to represent the image. Corners, for example, often have significance for visual tasks, and corner detectors have been constructed to identify them. The general class of such operators is known as *feature detectors* or *interest operators*. They are closely related to the biological phenomenon of visual attention. The attention of human observers, for example, is naturally associated with specific types of visual events, many of which have been described in terms of image-based features.

In practice, an interest operator should identify image locations that are stable under slight changes in the image and slight changes in viewpoint. The interest operator should also abstract the image in terms of a manageable number of features.

Perhaps the most famous of the feature detectors is the *Moravec interest operator*. The Moravec interest operator [244] produces candidate match points by measuring the distinctiveness of local image structure. The Moravec operator defines the variance measure at a pixel (x, y) as

$$\text{var}(x, y) = \left\{ \sum_{k,l \in S} [f(x, y) - f(x + k, y + l)]^2 \right\}^{\frac{1}{2}},$$

where

$$S = \{(0, a), (0, -a), (a, 0), (-a, 0)\}$$

and a is a parameter. The variance is computed over a neighborhood, and the minimum variance is computed by

$$\text{Moravec}(x, y) = \min_{(\delta x, \delta y) \in N \times N} \text{var}(x + \delta x, y + \delta y),$$

and then only local maximal values of the operator that exceed a specified threshold are retained.

The Moravec operator is designed to identify points in an image with high variance, such as corners. Although points with high variance may be of interest, it is difficult to say precisely to what the detector will respond. Many other feature detectors exist;

Figure 4.6. The binary acquisition target. The target is designed to be easy to identify and to provide target pose information. (Reprinted, with permission, from Maitland and Harris, "A Video-Based Tracker for Use in Computer Surgery [220], p. 610.)

for example, Nagel [256] developed a detector designed to respond well to intensity patterns that appear near corners in an image. Unfortunately, the relationship between the distribution of image intensities identified as "corners" by Nagel's corner detector only indirectly correspond to corners in an image. Thorpe [354] surveyed a number of different feature point detectors.

Rather than relying on naturally occurring image intensity patterns, another alternative is to design a visual feature that will be prepositioned in the environment to simplify later visual acquisition. A number of these visual targets have been proposed. The binary acquisition target (BAT) [220] is typical (see Figure 4.6).

The BAT is placed in the environment at a position that must be localized visually. (In the application considered in [220] the BAT is placed on a pointing instrument.) Very simple image processing based on local mean removal and the identification of connected components is used to obtain the outline of the target, but more complex operations such as those described in the following section on edges could also be used. The BAT is planar and of known size, permitting the recovery of the 3-D position and orientation of the BAT provided that the system has been properly calibrated.

4.4.6 Edges

Many images can be described in terms of the structure of changes in intensity in the image. One commonly occurring intensity variation is rapid change in intensity: an edge. A *step edge* in an image is an image intensity contour across which the brightness of the image changes abruptly. These are frequently associated with the projection of actual object boundaries in the scene. Edges, and step edges in particular, are popular representations of images. They have an intuitive appeal as a "cartoonlike" description of an image, and there is substantial evidence that primate visual processing is associated with edgelike representations. Edges also provide a compact representation of the image and can provide an expressive representation of the salient image features as well. This is especially true of many man-made environments. Unfortunately edges do not form a complete (i.e., information-preserving) representation of the underlying image, nor can they be extracted in a reliable and robust manner under all imaging conditions. It is also the case that certain classes of image are not well described by edges. Perhaps the largest drawback to the use of intensity edges as a representation of objects is that not all abrupt changes in intensity are the result of object edges, nor do all object edges result in changes of intensity. Thus the term *edge detection* is not completely correct, but the term has widespread use in the literature, and we shall use it here.

A common mechanism for extracting edge structure from an image is to perform the computation in two stages: first extract candidate edge elements (*edgels*) from the image and then combine the edge elements into longer extended edge structures.

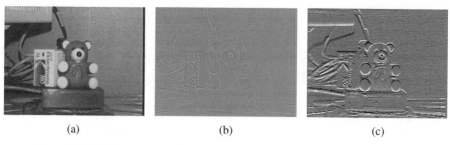

(a) (b) (c)

Figure 4.7. Sobel operator. (a) Original (I). (b) $\Delta_1 I$. (c) $\Delta_2 I$.

If a step edge is associated with an intensity change, the process of detecting step edgels can be formulated as the task of identifying image locations associated with a large change in intensity. If we assume that an image is a continuously differentiable function, we can examine the gradient of the image for candidate locations. The gradient of a function $f(u, v)$ is the vector $\nabla f(\mathbf{u}, \mathbf{v}) = [\partial f/\partial \mathbf{u}, \partial f/\partial \mathbf{v}]$. Large values or peaks in the magnitude of the gradient should be associated with step edgels.

Many different discrete approximations to the gradient operator exist; Roberts [319], Prewitt [305], and Sobel [299] proposed relatively simple image differencing schemes that approximate the gradient within a fixed size window. If Δ_1 and Δ_2 are orthogonal directional derivatives of the image intensity, the magnitude of the image-intensity gradient is given by $\sqrt{\Delta_1^2 + \Delta_2^2}$, and the direction of the image-intensity gradient is given by $\tan^{-1}(\Delta_2/\Delta_1)$. For example, the Sobel operator is implemented as a correlation of the image with Δ_1 and Δ_2, where Δ_1 and Δ_2 are given by

$$\Delta_1 = \begin{bmatrix} -1 & 0 & 1 \\ -2 & 0 & 2 \\ -1 & 0 & 1 \end{bmatrix} \qquad \Delta_2 = \begin{bmatrix} 1 & 2 & 1 \\ 0 & 0 & 0 \\ -1 & -2 & -1 \end{bmatrix}$$

The effect of applying the Sobel operator to an image is shown in Figure 4.7.

Unfortunately, derivative-like operators tend to amplify any noise present in the image, and thus operators like Sobel tend to perform poorly unless the image is first preprocessed to reduce any noise that may be present.

Equation (4.5) can be used to examine the frequency response for each of the Sobel filters. For Δ_1, for example, the transfer function $\hat{\Delta}_1(k_1, k_2)$ is given by

$$\hat{\Delta}_1(k_1, k_2) = \sum_{\alpha_1=-\infty}^{\alpha_1=+\infty} \sum_{\alpha_2=-\infty}^{\alpha_2=+\infty} h(\alpha_1, \alpha_2) e^{-i(\alpha_1 k_1 + \alpha_2 k_2)}$$

$$= -2i(\sin(k_1 + k_2) + \sin(k_1 - k_2) + 2\sin(k_1)); \tag{4.8}$$

$|\hat{\Delta}_1|$ is plotted in Figure 4.8. Because Δ_1 has considerable power at high frequencies, it can be expected to perform poorly in the presence of noise. The use of an initial filtering stage to remove higher frequencies will make operators like Sobel much more stable.

A second major problem with gradient-based operators is that the output of the operator must be searched to find and identify local maxima and minima (known as *peaks*) in the image. Peaks can be very difficult features to find. The use of second derivative operators reduces this problem because the search for peaks can be replaced with a search for

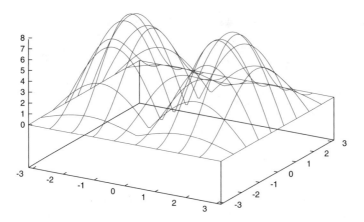

Figure 4.8. Frequency response of Δ_1.

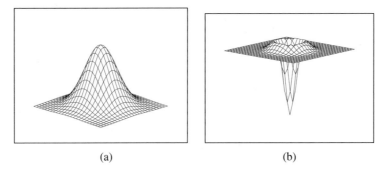

(a)   (b)

Figure 4.9. Laplacian of Gaussian. (a) 2-D Gaussian. (b) Laplacian of
the Gaussian.

zero-crossings. There are a number of possible second derivative operators that can be
considered. Perhaps the most popular of these is the Laplacian

$$\nabla^2 = \frac{\partial^2}{\partial x^2} + \frac{\partial^2}{\partial y^2}.$$

The Laplacian is a nondirectional second derivative operator.

As is the case with gradient-based methods, the Laplacian operator amplifies high
frequencies in the image and hence is susceptible to noise. Again one strategy for reducing
the effect of any noise is to prefilter the image with a low-pass filter such as the Gaussian
and then to apply a derivative operator. The Gaussian is given by

$$G(x, y) = \frac{1}{2\pi\sigma^2}e^{-\frac{x^2+y^2}{2\sigma^2}}.$$

The Laplacian of the Gaussian $\nabla^2(G * I) = (\nabla^2 G) * I$ operator and the Difference of
Gaussians (DOG) operators use this type of approach and compute zero-crossings in the
second derivative rather than peaks in the first derivative [227]. The $\nabla^2 G$ operator is an
isotropic edge detector; that is, it is not selective to the orientation of the edge data. The
operator $\nabla^2 G$ is also known as a *Mexican hat* operator owing to the shape of the amplitude
profile (see Figure 4.9).

A full treatment of the use of $\nabla^2 G$ as an image operator is given by Marr and Hildreth in [227]. Their use of $\nabla^2 G$ to identify edges was based not only on the desirable signal processing properties of the operator but also on its ability, through different choices of the parameter σ, to localize structure at different scales. The use of the same operator at different spatial scales is an important concept in the processing of visual images. Real scenes are characterized by structures of different sizes owing to the physical process operating at differing scales and task-specific considerations. One particular advantage of the $\nabla^2 G$ operator over the earlier edge filters is that it made this scale dependency explicit. Figure 4.10 shows the output of the Laplacian of the Gaussian operator when applied to the same image for different choices of the scale parameter σ.

Many different image operators can be used to analyze an image at different scales. The most common class of operators are *bandpass operators*; these are operators that respond only to structure having a particular range of spatial frequencies.

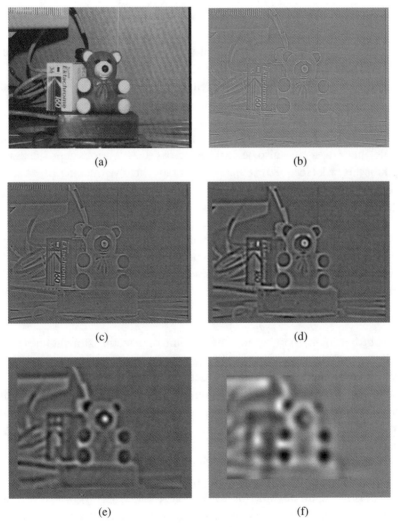

Figure 4.10. Laplacian of the Gaussian for different choices of σ. (a) Original. (b) $\sigma = 1.0$. (c) $\sigma = 2.0$. (d) $\sigma = 4.0$. (e) $\sigma = 8.0$. (f) $\sigma = 16.0$.

Many different edgel detectors have been proposed in recent years. More recent detectors have been constructed based on optimally detecting edges under certain assumptions and criteria. Of these, Canny's [65], Shen and Castan's [333], and Deriche's [94] are perhaps the best known. Each of these edge detectors can be proven to be optimal detectors under slightly different criteria; Canny assumes that the edge detector is to be implemented as a filter with a finite support region, Shen and Castan use a slightly different optimality criterion from that of Canny, whereas Deriche develops a filter with an infinite support region. Canny's edge detector is well approximated by peaks identified in the first derivative of a Gaussian-filtered version of the image. The Canny edge detector is described in some detail in Figure 4.11, and the set of edges obtained when applying Canny's operator to Figure 4.7(a) is given in Figure 4.12.

Finding and matching edgels   The second stage in many edge detection operators involves the localization of zero-crossings or peaks in the output of a filtered version of the image. This process will ideally obtain the location of edges to subpixel accuracy. Various techniques exist for finding the location of an edge, but most involve fitting a local continuous surface to the filter output and then solving the fit for the location of the zero-crossing or peak. Edges associated with peaks below a given threshold or with zero-crossings associated with low magnitude gradients are discarded.

Edges are typically coded by the strength (either the magnitude of the peak or the gradient) and also their orientation. This information can then be exploited in later edge aggregation or matching processes.

If edges are detected at different scales using the Laplacian of the Gaussian operator, for example, then edges must also be matched across scale. Various approaches have been suggested for this task (see [383, 189, 388]), but most involve tracking edges across scale based on features of the filters used and the unlikelihood that, for small changes in scale, the location of the edge will move a considerable distance in the image.

Aggregating edgels   Individual edgels detected using an edge detector may be aggregated into more complex edge structure before undergoing later processing. The process of aggregating edges tends to remove spurious results from the edge detection phase and often results in considerable data reduction. Two approaches are described below.

Hough transform   Consider the problem of detecting straight lines in an image from a collection of edgel measurements (x_i, y_i). Each measurement (x_i, y_i) can be thought of as "voting" for the presence of edge structure passing through this point. If the edge is represented as $y = mx + b$, the measurement (x_i, y_i) provides support for the set of lines that pass through (x_i, y_i), or, equivalently, for the set of values (m, b) that satisfy $y_i = mx_i + b$. The Hough transform [29] provides a voting scheme to combine individual (x_i, y_i) measurements to obtain (m, b).

The Hough transform maintains an accumulator array $A(m, b)$, which is initialized to zero and represents a discretized version of all possible (m, b) pairs. Whenever a (x_i, y_i) measurement is made, all possible (m, b) cells in A that satisfy $y_i = mx_i + b$ are incremented. When all measurements have been processed, the elements of the accumulator array vote for the most likely edge(s). Note that this particular parameterization of a line

Although the Canny edge detector can be described as the identification of peaks in the first derivative of a Gaussian-smoothed version of an image, in practice the Canny detector involves several manually selected parameters.

1. **Noise suppression** The image is convolved with a symmetric 2-D Gaussian filter $G(\sigma_1, \sigma_1)$ in order to suppress noise in the input.

2. **Directional differentiation** The image is filtered in the x and y directions with a 1-D Gaussian filter $G(\sigma_2)$ and then differentiated along that direction. Because $\frac{d}{dx}[G(\sigma_2) * f(x,y)] = [\frac{d}{dx}G(\sigma) * f(x,y)]$, this is typically implemented as a convolution with a directional derivative of a 1-D Gaussian, that is, a convolution with

$$\frac{dG(x)}{dx} = \frac{-x}{\sqrt{2\pi}\sigma^3} e^{\frac{-x^2}{2\sigma^2}}.$$

From the computed x and y gradient values, the magnitude and orientation of the edge are computed in a manner similar to the Sobel operator.

3. **Nonmaximum suppression** Maximum outputs in the magnitude of the image gradient must be identified. This is accomplished by suppressing outputs in the gradient magnitude perpendicular to the edge direction rather than suppressing outputs parallel to the edge. This "thins" edges but introduces problems at points on edges with high curvature such as corners. Theoretically this suppression could be accomplished at each candidate edge pixel by differentiating the magnitude of the gradient in a direction perpendicular to the edge and examining the derivative to ensure that this pixel is a maximum. More commonly individual pixels surrounding each candidate pixel are examined to ensure that the candidate pixel gradient value is greater than the gradient values of adjacent pixels perpendicular to the line direction. Pixels that are not maximal are suppressed.

4. **Edge Thresholding** Candidate edge pixels whose gradient magnitude falls below a threshold are discarded. Canny proposes the use of a threshold with a memory (a "hysteresis" method) to perform this thresholding. An upper and lower threshold are used. If the pixel gradient is above the upper threshold, the pixel is identified as an edge. If the pixel gradient is below the lower threshold, the pixel is identified as nonedge. Pixels that lie between these two values are accepted if they are connected to pixels with a strong response (greater than the lower threshold). Canny recommends that the ratio of high-to-low limit be in the range 2 or 3 to 1.

Figure 4.11. Canny edge detector.

Figure 4.12. Canny edge map.

is not ideally suited to use with the Hough transform, and other parameterizations based on representing the orientation of an edge are preferred (e.g., perpendicular distance from the origin and orientation as an angle).

Different parameterizations of edges and other structures, including circles and arbitrary contours, can be processed using variations on the Hough transform; in particular, the generalized Hough transform generalizes the Hough transform to arbitrary contours. The key requirement is a parametric definition of the geometric feature of interest that allows specific pixels to vote for specific arrangements of the object of interest. The Hough transform is an effective mechanism for mapping edgels onto more complex structures such as geometric shapes or for classifying the edgels into known contours. Key limitations of basic Hough transform methods are the limit of resolution posed by the discretization of the accumulator array, and the tendency of complex forms to lead to high-dimensional accumulator arrays and hence substantial space requirements.

Line approximation   Rather than using the edgel structure to provide support for a particular structure such as a geometric shape, an alternative approach is to group the edgels into edge chains and then to approximate these edge chains by longer line segments.

A popular strategy for grouping edges together is to pose the grouping task as a graph search for a minimum cost path. Each edgel is mapped to a node in the graph, and the cost between two nodes depends on their proximity, relative orientation, and contrast. The graph is then searched for a minimum cost path from one node to another, and the best sequence is used to approximate the line (see Section 5.3.1 for a description of a general graph search algorithm). A major difficulty in applying this type of strategy is determining a tolerance for joining two nodes in the graph (i.e., edges) together. If the threshold value is set too low, edgels tend not to be joined together, and the recovered edge chains are short and disconnected. If the value is set too high, edges are connected even when they should not be, and spurious curves are generated.

Once edge chains have been identified, it is often useful to merge the edge chains into longer polygonal lines. Again many techniques have been proposed for this. One approach known as *recursive splitting* is described by Pavlidis [291]. The recursive splitting algorithm joins the first and last points in a contour chain by a straight line and then examines the maximal distance e_m from the line and the contour. For a given threshold ϵ, if $e_m < \epsilon$, then the contour is well approximated by the straight line and the process completes. Otherwise, the line is split in two at the contour point where the distance is e_m, and the algorithm then operates recursively on the two halves.

Although many methods can be used on simple unambiguous data, the extraction of curves from complex images remains a difficult problem. Significant difficulties relate to the completion of inherently intermittent and noisy edge data and the interpretation of crossings between different curves that can lead to alternative interpretations.

Some thoughts on edges Many researchers have assumed that zero-crossings obtained from $\nabla^2 G$ operators or some other more or less complex edge detector are a reasonable starting point for image processing. These works assume that (1) zero-crossings can be found, (2) that they signal the presence of structure in the scene (typically inferred to be edges), and (3) that structure in the scene will give rise to edges. Attempting to code the input entirely using zero-crossings obtained from bandpass filters can be problematic. Daugman [91] and Mayhew, Frisby, and Gale [233] have identified visual tasks that are solvable by humans but are not codable using zero-crossings alone, suggesting that edge-base representations are not complete and thus may miss salient features. To overcome these problems, researchers have attempted either to extract more than just zero-crossings from the image (such as zero-crossings and peaks [233], peaks and ridges [87]) or to use the entire filtered signal to represent the scene. This latter approach is considered in the following two sections.

4.4.7 Image Filters

Rather than comparing two images by convolving the images with filters, extracting the edges, and then comparing the edges, one alternative is to match the convolved images directly. This is the approach taken by Jones and Malik [175]. Given two images I_1 and I_r, the appropriate shift should be determined by having convolved versions of the images agree. If k filters are applied to the images, the correct shift would be the shift that minimizes

$$e_m = \sum_k |F_k * I_r(i, j) - F_k * I_1(i + h, j + v)| ,$$

where F_k is the set of filter banks to use and e_m is the error measure.

If the filter banks F_k localize structure in the image, this type of approach is likely to succeed provided that a single shift exists at an image location that aligns the images. If no such shift exists, as would occur near object boundaries or if semitransparent surfaces exist in the image, then a single shift will not exist and the method will fail. When combining filter outputs with competing best-shift solutions, the overall shift will be a function of the relative channel amplitudes, and these may not be appropriate.

4.4.8 Local Phase Differences

Combining the entire filtered image as proposed in the previous section will be influenced by the relative intensity of the signal. An alternative is to analyze the structure of the signal independently of its amplitude. If the two filtered images can be locally approximated by sinusoids, the difference between the signals can be described in terms of their local phase difference and the local change in amplitude. The underlying concept is that local amplitude variation encodes the intensity difference between the two images, whereas the local phase difference encodes the shift or disparity.

If the two images to be compared are labeled $I_l(x)$ and $I_r(x)$, then by convolving these signals with a quadrature filter pair such as a complex Gabor (Gabor(ω, σ)) kernel with central frequency ω and standard deviation σ, we obtain two complex responses $L(x)$ and $R(x)$. For appropriate choices of ω and σ, the output of this convolution will be tightly bandpassed versions of the input signal and will thus satisfy the local sinusoidal approximation. Because the Gabor filter is a quadrature pair, various mechanisms exist for recovering the local amplitude and phase differences. One simple mechanism for obtaining the local phase difference would be to extract the absolute phase from the left and right images and then simply subtract them [328]. Although conceptually simple, in practice this approach is quite sensitive to image variations and to a problem known as the *phase wraparound effect*. More sophisticated phase-matching mechanisms exist (cf. [171, 173]).

4.4.9 Summary

There is a wide array of different mechanisms for representing an image to make it more suitable for later processing. Unfortunately, many techniques work well in controlled test environments but then fail when applied in the real-world operational environment.

The essential function of the techniques presented in this section is to allow portions of two images to be compared under a wide range of viewing conditions. Given this ability to compare images or parts of images, vision becomes a powerful sensor for mobile robots, and it can be used to recover environmental structure or to localize the robot in its environment without emitting additional energy into the environment.

4.5   Obtaining Depth

A single perspective camera is unable to localize structure in three dimensions; it obtains the direction to the structure but not the distance to it. If depth information is required, then some other mechanism must be used to recover this missing dimension. Many of these techniques require the identification of corresponding image features in two or more images, which is the task considered in the previous section.

4.5.1 Ground Plane Assumption

Suppose that the object to be localized lies on a particular known plane, typically the ground. Then this information, coupled with a calibrated camera, is sufficient to localize the structure in three-space. Let $A = [a_1, a_2, a_3, a_4]$ and $A[x, y, z, 1]^T = \mathbf{0}$ be the equation of the plane upon which structure resides. Given an image point (u, v) from a calibrated perspective camera $\tilde{\mathbf{P}}$, the 3-D point that corresponds to this image point can be found from

$$\begin{bmatrix} \tilde{\mathbf{P}}_1 - u\tilde{\mathbf{P}}_3 \\ \tilde{\mathbf{P}}_2 - v\tilde{\mathbf{P}}_3 \\ A \end{bmatrix} \begin{bmatrix} x \\ y \\ z \\ 1 \end{bmatrix} = \begin{bmatrix} 0 \\ 0 \\ 0 \end{bmatrix}. \tag{4.9}$$

The ground-plane assumption finds application in a number of restricted environments such as road following. Suppose that an autonomous vehicle is to navigate by sensing road markings; then, whenever a road marking is found at (u, v), the road marking's 3-D position relative to the robot can be determined using (Eq. 4.9).

In practice it may not be necessary to determine $\mathbf{A}$ and $\tilde{\mathbf{P}}$ explicitly, but instead the calibration of (u, v) to (x, y, z) can be accomplished directly from the ground plane.

4.5.2 Multiple Cameras

Suppose that instead of using just one camera to view the scene, multiple cameras are available. The two-camera approach is known as *stereo vision*, or *binocular vision*, whereas the three-camera approach is known as *trinocular vision*. Approaches with as many as five and six cameras are described in the literature.

When a scene is viewed by two or more cameras, points in the world are mapped onto different image points in the different cameras. In general a point will have different horizontal and vertical positions in each camera. If $X = [x \ y \ z \ 1]^T$ is an arbitrary point in three-space described in homogeneous coordinates, then pinhole camera i maps X to the point as follows:

$$(u_i, v_i) = \left(\frac{(\tilde{\mathbf{P}}_i X)_1}{(\tilde{\mathbf{P}}_i X)_3}, \frac{(\tilde{\mathbf{P}}_i X)_2}{(\tilde{\mathbf{P}}_i X)_3} \right)$$

If the calibration matrices $\tilde{\mathbf{P}}_i$ are known, then the 3-D point (x, y, z) that gives rise to the projections can be found by solving

$$\begin{bmatrix} (u_i \tilde{\mathbf{P}}_i)_3 - (\tilde{\mathbf{P}}_i)_1 \\ (v_i \tilde{\mathbf{P}}_i)_3 - (\tilde{\mathbf{P}}_i)_2 \\ \cdots \end{bmatrix} \begin{bmatrix} x \\ y \\ z \\ 1 \end{bmatrix} = \begin{bmatrix} 0 \\ \cdots \\ 0 \end{bmatrix}.$$

Provided 1.5 or more views of the same point are available, this equation can be solved using least squares to determine (x, y, z). Unfortunately, determining the corresponding image points in the two or more views may not be particularly easy. In fact, determining this correspondence is considered to be the hard problem in stereopsis. (Almost all of the techniques described in Section 4.4 have been used as a mechanism for establishing this correspondence.)

The classical technique in static stereopsis is to consider all possible matches and to then discard those matches that violate a set of matching criteria. The problem is that there can be a large number of possible matches, and the selection of a set of criteria that is stable and does not discard potentially good matches is very difficult [171].

A vast number of stereopsis algorithms exist in the literature. The output of these algorithms is usually represented as a *depth map* (see Figure 4.13). These are retinotopic maps of the recovered disparity at that pixel. In Figure 4.13 white pixels are closer to the cameras.

Stereopsis is an attractive technique for recovering depth because very few assumptions are required. However, several points to consider are as follows:

- The key challenge in stereopsis is the correspondence problem: matching the projection of an object in one camera with its projection in the other. The correspondence process may require considerable assumptions about the robot's

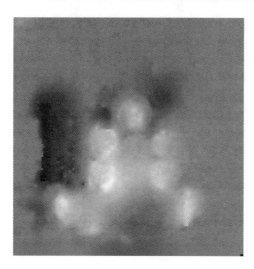

Figure 4.13. Stereo disparities recovered from the central portion of Figure 4.7(a).

environment that may not hold in practice. A number of image features and techniques that can be used to establish this correspondence are discussed in Section 4.4.

- The cameras can be convergent or parallel. For stereopsis to take place, the structure of interest must be visible in each camera's view. Ideally, the cameras will all fixate the region that contains the structure of interest. This becomes problematic if the cameras are fixed and different regions of space are of interest.
- The accuracy of the triangulation process in stereo vision is limited by the size of the pixels and the camera geometry. If the cameras are placed close together, the accuracy will be poor, but the correspondence process will be simplified because objects will appear very similar in the two camera's views. As the cameras are placed farther apart, the increased baseline improves accuracy, but the matching process becomes more difficult.

4.5.3   Model-Based Vision

Many robotic systems operate in a known (or partially known) environment. If special-purpose or naturally occurring features can be reliably extracted from the environment, a representation of the metric space around the robot can be used with visual routines that recover the features to estimate the robot's pose within the environment. In a typical application (e.g. [193]), a computer-aided design model of the robot's environment is constructed with salient visual features identified. At every motion of the robot, features are extracted from the visual field and these are compared with their predicted position. A mechanism such as Kalman filtering (see Section 3.9.2) is then used to update the robot's position.

Naturally occurring targets can be entities such as walls, signs, or doorways in the environment. King and Weiman [185], for example, have devised a navigation system using light fixtures mounted on the ceiling as visual targets (see also [228]). If special-purpose targets are available, these targets can be made very robust. One such technique (see [153]) places special-purpose targets on the ceiling that are then localized using a vertically mounted camera based on the robot. Because the distance from the robot to the ceiling-mounted target is known, an appropriately designed target can be used to localize the robot.

4.5.4   Floor Anomaly Detection

For robots moving over the floor, one essential measurement task is the verification of the floor plane in front of the robot. Robots that do not sense anomalies in the flat floor may suffer a catastrophic failure when faced with a flight of stairs or an open floor-access panel. Thus, being able to verify the ground-plane assumption may be a critical requirement, especially in industrial robotic applications.

Various sensor techniques exist to verify the ground plane. Perhaps the simplest approach is to use a laser stripe sensor (see Section 4.7.1) to probe the ground in front of the robot. A floor anomaly detection system using a laser striper based on BIRIS (see Section 4.7.2) was implemented as part of the ARK project. Although relatively inexpensive, this type of approach suffers from a number of problems. A line striper provides a one-dimensional probe of the floor, whereas the floor is two-dimensional, and thus the line must be swept through space to provide complete floor coverage in the direction in which the robot is to move. Figure 4.14 shows a BIRIS-based floor anomaly detector mounted on a Cybermotion platform.

An alternative technology is stereo vision [170]. The general stereo problem is simplified because the objects to be viewed are known to lie near the ground plane. Thus the input images can be warped to bring the floor plane into exact alignment before matching takes place – a procedure that simplifies the matching process [63]. The floor anomaly detection process described in [170] uses a robust statistical technique known as mixture models [172] to group raw disparity measurements into three pools: pixels consistent with the floor-plane model, pixels near the floor plane (anomalies), and pixels that could not be classified.

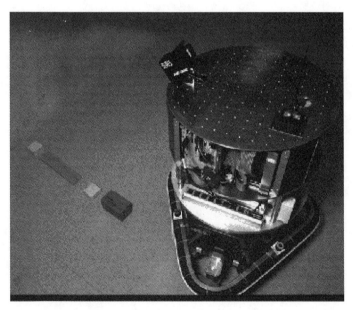

Figure 4.14. BIRIS-based floor anomaly detection. (Reprinted by permission from the National Research Council of Canada (NRC).)

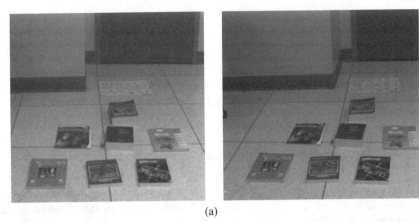

(a)

(b)

Figure 4.15. Stereo-based floor anomaly detection. (a) Stereo pair of the floor. (b) Measurements consistent with obstacles (left), the floor (center), and outliers (right). Intensity encodes class probability with white representing high probability.

4.5.5 Ego-Motion

Suppose that a robot is equipped with a video camera with which it views the world while moving through it. Can the changing visual field be used to estimate the robot's motion (its ego-motion)? Figure 4.16 sketches the geometry of the situation. When the robot's camera is at C_1, the robot views point M. The robot then moves by an unknown amount T, rotates by an unknown amount R, and reviews point M from C_2. What can be inferred about the unknown robot motion R and T by the projections m_1 and m_2?

Clearly if m_1 and m_2 are corresponding images of the same point, then $\mathbf{C_1 m_1}$, $\mathbf{C_2 m_2}$, and $\mathbf{C_1 C_2}$ must all lie in the same plane. This can be expressed compactly as

$$\mathbf{C_1 m_1} \cdot (T \times R \mathbf{C_2 m_2}) = 0.$$

This relationship is independent of the magnitude of T, and thus the absolute motion of the camera between the two views cannot be determined. This limits the direct application of monocular ego-motion in robotic applications. Various techniques for recovering R and T up to this scale factor exist (see [118] for a review), but perhaps the most straightforward mechanism is to use standard nonlinear minimization techniques to minimize

$$\Phi(R, T) = \sum \mathbf{C_1 m_{i,1}} \cdot (T \times R \mathbf{C_2 m_{i,2}}) = 0$$

subject to the constraint $|T| = 1$.

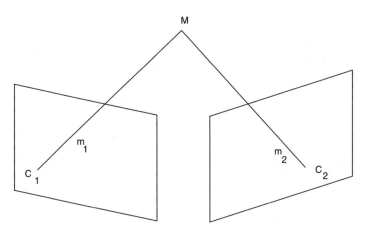

Figure 4.16. Motion constraints.

4.6 Active Vision

Many different technologies are encompassed under the umbrella term *active vision* [7]. Blake and Yuille [40] identify structure from controlled motion, tracking, focused attention, prediction, and sensing strategies as key components of active vision. Each of these techniques can be applied to sensing for mobile robots. For example, active vision research in object tracking is obviously useful for the tracking visual landmarks as the robot moves.

Fundamental to active vision approaches is the concept that manipulation of the sensor can be used to direct the sensor, and hence any associated processing, to that portion of the scene that is most relevant. Many different techniques are presented in the literature to accomplish this direction of attention, but two will be discussed here: foveated sensors and stereo heads.

4.6.1 Foveated Sensors

Perhaps the primary goal of active vision systems is to attend to salient events in the world. If a system is attending to some event, ideally the camera should acquire a larger number of intensity samples per unit area near the center of the image (known as the *fovea* after the biological structure) than in the periphery. This nonuniform sampling has two positive benefits: it allows image compression and it permits a higher sampling rate in the fovea, where more information is needed, than would be possible with a uniform sensor having the same bandwidth. Figure 4.17 shows a foveated sampling of Figure 4.7(a).

Foveated sensors decrease the distance between samples as a function of image eccentricity. Most commonly, the sampling distance is a linear function of eccentricity, which introduces a topological mapping from the linear sampling case to the foveated sampling, which is known as *log-polar*.

There are two general approaches to the construction of a foveated sensor. The first is to use a standard charge-coupled device (CCD) sensor and to foveate the image in software (e.g., [44]). This limits the sampling in the fovea to the sampling rate of the standard CCD but is easier to implement. A second alternative is to fabricate the appropriate sensor (e.g., [370, 285]). Much higher density sampling in the fovea is possible and it is also possible to construct the sensor to provide nonlinear readout of the sensor elements.

Figure 4.17. Foveated image. Foveated images have a nonuniform sampling with a higher sampling in the center of the image.

4.6.2   Stereo Heads

One class of active vision sensors that has received considerable attention in the past few years is the design of binocular robotic vision systems or active stereo heads. Active stereo head design is an emerging technology, and many different head designs are reported in the literature (e.g., [251]). Binocular stereo heads have the problem of positioning and directing two cameras and pointing them in some direction, as do biological systems. (See Figure 4.18 for a typical stereo head.) Because the heads themselves are modeled on a biological system, the design of stereo heads is often described in anatomical terms. There are two basic models for describing human eye movements: the Helmholtz and Fick systems (see [159] for a review). Under the Helmholtz model, the eyes are rotated about a horizontal axis first (tilt) and then about the vertical axis (pan). Under the Fick model, the eyes are first rotated about the vertical axis (pan) and then about the horizontal axis (tilt). The Fick model is also known as the gunsight model. Under either model the eyes can rotate about the optical axis (torque). Robotic stereo heads are typically built using one of these two models.

Models of human eye motions are predicated on the primarily rotational nature of human eye motions. Robotic devices have considerably more freedom, and robotic heads have been built with variable baselines: it is quite common for robotic heads to translate individual cameras as well as to rotate them.

Under either the Fick or Helmholtz model of camera movements, the two cameras can be raised or lowered independently. But for a stereo head to be more than just two separate aiming mechanisms, the motions of the two cameras are usually controlled as a single logical unit. For stereopsis to provide information about structure in the environment, that structure must appear in both camera views, and one technique for ensuring that some structure appears in both camera views is to have the optical axes of the two cameras intersect at some point in space. For this to happen most stereo heads are constructed so that either they cannot raise or lower their cameras independently (e.g., [85, 74, 119]) or control the vertical orientation of the cameras as a single logical unit (e.g., [241, 277]).

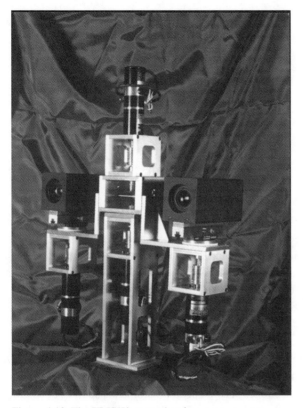

Figure 4.18. The TRISH2 stereo head.

There are a number of different ways in which the orientation of the two cameras with respect to their common plane can be specified. One way is to refer to the two cameras as separate pan units having individual pan angles. A somewhat more useful notation is to talk about the vergence and version angles. The *vergence angle* is the angle subtended by the two optical centers of the cameras measured at the fixation point. A vergence angle of zero corresponds to a target at infinity. The *version angle* is the angle from the center of the line passing through the optical centers of the two cameras to the fixation point. A version angle of zero corresponds to a target directly in front of the stereo head. When a stereo head fixates a particular point in space, a region of space is brought into registration in the left and right images. This region of space is known as the *horoptor*. Active binocular systems typically only consider matches that are near the horoptor; that is, have near zero disparity.

The most general binocular stereo head would have 12 positional and orientational degrees of freedom. Each camera could be placed with arbitrary position and orientation. Because stereo heads are often designed to mimic a biological structure, most heads are built with considerably fewer degrees of freedom.

In the case of zero torsion, the horoptor curve consists of two parts: a circle lying in the plane containing the nodal points of the two cameras, known as the longitudinal horoptor, and a vertical line perpendicular to the circle, known as the vertical horoptor [365, 159]. The longitudinal horoptor is also known as the Vieth–Müller circle. This circle remains unchanged as the cameras fixate different points along the circle. The vertical horoptor does

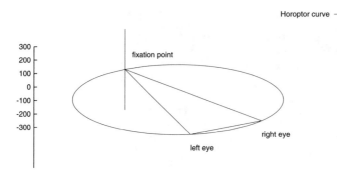

Figure 4.19. Horoptor curve.

not necessarily intersect the longitudinal horoptor at the fixation point, although it does in the case of symmetric fixation. A sketch of the horoptor curve is given in Figure 4.19.

Because stereopsis is typically performed in the region of space with near-zero disparity, techniques that warp the horoptor towards structure of interest – such as the floor – are often utilized in active stereo systems.

4.7   Other Sensors

Standard vision sensors suffer from two fundamental problems: they have a limited field of view and the nature of the imaging process does not encode the absolute distance to an object. This introduces serious problems in tasks such as determining ego-motion from monocular images (see Section 4.5.5). To overcome these limitations, active illuminants, techniques that expand the sensor's field of view, and visual sensors combined with other techniques such as laser sensors have been proposed.

4.7.1   Light Striping

One procedure for augmenting vision is to illuminate the scene with a "structured" known light source, that is, an illumination pattern that can be used to provide additional information and resolve ambiguity. Perhaps the most powerful of these techniques is known as *light striping*. The basic geometry of light striping is shown in Figure 4.20. A line is projected into the scene, and the point at which it strikes scene structure is sensed by a camera. Various light sources are possible, but laser sources are common owing to the highly collimated nature of the beam.

A line projected into the scene allows recovery of the depth of the point at which the light beam strikes an object by triangulation. If a coordinate system is defined coincident with the optical axis of the camera, the computation is simplified. If the source is located a distance d away from the optical axis, with angle Ω between the x axis and the direction of the light projection, then the distance z can be recovered from the projection of the line x' in the camera as

$$z = \frac{fd}{f\cot(\Omega) + x'}.$$

The simplest light structure is a line, but more complex 2-D patterns can be used to maximize observability. Off-the-shelf laser systems are commonly available. For example,

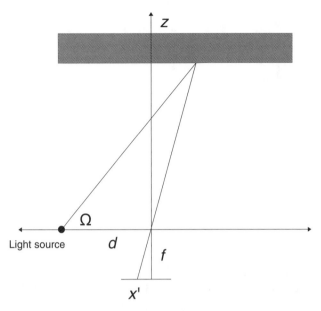

Figure 4.20. One-dimensional line stripe geometry.

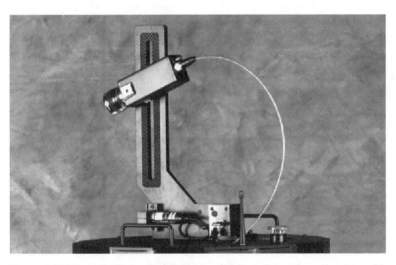

Figure 4.21. Nomadic Technologies Sensus 500 laser line striper. (Appears with the kind permission of Nomadic Technologies.)

Nomadic Technologies offers a laser striping system on their line of robots (see Figure 4.21). Although line striping systems do obtain absolute distance information, the approach is not without its limitations. The entire system must be calibrated, and accuracy is limited by the system optics, the camera resolution, and the frame buffer size. Common line stripers are very fast along the single line because no physical motion is required, but it may take considerable time to scan a volume of space with such devices. Surfaces that either absorb or fully reflect the illuminant beam are problematic.

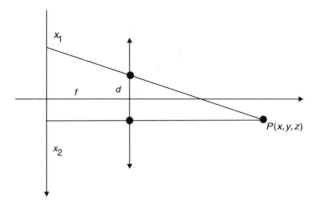

Figure 4.22. BIRIS optics.

4.7.2 BIRIS

BIRIS is a single-camera stereo system [39]. It is based on the concept of constructing a camera with two pinholes or irises (hence BI–IRIS), as shown in Figure 4.22. Because there are two irises in the camera, a pair of "stereo" images are produced on the image plane. The imaging mechanism cannot distinguish between the images projected through the two irises, and thus the viewed image is the superposition of the two projections (i.e., it appears to be a blurred image of the scene). If the two "pinholes" are located at $(\pm d, 0, 0)$, and the camera has focal length f, then a point $P(x, y, z)$ is imaged at (x_1, y_1) and (x_2, y_2) where

$$x_1 = -d - f(x + d)/z$$
$$x_2 = d - f(x - d)/z$$
$$y_1 = y_2 = -fy/z,$$

and given the correspondence between (x_1, y_1) and (x_2, y_2), the point P can be recovered as

$$(x, y, z) = \left(\frac{2d(x_1 - x_2)}{x_2 - x_1 - 2d}, -\frac{2dy_1}{x_2 - x_1 - 2d}, \frac{2df}{x_2 - x_1 - 2d} \right).$$

Passive BIRIS attempts to estimate range directly from stereo correspondence using this double image. The separation between the "pair" of images provides a range estimate. The difficult problem, in passive BIRIS is to solve the correspondence problem, that is, to identify corresponding image features in the same image. One mechanism to avoid this problem is to illuminate the scene with a laser and to use the image of the laser beam as the only set of targets to match. This is known as an active BIRIS system. A laser line projected into the image perpendicular to the line connecting the two irises provides an active target to match. This greatly simplifies stereo correspondence.

The laser line used by the BIRIS system is typically projected so that it is parallel to one of the natural axes of the image. The line thus intersects each row (or column) of the image exactly once, and its image can be detected by simply looking for the brightest spot on each scanline. Using a frequency selective filter in front of the camera can further simplify the detection process and is one of the advantages of using a laser source. A refinement is to project multiple laser lines simultaneously so that more data can be extracted from a single image (and a single position of the system)[39]. Note that full $2\frac{1}{2}$-D images are still relatively slow because scanning of the entire image is needed.

4.7.3 Structured and Unstructured Light

An obvious extension to line striping technology is to project a 2-D pattern rather than a 1-D line. This concept is known as *structured light*. The measurement process is identical to the process used for line striping. Given the projection of a pattern onto an environmental surface structure, the location of the pattern in the image provides depth information. Various 2-D projective patterns have been proposed, and given the recent emergence of inexpensive, lightweight computer-controllable projectors, dynamic 2-D projected displays are beginning to emerge.

4.7.4 LaserEye

LaserEye is a combined range and video sensor consisting of a camera and a laser range finder [169] arranged so that the optical axis of the camera and the laser beam are parallel or coincident. The range finder uses the time-of-flight principle and provides a single-depth measurement for each orientation of the entire sensor while the video camera obtains a standard video image of the scene. Measuring distances to objects in the scene requires pointing the sensor at each of them in turn and reading their depth. LaserEye utilizes a motorized pan-and-tilt system to point the entire assembly at the structure to be examined.

LaserEye has four degrees of freedom: two extrinsic (head pan and tilt) and two intrinsic (camera zoom and focus) (see Figure 4.23). The head can tilt in any direction between 65° below and 95° above the horizon, and the panning range covers 360°; the head can rotate with speeds exceeding 180° per second.

The range finder measures distance to an object in the center of the camera's field of view. In the university prototype, colinearity of the camera's optical axis and that of the range finder is achieved by using a "hot mirror" (one that reflects infrared and transmits

 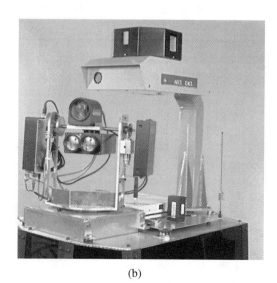

(a)   (b)

Figure 4.23. LaserEye: Integrated laser and video sensor. (a) University prototype. (b) Industrial unit.

visible light) placed in front of the camera lens. The mirror transmits the visible light from the observed scene to the camera with minimum attenuation. The hot mirror reflects the transmitted infrared beam and sends it in the direction of the optical axis of the camera. The returning pulse is reflected by the hot mirror again and projected on a detector in the range finder [169]. The industrial unit introduces a small vertical disparity between the center of the video image and the distance obtained by the laser. A single range measurement takes 0.12–0.5 s, depending on the selected accuracy. The time required to point the head in a new direction depends on the required rotation.

By combining vision with a single depth measurement, LaserEye is capable of performing tasks that are impossible with either a single video camera or a distance measurement system alone. LaserEye has been used, for example, to identify known landmarks visually by servoing in on them using the extrinsic and intrinsic degrees of freedom available with the device and then "shooting" them with the laser to determine distance. The distance to a known landmark coupled with the pan-and-tilt angles is a strong cue to the robot's pose. LaserEye is used on the ARK robot (see Section 9.4).

4.7.5   COPIS and Paracamera

One problem with a standard video source is the limited field of view that is available. Because a robot cannot respond to something it cannot sense, limited-view, single-camera robots tend to perform poorly under general conditions. Various techniques have been proposed to overcome this problem. Multiple camera solutions, active panning, and even fish-eye lenses have been suggested. An alternative is to use specially designed mirrors to bring a larger portion of the environment into the field of view of the camera. This is the approach taken by COPIS (conic projection image sensor) [384, 385] and Paracamera [89]. The Paracamera is shown in Figure 4.24.

Systems such as Paracamera and COPIS use a conic or similar mirror to project a 360° view of the environment into a single CCD camera mounted directly below the mirror. The field of view is limited only by the vertex angle of the conic mirror and the visual angle of

Figure 4.24. The Paracamera vision sensor. The Paracamera sensor is attached to a standard CCD camera and obtains a 360° view of the scene. (Appears with the kind permission of Cyclovision Technologies.)

the camera. The sensor obtains a radial view of its environment; the robot is situated in the center of the image with the environment displayed radially about it. COPIS has been used successfully to navigate in structured known and unknown indoor environments [385].

4.8 Further Reading

4.8.1 Computer Vision

There is an extensive computer vision literature. The classic text of [29] is slightly dated, and more recent texts, including [157], [259], [369], and [118] exist, as do collections of major papers in the field [124]. Implementations of various low-level image-processing algorithms can be found in [287]. Shading analysis, in particular, is especially well covered in [157].

4.8.2 Stereo Vision

Reference [160] provides an in-depth treatment of biological research in stereo vision, and details of binocular stereopsis algorithms can be found in [226, 137], whereas [22] (see also [23]) describes a trinocular stereopsis algorithm.

4.8.3 Signals and Systems

The classic text is Oppenheim [273].

4.8.4 Local Phase Differences

A number of different techniques for measuring the phase difference exist in the literature (see [171] for a review). Different filter families as well as different computational mechanisms for recovering the phase difference are possible. Note that for the technique to work the images must be brought into rough alignment before processing. This requires a control structure to preshift or warp the images, and thus phase-difference measurements are usually applied within a larger control structure. It is also important for a phase-difference algorithm to identify regions of the image for which the local sinusoidal signal model breaks down. Various techniques exist to detect these regions (e.g., [173]).

4.8.5 Active Vision

An overview of active vision work can be found in [86] and [40]. A large literature exists on the design of robotic heads, including [74, 119, 251, 277, 241].

4.9 Problems

1. Describe the optical and physical phenomena in the world that can lead to intensity edges in images.
2. Implement an edge detector, for example the Sobel detector, and compare its output with that of the Canny–Deriche edge detector.
3. One technique for localizing a robot in an office environment is to place targets on the ceiling to identify locations uniquely and to define a local orientation. One possible target consists of a large filled circle drawn on a contrasting background (to define position) and a second smaller filled circle outside the larger circle used to define local orientation. Implement an algorithm to find the two circles in an image. One

approach would be to use edge detection coupled with the Hough transform to find the centers of the circles, but other approaches are certainly possible.

4. Implement a system to drive a robot down the center of a hallway by using vision to track salient features in the hall. The best selection for salient features will depend upon the nature of hallways in your environment but could include such things as the orientation of ceiling tiles or the wall–floor boundary.

5. One straightforward technique for measuring stereo disparity is to assume that the epipolar lines are coincident with the scan rows, to perform simple correlation between the left and right images, and to choose the shift corresponding to the maximum correlation as the correct match. Implement such a stereo algorithm and try it out on real imagery. Can you identify problematic regions in your environment? Try normalized cross-correlation of mean corrected versions of the imagery. Does this improve the algorithm's performance?

Part three

Reasoning

Given a robot that can move and sense its environment, the remaining task is planning intelligent motions.

Chapter 5 looks at the fundamental computational tasks, tasks that must be addressed for a mobile robot to move intelligently through its environment: how the environment should be represented, how the robot should be represented, and how to plan given these representations.

The software environment within which the control programs of modern mobile robots execute can be likened to mobile operating systems. The various tasks that provide overall robotic control must compete for scarce computational and sensor resources and must meet soft and hard real-time constraints. To meet these requirements, various architectures and strategies have been proposed to provide a framework within which the controlling processes exist. Chapter 6 examines how the various computational components that make up a mobile robot can be put together, that is, the software environment or operating system, within which the computational tasks compete for the scarce resources onboard or offboard the robot.

Chapter 7 considers pose maintenance – a necessary task in many robotic systems. This allows a robot to use and construct maps, which are covered in Chapter 8.

Chapter 9 provides case studies of mobile robotic systems operating in the world today. Existing systems must not only meet demanding technological requirements but must also meet economic constraints. Given their relatively high cost, industrial autonomous robotic systems find application only in situations characterized by being inhospitable, remote, or dangerous to a human operator.

5

Representing and reasoning about space

... They assume the end, and consider how and by which means it is attained, and if it seems easily and best produced thereby; while if it is achieved by one means only they consider how it will be achieved by this and by what means this will be achieved, till they come to the first cause, which in the order of discovery is last . . .*

"That's something I could not allow to happen."†

Robots in fiction seem to be able to engage in complex planning tasks with little or no difficulty. For example, in the novel *2001: A Space Odyssey*, HAL is capable of long-range plans and reasoning about the effects and consequences of his actions [75]. It is indeed fortunate that fictional autonomous systems can be presented without having to specify how such devices represent and reason about their environment. Unfortunately, real autonomous systems must make explicit any internal representations and mechanisms for reasoning about them. This chapter considers some of the fundamental computational tasks that must be addressed by a mobile robot: how space should be represented, how to represent the robot itself, and how the robot can reason with respect to its representation of space. These are fundamental tasks for a mobile robot that must plan complex strategies and long-term plans.

5.1   Representing Space

Although it may be possible to carry out a number of complex tasks without an internal representation of the robot's environment, many tasks require such a representation. The most natural representation of a robot's environment is a map. In addition to representing places in an environment, a map may include other information, including reflectance properties of objects, regions that are unsafe or difficult to traverse, or information of prior experiences. An internal representation of space can be used by a robot to preplan and preexecute tasks that may be performed later.

A robot's internal representation of its space is typically required for at least three different classes of task:

---

* Aristotle, *Nicomanchean Ethics*.
† The robot HAL planning and reasoning about future actions in *2001* [75].

1. To establish what parts of the environment are free for navigation. This is a requirement to represent and manipulate the part of the environment that is free of obstacles. This region is known as *free space*.
2. To recognize regions or locations in the environment.
3. To recognize specific objects within the environment.

   The second and third requirements entail representing and manipulating the portion of the environment that is occupied.

So how should a robot represent its environment? Perhaps the simplest solution would be to let the environment represent itself and not to construct an internal representation of the environment at all. This is a fundamental tenant of the subsumption architecture for robotic control in which the environment, as measured by the robot's sensors, acts as its own representation [58]. One difficulty with this type of approach is that, because no internal representation of space exists, all planning and manipulation of the environment must take place on the external (or real) environment itself. According to this approach, plans can only be based on instantaneous sensory input. Long-term planning is difficult to accomplish, although *reactive planning* – planning based on reacting to the current state of the environment – is attractive for real-time, low-level planning.

If an internal representation is to be constructed, what primitives should be used in this construction? Representations based on objects, features or symbolic entities, spatial occupancy, places, task specific information routes, and procedural information have been proposed. In general, spatial representations can be divided into two main groups: those that rely primarily on an underlying metric representation and those that are topological.

5.1.1   Spatial Decomposition

Perhaps the most straightforward representation of space is to sample discretely the two- or higher-dimensional environment to be described. The idea here is to represent *space itself* as opposed to representing individual objects within it. This precludes having to discriminate or identify individual objects. This sampling can be performed in various ways using a number of different subdivision methods based on the shapes of the objects or, more commonly, by defining a sampling lattice embedded in space and sampling space at the nodes so defined. The simplest method is to sample space at the cells of a uniform grid. Samples taken at points in the lattice express the degree of occupancy at that sample point: Is space empty, full, or partially full? If the samples are binary, then in two dimensions the grids are known as *bitmaps*. Otherwise, in two dimensions the grids are known as *pixel maps* or *occupancy grids*. In three dimensions the sampling elements are known as *voxels* or *volume elements*.

The main advantage of a regular lattice representation is its extreme generality: no strong assumptions are made regarding object type. The grids can represent anything. The main disadvantage of this type of representation is that the grid resolution or fidelity is limited by the cell size and the representation is storage intensive even if much of the environment is empty or occupied. For example, for a $15 \times 15 \times 15\,\mathrm{m}^3$ environment with a 3-m accuracy, 125 cells will be required, whereas for a $100 \times 100 \times 100\,\mathrm{m}^3$ volume with a 1-cm accuracy (such as would be appropriate for an office or laboratory area) 10^9 cells will be needed. A voxel-based representation is hardly suitable for large volumes of space.

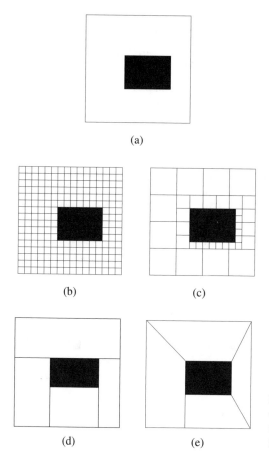

Figure 5.1. An environment and five different spatial decompositions of it. (a) Sample environment. (b) Uniform. (c) Quadtree. (d) BSP. (e) Exact.

In addition to representing the level of occupancy at particular locations in space, elements of the lattice can also be tagged with other attribute information such as the confidence of the occupancy value, the safety or desirability of occupying the cell, terrain information, and so forth. Figures 5.1(a) and (b) show a sample environment and its voxel-based representation. Clearly many of the cells contain essentially the same information (space is either occupied or empty).

Given the simplicity of a grid-based representation but the unrealistic storage requirements needed to represent each cell of the grid explicitly, one alternative is to take advantage of the fact that many of the cells will have a similar state, especially those cells that correspond to spatially adjacent regions. Two general approaches to addressing this storage problem along these lines have been developed. One alternative is to represent space using cells of a nonuniform shape and size, but more commonly a recursive hierarchical representation is used. The most common such example is the *quadtree*.

A *quadtree* [326] is a recursive data structure for representing a square two-dimensional region. It is a hierarchical representation that can potentially reduce storage and aid in certain types of computation. Begin with a large square region that encompasses all of the necessary space. Cells that are neither uniformly empty or full are subdivided into four equal subparts. Subparts are subdivided in turn until either they are uniformly empty or full or until an a priori resolution limit is met. A sample environment and its quadtree representation are given in Figures 5.1(a) and (c). As illustrated in Figure 5.1(c), obstacle boundaries are represented at the finest resolution, whereas large empty (or full) spaces are represented at much coarser resolutions.

The three-dimensional analog of the quadtree is an *octree*. Start with a cube. Recursively subdivide each dimension to achieve homogeneity. In 3-D there are $2^3 = 8$ subcells, hence "oct" tree. Higher N-dimensional versions are possible based on hypercubes subdivided into 2^N subparts.

How good are these representations in terms of saving space? The worst case is the complete subdivision into smallest cells. Thus, in the worst case, quadtree representations are worse than uniform subdivision owing to the extra overhead involved in the quadtree representation. In general, the number of cells varies roughly with the area (or surface, in 3-D) of the obstacles being described. Thus, for environments where most of space is free or occupied, quadtree-like representations are very suitable.

Hierarchical representation systems based on a power of two decomposition are popular in part because of the binary nature of the decision process involved in search. Unfortunately not all space is well characterized by this power of two representation, nor are all environments aligned with power of two boundary planes. Consider, for example, what would happen to the object represented in Figure 5.1(b) if the black object were to be rotated by 45°. Very different representations of what are essentially the same shape would result. Two alternative spatial decomposition methods that are not quite as restrictive as quadtree representations are *binary space partitioning trees* (BSP trees) and the exact decomposition method.

A BSP tree is a hierarchical representation used extensively in computer graphics but which has general application to the task of representing space. It is a hierarchal representation within which a rectangular cell is either a leaf or is divided into two BSP trees by a plane parallel to one of the external boundaries of the environment. Figure 5.1(d) shows a potential BSP representation of the free space depicted in Figure 5.1(a). The free space is divided into regions by lines parallel to the outer boundaries of the environment. Note that each new boundary divides a cell into two but not necessarily in the center of the region. BSP trees provide the same binary space-splitting characteristic of quadtrees but do not enforce the rigor of exactly even subdivision. A BSP representation of a given space is not necessarily unique, and depending on the choice of division planes, radically different representations of the same space are obtained.

Another alternative is to subdivide space exactly rather than requiring a hierarchy such as those introduced by quadtree or BSP decompositions. Free space is simply broken down into nonoverlapping regions by planes such that the union of the parts is exactly the whole. Figure 5.1(e) provides a sample decomposition of the free space shown in Figure 5.1(a). The primary advantage of the exact decomposition method is that it is exact. Unfortunately, as with the BSP approach, the exact decomposition method is not unique because there is no simple rule for how to subdivide space.

When decomposing space into regions, it is not necessary to have the regions constructed so that they do not overlap. For example, Brooks [55] proposes a spatial representation based on describing space in terms of overlapping generalized cones. Each cone is formed with a straight spine and with a cross section perpendicular to the spine. The free space is described in terms of these overlapping regions. The spines of the cones and the intersections of the spines are used to form the edges and nodes of a graph that represents the freespace.

5.1.2 Geometric Representations

Geometric maps are those made up of discrete geometric primitives: lines, polygons or polyhedra, points, polynomial functions, and so forth. Such maps have the advantage of being highly space-efficient because an arbitrarily large region of space can be represented by a model with only a few numerical parameters. In addition, geometric maps can store occupancy data with almost arbitrarily high resolution without becoming liable to the storage penalties incurred by techniques based on spatial sampling.

Geometric maps used in mobile robotics are composed of the union of simple geometric primitives; for example, points, polygons, and circles in 2-D, or cubes and ellipsoids in 3-D. Such maps are characterized by two key properties:

- The set of basic primitives used for describing objects.
- The set of composition and deformation operators used to manipulate objects.

Although simple Platonic solids are sufficient for basic navigation tasks, more elaborate modeling, grasping, or landmark recognition problems motivate the use of more sophisticated primitives. Roughly in order of increasing expressive power or complexity, key classes of geometric primitives in common use include the following

- 2-D maps
  - Points
  - Lines, line segments and polylines (piecewise linear curves). For an example of a map based on this type of representation, see Figure 5.2.
  - Circles and arcs of circles
  - Polynomials
  - Polyhedra
  - Splines
- 3-D maps
  - Points
  - Planar surfaces
  - Regular polyhedra, general polyhedra
  - Surface patch networks
  - Circles and ellipsoids
  - Superquadrics [30, 295]. See Figure 5.3.
  - Tensor product surfaces, NURBS (Nonuniform rational B-splines) [117] and related spline surfaces.

Given a potential representation framework, basic operators for manipulating these primitives include the following:

- Rigid transformations (translation, rotation)
- Conformal transformations (shape-preserving transformations)
- Affine transformations

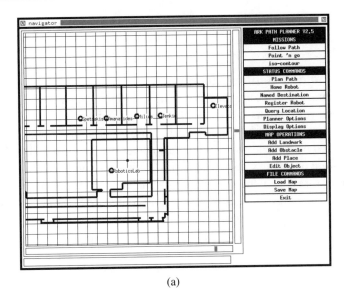

(a)

```
landscape newworld;
  unit meter;
  width 22.500000 to 45.500000;
  height 12.000000 to 28.500000;
  elevation 0.000000 to 2.200000;
  begin
    name (43.541718,23.182617) "Elevator";
    name (33.433750,17.051640) "Robotics Lab";
    obstacle boundary2: wall;
      extent (39.849998, 25.200001) to (39.849998, 21.400000);
      elevation 0.000000 to 0.000000;
    end;
    obstacle boundary6: wall;
      extent (38.496956, 12.395000) to (38.496956, 12.065001);
      elevation 0.000000 to 0.000000;
    end;
end.
```

(b)

Figure 5.2. A sample map and a sample definition of an Environment from the ARK project (see Section 9.4). The world is specified in terms of 2-D primitives, which are then used to construct an occupancy grid representation of space. The 2-D map is based primarily on lines and polylines. View (a) shows the graphical presentation of the map, whereas view (b) shows a sample map definition in the underlying map definition language. Note that (b) does not generate (a).

- Warpage
- Boolean set operations (constructive solid geometry: union, intersection, etc.)
- Regularized Boolean set operators.

The primary shortcoming of geometric model-based representations relates to the fact that they can be difficult to infer reliably from sensor data. Three fundamental modeling problems are regularly encountered:

Figure 5.3. Sample superquadrics. The parametric equation of a superquadric ellipsoid $e = (e_1, e_2, e_3)^T$ is given by

$$e = \begin{pmatrix} a_1 C_u^{\epsilon_1} C_v^{\epsilon_2} \\ a_2 C_u^{\epsilon_1} S_v^{\epsilon_2} \\ a_3 S_u^{\epsilon_1} \end{pmatrix},$$

where $-\pi/2 \leq u \leq \pi/2$, $-\pi/2 \leq v < \pi/2$, $S_w^{\epsilon} = \mathrm{sgn}(\sin w)|\sin w|^{\epsilon}$, and $C_w^{\epsilon} = \mathrm{sgn}(\cos w)|\cos w|^{\epsilon}$. $0 \leq a_i \leq 1$ are aspect ratio and scale parameters, and $\epsilon_i \geq 0$ are squareness parameters.

1. Lack of stability – the representation may change in a drastic way given a small variation in the input.
2. Lack of uniqueness – many different environments may map to the same representation.
3. Lack of expressive power – it may be difficult (or impossible) to represent the salient features of the environment within the modeling system.

These difficulties arise because individual model parameters are difficult to estimate reliably and especially because, for a scene described by multiple model classes, it can be exceedingly difficult to associate specific models reliably with particular sets of measurements. The lack of stability refers to the fact that the geometric models generated as the result of a particular set of observations may vary rapidly with small variations in the input data. Formally, the stability of a modeling function is defined as the ratio of the variation in the output parameters to changes in the input. Given the model parameters $\mathbf{G}$, and a function of changes $\mathbf{I}h$ to the input parameters $\mathbf{S}$,

$$\kappa = \lim_{h \to 0} \frac{|\mathbf{G}(\mathbf{S} + \mathbf{I}h) - \mathbf{G}(\mathbf{S})|}{h}$$

The lack of uniqueness in a representation occurs because many modeling systems, especially those that have substantial expressive power and that approximate the input data rather than expressing it exactly, can express a single set of observations in more than one way. This issue is sometimes partially addressed by using models extracted following the principle of minimal description length. Approaches based on this principle associate a cost with each model used and its approximation errors and attempt to find a single model (from a set of alternatives) that minimizes the total cost.

One approach to addressing instability (as well as uniqueness) is to regularize the problem by introducing a stabilizer that acts to damp variations in the modeling system with (small) variations in the input (see Section 3.1). Recall that a stabilizer is a criterion that serves to bias the model-fitting process toward specific types of solutions. Although formal Tikhonov regularization can be used, a more ad hoc approach is frequently applied in which the stabilizer is simply an additional term used in the model fitting stage. Typical stabilizers include the following:

- Discarding data points that do not have nearby neighbors.
- Preferring line segment models that are straight, aligned with preferred directions, or parallel to other models.
- Preferring line segment models that are long.
- Preferring models are the most compact possible for a given set of data points (for curves, circles, polygons, and superquadrics).
- Preferring models that have uniform or low curvature.
- Preferring models with uniform data coverage.

For example, fitting a superquadric or superquadratic function to an incomplete set of data points often leads to an optimization problem with a very shallow minimum, that is, the precise value of the optimal superquadric parameters is difficult to establish precisely. A wide range of possible superquadric shapes are equally good in terms of their fit to the data but often look quite different. One potential solution to this problem involves adding an additional term to the fitting procedure to select the possible model with the smallest volume preferentially. A secondary problem with superquadrics, and other complex models in general, is that the objective fitting function is nonconvex. Thus, simple gradient descent is insufficient to find the globally optimal values of the model parameters. To address this, a variety of nonconvex optimization procedures can be used, including Levenberg–Marquardt optimization and simulated annealing (see [304]).

Geometric models can suffer from a lack of expressive power in that they are not well suited to expressing *distributions* of measurements and the associated error models. That is, geometric objects are usually inferred from groups of data points, and the underlying statistics of the data are discarded. This is what makes geometric models concise, but if aspects of the original distribution are important, then they must be explicitly represented. Basic error models that are used to express misfits between geometric models and data include means or standard deviations, or both, of uniform or Gaussian distributions. Although better than ignoring the data misfits, such error models may fail to capture the complex distributions associated even with simple sensors such as sonar.

Despite these shortcomings, geometric models provide a concise expression of environmental data and one that can be readily used for higher-level processing. The discrete nature of geometric models makes them well suited to semantic interpretation and reasoning. If geometric models of the environment can reliably be inferred, they can readily be manipulated by inference system.

5.1.3 Topological Representations

Geometric representations rely on metric data as the core of the representation. Unfortunately these metric data are likely to be corrupted by sensor noise at the very least. To avoid reliance on error-prone metric data, a nonmetric topological representation can be used.

The representations of large-scale spaces that are used by humans (and other organisms) seem to have a topological flavor rather than a geometric one [286]. For example, when providing directions to someone in a building, directions are usually of the form "go down the hall, turn right at the cooler, open the first door on your left," rather than in geometric form.

The key to a topological relationship is some explicit representation of connectivity between regions or objects. In its purest form, this may involve a complete absence of metric data. A topological representation is based on an abstraction of the environment in terms of discrete places with edges connecting them; for example, a graph $G = (V, E)$, where V is a set of nodes or vertices and E is the set of edges that connect them. It is often the case that the graph G is embedded in some metric space – the edges have length, and the edges are oriented with respect to the nodes.

The use of graphs, and in particular embedded graphs with edges and vertices augmented with various labels, has been exploited by many robotic systems to represent the environment. The following example from [112] is representative. The robot's environment is modeled as a graph whose vertices correspond to visual landmarks placed on the ceiling within the robot's environment. Each landmark is unique and also defines a local orientation. The landmarks are localized using a camera mounted on the robot that points directly up. A graph-based representation of a sample environment is shown in Figure 5.4. Each vertex corresponds to one of the unique landmarks, whereas edges correspond to known straight paths between landmarks. Each edge in the graph is labeled by the distance that needs to be traveled along this edge to arrive at the next landmark. Edges are also labeled to show their direction with respect to the local orientation defined by the landmark. The robot has no real understanding of the geometric relationship between locations in the environment; locations are only linked by their (augmented) topological

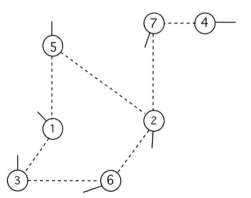

Figure 5.4. Graph-based representation of a robotic environment. Vertices correspond to known landmarks and edges to the paths between them.

representation. Nevertheless, the representation does encode sufficient information for the robot to conduct point-to-point motion. The representation is also extremely compact.

A variety of authors have considered problems of exploration, search, and navigation in the context of a graph-like world. This abstraction permits a range of graph-theoretic techniques to be employed directly. The issue of exploration in graph-like environments is discussed further in Section 8.3.

5.2   Representing the Robot

Mobile robots come in varying shapes and sizes with a variety of capabilities. In the most general case, a robot can be represented in configuration space, but for many autonomous vehicles more simple representations suffice.

5.2.1   Configuration Space

Configuration space (or C-space) is a key construction and formalism for motion planning. A configuration q of the robot A is a specification of the physical state of A with respect to a fixed environmental frame F_w [202]. Consider a rigid robot A capable of translating and rotating in the plane. The configuration of A could be represented as $q = [x\ y\ \theta]$ in that q completely defines the configuration of the robot. For more complex robots, such as limbed or articulated robots, the structure of q can be considerably more complex. A limbed robot's configuration might include a rigid pose for some origin associated with the robot, as above, augmented with the joint angles of each of its limbs. The configuration space of A is the space $\mathcal{C}$ of all possible configurations of A. The space $\mathcal{C}$ defines all of the valid configurations of the robot in its environment.

The physical construction of the robot may prohibit certain configurations, as may the presence of obstacles in the environment. For example, a circular robot with radius r may move no closer than a distance r from any object, thus constraining the possible configurations of the robot and reducing the size of the accessible portion of the robot's configuration space. Constraints of this form can be written as

$$G(q) = 0, \tag{5.1}$$

where q is the robot pose, and are known as holonomic constraints. For any real-world obstacle, we can transform it into a set of points in configuration space and produce a relation of the form in Eq. (5.1). The region of space rendered inaccessible by a real-world obstacle is called a *configuration space obstacle*. In general, planning a path to avoid C-space obstacles in the presence of only holonomic constraints is straightforward. The portion of the environment that is accessible to the robot, that is the free space, is represented by an analogous region of the configuration space denoted by $\mathcal{C}_{\text{free}}$. Constraints on the *derivatives* of the robot motion that cannot be integrated out (i.e., reduced to holonomic constraints) are knows as *nonholonomic constraints* [202]. These take the form

$$G\left(q, \frac{dq}{dt}, \frac{d^2q}{dt^2}, \dots\right) = 0. \tag{5.2}$$

Nonholonomic constraints include restrictions on what velocities (tangents in the configuration space) are allowed. Nonholonomic constraints reduce the range of allowed differential motions and *greatly complicate the motion planning problem*. The essence of the problem caused by nonholonomic constraints is that for the robot to move from one admissible state to another, even if the states are "adjacent" to one another, a trajectory of arbitrary complexity may be required. Common examples of vehicles with nonholonomic motion constraints are automobiles and vehicles with trailers. Parallel parking is a familiar illustration of the type of difficulty associated with even this simple path-planning problem. Other contexts in which nonholonomic constrains occur include when there is a rolling contact, such as with a fingered hand on a surface, or when conservation of angular momentum is a significant factor, as in the case of free-flying robots. A standard nonholonomic constraint for mobile robots is a constraint on the *radius of curvature* that can be executed in the trajectory of the robot (i.e., a limit of the sharpness of the turns that are possible). For problems involving a bounded radius of curvature, optimal length paths in obstacle-free environments are always composed of a sequence of circular arcs.

To make the relationship between holonomic and nonholonomic constraints more concrete, consider the configuration space representation of a synchronous drive robot *A* as described in Section 2.1.1. This robot can control the velocity at which its wheels turn and the direction in which they point. The configuration space representation of *A* could be given by $q = [x\ y\ \theta]$. Suppose that the radius of the robot is r and that there is one infinitesimally small obstacle at the origin. Then this obstacle results in a holonomic constraint on the robot of the form

$$x^2 + y^2 > r^2.$$

If the robot moves at a velocity v, then

$$dx/dt = v\cos(\theta)$$
$$dy/dt = v\sin(\theta)$$

and $dx\sin(\theta) - dy\cos(\theta) = 0$; that is, the robot moves in a straight line in the direction it is facing. This is a nonholonomic constraint of the form given in Eq. (5.2) because it involves q and q', and q' cannot be eliminated. Omnidirectional robots (see Section 2.1.2) do not suffer from this constraint. Path planning for robots that incur holonomic constraints is known as *holonomic path planning*, which is significantly different from path planning for nonholonomic robots (*nonholonomic path planning*). In the presence of nonholonomic constraints, even simple problems such as finding a minimum-length trajectory through a cluttered environment can be exceedingly difficult.

Controllability refers to being able to move between arbitrary points in state space. Nonholonomic systems are not locally controllable, yet they are in many cases globally controllable. Common approaches to nonholonomic motion planning for mobile robots can be divided roughly into methods that perform complete search (often based on discretization), iterative refinement methods, and methods that use specific well-behaved controls but deal poorly with obstacles.

5.2.2   Simplifications

The major problem associated with representing a robot in configuration space (or C-space) is that the configuration space representation of obstacles and the resulting dimensionality of the search space for motion paths can be very large and hence expensive to

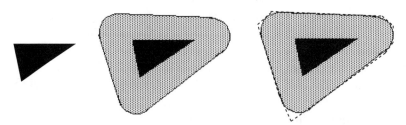

Figure 5.5. Effect of dilation. A triangle undergoes dilation by the robot's radius followed by a polynomial approximation of the resulting boundary.

search. Various simplifications have been proposed to reduce the complexity of the C-space representation and thus the cost associated with representing objects and path planning.

The classic simplification is to assume that the robot can be represented as a point and is capable of omnidirectional motion. This is known as the *point robot assumption*. The obvious problem with this simplification is that autonomous vehicles are not points and many robot designs introduce nonholonomic constraints. If the robot is shrunk to a point, and subsequent processing uses this point representation to plan operations such as paths to follow, it will be important to integrate knowledge of the true size and shape of the robot as well as any nonholonomic constraints into the path execution process. One mechanism for dealing with the nonzero size of the robot is to assume that the robot has a circular cross section and then to *dilate* all obstacles in the environment by an amount equal to the robot's radius, as shown in Figure 5.5. The dilation operation (also known as a Minkowski sum) for an object can be computed by taking the union of the object's shape with a set of circles (or spheres in three-dimensions) placed at every point on the object's boundary. Polygonal obstacles can be described as a set of lines and arcs of circles after dilation. In Figure 5.5 a polygonal object is dilated by the robot's radius and then reapproximated by a polygon. Object dilation can make the resulting environment much more complex as simple corners are dilated into smooth shapes. It is also worth noting that if these complex shapes must be represented by some set of primitives such as polygons, the resulting objects will only approximate the robot's environment.

5.3   Path Planning for Mobile Robots

Motion planning under various types of constraints is an extremely broad field in its own right, and we will survey only a few of the key issues. The basic path planning or trajectory planning problem refers to determining a path in configuration space between an initial configuration of the robot and a final configuration such that the robot does not collide with any obstacles in the environment and that the planned motion is consistent with the kinematic constraints of the vehicle. The initial configuration is known as the *start location* or pose, and the final location or pose is known as the *goal*.

This basic problem can be augmented in several ways, as follows:

- It is often of interest to consider the minimum length path.
- Alternative formulations of a minimum cost path are also sometimes important. In particular, the minimum time path is not necessarily the same thing as the minimum length path. A common case in which these two can differ occurs when

the maximum vehicle velocity is a function of the curvature of the path, as is the case with many synchronous-drive vehicles. As a consequence a minimum-length path may involve lower vehicle velocities than a longer but lower curvature (and hence faster) alternative path.

- Environments with moving obstacles can present significant additional challenges.
- There has been recent interest in algorithms that can operate under time constraints. A particular class of interest is *anytime algorithms* [392]. These provide some solution whenever they are interrupted, but such algorithms exhibit monotonically improving solution quality with increased computation time.
- It may be of interest to select paths that satisfy other constraints as well as terminating at the goal; for example, to choose "safe" paths or paths that permit the robot to sense certain landmarks in the environment [264].

Motion planning entails considering the abilities of the robot and the structure of the environment (and hence any obstacles). A "standard" path-planning algorithm relies on a number of common formalisms and simplifications of the environment as follows:

- A rigid robot A, which is often modeled as a point robot.
- The environment W, which is static and known. The environment is also known as the domain or workspace of the robot.
- The domain of the robot has a defined Euclidean space: R^N, often R^2 or R^3.
- A set of known obstacles $B_1, B_2, \ldots, B_q$ in W.
- The robot travels in straight line segments perfectly.

The general path-planning problem is to find a path t, which from some initial state A leads the robot to the goal. A significant literature on path planning exists. Algorithms are constructed based on different theoretical assumptions and requirements concerning the following:

- **Environment and robot.** The structure of the environment, the robot's capabilities, its shape, and so forth.
- **Soundness.** Is the planned trajectory guaranteed to be collision free?
- **Completeness.** Are the algorithms guaranteed to find a path, if one exists? *Resolution complete* algorithms are complete up to the limits imposed by the resolution.
- **Optimality.** The cost of the actual path obtained versus the optimal path.
- **Space or time complexity.** The storage space or computer time taken to find solution.

To render the planning problem tractable it is often necessary to make a variety of simplifications with respect to the real environment. After an algorithm has been developed based on some set of assumptions, it must actually run in the real world. Idealized algorithms for path planning must be augmented to deal with many annoying realities when applied in the field; moving obstacles, motion constraints, complex definitions of a goal, optimization criteria or side conditions, and, as always, uncertainty.

```
1.      Procedure GraphSearch(s, goal)
2.      OPEN := {s}.
3.      CLOSED := { }.
4.      found := false.
5.      while (OPEN ≠ ∅) and (not found) do
6.              Select a node n from OPEN.
7.              OPEN := OPEN - {n}.
8.              CLOSED := CLOSED ∪ {n}.
9.              if n ∈ goal then
10.                     found := true.
11.             else
12.                     begin
13.                             Let M be the set of all nodes
14.                             directly accessible from n
15.                             which are not in CLOSED.
16.                             OPEN := OPEN ∪ M.
17.                     end
18.     end while
```

Figure 5.6. General graph search algorithm.

5.3.1   Searching a Discrete State Space

Searching and search algorithms form a fundamental component of many robot path-planning algorithms. Given a search space, a set of possible problem states, and a state transition function to determine the states directly reachable from any given state, a *search method* is an algorithm to control the exploration of the state space in order to identify a path from some initial state to the goal.

Graph search   A large literature exists on searching (cf. [268]), but the simplest graph search algorithm expands nodes in turn from a start node until the goal is reached. The basic algorithm is provided in Figure 5.6.

Given a state transition function, a graph G with start node s and set of goal nodes *goal*, the general graph search algorithm depiction in Figure 5.6 determines if a path exists from s to an element of *goal*. The algorithm operates by maintaining a list of nodes that have been visited (*CLOSED*) and a list of nodes that have been visited but might lead directly or indirectly to the goal (*OPEN*). The algorithm continues until either the goal is found (in which case *found* is true), or until the set *OPEN* becomes empty (in which case *found* is false).

As described, the search algorithm only determines if a path exists from the start node to one of the nodes in the set of goal nodes. Additional structures must be maintained if the actual path that was found from the start to the goal node is to be obtained.

In line 6 of the graph search algorithm, a node n is selected from the set of *OPEN* nodes for further exploration, and in line 16 additional *nodes* are added to the set. Different strategies for representing this set and choosing n results in different search algorithms. If *OPEN* is a stack (rather than a set), then a depth first search results. If *OPEN* is a queue, then a breadth first search results. Rather than a static mechanism to order the elements of *OPEN*, an alternative is to order nodes in *OPEN* through the use of an evaluation function $f(n)$. By convention, smaller values of $f(n)$ indicate that n is more likely to be on the optimal path. The general search algorithm is then modified at line 6 to choose the node n in *OPEN* with the smallest value of $f(n)$.

Consider some possible formulations of the evaluation function $f(n)$. Suppose that no link has a zero or negative weight; then $f(n)$ could be the cost of the shortest path from the start node that passes through n. The process of evaluating $f(n)$ can then be accomplished in line 16 by noting that $f(n) = link + f(parent)$, where *parent* is the node in the graph that was expanded to obtain n, and *link* is the cost associated with moving from *parent* to n. This is known as best first search [381].

Best first search is said to be *uninformed* in that, although it knows the cost from the start node to the current node, it knows nothing about the direction or distance from the set of explored nodes to the goal node. Now suppose that $f(n) = g(n) + h(n)$ is the cost function, where $g(n)$ is the estimated cost from the start node to node n and $h(n)$ is the estimated cost from node n to the goal node. This is known as algorithm A [268]. If $g(n)$ is an upper bound on $g^*(n)$, the minimum cost path from the start node to n, and if $h(n)$ is a lower bound on $h^*(n)$ the minimum cost path from node n to the goal node, then algorithm A is known as algorithm A* [268] and the search algorithm will find the optimal path from the start to the goal. If a heuristic search algorithm finds the closest solution to the root (the best solution), we can call it *heuristically adequate*.

If no path exists from the start to the goal, then the basic graph search algorithm will eventually evaluate every possible reachable state before returning false. Thus, failure can take a considerable length of time to detect. Although effective, simple graph searching – especially without an informed evaluation function – is likely to be too slow for robot path planning for a reasonably sized search space.

Dynamic programming Dynamic programming is another general purpose technique that can be used for path planning. Dynamic programming can be described as a recursive (or iterative) procedure for evaluating the minimum cost path to any point in the environment from some source. To use this method, the problem of interest must adhere to Bellman's principle of optimality, which can be stated, in this context, as an assertion that, given three points A, B, and C, the optimal path from A to B via C can be computed by determining the optimal path from A to C and from C to B. In general, the environment must be discretized, and moving from one location to an adjacent location is assigned a specific cost that may be spatially varying but must be temporally invariant. The discretized environment is referred to as a *cost table* and indicates the cost associated with moving from the goal to any location represented by a cell in the table. The idea is to compute the cost of each cell in the table incrementally by simply computing an increment to the cost of an adjacent cell for which the cost is already known, if such a cell exists. In an attempt to compute the path to a specific set of goal locations efficiently without completing the entire cost table, heuristic functions are often used to expand specific nodes in the cost table preferentially (and avoid completing the entire table).

5.3.2 Constructing a Discrete Search Space

Given techniques to search a state space for a path for the robot, it remains to take an environment and construct a state space to represent it. One straightforward approach is to take a geometric representation of the free space and discretize it using, for example,

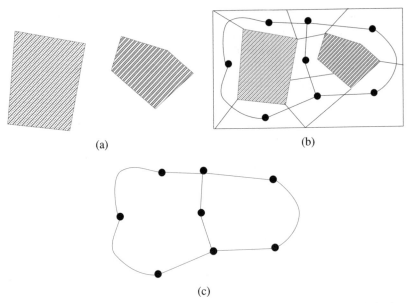

(a)

(b)

(c)

Figure 5.7. Constructing a graph-based representation. The environment (a) is broken down into connected discrete regions (b), which form the nodes of the graph representing space (c).

one of the methods described in Section 5.1.1. A graph is then constructed in which adjacent cells in the discretization are connected. Cells that would result in robot–obstacle collision are removed from the representation, and the resulting graph is searched. This approach can potentially result in a large search space – especially if the robot's workspace is discretized at a fine resolution. The process of constructing a graph-based representation of a workspace is illustrated in Figure 5.7.

Other mechanisms for mapping the robot's environment onto a discrete searchable space include visibility graph and Voronoi graph construction techniques.

Visibility graph planning   The *visibility graph* or *V-graph* is a technique that produces a minimum-length path from start to goal by solving a simple graph traversal algorithm. The visibility graph $G = (V, E)$ is defined such that the set of vertices is made up of the union of all of the verticies of the polygonal obstacles in the environment as well as the start and end points. The edges of the graph connect all vertices that are visible to one another; that is, the straight line connecting them does not intersect any obstacle (see Figure 5.8). Once the construction is complete, a graph has been constructed whose verticies are a subset of the verticies of the obstacle and the start and goal node, and the edges connect locations that can be traversed directly without hitting any obstacles. The problem of finding the shortest path from the start to the goal can then be reduced to the problem of finding the shortest path from the start node to the end node in the resulting graph. This is an example of a roadmap approach to path planning [202]. Algorithms for efficiently constructing the set of visability edges and searching the resulting graph exist with running time $O(N^2)$. The task of searching a graph for a path from one node to another is discussed in Section 5.3.1.

Because no path on the final graph can pass through an obstacle vertex that is concave with respect to the obstacle it defines, only convex obstacle vertices ever need be

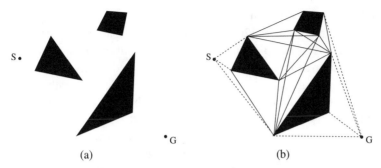

(a) (b)

Figure 5.8. Visibility graph construction. Vertices in (a) are connected if the straight line joining them does not intersect the obstacles' interior; thus, the links of the graph also include the edges of the obstacles in (b). Links between polygon vertices in (b) are drawn in solid lines, whereas links between the vertices and the start and goal nodes are drawn in dotted lines. Note that only the dotted lines change as different start and goal locations are chosen.

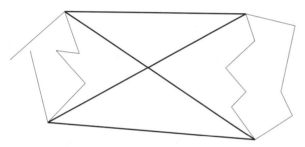

Figure 5.9. Tangent graph. Any path that would have intersected the obstacles must take one of the dark lines cotangent with the obstacles instead.

considered. Further, it can readily be shown that for any pair of obstacles there are at most only four edges that actually need to be included: those that are "cotangent" with the two obstacles (see Figure 5.9). This more efficient construction of a visibility graph is known as a *tangent graph*.

One unfortunate feature of a path found using a visibility graph is that the path passes through vertices and is arbitrarily close to the edges of obstacles. Because the path passes through vertices but not through the interior of any object classifies it as a *semifree path*. Further, the technique does not take into account the size of the robot but makes the assumption that the size of the robot can be ignored. These problems can be overcome in part by dilating all of the obstacles in the environment by the radius of a bounding circle for the robot finding the path (see Figure 5.5). For noncircular robots, however, this method is not complete; that is, in some cases it may not find a path even if one exists.

Voronoi diagrams A common problem with visibility graph planning is that the resulting plans bring the robot close to the boundaries of the obstacles. An alternative approach is to plan paths that keep the robot as far as possible from all of the obstacles in the environment.

The *generalized Voronoi diagram* is the locus of points equidistant from the closest two or more obstacle boundaries, including the workspace boundary [203]. The set of points in the generalized Vornoi diagram has the useful property of maximizing the clearance between the points and obstacles [202]. For a closed free space with compact obstacles, the Voronoi diagram is made up of continuous curves. Thus, at any point on the Voronoi diagram the distance to nearby obstacles cannot be increased by any (differential) motion local to the Voronoi diagram contour. If a robot were to follow the paths defined by the Vornoi diagram then it would not only avoid obstacles, but it would locally maximize the distances to them.

Given an identified start and end position, a robot could move directly away from its nearest obstacle until it moved to a point laying on the generalized Voronoi diagram. It could then follow the set of arcs and straight line segments that make up the Voronoi diagram until reaching a position from which it could move directly towards the goal location while maintaining a maximum distance from environmental obstacles [271, 348].

The major problem with this type of planning is the relatively long path lengths associated with the use of the Voronoi diagram. In short, the technique is often too conservative about approaching obstacles to be attractive.

5.3.3 Searching a Continuous State Space

Rather than searching through a discrete space that represents the state of the robot, an alternative is to model the configuration space of the robot as a continuous space and to consider path planning as the determination of an appropriate trajectory within this continuum.

Potential fields Path planning using artificial potential fields is based on a powerful analogy: the robot is treated as a particle acting under the influence of a potential field U, which is modulated to represent the structure of free space [182]. Typically, obstacles are modeled as carrying electrical charges, and the resulting scalar potential field is used to represenet the free space. The robot is modeled as a charged point having the same charge as obstacles in the environment. Collisions between the obstacles and the robot are avoided by the repulsive force between them, which is simply the negative gradient of the potential field. Attraction towards the goal is modeled by an additive field, which in the absence of obstacles, draws the charged robot towards the goal.

More formally, an artificial differential potential field $U(q)$ is constructed from components associated with the goal ($U_{goal}(q)$) and any obstacles ($U_{obstacles}(q)$). The net artificial potential felt by the robot is produced by summing these as follows:

$$U(q) = U_{goal}(q) + \sum U_{obstacles}(q). \tag{5.3}$$

This can then be used to produce an artificial force field defined by

$$F = -\nabla U(q) = -\begin{pmatrix} \partial U/\partial x \\ \partial U/\partial y \end{pmatrix}.$$

Robot motion can then be executed by taking small steps driven by the local force.

Modeling the environment involves determining field functions for each of the obstacles and for the goal. Typically, as shown in Figure 5.10(a), U_{goal} is defined as a parabolic attractor; for example,

$$U_{goal}(q) = \alpha \, dist(q, goal)^2,$$

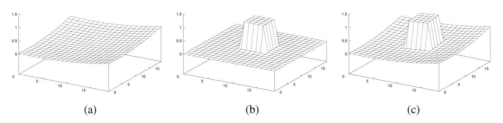

Figure 5.10. Potential fields. (a) Goal field. (b) Obstacle field. (c) Sum.

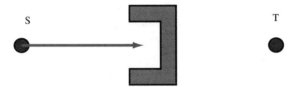

Figure 5.11. A robot trap. The potential field associated with this obstacle can easily exhibit local minima that prevent the robot from reaching the goal.

where dist( ) is the Euclidean distance between the state vector q and the goal state goal.

The repulsive force of an obstacle is typically modeled as a potential barrier that rises to infinity as the robot approaches the obstacle, such as

$$U_{\text{obstacle}} = \beta \, \text{dist}(q, \text{obstacle})^{-1},$$

where *dist* is the Euclidean distance between the robot in state q and the closest point on the obstacle (see Figure 5.10(b)). The repulsive force is computed with respect to either the nearest obstacle or summed over all obstacles in the environment. Using only the nearest obstacle can improve computational efficiency at the expense, in principle, of possibly less desirable trajectories. In practice, the potential computation is performed only over obstacles in the immediate vicinity of the robot under the assumption that distant obstacles are irrelevant and exert negligible effects (in principle, if the effects of all obstacles are being summed, distant obstacles can exert nonnegligible effects, but this may be regarded as a disadvantage).

The robot simply moves downhill in the direction provided by the local field gradient. Path planning based on artificial potential fields has a number of attractive features: spatial paths are not preplanned and can be generated in real time; planning and control are merged into one function, which simplifies the overall control structure; smooth paths are generated; and planning can be coupled directly to a control algorithm. A key issue for path planning using potential fields is knowing how to deal with local minima that may occur in the field [188, 14, 182]. It is straightforward to construct potential fields that will trap a robot as it moves down the potential field (see Figure 5.11). Because of this limitation, potential fields are most commonly used for local path planning.

It is possible to incorporate the idea of a potential field within a long-range planner to avoid these local potential minima, for example, Hwang and Ahuja [164] describe a system in which the global planner uses a graph-like representation of the connectivity between minimum potential valleys in the potential field, whereas the local planner uses a simple potential field system to drive the robot. Another approach is to perform discretized search with costs associated with each location tied to the potential field. Zelinsky and Yuta [390] construct a potential field within a discrete grid and then search through this distance transform for a path that reaches the goal.

Rather than dealing with the local minima in an initial planning step, another alternative is to use some sort of active search whenever the robot enters a local minimum [202], or to employ heuristics [97] to escape from the local minimum traps. Common approaches include the following:

- Backtracking when a local minimum is encountered, with a specific avoidance procedure when a sufficient "backup" has been accomplished.
- Taking some number of random steps when a local minimum is detected. Randomized plans attempt to overcome local traps or minima by introducing a stochastic step within the planning process. The *randomized path planning* (RPP) algorithm [31, 202] iteratively applies a hill-climbing algorithm to search for the goal. At every local minimum, the planner generates up to K (K is approximately 20) random walks for the local minimum of some length. If one of these random motion paths reaches a better minimum, the robot restarts the search process from this new (local) minimum. If, on the other hand, the random search process does not find a new minimum, one of the states in the random paths is used for a new starting point for the search.
- Invoking a procedural planner, such as a wall follower, when a local minimum is encountered.
- Increasing the potential when the robot visits a region to cause it to be repelled by previously visited regions.

Each of these methods has advantages as well as shortcomings. In particular, most methods for escaping local minima depend on being able to *detect* that the robot has entered a local minimum. In general, the robot does not land exactly at the minimum (owing to noise and errors in sensing and actuation) but oscillates about it – as such, simply observing the minimum can sometimes be problematic.

One formal way to avoid local minima completely is to use a form of potential field that is assured to be free of them. Such a minimum-free function is called a *global navigation function*. In general, saddle points cannot be precluded [188, 318], but it is possible to find an almost global navigation function that only has a finite number of saddle points so that small perturbations in the robot's position allow it to escape. In practice, these small saddle points, which constitute a set of measure zero within the free space, can occupy a finite nonzero volume of the free space due to noise and numerical imprecision.

One such global navigation function is based on using a harmonic potential field [78, 77], obtained by solving Laplace's equation $\nabla^2 u(x, y) = 0$. This can be visualized as solving a flow problem for either current or fluid moving from the source location to the goal. Because this type of model is conservative – flow cannot be created or destroyed except at the source and sink – no local minima are possible. This can be proven formally using the Gauss integral theorem [81] in the continuous case, or Kirchoff's law in a discrete grid. The primary disadvantage of this type of field is that the computational cost of obtaining a solution is substantial. In low-dimensional discretized environments, such algorithms can be effectively applied, but the computational cost rises quickly as the number of cells in the discretization grows. Additional complications include the desirability of the final solutions that are obtained and selection of the appropriate boundary conditions for the problem. A final issue relates to quantization: Although there may be no local minima, the gradient of the potential field can be arbitrarily small, making trajectory planning impossible.

Several groups are investigating efficient solution techniques, including solid-state analog solution chips as well as reformulating the underlying computation. For example, the computational cost associated with solving Laplace's equation can be reduced by applying Green's theorem to replace an integral over the surface area that makes up the robot's environment with an integral around the boundary. The boundary integral equation [224] method can be used to reduce significantly the computational costs associated with the use of harmonic potential fields.

Vector field histogram Various heuristics based on ideas similar to a potential field have been used for robot control. The *virtual field force* (VFF) algorithm [46], for example, constructs an occupancy grid on-line and then has obstacles (and the goal) exert forces on the robot. As in potential-field approaches, these forces drive the robot towards the goal while driving it away from obstacles. Unlike a true potential field however, the VFF algorithm only considers forces from a small local neighborhood around the robot.

Experiments with the VFF algorithm identified a number of concerns, many of which were related to the fact that the algorithm reduces the spatial distribution of forces to a single vector quantity. Detailed information concerning the local distribution of obstacles is lost. The *vector field histogram* (VFH) algorithm [47] overcomes this concern by constructing a local *polar* representation of obstacle density. The local region around the robot, defined by a circular window of width w, is divided into angular sectors, and obstacles within each sector are combined to obtain a measure of that sector's traversability. A threshold is set and sectors above the threshold are termed impassable, whereas sectors below the threshold are identified as candidate directions for the robot. The candidate region most closely aligned with the robot's preferred direction of motion is chosen as the appropriate direction of travel. The robot and obstacles are defined in a preexisting occupancy grid C expressed in Cartesian coordinates as (x_r, y_r) and (x_i, y_j). The orientation of the obstacle (and hence the *vector direction*) is given by

$$\beta_{i,j} = \arctan \frac{y_j - y_r}{x_i - x_r}, \tag{5.4}$$

whereas the *vector magnitude* is given by

$$m_{i,j} = c_{i,j}^2 \left(a - b d_{i,j}^2\right), \tag{5.5}$$

where $c_{i,j}$ is the certainty of cell $C_{i,j}$ in the grid, $d_{i,j}$ is the distance of cell $C_{i,j}$ from the robot, and a and b are constants that must satisfy the relation

$$a - b \left(\frac{w - 1}{2}\right) = 1. \tag{5.6}$$

```
Visualize a direct path SG from the start S to the goal G.
while the goal G is not achieved, do:
  begin
    while the path SG to the goal is not obstructed, do
      begin
        move towards the goal,
        if the path is obstructed then
          begin
            mark the current location as p
            circumnavigate the object until the robot either:
            (a) hits the line SG again and can move towards G,
             in which case you do so;
            (b) returns to where p
             in which case G is unreachable.
          end
      end
  end
```

Figure 5.12. Bug algorithm.

A more recent variation referred to as the VFH+ was developed for the *GuideCane*, a robot developed to serve as a navigation device for the blind [368]. In this variation, the vectors used are enlarged to account for the width of the robot. The specific motion direction within the preferred region is chosen based on the width of the preferred region. If the region is narrow, the robot drives down the center of the region. If the region is wide, the robot moves in a direction closest to the goal direction that stays within the preferred region while avoiding the edges of the region by a specified safety margin.

Bug algorithm   In many cases, a global map of the environment is not available when the robot must begin moving towards its goal. As we have seen, potential field-based planning is an example of a local planning method that can be used in such a situation. Unfortunately local potential field-based path planners cannot be guaranteed to find a path to the goal. Under appropriate circumstances, it is possible to devise planning methods that can be used in the presence of uncertainty that provide performance guarantees. The bug algorithms [216] are such a class of algorithms. These algorithms are used for path planning from a starting location to a goal with known coordinates, on the assumption of a holonomic point robot with perfect odometry, an ideal contact sensor, and a infinite memory.

Both algorithms operate by switching between two simple behaviors: (1) moving directly towards the goal location and (2) circumnavigating an obstacle. The basic form of the bug algorithm is described in Figure 5.12.

The bug algorithm is guaranteed to get to the goal location if it is accessible. Note that this trajectory can be arbitrarily worse than the length of an optimal trajectory. Figure 5.13 illustrates the performance of the algorithm.

One source of the cost associated with the bug algorithm is due to the requirement that the robot return to the line SG after circumnavigating an obstacle. A more efficient strategy is to move towards the target directly as soon as a straight-line path is feasible. An alternative strategy is to move towards a point on the line SG closer to G than the intersection point with the current obstacles. These two improvements are the basis of

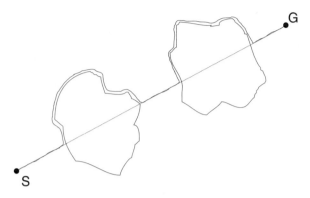

Figure 5.13. Bug algorithm example.

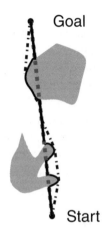

Figure 5.14. Distbug algorithm example. The dotted line shows the straight-line path. The solid line shows the path generated by the bug algorithm. The dash dotted line shows that generated by visbug.

the distbug and visbug algorithms, respectively [217, 179] (see Figure 5.14). The bug algorithm can be further extended to obtain a space exploration algorithm. If one assumes that every object is visible from some other object, depth-first search using a variant of the bug algorithm allows the entire space to be searched [215].

5.3.4   Spatial Uncertainty

Many algorithmic approaches to navigation emphasize a particular aspect of the overall problem while making simplifying assumptions in other regards. Consider the family of bug algorithms (see Section 5.3.3) as an example. The abilities of the robot to know when it has returned to a specific point, to know when it has returned to a line in space, and to follow the boundary of an object accurately are key to these algorithms. Failure to meet these requirements leads to failure of the path-planning algorithm.

A key problem when transferring idealized path-planning algorithms to a real robot is the issue of spatial uncertainty. The problem of determining whether the current location (x_i, y_i) is the same as some other point (x_k, y_k) is not always easy to answer. Ideally the position of a robot in configuration space can be represented as a probability density function (PDF) to denote the probability that the robot is at each point in space. Unfortunately it is often not practical to compute such a representation because it is not possible to model the evolution of the PDF accurately as the robot moves or sensor measurements are made (exceptions include *Markov localization*, which is discussed later).

For geometric representations of space, a simplification that is used to approximate spatial uncertainty is to represent the robot by its pose $[x, y, \theta]$ as well as the matrix of the error covariance (i.e., the error covariance matrix):

$$\begin{bmatrix} \sigma_{xx} & \sigma_{xy} & \sigma_{x\theta} \\ \sigma_{xy} & \sigma_{yy} & \sigma_{y\theta} \\ \sigma_{x\theta} & \sigma_{y\theta} & \sigma_{\theta\theta} \end{bmatrix}.$$

The diagonal terms represent the variances in the error in each individual dimension, and the off-diagonal terms reflect correlations between the errors in the different axes. This model for uncertainty in the form of a covariance matrix is closely related to the assumption that errors are normally distributed.

By representing the spatial uncertainty of the robot as a covariance matrix or in some other geometric manner, it is possible to incorporate this information into most path-planning algorithms. For example, [264] uses such an approach to plan paths that minimize the maximum expected uncertainty of the robot when planning a path in a grid-based representation of space.

For topological representations uncertainty appears in two distinct ways: (1) uncertainty that the robot is in a place represented by a node, and (2) uncertainty as to which node the robot is in, assuming that it is in one. For an appropriate environment these problems can be engineered away, but in some cases it is very difficult to deal with these problems, and topological representations turn on these types of uncertainty.

One approach to the management of spatial uncertainty in topological representations is the use of Partially Observable Markov Decision Processes (POMDPs). This technique associates observables with the nodes of a topological representation of space and represents the robot as a distribution of probabilities over the graph [190]. Robot actions are associated with changes in the robot probability distribution; for example, forward motion increases the probability that the robot is at a more forward node than the one it was occupying. As the robot moves and observes its environment, this probability distribution can "coalesce" into a very high probability at a single node (e.g., at a junction of hallways where the sensor data are definitive), or it can diffuse when the robot encounters a region with ambiguous percepts.

5.3.5   Complex Environments

The path-planning algorithms described earlier in this chapter make various simplifications concerning the robot's environment that are unlikely to be met in practice. Several algorithms have been proposed to extend the applicability of algorithms designed for a constrained environment to more general environments. These extensions include those discussed in the following paragraphs.

Dynamic environments   Rather than requiring all obstacles to be static, the objects are permitted to move. If the motion of the objects is known a priori, then the problem is quite similar to path planning with known static objects. For example, [180]

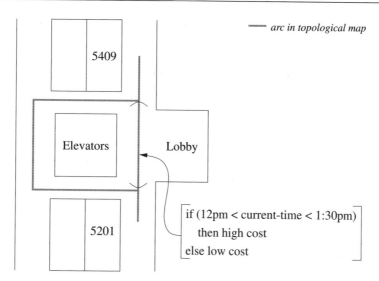

Figure 5.15. A high-level view of a sample-learned rule for an indoor path planner. Haigh's system learns actual traversal costs. (Figure appears with the kind permission of K. Haigh.)

describes an algorithm for this type of generalization for polyhedral objects with known positions and motions.

One approach to dealing with environmental change, proposed by Haigh, is to use *situation-dependent rules* that determine costs or probabilities of actions as a function of the environment [141, 140]. Changes to the environment are expressed in rules that capture the fact that actions may have different costs under different conditions. For example, a path planner can learn that a particular highway is extremely congested during rush hour traffic, whereas a task planner can learn that a particular secretary does not arrive before 10:00 a.m. Figure 5.15 shows a sample rule for an indoor route planner; the sample rule avoids the lobby during lunch hour. Once these patterns have been identified from execution traces and then correlated to features of the environment, the planner can predict and plan for them when similar conditions occur in the future.

Haigh suggests that such rules can be learned using an approach that consists of processing execution episodes situated in a particular task context, identifying successes and failures, and then interpreting this feedback into reusable knowledge. The execution agent defines the set of available situation *features*, $\mathcal{F}$, whereas the planner defines a set of relevant learning *events*, ε, and a *cost function*, $\mathcal{C}$, for evaluating those events.

Events are learning opportunities in the environment for which additional knowledge will cause the planner's behavior to change. *Features* discriminate between those events, thereby creating the required additional knowledge. The *cost function* allows the learner to evaluate the event. The learner then creates a mapping from the execution features and the events to the costs as follows:

$$\mathcal{F} \times \mathcal{E} \to \mathcal{C}.$$

For each event $\varepsilon \in \mathcal{E}$, in a given situation described by features $\mathcal{F}$, this learned mapping predicts a cost $c \in \mathcal{C}$ that is based on prior experience. Haigh calls this mapping a *situation-dependent* rule. Each planner in the system can then use the learned rules to create plans tailored to the situations it encounters in its environment. The approach is relevant to planners that would benefit from feedback about plan execution.

Outdoor environments   In outdoor environments space may not be traversable omnidirectionally. It may be easier for a robot to go across a grade rather than up or down it. (The same problem occurs to a lesser degree in indoor mobile robotics with ramps.) Vegetation, roads, direction to the sun, and time of day are all things that may constrain terrain traversability. The planner must take such information into account when planning paths. An issue that is particularly conspicuous in outdoor environments is the presence of *negative obstacles*,* holes or depressions in the ground that must be avoided but are not associated with space-filling obstacles but irregularities in the terrain. Negative obstacles are particularly difficult to detect.

Unknown environments   One major flaw with many classical path planners is the assumption that the environment is known in advance. In a typical application the robot thinks, plans its path, and then begins to execute it. If the world model is inaccurate, then at some point during the executing of the plan the robot may encounter an event that makes the plan being executed invalid, and the robot must replan. The initial plan has been wasted. Because it is often the case that the initial plan will not survive contact with the environment, an alternative to expending considerable effort to generate a complete plan initially is to generate an approximate plan quickly and to begin to execute it, refining the plan as the robot moves.

Methods that explicitly deal with the need to replan and can reevaluate the path as it is being executed are known as *on-line algorithms*, and the trajectory they produce is sometimes referred to as a *conditional plan*. A true on-line algorithm should be able to generate a preliminary trajectory even in the complete absence of any map. Despite such a handicap, on-line planners can be developed that are complete and can generate efficient paths in certain environments. The bug algorithm (Section 5.3.3) is an example of a simple on-line algorithm for path planning. For algorithms such as this that may not guarantee an optimal trajectory, the *competitive ratio*, which compares the difference between their output and the optimal path, is a useful performance measure. Motion in unknown environments is discussed further in Chapter 8.

Probabilistic path planning   For complex spaces or complex robots with many degrees of freedom, it may not be practical to search the entire configuration space fully. A number of heuristic techniques have been proposed to search through these high-dimensional spaces without resorting to an exhaustive search. Because these techniques are heuristic, we cannot be assured that they will always find a path even though one exists, but if they do find a path it will take the robot from some initial configuration to a specified goal configuration.

The *randomized path planner* (RPP) [31, 202] discussed in Section 5.3.3 can be used in these highly complex searches. Because the RPP follows the gradient, it can potentially avoid the expensive search required to find the goal. Unfortunately the RPP encounters

---

* The term "negative obstacle" is attributed to Bob Bolles in the context of the U.S. unmanned ground vehicle project.

a number of problems when applied to highly complex searches with many degrees of freedom. It is difficult to know what length of random walk is sufficient to escape from a local minimum. How often should different random searches be conducted before giving up and assuming that the goal is not reachable? Perhaps the biggest difficulty with applying the RPP to complex search spaces is that a stochastic walk is unlikely to lead the planner out of tight regions of the C-space.

A more sophisticated technique for probabilistic path planning is described in [181]. This algorithm operates in two phases, a *learning phase* in which a roadmap is constructed within the C-space, and a *query phase* in which probabilistic searches are conducted using the roadmap to speed the search.

Learning phase An undirected, acyclic graph is constructed in the robot's C-space in which edges connect nodes if and only if a path can be found between the nodes (which correspond to locations in the C-space). The graph is grown by randomly choosing new locations in C-space and attempting to find a path from the new location to one of the nodes in the graph while maintaining the acyclic nature of the graph. This process relies on a local path planner to identify possible paths from the randomly chosen location and one or more of the nodes in the graph.

The choice of when to stop building the graph as well as the design of the local path planner are application specific, although performance guarantees are sometimes possible.

Query phase When a path is required between two configurations, say s and g, paths are first found from s to some node $\bar{s}$ in the roadmap and from g to some node $\bar{g}$ in the roadmap. The roadmap is then used to navigate between $\bar{g}$ and $\bar{s}$. Note that after every query the nodes s and g and the edges connecting them to the graph can be added to the roadmap.

As in the learning phase, the query phase relies on a heuristic path planner to find local paths in the configuration space.

This roadmap approach has a number of advantages over algorithms similar to the RPP algorithm. Rather than generating the initial nodes randomly, it is possible to seed difficult areas with many nodes during the learning phase, thus giving the algorithm a better chance to find suitable paths even in challenging environments.

5.4   Planning for Multiple Robots

Motion planning for multiple robots involves some specific issues distinct from those relevant to single robot systems. In particular, the individual robots must avoid collision with one another, and they may have to coordinate their actions either to behave efficiently or to allow them to share information. Approaches to multirobot planning can be grouped into those that use a single centralized omniscient planner and those that involve distinct independent planning systems known as decoupled planners [202].

A typical example of centralized planning is the exact cell decomposition method for motion planning of two discs proposed by Schwartz and Sharir [331]. Centralized planning, although conceptually much simpler, cannot be applied to systems where the individual agents are not in complete communication. As a result, decoupled planning is the approach of choice for real multirobot systems.

Decoupled planners, such as prioritized planners [115], path-coordination or dynamic multiagent planners [60] require no central planner but rather considerable communication initially and often during the execution of the motion. Within the class of decoupled planners, Azarm and Schmidt [24] distinguish between distributed planners based on master–slave relationships [389], and traffic–rule-based dynamic planners [3]. Mutual exclusion across spatial resources demands static environments similar to centralized planners, whereas sensor-based planners [143] suffer from the same limitations as the unirobot reactive control methods.

5.5   Further Reading

Latombe's book [202] provides an effective theoretical survey of robot path planning.

5.6   Problems

1. Implement a potential field path-planning method and compute a 2-D trajectory across a rectangular room with several nonconvex obstacles in it.
2. Repeat the problem above using a 3-D environment and potential field. How does the computation time vary with respect to the number of obstacles and the dimensionality of the space?
3. Modify your potential field method from Problem 1 (or 2) so that the potential field is only computed in the vicinity of the robot. How does the computed trajectory differ? Can this approximation ever lead to results substantially different from those for the field computed over the entire environment? (Justify your answer.)
4. Use the simulator for the ideal disk-shaped synchronous robot developed in Chapter 2 to implement the BUG algorithm.
5. Write a program to construct a Voronoi diagram of a closed environment containing obstacles constructed of line segments. Use the Voronoi diagram to implement a Voronoi-based path planner. How do you plan paths from start and goal locations not located on the Voronoi diagram?
6. Implement the visibility graph-based path planner for an environment composed of polygonal obstacles. How efficient is your determination of vertex–vertex visibility?

6

Operating environment

Robotic systems, and in particular mobile robotic systems, are the embodiment of a set of complex computational processes, mechanical systems, sensors, and communications hardware. The problems inherent in integrating these components into a working robot can be very challenging. This task is complicated by the nonstandard nature of much robotic equipment. Often the hardware seems to have been built following a philosophy of "ease of design" rather than with an eye towards assisting with later system integration. For example, at the hardware level the robot's wheels rotate in encoder counts, sonar sensors return clock ticks to the first returned echo, and the hardware interfaces are usually very specialized. Even if the devices provide standard interfaces such as through a VME bus, serial connections, or via some other standard protocol, the actual command stream can be very device specific. These factors impede abstraction, portability, rapid prototyping, modularity, and pedagogy. Software developers must write layers of code to divorce the low-level interface from higher-level software functions. Because this layer is required for each software device, a large amount of code must often be developed before the first robotic application can be run. The complexity of these underlying software and hardware components can have serious effects on the type of tasks that can be accomplished by the robot, and failures in higher-level software can often result from unidentified bugs or features in this lower layer; these bugs can be very difficult to detect and excise.

Early autonomous robots (e.g. [247]) were more concerned with the process of actually getting the robot to move rather than with considering the limitations of the control architecture on the performance of the vehicle. Take the example of the Stanford Cart, shown in Figure 1.3(c), that was capable of performing limited point-to-point navigation in an unknown but static environment:

> After rolling a meter it stopped, took some pictures, and thought about them for
> a long time. Then it planned a new path, executed a little of it, and paused again.*

The structure of the software that controlled the cart can be thought of as a sequence of separate computational units or modules, each one of which is processed serially with the output of one action forming the input to the next. A top-level description of the software underlying the motion of the vehicle might be described along the lines of the following:

1. Take nine images of the environment with a camera mounted on a sliding track. Identify interesting points in one image and then determine their location in the other eight images to obtain depth estimates of the scene.

---

* Moravec, 1984, p. 274 [247].

2. Integrate this information within a global world representation.
3. Correlate the current image set with the previous image set to estimate the robot motion.
4. On the basis of the desired motion, the estimated robot motion, and the current estimate of the robot's environment, determine the direction in which the robot is to move.
5. Execute the motion.

The result of the execution of these steps was that the robot moved in lurches roughly 1 m every 10 to 15 minutes.

Although the overall system performance seems mediocre by modern standards, the structure of the underlying system architecture is the basis of many of today's mobile robot systems. This _horizontal decomposition_ or _functional decomposition_ of the robotic task breaks the problem of driving the robot into separate functions or components, each of which must be processed in turn with the output of one module acting as the input to the next.

6.1 Functional Decomposition

Functional or horizontal decomposition is the classical top–down methodology used in the design of many existing autonomous robot systems. The world is processed and represented using a discrete set of actions, times, and events. Hu and Brady [162] describe the modules that make up the classic horizontal decomposition of a control system as modules to deal with

- **Perception.** A module to gather information from the environment.
- **Model.** A module to build an environmental model from the robot's perception of its environment.
- **Plan.** A module to construct a plan of action for the robot.
- **Execute.** A module that moves the robot based on the plan.
- **Motion Controller.** A module to provide low-level control of the robot.

A graphical description of this classic horizontal decomposition of the control system is shown in Figure 6.1.

Within a horizontal control system the individual modules operate in a deterministic fashion. It is interesting to note that the system cannot operate until all modules have been coded. Traditional deliberative architecture is based on sensing followed by planning. This is also known as the _sense–plan–act_ or the _sense–model–plan–act cycle_.

The Stanford Cart exemplifies the use of top–down control [244, 245, 246]. More recent and more complex robots also use this top–down control method. As an example, consider the Autonomous Land Vehicle (ALV) robot Alvin [364]. This early outdoor autonomous vehicle was designed to navigate on- and off-road, exhibiting goal-directed autonomous behavior such as road following, obstacle avoidance, cross-country navigation, landmark detection, map building and updating, and pose estimation. The overall software structure of Alvin is given in Figure 6.2. The system software consists of five primary modules:

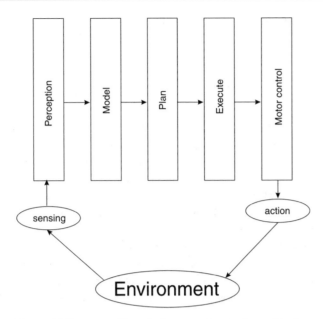

Figure 6.1. Decomposition of robot operational software into horizontal structures.

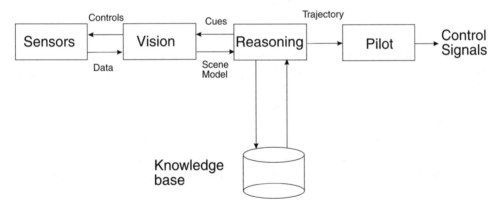

Figure 6.2. The ALV system configuration.

- **Sensors.** A module to deal with the sensors mounted on the robot. Alvin relied on a laser sensor plus a CCD camera mounted on a pan-and-tilt unit to sense the group in front of the robot.
- **Vision.** A module that produces a description of the road in front of the vehicle as a scene model given the output of the sensor module.
- **Reasoning.** The executive controller of the ALV. This module is responsible for overall control of the robot. Given a scene model, the reasoning system builds a reference trajectory to keep the vehicle on the road.
- **Knowledge base.** An a priori road map including significant environmental features.
- **Pilot.** A module that performs actual driving of the vehicle.

These functional modules form a network with well-defined information flow paths. Information from the sensors provides input to the vision module, which generates scene models for the reasoning module, and so on. As can be seen in Figure 6.2, there is an explicit flow of information from the sensors, through vision and reasoning, to the pilot and an implicit flow of information from the pilot back to the sensors through the environment and the robot's actions upon it.

The standard criticism of systems based on a horizontal decomposition model is the structure's inability to react rapidly, for example, in case of an emergency. To see this, observe that for the robot to respond to some critical external condition, the robot must sense, model, and plan, before beginning to act. (This is sometimes known as the SMPA – Sense–Model–Plan–Act cycle.) Horizontal decomposition systems tend to have a long latency time built into the system, although there have been attempts to address this by specifying temporal constraints (see [361]).

In addition to latency problems, horizontal decomposition systems often make the traditional assumption that the world remains static between successive activations of the perception module. It is assumed that the robot is the only active agent in the environment. Conditions that violate this assumption – such as moving obstacles – can cause problems for the robot.

Horizontal decomposition systems must deal with the problem of organizing information and its representation within the robot. Two standard mechanisms have emerged to address this issue: hierarchical- and blackboard-based systems.

6.1.1   Hierarchical

Hierarchical systems decompose the control process by function. Low-level processes provide simple functions that are grouped together by higher-level processes in order to provide overall vehicle control.

The Autonomous Benthis Explorer (ABE) [52, 387] underwater robot provides a typical example of hierarchical control. The ABE utilizes a distributed hierarchical control architecture organized into two broad layers. The lower layers provide low-level control of the robot's sensors and actuators, its attitude and depth sensors as well as thruster control, whereas the higher-layer levels provide mission planning and operational activity monitoring of the lower levels.

Although the NASA–NBS Standard reference model for telerobot control system architecture (NASREM) [5] utilizes a hierarchical as well as a blackboard control architecture, the NASREM system is a classic example of a hierarchical control system. NASREM's control system is hierarchically structured into the following multiple layers:

1. **Coordinate Transform.** Transform representations to world coordinate systems and deal with output servoing.
2. **Primitive.** Compute mechanical dynamics.
3. **E-move.** Obstacle detection and avoidance.
4. **Task.** Transformation of tasks to be performed into effector movements.
5. **Services Bay.** Task sequencing and scheduling.
6. **Service Mission.** Resource allocation

NASREM couples this strict hierarchical control system with a global database or blackboard. Blackboard representations are described in the following section.

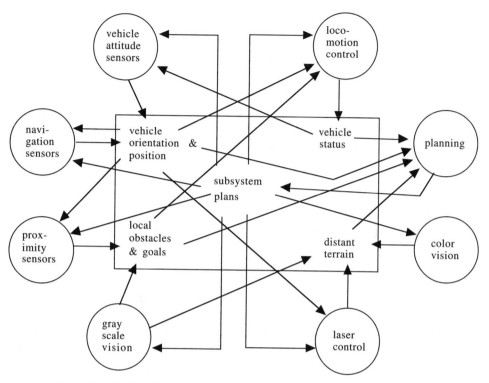

Figure 6.3. Blackboard system from GSR.

6.1.2 Blackboard

Hierarchical systems decompose the control task into separate units and attempt to minimize the communication between units. Blackboard-based systems rely on a common pool of information (or blackboard) shared by the independent computational processes that act on the blackboard (see Figure 6.3). The GSR system [144], an autonomous robotic system designed to navigate from one known geographic location to another over unknown natural terrain, is a typical blackboard-based system. In order to complete its global task the robot is required to develop a terrain map of the territory. GSR uses a blackboard to represent information and to pass information from one software module to another. Fundamental to any blackboard-based system is a mechanism to provide efficient communication between the various computational agents and the blackboard.

Blackboard-based systems provide a loose coupling between each subsystem, permitting the straightforward exchange of information between the subsystems, and they provide a clear and consistent representation of information that can be used by each individual subsystem. GSR implements the blackboard using tightly coupled microprocessors with a local area network connecting them, but software-only implementations are also possible.

Although blackboard systems offer a natural mechanism for providing a common pool of information to a number of parallel computational tasks, the shared database can lead to bottlenecks in terms of processing. In addition, the asynchronous nature of the blackboard system can make software development difficult and can lead to subtle timing errors between the various computational modules.

6.2   Reactive Control

Whereas the horizontal or functional decomposition of the control task is based upon planning, reactive control [16], situated agents [2], embedded systems [177], motor schema [15], subsumption [56], or reflexive behavior [292] directly couple sensors and actuators (see Figure 6.4). The reactive control paradigm is based on animal models of intelligence – the overall action of the robot is decomposed by behavior rather than by a deliberative reasoning process. Behavior-based mechanisms were introduced to deal with a number of difficulties encountered in adapting classical planners to deal with low-level robot control. In particular, classical planners encounter difficulties with the following [58]:

- **Multiple goals.** Unlike classical planners, which typically attempt to satisfy some single overall goal, low-level robot control must meet several goals simultaneously. The controller must provide for vehicle safety while executing commanded motion, while processing sensor input, and while dealing with communication tasks. Each of these tasks has a time-critical nature, and the deterministic, discrete model of processing is not well suited to the task of meeting multiple goals.
- **Multiple sensors.** The sensors on a robot have real-time constraints. Data must be retrieved rapidly, or they may be overwritten by subsequent measurements. Likewise, the data were acquired at a particular point in space-time and must be identified as such, or they will be analyzed inappropriately. Individual sensors may have different time constants; some return results almost instantly, whereas others may take a tenth of a second or longer to return a value.

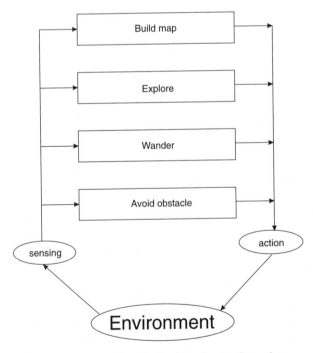

Figure 6.4. Decomposition of robot operational software into vertical structures.

- **Robustness.** The low-level system must be relatively insensitive to conflicting, confounding, or missing data from one or more of the robots sensors.
- **Extensibility.** The control system should be easily modified to deal with changes in sensor, task, or locomotive configurations.

Common to most reactive systems is that goals may not be represented explicitly, but rather they are encoded by the individual behaviors that operate within the controller. Overall system behavior emerges from the interactions that take place between the individual behaviors, sensor readings, and the world.

6.2.1   Subsumption

Perhaps the best known of the reactive control architectures, *subsumption control* systems, consist of a number of behavior modules arranged in a hierarchy. Different layers in the architecture take care of different behaviors. Lower layers control the most basic behaviors of the device, whereas the higher behavior modules control more advanced functions. The overall structure is similar to hierarchical motor patterns as they are used in ethology (see [358]).

The subsumption architecture introduced the concept of providing levels of competence – "an informal specification of a desired class of behaviors for a robot over all environments it will encounter" [56]. The basic levels of competence are as follows:

0. Avoid contact with objects.
1. Wander aimlessly around without hitting things.
2. "Explore" the world.
3. Build a map of the environment.
4. Notice changes in the environment.
5. Reason about the world in terms of identifiable objects.
6. Formulate and execute plans.
7. Reason about the behavior of objects and modify plans accordingly.

Each level of competence includes all earlier levels. A subsumption architecture consists of a set of independent behaviors or experts that directly map sensation to action. The behaviors are organized in a static hierarchy in which lower levels of competence have an implicit priority over higher ones.

The final emergent behavior of the system is the set of reactions that emerge from the various modules provided to achieve each of these levels of competencies. The incremental way in which subsumption architectures are constructed makes them fairly straightforward to implement and allows for a great deal of experimentation and flexibility in terms of system design. However, given the random nature in which the conditions that trigger the various individual behaviors are met, the behavior that emerges from a subsumption architecture can be very difficult to judge a priori, and it can be very difficult to prove performance or timeliness bounds for a given subsumption implementation. Debugging a subsumption architecture can be problematic.

Initial implementations of the subsumption architecture were based on a collection of separate processors, each of which simulates a finite state machine. Various researchers have since utilized the same concept but have built different implementations using fewer processors and generalizing the computational abilities associated with each behavior (see [136], for example).

Perhaps the most sophisticated subsumption-based system is the six-legged walking robot Atilla described in [57]. Here the robot control system is implemented as a series of competency layers, each specifying a behavior for the robot. Elements in the layers are each implemented as augmented finite state machines. The levels of competence in this autonomous system are stand-up, simple walk, force balancing (used on rough terrain), leg lifting (to climb over small obstacles), using whiskers (to sense obstacles), using pitch stabilization, prowling, and steered prowling.

6.2.2   Motor Schema

Motor schema [15] are individual motor behaviors, each of which react to sensory information obtained from the environment. The output of each schema is a velocity vector that represents the direction and speed at which the robot is to move for that schema given the current sensed view of the environment. Individual schema include [13] the following:

- **Move-ahead.** Move in a general compass direction.
- **Move-to-goal.** Move towards a discernible goal.
- **Avoid-static-obstacle.** Move away form a detected barrier.
- **Stay-on-path.** Move towards the center of a path.

Individual schema are sometimes displayed as needle diagrams, but in reality they are not; they are simply the vector output of a computation based on a local internal state and the current input sensor values of the robot. Note that each schema is relatively straightforward to compute.

At any point in time a given set of schema are active, and the outputs of the members of the active set of motor schema are combined as a normalized vector sum. This should be contrasted with the "winner take all" approach of the subsumption architecture described in Section 6.2.1.

6.2.3   Continuous Control

Much of the work on the reactive control of a mobile robot is based on a discrete controller. An alternative approach is simply to consider the low-level control as the development of a control system (in the classical sense) that transduces continuous inputs to some continuous outputs. An obvious advantage of this type of approach is that a very large literature on control theory exists, and this body of work can be brought to bear on the problem. Van Turennout et al [371] describes a system for wall-following based on the construction of an analog controller. Essentially the controller produces values for the forward speed v and rate of turn ω based on a measured distance from the wall and a desired position along the wall.

6.2.4   Integrating Reactive Behaviors

If a reactive system can be built to provide control for a limited task, one obvious extension is to build different reactive systems for different portions of the robot's mission and to swap between the different reactive systems as required. Various mechanisms have been proposed to allow the specification of which set of behaviors should be operational and for how long. These include DAMN [292, 293] (Distributed Architecture for Mobile Navigation), RPL [236] (Reactive Plan Language), CIRCA [253], and many others. Here we discuss BDL [322], RAP [123], and TCA [335] in some detail.

BDL The task of integrating multiple behaviors on a task-specific basis has been considered at the University of Massachusetts Mobile Perception Laboratory (MPL). Based on HMMWV chassis, the MPL robot was designed to perform autonomous driving on and off roads. Overall control of the robot is accomplished via a collection of independent perception-action processes that are executed concurrently. Each process converts sensory data into some type of action. A global blackboard is used for communication between processes [322].

The overall behavior of the robot is defined by the set of processes currently running. Different behaviors are instantiated by providing a mechanism to allow different sets of behaviors to be enabled under specific circumstances.

BDL is based on an augmented finite state machine model (see Figure 6.5). Transitions between states are controlled by external events, and associated with each state is a *run set*, the minimum set of behaviors to be executing, and a *kill set*, the behaviors that must not execute when the robot is in this state.

RAP The RAP system [123] provides an Animate Agent Architecture to integrate and interface between reactive control modules. It allows continuous reactive

```
PROCS = {
    rf "driveOnRoad",
    tl "checkTrafficLight",
    vs "vehicleStop",
    dm "distanceMonitor"
}
STATES = { drive, wait, stop }
EVENTS = { red, green, done }
MSGS = { distance }
WHILE drive(d) {
    SET distance = d;
    RUN rf, tl, dm;
    EVENT red GOTO wait;
    EVENT done GOTO stop;
}
WHILE wait() {
    KILL rf;
    RUN vs, tl;
    EVENT green GOTO drive;
}
WHILE stop() {
    RUN vs;
    KILL rf, tl;
}
```

Figure 6.5. Behavior description language representation.

primitives to be grouped together and executed in sequence or in parallel to perform complex tasks.

Underlying the RAP system is the concept that individual reactive behaviors are executed in parallel and the state of the individual behaviors, the robot, and the environment can be queried by the RAP controller. On the basis of this state information, and on asynchronous events generated by the reactive behaviors, different behaviors can be scheduled and sequenced to generate more complex plans.

TCA The Task Control Architecture [335] is a control and communications protocol and interface for mobile robot systems. It provides an interface and standard formalism for structuring a mobile robot system composed of different tasks and processes. In particular, it provides mechanisms for managing multiple processes constituting a mobile robot application, executing and synchronizing communications between them, and scheduling error recovery or exception handling. Although well-suited to medium term task management, TCA is not well suited to real-time operations. In that context, it is best used in conjunction with a real-time scheduler. TCA and related derivative systems called TCX and IPC have been used on the Mars Explorer prototype called Ambler, the lunar explorer prototype called Ratler, and on the Tessalator tile inspection robot as well as various simulators. TCA has been adapted to a variety of common computing platforms, including SUN solaris, VxWorks, Microsoft windows, SGI IRIX and MacOS.

6.3   High-Level Control

It has been clear since the earliest autonomous robot systems were designed that a procedural representation is not an ideal mechanism for achieving the complex missions that are desired. Consequently, alternative mechanisms, mostly based on logical formalisms, have been proposed to provide high-level robotic control.

Perhaps the most straightforward approach to higher-level control or task planning is to treat the robot as an abstract entity and to apply classical artificial intelligence techniques to specify more complex tasks. As an example, consider the task of having an autonomous robot collect a set of obstacles (pallets) in an environment while on its way to reach some goal. Peng and Cameron [294] describe a system in which simple Prolog programs are used to derive sequences of robot motions that collect the pallets. If ORIGINAL is a set of pallets to be collected, then the Prolog program FINDORDER (from [294]) (see Figure 6.6) determines the sequence in which the pallets should be collected and hence the appropriate robot motions to collect them. In FINDORDER, PERMUTATION(X,Y) is true if X is a permutation of Y, and PATH(A,B) is true if the robot can move from A to the goal given that the pallets in B have not yet been collected. Execution of the Prolog program will determine a sequence of robot motions that will cause the robot to collect the pallets. Note that PATH requires a considerable amount of knowledge concerning the robot's environment and its abilities.

This particular high-level control system is made simpler owing to the limited world representation. From the task planner's point of view, the world can be described by exactly which set of pallets have not yet been collected and the robot's current position. More complex tasks require more complex representations. Marco et al. [225] describe the use of Prolog for the strategic control of autonomous underwater vehicles. In this aquatic system,

```
findorder(Original,Result):-
    permutation(Original,Result),
    sortbypath(Result).
sortbypath([ ]).
sortbypath([ P1|Prest ]):-
    path(P1,Prest),
    sortbypath(Prest).
```

Figure 6.6. Findorder program.

```
done :- current_phase(mission_abort).
done :- current_phase(mission_complete).
execute_mission :-
    initialize_mission,
    repeat,
    execute_phase,
    done.
initialize_mission :-
    ood('start networks',X),
    asserta(current_phase(1)),
    asserta(complete(0)),
    asserta(abort(0)).
execute_phase :-
    current_phase(X),
    execute_phase(X),
    next_phase(X),
    !
```

Figure 6.7. Strategic control in Prolog. (Adapted from Marco, Healy, and McGhee, "Autonomous Underwater Vehicles: Hybrid Control of Mission and Motion [225], p. 175.)

prolog is used to provide a high-level language within which overall mission control can be defined. In [225] a mission is defined in terms of a sequence of phases (see Figure 6.7). Essentially, the mission is complete or DONE if the CURRENT_PHASE can be established as being either MISSION_ABORT or MISSION_CCOMPLETE. A mission is commanded by EXECUTE_MISSION, which attempts to establish each of the mission phases in turn, starting with phase 1. The prolog language is extended by a set of predicates (such as ODD()), which, when evaluated, cause an external action as a side effect and return the success or failure of that side effect as their value. Here ODD('START_NETWORKS',X) performs low-level initialization of the robot.

This type of high-level control provides a well-established mechanism within which a number of different low-level experts or modules can be assembled to accomplish complex, long-term tasks. The order of assembly of these tasks is a simple permutation of a set of tasks (as in the pallet collection system of [294]), or is a predefined sequence of tasks (as in the autonomous aquatic system of [225]). Much more complex sequences of simple tasks can certainly be assembled, and languages such as Prolog provide considerable support for searching through assemblies of simple tasks to achieve high-level goals.

As the search task becomes more complex, a fundamental problem that must be dealt with is the frame problem. The *frame problem* is the task of representing the changes and the invariants in the state of the world when operators are applied. There are many potential approaches to dealing with the frame problem. One approach is to provide a set of logical axioms known as *frame axioms* that express these invariants. Unfortunately a large number of frame axioms may be required for even trivial domains. One simple mechanism for addressing the frame problem is to make the assumption that nothing changes that is not explicitly described by an operator. This is the approach taken by the STRIPS system.

6.3.1 STRIPS

STRIPS [122] represents the world by a set of logical formulas. In STRIPS, procedures or actions are represented by operators. These operators consist of a precondition, an add list, and a delete list. Given a description of a world state s, a STRIPS action includes a precondition, the condition that must be true in order for the rule to be performed. Hence, the following rule from [381] that deals with picking up blocks:

$$\text{PICKUP}(x)$$

precondition :	$\text{EMPTYHAND} \wedge \text{Clear}(x) \wedge \text{On}(x, y)$
delete :	$\text{EMPTYHAND}, \text{Clear}(x), \text{On}(x, y)$
add :	$\text{INHAND}(x)$

PICKUP can only be used if EMPTYHAND is true and for some x and y the predicates $\text{Clear}(x)$ and $\text{On}(x, y)$ hold. The action of the rule $\text{PICKUP}(x)$ is to remove from the database of logical formulas EMPTYHAND, $\text{Clear}(x)$, and $\text{On}(x, y)$ and to add to the set of logical formulas $\text{INHAND}(x)$.

6.3.2 Situation Calculus

A small amount of experimentation with systems such as STRIPS or the generation of complex plans using Prolog illustrates a requirement to be able to reason about time, actions, and plans. The *situation calculus* [234] is a formal calculus of situations that has become a standard approach to the problem. The situation calculus is a first-order language for representing dynamically changing worlds in which all of the changes are the result of named *actions* performed by some agent. Following [381], to express in the situation calculus that B is on A and that A is on a "table" in some state s, one could write

$$\text{On}(B, A, s) \wedge \text{On}(A, \text{Table}, s).$$

Operations in the situation calculus can be thought of as functions that generate new situations. For example, to put x on the table, we can define a function "Putontable" that may have to do something very complicated in the real world, but in terms of the logic,

$$\forall s \forall x [\neg \text{On}(x, \text{Table}, s) \Rightarrow \text{On}(x, \text{Table}, \text{Putontable}(x, s))].$$

Note what Putontable does; it simply returns a state in which $\text{On}(x, \text{Table}, \text{Putontable}(x, s))$ is true. Given a description of the environment and a sufficient description of the effects of actions, the environment, and the set of valid operations within that environment, proofs can be constructed that determine if certain environmental configurations are possible. These logical proofs require a certain set of actions to be performed in a particular sequence (Putontable actions in the above toy example). If performing a Putontable action agrees with the logical definition of the Putontable situation function, the sequence of Putontable evaluations within the proof corresponds to the set of actions that must be taken in the real world to effect the desired final result.

The Golog [207] system uses the situation calculus to define complex actions for general systems and for mobile robots in particular. Golog programs are defined in an imperative programming language that uses common language control structures. In Golog, if α is an action and s a situation, the result of performing α in s is represented by $do(\alpha, s)$. The actions in a given domain can be specified by providing (1) *precondition axioms* that state the conditions under which the action can be performed, and (2) *effects axioms* that specify how the action affects the world's state. Golog has been used to provide control for a number of robots, including an RWI 21 and a Nomad 200 for delivery tasks [351].

6.3.3   GRAMMPS

The GRAMMPS (Generalized Robotic Autonomous Mobile Mission Planning System) is a mission planning and execution module [61, 62] that provides high-level control of one or more mobile robots. The GRAMMPS system can be thought of as a mission planner that distributes one or more strategic goals to one or more robots. Each individual system goal is represented by a software module that continually plans actions that will cause the individual goal to be achieved. GRAMMPS takes the results of these plans and allocates goals to individual robots so as to optimize overall system performance.

6.4   Artificial Neural Networks

Artificial Neural Networks (ANNs) have found applications in a wide variety of areas, and a survey of their applications for intelligent vehicles and robotics can be found in [302]. In particular, neural networks have been applied to transform transducer inputs from video to range sensors to steering control signals directly. Perhaps the most famous application of neural nets to robotics is the ALVINN system (and related offshoots), which has been used to control the motion of the Carnegie–Mellon University's Autonomous Land Vehicle (ALV) while driving along roads and highways.

Although many different neural network architectures have been developed, perhaps the most common approach is the fully connected feed-forward network organized as an input layer, a set of one or more hidden layers, and an output layer (often consisting of a single output unit). ALVINN uses a feed-forward network to transform an input image of the road ahead into a steering direction for the vehicle (see Figure 6.8).

The neural net used for ALVINN [302] is composed of an input "video retina" of 30×32 pixels, a middle layer of 4 hidden units, and an output layer of 30 steering direction units indicating the direction in which the vehicle is to steer. Activations are passed forward through the units, and the output unit with the highest activation level determines the steering direction.

The output layer of ALVINN is an example of an output encoding using *radial basis functions*. In such an output encoding, the output units represent discrete sample locations in a continuous (potentially high-dimensional) vector space of interest. Each unit encodes a probability that the specific value it represents is correct (these are sometimes portrayed as probabilities of being correct).

While driving, each unit (neuron) in the network computes an output value based on the product of the input values available to that unit and the weights that this neuron assigns

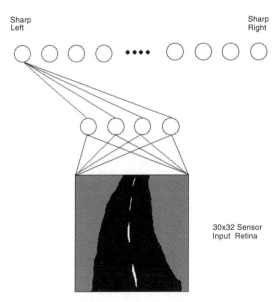

Sharp
Left

Sharp
Right

30x32 Sensor
Input Retina

Figure 6.8. ALVINN network architecture.

to each of its inputs. If x_i is the set of values available to the jth unit, the unit's output is computed as $g(h_j)$, where $h_j = \sum_i w_{j,i} x_i$, and g is a sigmoid function typically of the form

$$g(h) = \tanh(h) = \frac{e^h - e^{-h}}{e^h + e^{-h}}.$$

Note that information flows from the input through each unit to the output layer. Each node j is defined by its set of weights $w_{j,i}$. The entire network is thus defined by the weights associated with each neuron, and the process of training a neural network involves assigning the weights $w_{j,i}$.

The neural network used in ALVINN, like many others, is trained using the *backpropogation algorithm* [377, 235]. The "backprop" algorithm is a supervised learning technique; that is, it requires a training phase during which a supervisor signal is present that provides the correct result for each of a series of training examples. By constructing a neural network such that the function computed by each simulated neuron is a smooth differentiable function (as is the case here), the derivative of the final output error with respect to each weight in the network can be computed. As a result, output errors can be propagated backwards through the network (hence the name of the algorithm), and the final output error can be improved by incrementally modifying the individual weights in the network (typically by some form of gradient descent) (see Figure 6.9).

In the training phase the network is presented with a series of (input, answer) pairs. The network's current output is compared with the correct steering angle as presented by a human operator, and the error is used to correct the weights so as to reduce the network's error on this input. For a given training example with training output t_k and network output out_k, the residual can be defined as

$$E(x) = \frac{1}{k} \sum_k (t_k - \text{out}_k)^2.$$

1. **Weight initialization** Set all weights to some initial random value.
2. **Activation calculation** Given an input t_k compute an output computation of the network out_k and compute the output of each of the hidden hidden units of the network. That is, each individual unit computes an output $g(h_j)$, where $h_j = \sum_i w_{j,i} x_i$.
3. **Weight training** Start at the output units and work backwards to the hidden layers recursively. Weights are adjusted by

$$w_{j,i}(t+1) = w_{j,i}(t) + \eta \delta_j O_i,$$

where η is the learning rate, δ_j is the error gradient at unit j, and O_i is the output of unit i.
The gradient of the error δ_j is given by
- For an output unit:

$$\delta_j = (T_j - O_j) g'(h_j),$$

where T_j is the activation for output unit j that is required for output k.
- For a hidden unit:

$$\delta_j = g'(h_j) \sum_k \delta_k w_{k,j},$$

where δ_k is the error at unit k to which a connection points from hidden unit j.
4. Iterate until the units converge.

Figure 6.9. Backpropagation learning algorithm.

Individual weights are then adjusted to reduce E. The backpropagation delta rule adjusts all of the weights based on the output residual, starting with weights on the output nodes and working back towards the input. As the weights are adjusted for each input, the order, frequency, and content of the training set are critical to the eventual performance of the system. Once trained, the network enters an operational mode in which input data are transformed directly into an output response.

Because ALVINN is based upon a supervised learning algorithm, it is necessary to present ALVINN with a sufficiently rich set of training data. Although originally ALVINN was intended to be trained using simulated imagery, this approach proved to be time-consuming and not particularly robust because it is difficult to generate high-fidelity simulations that cover the range of encountered scenes. Thus, ALVINN is trained "on the fly" using real data. A human operator drives the vehicle, and ALVINN uses the human operator's response and the machine retina to learn the mapping from imagery to steering direction. This accounts for ALVINN's response to a given input.

One drawback with this approach is that human drivers tend to be quite good, and the operator keeps the vehicle centered on the road. Thus, the neural net is rarely exposed to "bad" driving situations and does not learn to recover from them. To overcome this problem, ALVINN's training set is augmented by slightly shifted and rotated versions of the input with appropriate "recovery" steering directions.

As is the case with many supervised neural networks, ALVIN suffers from a number of classic problems such as the following:

- **The net can overlearn.** That is, the net can be more influenced by more recent elements of the training set than by older ones. Thus, in generating a training set, old exemplars must be maintained, and ALVINN uses a buffer of old and new training data points to avoid being unduly influenced by more recent events.
- **The training set may not cover a rich enough set of inputs.** This is partially addressed as described above, but an additional constraint was added to have ALVINN learn only a single road type at a time (such as a single-lane road) in order to restrict the type of environment. Early trials clearly demonstrated the need to expose the net to a wide variety of imaging conditions. For example, if ALVINN had never been presented with a road passing under a bridge during training, a bridge encountered during executing would present a very novel input vector and could result in an unexpected steering direction.

ALVINN successfully drove the ALV under various environmental conditions and was trained to run on various types of roads: one-lane, two-lane, and so forth. In order to apply ALVINN to multiple road types, a number of different approaches were considered. One approach trained different ALVINN networks on different road types and then during the run phase each of the networks was executed in parallel with the winning network driving the vehicle. The arbitration between the various networks was controlled either via a rule-based arbitration scheme or alternatively through another neural network, leading to the development of the MANIAC system [174].

6.5   Genetic Algorithms

Genetic algorithm techniques have also been applied to low-level robotic control. Bekey [36] used a genetic algorithm to generate gaits for a six-legged robot called Rodney. Each leg was controlled by a simple neural net, and the nets for each of the legs were linked. The weights of the neural nets were learned using a staged evolution approach. Initially a genetic algorithm was used to obtain a stable oscillation motion of individual legs. In a second stage, a sequence of leg motions was evolved that produced the maximum amount of forward movement along the body axis in unit time. The result of this learning process was that Rodney learned the tripod gait.

Genetic algorithms, like neural networks, have been used to learn the mapping from sensor data to world models or from sensor signals to steering commands for collision avoidance.

6.6   Hybrid Systems

For almost all robotic tasks, neither a completely deliberative nor completely behavioral design of robot control systems is appropriate. Rather, many robotic systems use a combination of deliberative and reactive subsystems. Low-level control requires a real-time response to external events and has a decidedly continuous flavor, whereas higher-level processing is often better expressed as a discrete set of operations or tasks that must be accomplished. In order to take advantage of the best of both approaches, over-all robotic control is frequently a hybrid of a discrete blackboard, hierarchical, or other high-level control algorithm with a continuous, "functional" low-level controller. Because discrete and continuous systems are better understood as independent systems rather than in combination, most hybrid systems provide a clear demarcation between the functional and behavioral modes of control. There are no standard names for the various levels of control within a hybrid system, although upper levels are often referred to as *strategic control* or *task control*, whereas lower levels are referred to as *execution control* or *reactive control*.

The autonomous robot architecture (AuRA) planner [13, 16] system can be thought of as a hierarchical planner composed of modules to plan missions (the *mission planner*), a *navigator* that accepts a start and goal point from the mission planner and determines a piecewise linear path, and a pilot to implement leg-by-leg motion. The pilot chooses from a repertoire of available sensing and motor behaviors (schema) [15] that are to be active for each stage of the plan. This schema set is chosen so that, based on the a priori world model and the path length to be completed, the schema set is the most appropriate set for this portion of the task.

This concept of a layered control architecture for mobile robot control also exists with the Oxford Autonomous Ground Vehicle (AGV). The AGV employs four distinct layers of control. Its distributed real-time architecture (DRTA) is a hybrid of hierarchical and subsumption approaches [161]. The top layer (Monitor and Reasoning) provides communication and task reporting, the Path Planner utilizes a topological map and provides point-to-point navigation based on large-scale regions, the Navigator maintains an estimate of the robot's position within the environment, and the obstacle avoidance layer uses sonar to build a local map and performs local obstacle avoidance.

The automated vehicle architecture is another example of hierarchical control (see Figure 6.10). Designed to provide control for autonomous vehicles with varying levels of human control, this control system is unique in that it is designed to work at the skill level as well as under a complete system with strategic, tactical, and skill levels of control [34].

Consider the robots of the ARK project as a more detailed example of a hybrid control regime. The ARK project [262] constructed a series of three robots to perform inspection and survey tasks in industrial environments (see Figure 6.11). Each of the three robots utilizes a hybrid control architecture in which the lower level (called the *reactive system*) was based on a continuous model, whereas the higher-level (known as the *navigator*) utilized a discrete, functional control model. ARK-1 and ARK-2 are based on the Cybermotion Navmaster platform, whereas ARK-lite is based on the Nomadic Technologies Nomad 200 platform.

The nature of the lower control levels in an autonomous robot is strongly influenced by the hardware provided by the manufacturer. As delivered, the Cybermotion Navmaster

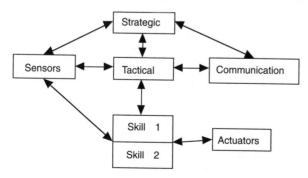

Figure 6.10. Automated vehicle architecture.

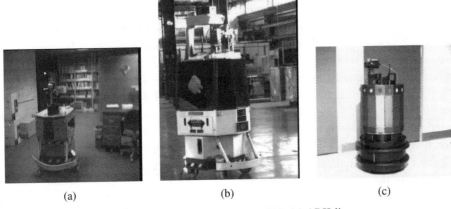

Figure 6.11. The ARK robots. (a) ARK-1. (b) ARK-2. (c) ARK-lite.

platform itself has very little support for onboard computation. An onboard serial bus connects small microprocessors that are dedicated to sensors or actuators. The robot supports several different drive modes, including velocity and position control modes. The Navmaster platform supports the notion of a safety-emergency or e-stop radius. Under software control, individual sensors can be enabled to halt the robot whenever an event is sensed within this e-stop radius. Whenever the e-stop circuit is triggered, the robot freezes in place until either the current movement command is aborted by some external agent or the e-stop circuit is cleared. The current command is not aborted unless this command abort is performed explicitly; rather, the e-stop circuit simply provides a way of arresting the robot until the condition is cleared, at which point the robot continues with whatever command was being executed. Thus, at the very lowest level, ARK-1 and ARK-2 rely on the e-stop circuit to provide limited continuous control. The robot can be controlled to move from point to point by higher levels of control (the navigator), whereas the reactive system (the e-stop circuit onboard the robot) is utilized to provide continuous real-time control. Because the ARK robot's tasks can readily be expressed in terms of point-to-point navigation, the navigator deals with the construction of long-term plans and then decomposes these plans into segments that can be interpreted by the controller on the ARK-1 or ARK-2 robots.

ARK-lite is based on the Nomad 200 platform, which provides direct access to the motor controllers and sensors. Thus, a more sophisticated reactive level of control is possible. ARK-lite utilizes a reactive control architecture based on a set of competing behaviors with a static priority for continuous, low-level control [320]. Each behavior is implemented as a finite state machine. At an even higher level, the ARK-lite robot has also been controlled using Golog; Tam et al [351] describes a cognitive robotics control layer built in Golog on top of the navigator control layer.

6.7   User Interface

The vast majority of mobile robotic systems work on a plane and are concerned with the task of point-to-point navigation. Thus, it is not surprising that the classic user interface to a mobile robot consists of a graphical display of a 2-D depiction of the environment. The display shown in Figure 6.12 is typical. The interface provides a 2-D

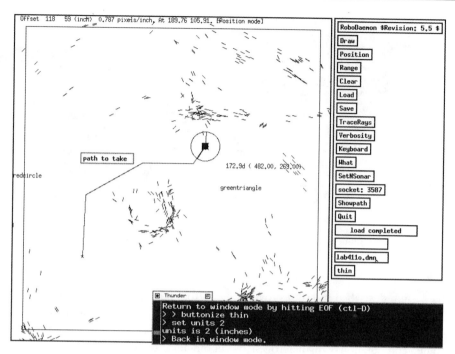

Figure 6.12. Typical mobile robotics graphics display.

representation of the environment with sensor measurements and the robot's motion and planned path overlayed. Buttons provide access to various onboard functions and for the selection of the robot's goal position.

In more complex environments, graphical depictions of the environmental layout, the by locations of walls and other obstacles, and landmarks may also be displayed. As the environment becomes more complex, more sophisticated user inputs may be necessary. For example, the immersive user interface for the ARK robot [20] uses a six-degree-of-freedom joystick and a head-mounted display to provide an immersive environment for the operator. In this system, the operator can "fly" through a simulation of the robot's workspace and can control the robot either robotically or by teleoperation (see Figure 6.13).

User interfaces for mobile robots are, in general, not well developed. Task-level control, point-to-point navigation, sensor-map fusion, and so forth are easily represented, and the information is conveyed to a user. Shared control of the vehicle and the representation of environmental maps and complex sensor readings are very difficult tasks.

6.8   Mobile Robot Software Development as Experimentation

Many mobile robot systems are designed for experimentation rather than as an end in themselves. For these experimental systems, neither performance correctness nor safety is as critical as the ability to provide straightforward access to the platform for multiple users. In recognition of these realities, a number of systems (e.g. [100]) provide an integrated environment for the development of algorithms and software for mobile robotics as opposed to complete application systems.

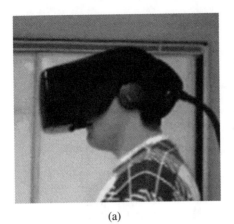
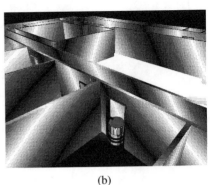

(a)   (b)

Figure 6.13. Immersive user interface. (a) Operator. (b) Operator's view. The operator wears a head-mounted display and can "fly" through the robot's environment using a joystick.

The system described in [100] provides a control and development interface for mobile robotics experiments that permits a single robot to be controlled, simulated, or both using any combination of manual experimentation, simple interactive programming, and distributed computation using heterogeneous computers. The control and communication structures for a particular robot are abstracted (transparently) by the interface.

Many of the concepts relating to incremental development and simulation are well established in other contexts, and the concept of an environmental simulator–controller for manipulator robots is commonplace. Results from manipulator simulations suggest that for the simulation to be effective, it should accurately model as many of the real-world effects as possible.

The development environment described in [100] is based on a single, primary software module known simply as the *robot daemon*. This module forms a robot-independent gateway for all communication to the physical robot. Alternatively, it allows the physical robot to be "replaced" by a simulation. For such a simulator to be useful, it must be able not only to simulate the robot itself but also the sensory feedback the robot receives. The daemon is capable of simulating the behavior of the robot and its sensors in the context of a prespecified simulated environment.

The robot daemon acts as a "service server" for the robot with a graphical inspection and interaction monitor. (The 2-D display in Figure 6.12 was generated by the system described in [100].) Communication with the daemon is accomplished via the Internet. The daemon establishes an Internet address and accepts messages (commands) from other processes running on machines connected to the network. The daemon defines an abstract, robot-independent, communication stream between user tasks and the physical robot (or its simulation). Because the communication stream is identical in either case, the robot-controlling task is unaware if the robot that is running is live.

Coupled to the graphics daemon and simulator is a command-line interface that allows the user to interact with the robot using a combination of semantic primitives: primitive robot commands, abstracted robot functions (e.g., *plan a path to location* (300, 300) *avoiding obstacles along the way*), system or interface commands (e.g., redraw the screen or launch a specified UNIX process), and simple control structures (e.g., conditional, goto,

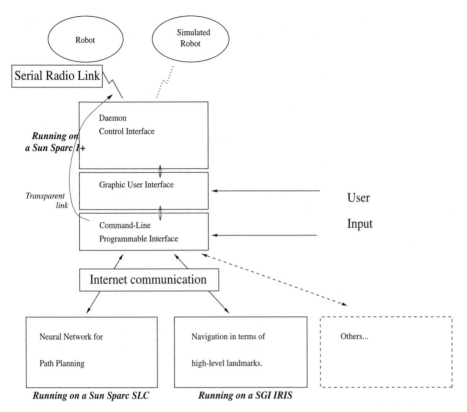

Figure 6.14. Functional units of an experimental system interface.

etc.). This allows very simple functions to be programmed interactively. These modules can be dynamically incorporated into the graphic user interface level and subsequently operated via the mouse. The relationship between the functional components of the robot daemon, including auxiliary processes, is illustrated in Figure 6.14.

The user interface can also incorporate high-level environmental models and can overlay the real robotic data (position, sonar sensor readings) with them. Such data can be manually drawn using the mouse, specified precisely in Cartesian coordinates, or generated automatically by another process. Once entered, the world model can then be used for sensor simulation or path planning alone or in conjunction with real data acquired from the robot.

The system can also be used for verifying the accuracy of the simulation module (by switching to simulation mode and simulating the sensors given the robot's current state). As an aid to debugging, the interface can optionally display the data transmitted to and from the robot as they are transferred, display the Internet communications taking place, display path-planning parameters and interim results, or graphically render the sensor data as they are acquired or simulated.

6.9   Multiple Robots

Although the vast majority of mobile robotic systems involve a single robot operating alone in its environment, a number of researchers have considered the problems and potential advantages of having a group of robots cooperate to complete some required task. For some specific robotic tasks, such as exploring an unknown planet, pushing objects [289, 232, 325], or cleaning up toxic waste, it has been suggested that rather than sending one very complex robot to perform the task it would more effective to send a number of smaller, simpler robots. Such a collection of robots is sometimes described as a *swarm* [37], a *colony*, or as a *collective*, or the robots may be said to exhibit *cooperative behavior* [288]. Using multiple robots rather than a single robot can have several advantages and leads to a variety of design trade-offs. Collectives of simple robots may be simpler in terms of individual physical design than a larger, more complex robot, and thus the resulting system can be more economical, more scalable, and less susceptible to overall failure.

Many different architectures have been proposed for the way in which the robots should be connected to perform a single task. Ueyama et al. [366] propose a scheme whereby complex robots are organized in tree-like hierarchies with communication between robots limited to the structure of the hierarchy. Hackwood and Beni [139] propose a model in which the robots are particularly simple but act under the influence of "signpost robots." These signposts can modify the internal state of the swarm units as they pass by. Under the action of the signposts, the entire swarm acts as a unit to carry out complex behaviors. Mataric [231] describes experiments with a homogeneous population of actual robots acting under different communication constraints. The robots either act in ignorance of one another, informed by one another, or intelligently (cooperating) with one another. As intracollective communication improves, more and more complex behaviors are possible. At the limit, where all of the robots have complete communication, the robots can be considered as appendages of a single larger robot (or robotic "intelligence").

Robotic collectives offer the possibility of enhanced task performance, increased task reliability, and decreased cost over more traditional autonomous robotic systems. Although they have this potential, many collective designs are neither more efficient, nor more reliable, nor more robust than a comparable single robot. In order for a collective to have these advantages it must be designed with these issues in mind.

The information-processing ability of a collective is dependent on a large number of factors, including the number of units, their sensing abilities, their communications mechanisms, and so forth [17, 269]. To understand more fully the properties of various designs of collectives, it is instructive to group collectives into classes and to determine the capabilities of each class.

Various classifications of robot collectives have been proposed. Dudek et al. [103, 104, 107] and, independently, Cao et al. [66] have proposed the classification of swarm, collective, or robot collaboration research by defining a taxonomy or collection of axes. Cao et al. identify group architecture, conflict resolution strategy, origins of cooperation, learning, and geometric problems as "research axes" or taxonomic axes within which cooperative robots can be compared, whereas Dudek et al. concentrate their taxonomy on the communication mechanisms and their expense. The primary purpose of these classifications is to clarify the result that different collective classes have very different capabilities.

The primary axes of the taxonomy of Dudek et al. include the following:

- **Size of the collective.** The number of autonomous agents in the collective.
- **Communications range.** The maximum distance between the elements of the collective such that communication is still possible.

- **Communications topology.** Of the robots within the communication range, those that can communicate with each other.
- **Collective reconfigurability.** The rate at which the organization of the collective can be modified.
- **Processing ability.** The computational model utilized by individual elements of the collective.
- **Collective composition.** Are the elements of the collective homogeneous or heterogeneous?

Physically building significant robot collectives poses many challenges. Many robot sensors (e.g., sonar, IR, RADAR, Laser, etc.) actively illuminate the environment with sound or light energy and then await the reflection of this energy from structures in the environment. If multiple robots utilize the same illuminating sensor technology, cross talk between the robots is possible and must be accommodated. Nevertheless, robot collectives provide the potential for significant improvement in task performance over that available with a single robot. They may also provide economic advantages over using a single robot. Even if robot collectives are not deployed with the objective of explicit collaboration, the incidental deployment of multiple robots in the same environment introduces problems of coordination and sensor cross talk that must be addressed.

6.9.1 Control Architectures

Given the set of possible control architectures that exist for a single mobile robot it is not surprising that there is a wide range of control architectures for robot collectives. For almost every element of the taxonomy described above, different architectures are possible. Rather than trying to survey the possible approaches, we present two specific examples here. These two examples were chosen because (1) they illustrate very different approaches to the task of controlling a collection of robots, and (2) the architectures have actually been deployed on (albeit small) collections of mobile robots.

Alliance Alliance [290] is a control architecture for collections of mobile robots that assumes that each of the robots is independently and individually controlled. Robots communicate through observing the behavior of other robots and the effect of other robot's actions on the task at hand.

Each robot operates under a subsumption architecture (see Section 6.2). In addition to lower control levels that provide for general vehicle safety, the subsumption architecture is augmented with high-level motivational behaviors that essentially provide a specific high-level control to the robot. Individual robots may have many different motivational behaviors only one of which is active.

The motivational behaviors are modeled as either *robot impatience* or *robot acquiescence*. The impatience motivation enables a robot to deal with a specific situation if the robot senses that other robots are not dealing with it. The acquiescence motivation causes a robot to decide not to deal with a specific situation if the robot senses that other robots are dealing with the task.

In the Alliance systems, robots are motivated to deal with tasks (or subtasks) that need to be accomplished, and are less motivated to deal with tasks (or subtasks) that appear to be well in hand. What is required, of course, is the ability of the robots to sense that a task (or subtask) is (or is not) being accomplished by other elements of the robot collective.

MARTHA   The MARTHA project [4] considers the control of a fleet of autonomous robots for transport tasks in highly-structured areas such as harbors and airports. Here it is assumed that a number of autonomous agents operating under centralized control will wish to navigate from point to point within the closed environment. Although the agents operate under centralized control, it is desirable to minimize the communication between individual agents and the central station.

Whenever an agent is assigned a task it formulates a plan and examines the set of resources required to complete the task. For example, a robot might be required to navigate through certain regions of the environment (known as cells in MARTHA) in a specific order to get to the goal. Each of the cells is a shared resource, and thus traversal through a specific cell requires merging the robot's plan with the plans of all the other robots operating in the environment. MARTHA provides an infrastructure and a communications mechanism so that a robot's plan can be validated and then merged with the plans of other operating robots. Plans that cannot be validated must be delayed until the deadlock condition which prevents the validation has been eliminated.

6.10   Further Reading

6.10.1 Neural Nets
A vast literature exists on neural networks, including [235], [148], [131], [130], and [393].

6.10.2 Subsumption-Based Systems
[58] provides a good introduction, whereas [57] describes a specific system in some depth.

6.10.3 Robot Collectives
[107] provides a survey of various robot collectives.

6.10.4 Searching and Planning
These topics are covered in most artificial intelligence textbooks, including [381].

6.11   Problems

1. Using the simple robot simulator developed in Chapter 2 (or ideally using a real robot if you have access to one), write a program that tries to keep the robot as close as possible to its initial position while avoiding any obstacles within 50 cm of the robot. Implement the code using a functional decomposition of the problem.
2. Repeat Problem 1 above, but implement the control software as a reactive system.
3. Repeat Problem 2 above, but take advantage of any multithreading primitives your implementation language supports. For example, if the implementation is in C, try

writing the reactive control software using pThreads, or if the implementation is in Java, trying using threads.

4. Extend the simple robot simulator developed in Chapter 2 so that it supports multiple robots, each controlled by a separate execution thread. Assume that robots can communicate with all other robots. Write an algorithm distributed over all of the robots to find a lost robot in the geometric environment. Place the lost robot in an unknown location and assume that the lost robot is found when one robot's simulated sensors touches the lost robot.

5. Extend your solution above so that it works even when individual robots are randomly killed (or put out of action) and if killed robots are later resurrected.

6. Extend your solution to Problems 4 or 5 so that communications only takes place with robots that are within some minimal radius R. Comment on the efficiency of your solution compared with the approaches possible in Problem 4.

7

Pose maintenance

"You are in a maze of twisty passages all alike."*

Even in simple games like Adventure or Zork, the task of navigation in an environment, especially an environment without distinguished locations, can be very difficult.

For numerous tasks a mobile robot needs to know "where it is" either on an ongoing basis or when specific events occur. A robot may need to know its location to be able to plan appropriate paths or to know if the current location is the appropriate place at which to perform some operation. Knowing "where the robot is" has many different connotations. In the strongest sense, "knowing where the robot is" involves estimating the location of the robot (in either qualitative or quantitative terms) with respect to some global representation of space: We can refer to this as strong localization. The weak localization problem, in contrast, involves merely knowing if the current location has been visited before (this is known as the "have I been here before" problem). In certain cases, complete qualitative maps can be constructed simply from weak positioning information [198, 197, 92]; thus, weak localization can be used to construct maps that can be used subsequently for strong localization. Between the extremes of the weak localization and the strong localization problems exist a continuum of different problem specifications that involve knowing where the robot is or estimating the robot's pose.

Given approximate estimates of a robot's position based on odometry and dead reckoning, and given a map of the environment and sufficient sensing, it is possible to maintain an ongoing estimate of the location of the robot with respect to the map. This process is sometimes known as *localization*, *pose estimation*, or *positioning*. The general specification of this problem starts with an initial estimate of the robot's location $\mathbf{q}$ in configuration space given by a probability distribution $P(\mathbf{q})$. Sensor based localization is based on the premise that we use sensor data $\mathbf{s}$ in conjunction with a map to produce a refined position estimate $P(\mathbf{q} \mid \mathbf{s})$ such that this refined estimate has an increased probability density about the true position of the robot. The map construction problem will be addressed in detail in Chapter 8. In this chapter, we generally assume that maps of the environment are available in various forms as needed.

In certain circumstances it may be necessary to infer the robot's position without an a priori estimate of its location. This type of positioning will be referred to as *global localization* by analogy with global function minimization, whereby an optimum must be

* From Zork, the Great Underground Empire, an early text-based computer game.

found without a reliable initial guess. A more common version of the localization problem is the need to refine an estimate of the robot's pose continually. This task is known as *pose maintenance* or *local localization*. The pose estimation problem (without an a priori estimate) is also known as the *drop-off problem*.

Perhaps the simplest approach to the pose maintenance task is to use open loop control* or odometry to keep track of how far the robot moves in each direction and then to sum these motions to produce a net displacement that can be added to an initial position estimate. Keeping track of how much one moves by observing internal parameters *without reference to the external world* is known as *dead reckoning*. This is the technique used to measure the distance traveled by an automobile using an odometer (note, however, that an odometer does not measure position or distance from a reference point but only the relative distance traveled). In the context of biology, dead reckoning (such as navigating a room with one's eyes closed) is known as *kinesthesia* or as *idiothetic* sensing.

Essentially all techniques for estimating elapsed motion must deal with measurement errors. These errors can arise from electrical noise, quantization, digitization artifacts, wheel slip, gear backlash, and other such sources. If dead reckoning alone is used for position estimation, these errors are added to the absolute pose estimate and accumulate with successive motions of the robot. This makes the general problem of maintaining an accurate absolute coordinate system very difficult, or potentially impossible, in the absence of some external reference for eliminating accumulated errors. Long-term localization, and associated tasks such as navigation and map construction, must make reference to the external world for position correction if positional accuracy is to be maintained. In general, this involves the use of sensory data for recalibrating a robot's sense of its own location within the environment. In some cases, it proves simpler to abandon absolute positioning in favor of only local position estimates or qualitative information (see Section 5.1.3).

A key step in the process of performing either local or global localization involves matching the set of current observations to some established map. Standard matching methods can be broadly classified into the following categories:

- **Data–data matching.** Directly matching the current raw data with predicted raw data (extracted from the map either by predictive modeling or using stored data sets).
- **Data–model matching.** Matching the observed data to more abstract models stored in the map (based on a model of how models and data are associated).
- **Model–model matching.** Matching models stored in the map to models generated from current observations.

Each of the techniques has been used with some success, and each has its particular domain of applicability, depending particularly on characteristics of the sensor and data acquisition methodology. In general, matching with raw data can reduce dependence on a priori assumptions about the environment but tends to be less robust unless the matching technique itself is very sophisticated (in which cases it resembles model–model matching).

---

* Open loop control refers to maintaining a model of the world based on the results you expect from your actions without actually making any observations of the outside world.

7.1   Dead Reckoning

Most devices for measuring position and distance are relative measurement tools (e.g., odometers). By counting the number of rotations executed by a vehicle's drive wheels, for example, and using knowledge of the wheel's size and the vehicle's kinematics, an estimate of the rate of position change can be obtained. Computing absolute coordinates thus involves the integration of such local differential quantities; for example, changes in position, orientation, or velocity. When someone walks in a silent, odor-free environment with his or her eyes closed, this is the form of position estimation to which that person is reduced. In the context of biological systems, this observation of internal parameters (for example, how many steps are taken) is referred to as *proprioception*.

To compute a robot's position x in the idealized error-free case with a velocity vector $\frac{dx}{dt}$ we have

$$\mathbf{x} = \int_{t_0}^{t_f} \frac{d\mathbf{x}}{dt} \, dt,$$

where the motion takes place over a time interval t_0 through t_f. More generally, for motion information from higher-order derivatives (such as acceleration) we can integrate repeatedly to recover position. This also implies, however, that errors in the sensing or integration process are manifested as higher-order polynomials of the time interval over which we are integrating. For discrete motions where positional change is expressed by a difference vector δ_i, we can compute the absolute position as

$$\mathbf{x} = \Sigma \delta_i.$$

This method of position estimation plays an important part in most mobile robot systems. It can have acceptable accuracy over sufficiently small steps given a suitable terrain and drive mechanism. Thus, from a known starting position the final position after several motions can be computed. For large or complex motions, however, the unavoidable errors in the individual position estimates have a major consequence. Simple scaling errors can readily be corrected, but more complex errors are essentially impossible to eliminate.

7.2   Simple Landmark Measurement

The fundamental approaches to position estimation are based on the solution of geometric or trigonometric problems involving constraints on the positions of landmarks in the environment. In principle, the problem is related to pose estimation of a landmark with respect to a fixed sensor. Important variations of the problem arise when the landmarks are unlabeled instead of labeled (that is, their individual identities are unknown), when the landmarks are difficult to detect, or when the measurements are inaccurate.

If we are willing to accept a suitably general definition of a landmark, essentially all methods for pose estimation can be described in the context of landmark-based methods. The primary factors governing the use of landmarks are as follows: Over what region can the landmarks be detected? What is the functional relationship between landmark measurements and position? How are errors manifested?

Additional factors that characterize a particular position estimation system include:

- Are the landmarks passive or active (i.e., are they energy emitters like radio beacons)?
- What is the sensing modality (e.g., vision, sonar, etc.)?
- What are the geometric properties of the landmarks (are they large or small, points or planes, etc.)?
- How easy is it to detect, identify, or measure a landmark?

A key issue in practice is whether the landmarks to be used are *synthetic* or natural. Artificial landmarks emplaced specifically for the purposes of robot localization are typically much easier to detect and can be uniquely labeled. Their optimal placement is an interesting issue. Naturally occurring landmarks, on the other hand, preclude having to modify the environment, but their stable and robust detection can be a major issue. Finally, the extent of the positional constraint provided by observations of a landmark depends on the sensor and the geometry of the landmark itself. Planar landmarks, for example, may provide only one-dimensional constraints on the robot's pose (distance along the normal to the landmark). This is true in the case of range sensing in particular because the measurements are invariant to translation parallel to the face of the landmark.

7.2.1 Landmark Classes

Landmarks can be active or passive, natural or artificial. Active landmarks are typically transmitters that emit unique signals and are placed about the environment. Active artificial landmarks avoid many of the problems commonly associated with passive, naturally occurring landmarks. Artificial landmarks are chosen to be highly visible to the underlying sensing technology but can still can be confused with naturally occurring structures. In general, the use of an artificial landmark – either active or passive – can extend the operational range of the underlying sensor technology relative to a natural landmark.

In principle, landmarks can be defined in terms of any sensing modality. Animals such as dogs and ants use judiciously applied chemical landmarks to define territorial boundaries [155]. From our point of view, the landmarks used by a dog are active because they *emit* odor, and they are *artificial* because the dog must place them itself (at positions it deems useful). The use of landmarks defined by odor has also been considered for robotic vehicles, although using a different set of chemical markers.

In the context of robotics, several primary sensing modalities are of particular interest for position estimation.

- Video-based sensing (i.e., computer vision) can be used in a wide variety of modes. In its simplest form, it can provide bearing and perhaps range to visually defined landmarks. The traditional lighthouse is a classic example of an artificial visual landmark. Artificial landmarks can be augmented by a unique barcode to facilitate their detection and assure their uniqueness. The use of naturally occurring landmarks can require highly complex image processing stages and even then reliable target detection can be problematic. That being said, many environments exhibit robust, naturally occurring landmarks that make excellent visual targets. For example, doors and door openings in corridor environments often make very good and very reliable visual landmarks.

- Laser transmission accompanied by video sensing deserves special mention. Retro-reflective landmarks can provide very long-range detectability. For example, one has been placed on the surface of the moon.
- Active radio beacons form a class of very well-established position estimation landmark. The LORAN terrestrial system has been in use for many years, and the U.S. Global Positioning System (GPS) is based on a network of satellites and can be used from almost any exposed outdoor location (see Section 3.8).
- Because sonar is ubiquitous and inexpensive, it has been considered for positioning despite its drawbacks in terms of beam dispersion, specular reflection, and background noise. It has been shown to work particularly well with large, simple geometric structures that are sometimes referred to as *geometric beacons*.

7.2.2   Triangulation

Triangulation refers to the solution of constraint equations relating the pose of an observer to the positions of a set of landmarks. Pose estimation using triangulation methods from known landmarks has been practiced since ancient times and was exploited by the ancient Romans in mapping and road construction during the Roman Empire.

The simplest and most familiar case that gives the technique its name is that of using *bearings* or distance measurements to two (or more) landmarks to solve a planar positioning task, thus solving for the parameters of a triangle given a combination of sides and angles. This type of position estimation method has its roots in antiquity in the context of architecture and cartography and is important today in several domains such as survey science. Although a triangular geometry is not the only possible configuration for using landmarks, it is the most natural.

Although landmarks and robots exist in a three-dimensional world, the limited accuracy associated with height information often results in a two-dimensional problem in practice; elevation information is sometimes used to validate the results. Thus, although the triangulation problem for a point robot should be considered as a problem with six unknown parameters (three position variables and three orientation variables), more commonly the task is posed as a two-dimensional (or three-dimensional) problem with two-dimensional (or three-dimensional) landmarks.

Depending on the combinations of sides (S) and angles (A) given, the triangulation problem is described as "side–side–side" (SSS), "side–angle–side" (SAS), and so forth. All cases permit a solution except for the AAA case in which the scale of the triangle is not constrained by the parameters. In practice, a given sensing technology often returns either an angular measurement or a distance measurement, and the landmark positions are typically known. Thus, the SAA and SSS cases are the most commonly encountered. More generally, the problem can involve some combination of algebraic constraints that relate the measurements to the pose parameters. These are typically nonlinear, and hence a solution may be dependent on an initial position estimate or constraint. This can be formulated as

$$\mathbf{X} = F(m_1, m_2, \ldots, m_n),$$

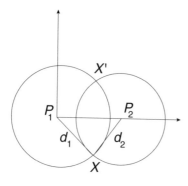

Figure 7.1. Simple triangulation example. A robot at an unknown location X senses the distances d_1 and d_2 to two landmarks P_1 and P_2. Up to a reflection, the robot can compute its position (but not its orientation).

where the vector $\mathbf{X}$ expresses the pose variables to be estimated and $\mathbf{M} = m_1, \ldots, m_n$ is the vector of measurements to be used. In the specific case of estimating the position of an oriented robot in the plane, this becomes

$$x = F_1(m_1, \ldots)$$
$$y = F_2(m_1, \ldots)$$
$$\theta = F_3(m_1, \ldots).$$

If only the distance to a landmark is available, a single measurement constrains the robot's position to the arc of a circle. Figure 7.1 illustrates perhaps the simplest triangulation case. A robot at an unknown location X senses two landmarks P_1 and P_2 by measuring the distances d_1 and d_2 to them. (This corresponds to the case in which beacons at known locations emit a signal and the robot obtains distances based on the time delay to arrive at the robot.) The robot must lie at the intersection of the circle of radius d_1 with center at P_1, and with the circle of radius d_2 with center at P_2. Without loss of generality we can assume that P_1 is at the origin and that P_2 is at $(a, 0)$. A small amount of algebra results in

$$x = \left(a^2 + d_1^2 - d_2^2\right)/2a$$
$$y = \pm\left(d_1^2 - x^2\right)^{\frac{1}{2}}.$$

In a typical application, beacons are located on walls, and thus the spurious solution can be identified because it corresponds to the robot's being located on the wrong side of (inside) the wall.

Although distances to landmarks provide a simple example of triangulation, most sensors and landmarks result in more complex situations. A common real-world situation is one in which relative bearing to the landmark is available but the distance is not. Consider, for example, a camera that can detect two small known landmarks. Assuming the camera has been calibrated (see Section 4.1.1), we can readily extract the angular separation between the landmarks from their positions on the image. Using the angular separation or *relative bearing* between two landmarks with known position constrains the robot's position to lie on a pair of circular arcs. If the robot can determine the clockwise enumeration of the landmarks (or label them uniquely), the position is constrained to only one of these two circles. Additional landmarks to which the bearing is known can provide a third constraint, and the intersection of these constraints uniquely determines the robot's position. The one exception to this is when the landmarks lie on a common circle, which

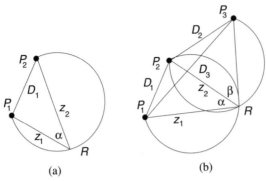

Figure 7.2. Bearing-based triangulation with landmarks.
(a) Two landmarks. (b) Three landmarks.

in turn implies the constraint circles are coincident (instead of merely intersecting at a pair of points) [343].

Sugihara was among the first to examine the use of computer vision formally for landmark-based pose estimation [343]. His emphasis is on the *computationally efficient* solution of the problem of bringing bearing measurements of indistinguishable landmarks into correspondence with a map. His solution has been improved by Avis and Imai [21].

The situation for two landmarks is illustrated in Figure 7.2(a). The robot senses two known landmarks and measures the bearing to each landmark relative to its own straight-ahead direction. This obtains the difference in bearing between the directions to the two landmarks and constrains the true position of the robot to lie on that portion of the circle shown in Figure 7.2(a). (Note that the mathematics admits two circular arcs, but one can be excluded based on the left–right ordering of the landmark directions.) The loci of points that satisfy the bearing difference is given by

$$D_1^2 = z_1^2 + z_2^2 - 2|z_1||z_2|\cos(\alpha),$$

where z_1 and z_2 are the distances from the robot's current position to landmarks P_1 and P_2, respectively.

The visibility of a third landmark gives rise to three nonlinear constraints on z_1, z_2 and z_3:

$$D_1^2 = z_1^2 + z_2^2 - 2|z_1||z_2|\cos(\alpha)$$
$$D_2^2 = z_2^2 + z_3^2 - 2|z_2||z_3|\cos(\beta)$$
$$D_3^2 = z_1^2 + z_3^2 - 2|z_1||z_3|\cos(\alpha + \beta),$$

which can be solved using standard techniques to obtain z_1, z_2, and z_3. Knowledge of z_1, z_2, and z_3 leads to the robot's position and orientation [38]. Using three landmarks also precludes any ambiguity if the landmarks cannot be labeled. More realistically, there can be noise in the landmark bearing estimates or even their labeling. This suggests the use of additional measurements either to improve robustness or validate the measurements. For simple validation, landmarks can be decomposed into groups, and a consistent estimate from each group can be sought. Betke and Gurvits [38] also describe an efficient algorithm for performing the estimation of the robot's pose when more than three landmarks are visible and the solution is overconstrained. By representing landmark positions in the complex plane, Betke and Gurvits show that it is possible to linearize the relationship between the geometric constraints. This permits a solution that can be computed in time that is a linear function of the number of landmarks given that certain constraints on the arrangement of the landmarks are satisfied.

The geometric arrangement of landmarks with respect to the robot observer is critical to the accuracy of the solution. A particular arrangement of landmarks may provide high accuracy when observed from some locations and low accuracy when observed from others. For example, in two dimensions a set of three colinear landmarks observed with a bearing measuring device can provide good positional accuracy for triangulation when viewed from a point away from the line joining the landmarks (e.g., a point that forms an equilateral triangle with respect to the external landmarks). On the other hand, if the robot is located on the line joining the landmarks, the position can only be constrained to lie somewhere on this (infinite) line. The quantification of this variation in accuracy with position is discussed in the next section.

Many different robotic systems rely on target triangulation to address the task of pose estimation. As one example, Yagi et al. [385] describe the use of the COPIS sensor (see Section 4.7.5) coupled with a map of salient features to locate the robot with respect to the map. The COPIS sensor obtains azimuth readings to vertical edges in the environment. Because the COPIS sensor is omnidirectional and the environment is constructed to be populated with vertical lines, a large number of azimuth readings are obtained surrounding the robot. The robot has an estimate of its current position, and it uses this estimate to establish correspondences between azimuth measurements and vertical features on the map. An optimization process is then used to find the true position of the robot.

Triangulation with uncertainty The ideal case of triangulation from range or bearing measurements is complicated somewhat by the fact that real sensor measurements have associated uncertainty. As a result, the position estimates produced by triangulation schemes provide probability distributions for the robot pose. Although the particular degenerate cases that lead to truly ambiguous pose estimates are, in principle, unlikely, the magnification of input error in the course of position estimation is a common occurrence (see Figure 7.3).

The relationship between the accuracy of the input measurements and the accuracy of the final estimate of the desired pose variables is formalized by the notion of the Geometric *Dilution Of Precision* (GDOP). This is a metric that expresses the variation in the output estimate X (i.e., the geometric variables constituting the pose) with variations in the input parameters S (i.e., sensor data):

$$\text{GDOP} = \frac{\Delta X}{\Delta S}$$

When we take the limit as ΔS approaches zero, this is equal to the Jacobian $\mathcal{J}$ of the measurement equation. In three-dimensional space, the *horizontal geometric dilution of precision* (HDOP) and *positional geometric dilution of precision* (PDOP) refer to the error sensitivity of only the horizontal or translational components, whereas the full GDOP may refer to the sensitivity of a larger class of variables. For example, in the context of (Section 3.8), GDOP is sometimes used to refer to the sensitivity of the system of variables,

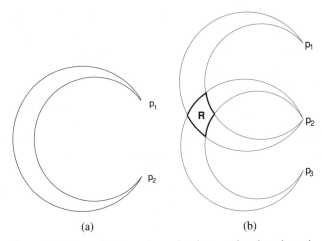

(a)   (b)

Figure 7.3. Pose estimates and associated uncertainty based on triangulation using imprecise bearings to (a) two landmarks where the
ambiguous region is the crescent and (b) three landmarks where the
ambiguous region is R.

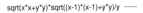

sqrt(x*x+y*y)*sqrt((x-1)*(x-1)+y*y)/y ——

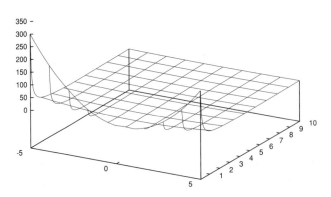

Figure 7.4. The GDOP for two landmarks at $(0, 0)$ and $(1, 0)$. The error
associated with the triangulation grows with distance from the targets
as well as for locations along the x-axis not found between the two
landmarks.

including the 3-D translation as well as the estimate of the local receiver's time clock
error.

Consider the simple landmark case shown in Figure 7.1. The GDOP is given by

$$\text{GDOP} = \mathcal{J} = \begin{bmatrix} d_1/a & -d_2/a \\ d_1(a-x)/ay & xd_2/ay \end{bmatrix}.$$

The magnitude of $\mathcal{J}$ is plotted in Figure 7.4. In Figure 7.4 the two landmarks are located at $(0, 0)$ and $(1, 0)$ and $\mathcal{J}$ is plotted over the range $x = -5 \ldots 5$, $y = 0 \ldots 10$.
$|\mathcal{J}|$ grows as the robot moves away from the x-axis. This is to be expected because the

effective separation between the two circles decreases as the robot moves away from the landmarks. Because the accuracy of most sensors decreases with range, the use of very distant landmarks is to be avoided if closer ones are available. What is slightly less obvious is the increase in the GDOP along the x-axis away from the region between the two landmarks. The error that would arise in any position estimate grows very quickly when both landmarks are on the same side of the robot and in line with it. Knowledge of the form of the GDOP can be used by the robot to select which landmarks are to be used if multiple landmark choices are available.

In practical situations robotic systems may encounter difficulties in uniquely identifying landmarks, or the position estimation may be unstable owing to landmark geometry. One approach to dealing with intermittently reliable landmark information is to combine landmark-based position information with position information from dead reckoning. This fusion of information from two sources has been effectively accomplished using a Kalman filter [51, 204, 375, 260] (Kalman filters are discussed in Section 3.9.2). Other approaches range from the closed-form calculation of position (pose) transformations [82, 154] to the use of neural networks [174, 278].

Sutherland and Thompson proceed under the assumption that landmarks can be uniquely identified but that they are costly to detect and that the estimated bearings are imprecise [344, 345]. They observe that the "area of uncertainty" (a threshold on the confidence of the pose estimate) can vary substantially with the particular subset of landmarks used and consider the selection of appropriate combinations of landmarks to produce an accurate pose estimate.

Few real-world systems have been demonstrated that can perform reliable pose estimation (and remapping) in environments incorporating substantial temporal change in their landmark layout. Typical approaches validate existing models against current measurements and eliminate those whose certainty falls too low [204, 206].

7.3   Servo Control

The use of sensor data, and in particular vision, for position estimation is complicated by the extreme difficulty of inverting the imaging transform to recover the locations of points in 3-D. Simply recognizing objects of interest is often difficult owing to phenomena such as perspective distortion, image noise, lighting and shadowing changes, and specular reflection (see Section 4.2). One of the simplest techniques for using sensor data (and specifically vision) to relate a robot's pose to that of a landmark is known as *image-based servoing* (or *visual servoing*), or, for more general classes of sensor, *sensor-based servoing*.

Servoing is typically applied to allow a robot to move to a specific target position using observed sensor measurements (hence it is also referred to as *homing*). This technique is based on storing a specific sensor image $\mathbf{I}(\mathbf{q}_{goal})$ associated with a target position $\mathbf{q}_{goal}$ for the robot and using the difference between $\mathbf{I}(\mathbf{q}_{goal})$ and $\mathbf{I}(\mathbf{q}_c)$ to move the robot from its current position $\mathbf{q}_c$ to the goal. The distance between the current robot location and the target position is assumed to be monotonically related to the distance in sensor space between the target sensor reading and the current sensor measurements. This monotonicity relationship typically holds when the robot is sufficiently close to the target position. Instead of some elaborate sensor interpretation to establish correspondence, sensor measurements acquired on-line are directly compared with the target sensor measurement through a simple method such as an L_2 (Euclidean) or L_1 metric. It is also possible to describe the image by a set of intermediate features $\mathbf{f(i)}$ and to use differences in these to express image variation. Examples of such features range from the pixel differences to landmark positions in the image, to energy in different bandpass channels. In general, given the image feature vectors, we assume that the discrepancy function

$$E(\mathbf{q}_c) = |\mathbf{f}(\mathbf{I}(\mathbf{q}_{\text{goal}})) - \mathbf{f}(\mathbf{I}(\mathbf{q}_c))|$$

is convex in the workspace of interest (which may have to be chosen to be suitably close to the target position).

The Jacobian $\mathcal{J}$ of the sensor image with respect to the pose parameters has the form

$$\mathcal{J} = \begin{bmatrix} \frac{\partial f_1}{\partial q_1} & \cdots & \frac{\partial f_1}{\partial q_n} \\ \vdots & \ddots & \vdots \\ \frac{\partial f_m}{\partial q_1} & \cdots & \frac{\partial f_m}{\partial q_n} \end{bmatrix}.$$

The local convexity assumption implies that the Jacobian of E (the *image Jacobian*) provides an indication of how pose changes are related to changes in E (for small motions because this is only a first-order approximation). For small pose changes, the image formation equation allows a linear approximation to be made, and then the pose change needed to produce a desired change in the image measurements can be computed as

$$\Delta \mathbf{q} = \tilde{\mathcal{J}}^{-1} \cdot \mathbf{f}.$$

As a result of the approximations used and sensor noise, actually attaining the target position usually involves an iterative approach. Moving the robot to $\mathbf{q}_{\text{goal}}$ then involves following a steepest descent strategy down the gradient of the discrepancy function from $\mathbf{q}_c$.

The key difficulties with sensor-based servo control are as follows:

- The mapping from pose to signals is not usually convex over large regions.
- The feature space may not be sufficiently robust or stable.
- No quantitative position estimate is produced, except at the "home" location.
- Servoing can only be used to return to previously visited poses (from which a sample image was acquired).

On the other hand, the technique has low overhead, is readily implemented, and makes only simple assumptions about the environment.

Sensor-based servo control can also be formulated with respect to a number of discrete target locations. This type of approach has been used to address the pose estimation problem (referred to as the *drop-off* or *global localization* problem) for outdoor robots [239]. The system relies on the creation of a precomputed database of panoramic views of the horizon. To solve the drop-off problem a panoramic view of the current environment is obtained, and it is compared with views in the panorama database. The best match is used to identify the robot's current location. The database represents the panorama in terms of the peaks and troughs in the skyline and hence is relatively insensitive to position differences and can be corrected for orientation errors. The use of raw sensor data to obtain pose estimates without scene reconstruction is also discussed in Section 7.5.

7.4   Kalman Filtering

To accomplish position estimation using external referencing, the disparity between the known and observed locations of obstacles provides an estimate of position to be used in correcting the drift in estimates from internal sensors. In Section 3.9.2 we saw how a Kalman filter could be used to combine pose estimates from dead reckoning and other measurements in an optimal manner. In the context of mobile robotics, the criteria that assure an optimal result are often violated. In practice, the response functions of real sensors (and of sonar in particular) vary nonlinearly with the robot's state variables. To account for this nonlinearity, a variant of the Kalman filter, the Extended Kalman Filter (EKF), is obtained by linearizing the model of the system (see Section 3.9.2).

Consider sonar as a particular example. The incorporation of sonar measurements entails several steps in addition to linearization of the system of equations. If a map of the environment can be taken for granted, observations from the sonar sensors can be associated with objects in the map through a correspondence process (this is essentially the same issue that arises in feature-based stereo and motion estimation, as seen in Chapter 4). The disparities between objects in the map and their observed positions based on the current estimated robot position yield estimates on the error in the current estimate's position qualified by the accuracy of the measurements, the accuracy of the map, and the reliability of the correspondence. Typically, the first two factors (sensor error and map accuracy) are quantified a priori, and the associated confidences are directly incorporated into the Kalman filter equations. Correspondence is typically handled differently. Initial correspondences can be computed in a variety of ways, depending on the types of measurement used (e.g., circular arcs or single points) and the type of data stored on the map (e.g., occupancy probabilities or line segments). One simple approach is to find the closest single explanatory feature on the map for each measurement given the current estimate of the robot's position. A more involved approach would be to find alternative objects to explain a given measurement, leading to a "multiple hypothesis tracking" framework.

Although the EKF is a powerful technique that often performs well under suitable conditions [204, 375, 260], it does have its shortcomings. Fundamentally, it depends on the acceptability of the linearization of the system being modeled, an acceptable estimate of the sources of error in the system, and on a well-behaved (e.g., Gaussian) error distribution. The actual responses from real sonar sensors, as one example, are substantially more complex than those captured by the comparatively simple models typically used in practice (they are highly nonlinear due to multipath sonar reflections, see Section 3.5). This, in turn, means that there is a potential for increasing error in the filter's estimates.

The sonar responses not correctly represented by the simplified sonar model are typically classified as outliers, and a threshold or gating function is used to discard them. This makes traditional EKF-based localization somewhat sensitive to the choice of a correct gating function: if too small, good data are discarded; if too large, outliers corrupt the estimates (discussed further in Section 7.4.1). Furthermore, if the error in the input pose estimate is even larger than the size of the gating function (e.g., if the robot goes over an unexpected bump), the mismatch between real data and models can lead to rejection of all the sensor data and divergence of the filter. In such cases, the EKF may lead to poor estimates and may even diverge (i.e., fail to converge to the correct estimate) [338, 45]. In addition to these concerns, the need for a simple relationship between geometric structures and observed measurements makes it difficult to apply such methods in some environments.

An alternative approach to the use of a single gating function is to use a variable scale thresholdlike function, such as that used in the Adaptive Localization at Multiple Scales (ALMS) method [219]. This method is based on using a collection of data points from multiple positions (which can be maintained on an ongoing basis). Because the ALMS approach has characteristics in common with many alternative approaches, we will examine this technique in further detail.

7.4.1   Adaptive Localization at Multiple Scales

Under the ALMS approach to localization, the process whereby a robot determines pose with respect to a mapped environment is performed in several stages. In each of these stages we will assume the existence of a geometric two-dimensional map of the environment based on lines that represent obstacles such as walls in the environment (see Section 5.1.2). The first stage, position calibration, is developed under the limited assumption that an estimate of the robot's position is available and that the robot's orientation is known accurately. The pose estimation problem is formulated as an optimization in terms of the extent to which the map explains the observed measurements. A refined version of the problem in which position and orientation are corrected simultaneously, given an initial coarse estimate, is referred to as local pose correction. Using the local pose corrector and an associated measure of agreements between observed and known landmarks allows global localization (where the robot has no initial estimate of its pose) to be formulated as a secondary optimization problem.

Most methods for model-based localization are based on a two-stage approach: models are first *matched* to observed data, and then the geometric relationships (i.e., disparity) between models and observations is used to obtain a position estimate. In the case of ALMS, the matching stage entails examining sensed data points and classifying each with respect to a target line segment (i.e., the line segment most likely representing the same object that the sensed data represent). The assumption is made that the closest line segment to a given sensed data point is the most likely target for that point [82, 219]. Every data point is associated with some model line. The estimation stage of ALMS is based on a voting procedure. Voting consists of computing a vector difference between each point and its target model and deriving a weighted sum of these correction vectors to give a new estimate of the robot's true position. This process is then repeated until the position can no longer be further refined. If the initial matches are sufficiently accurate, an estimate of translation and orientation could be computed with the solution of one nonlinear system [82].

Classification of data points   The purpose of classification is to match range data points with models representing the most likely object in the environment to which the sensor responded. The target model associated with each point is the model closest to the point. If we assume a small positional error, the data points should not be too far away from the objects they represent. It is a strong form of this assumption that permits the system of equations describing the localization process to be linearized in the construction of an EKF for localization. That is, the system is linearized about an operating point that is the correct robot position. In the approach described here, although it is assumed that

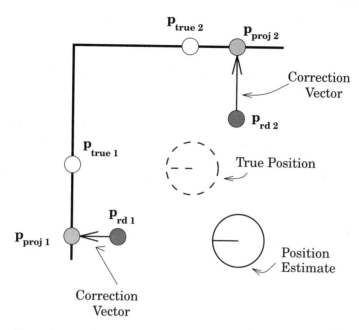

Figure 7.5. Projecting onto target line segments. By projecting range data points $p_{rd1,2}$ onto $p_{proj1,2}$, respectively, on their target line segment models, we can calculate the error in $p_{rd1,2}$ with respect to the true range measurements $p_{true1,2}$. The projected points only give information about the error perpendicular to the target line segment.

some fraction of the data is close enough to its correct position to be associated correctly, the method can cope with substantial errors and does not need to linearize the system.

From each data point and target line segment, a correction vector is obtained. The correction vector is the vector difference between the data point and its perpendicular projection onto the infinite line passing through the corresponding line segment. This vector represents the offset required to match the point exactly to the infinite line through the model (i.e., correct the error in the point that is perpendicular to the line [Figure 7.5]). An appropriate combination of the correction vectors from all the measurements used in the position estimate provides the estimate of the refined position.

It is important to note that only this perpendicular component of error observed from a single point may be corrected by the correction vector. This one-dimensional position constraint (and hence one-dimensional uncertainty) provided by each measurement comes from the geometric constraint that follows from matching to a one-dimensional (line) model. In fact, there is a weak constraint in the orthogonal direction that could be exploited using the knowledge that linear features in the environment have finite length. This lack of a two-dimensional constraint (i.e., a very large uncertainty in one dimension) is analogous to the aperture problem in motion estimation (see Section 4.4.2). In general, multiple measurements from nonparallel structures will provide sufficient constraints to avoid this problem. In some situations, however, this can be an issue. For instance, a robot in the middle of a long featureless hallway (such that the robot cannot see the ends) can only correct its position in the direction perpendicular to the main axis of the hallway. Movement along the axis of the hallway gives no displacement information because all parts of the walls look identical and therefore cannot be distinguished in order to calculate a displacement.

Weighted voting of correction vectors   Simple averaging across measurements is not an appropriate mechanism for combining the correction vectors because of the presence of outliers: measurements not associated with the correct model in the map. These can arise owing to incorrect correspondence, sensor noise, or imperfections in the map. As such, a robust averaging method is required. Simple gating using a heavyside (step) function suffers from instability and an absence of graceful degradation with respect to errors in the initial pose estimate. Rather, it is preferable to employ a continuous function with a long tail. If we consider each correction vector as $\mathbf{v}_i = (\Delta x_i, \Delta y_i)$, then the overall error vector $\mathbf{V} = (\Delta X, \Delta Y)$ can be calculated as follows:

$$\Delta X = \frac{\sum_{i=1}^{n} \omega(\|\mathbf{v}_i\|) \Delta x_i}{\sum_{i=1}^{n} \omega(\|\mathbf{v}_i\|)}$$

$$\Delta Y = \frac{\sum_{i=1}^{n} \omega(\|\mathbf{v}_i\|) \Delta y_i}{\sum_{i=1}^{n} \omega(\|\mathbf{v}_i\|)},$$

where the weighting factor ω is defined as

$$\omega(d) = 1 - \frac{d^m}{d^m + c^m}, \tag{7.1}$$

and where c is a constant and $\|\mathbf{v}_i\|$ is the norm (length) of the ith correction vector, which is simply the distance between the ith range data point and its target line segment (but not necessarily the distance to the infinite line through the target because a point could be closer to an infinite line from a line segment across the room than the true line segment).

In general terms, points close to their target line segments have a greater voting strength in the overall error vector than those far away. This separates the points loosely into two groups: close, highly weighted points, and far, lightly weighted points.

Although a simple threshold is essentially what is required as a weighting function, the discontinuity associated with a true step function can lead to instability. A sigmoid function, sometimes referred to as a "soft nonlinearity," provides a threshold that varies gradually. This is a blurred threshold and can be provided by several functions. The small values in the tail are appropriate for cases in which the error in the initial pose estimate is large. In these cases, many data points will be too far from their correct map models to be paired initially, and thus the long tail of the sigmoid provides a relatively equal weighting among these points (the weighting is low, but all are equally low). It prevents outliers from suddenly exerting their influence as a specific threshold is passed such as when the robot's pose is incrementally corrected (the shape of this transition is governed by the value of c in Eq. (7.1)). This is a major advantage over a heavyside weighting function in that it is not unstable as a function of increasing position error. Table 7.1 provides a summary of alternative weighting functions and illustrates the reason a sigmoid is the best choice.

Convergence of the estimate   In general, pose estimation methods involve nonlinear matching processes followed by either linear or nonlinear estimation processes. As a result, many position estimators only produce a correct position estimate if they

Table 7.1. *A comparison of possible weighting functions.*

Function type	Sample expression	Features	Disadvantages
Step	$step(\text{-}d\text{-}c)$	Constant weight for small d: points close to their paired models are weighted equally and high	Zero weight for large d, so distant data points can never contribute to the overall error vector; transition is too abrupt
Piecewise linear	$1 - \dfrac{1}{d_{run}}(d - d_{lin})$	Constant weight for small d	Zero weight for large d
Sigmoid	$1 - \dfrac{d^m}{d^m + c^m}$	Nearly constant weight for small d, small but *nonzero* weight for large d (allowing distant points to contribute to the overall error vector), smooth transition	
Inverse	$\dfrac{1}{d}$	Small but nonzero weight for large d	Too large and nonuniform weight for small d: weighting would be too sensitive to even minor sensor noise or map imperfections
Exponential	e^{-d}	Small but nonzero weight for large d	Nonuniform weight for small d: this suffers from the same effect as the inverse function, except that the weighting is bounded

are given a sufficiently accurate initial guess. This is due to the interdependence of the solutions to the classification and estimation procedures: accurate estimation depends on accurately associating measurements and map information. As the position estimate for the robot changes, the point–target correspondences can vary substantially. Not all points may be properly classified initially, but only a few are needed to start moving the position estimate in the right direction, because incorrect correspondences tend to be randomly distributed and hence are readily outweighed by correct ones.

In our example, this is addressed, in part, through the use of a sigmoid weighting function parameterized by the scale constant c (see Eq. (7.1)). A large value of c provides better

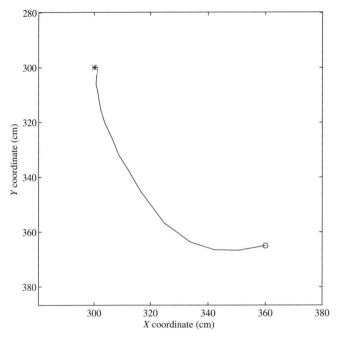

Figure 7.6. The path of convergence of the position estimate from the initial position marked ○ to the true position marked *. Note that the estimate does not move directly toward the true position initially but does move close enough that the more precise iterations can later do so.

noise immunity, whereas a small c provides better accuracy given a good prior estimate. To achieve noise immunity (or stability) while retaining an accurate final estimate, we use a multiscale computation. That is, we progressively decrease the value of c in Eq. (7.1) as the iterations proceed. This allows many measurements to participate in calculating the first refined pose estimate, whereas final position refinement is dependent only on measurements that are almost certain to be correctly attributed to known models. This coarse-to-fine strategy provides progressive shift in emphasis from coarse detection of an attractor to accurate estimation.

The key to this process is a reliable initial classification of sensor data points with the appropriate models of objects that produced them. In practice, this depends to a large extent on the distribution of objects in the world.

The path of the position estimate as it converges to the true position can be seen in Figure 7.6. The position estimate (shown by ○) may not necessarily initially move *directly* toward the true position (shown with an *) because the emphasis is on noise immunity rather than high precision at this point. As the position estimate gets closer to the true position, the emphasis shifts from noise immunity to accuracy, and the path takes a more direct approach.

Multiscale local correction results   The convergence properties of the position estimator are illustrated below using initial position estimates whose error ranged up to 300 cm (10 ft) in both the x and y directions from the robot's actual position, which is described using position calibration.

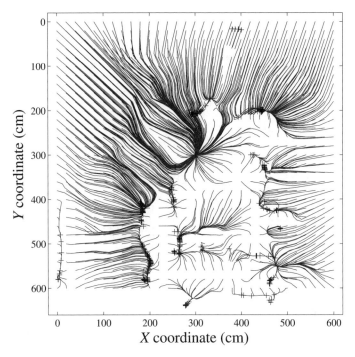

Figure 7.7. Paths of convergence, shown by lines originating initial position estimates (circles) and leading to final position estimates. The true robot position is in the center of the rectangle.

Actual positions were measured manually to within 0.5 cm using a tiled grid on the floor of the test area. Figure 7.7 shows the convergence of the position estimates as a function of initial position. Each line connects an initial estimate (small circles covering the map) to a final estimate. The true robot position is in the center of the map at $(x, y) = (300, 300)$ (where many solutions converge). Figure 7.8 shows more clearly the region around the true location for which the estimated robot position converges correctly. For example, any initial estimate in the upper-left or within 1 m of the true position converges to the correct solution. The other initial estimates do not converge correctly owing to incorrectly classified measurements. "Correct convergence" for this figure is defined as a final position error of less than 2 cm. Position estimation errors after convergence tend to be on the order of 2 cm or less in moderately well structured environments such as the office space depicted earlier.

Comparative behavior The utility of the multiscale, coarse-to-fine approach is most evident in the presence of outlier data or map inaccuracies. Figure 7.9 shows the map and data (only the data seen from the indicated robot position) but with synthetic noise added to the data points and the models (model noise can result from an incomplete model of the environment, changes to the environment since the model was constructed, and various other sources). Using these data, position estimation was computed from various different initial estimates sampling the environment. For each initial position estimate, the final error was recorded, providing an indication of how the final pose estimated varied with input error and when it diverged.

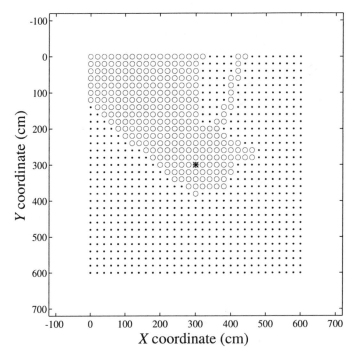

Figure 7.8. Initial position estimates that converge to the correct position of the robot (circles indicate successful convergence within 2 cm of true position). The filled dot in the center is the correct position. Open circles correspond to correct convergences. Dots correspond to convergence failure.

This process was performed using three different data-matching and localization procedures: large and small fixed-size rectangular classification windows and a variable-sized window based on the ALMS procedure.

Figure 7.10 illustrates the effect of the three scaling approaches on final error as well as the region of convergence. The radii of the circles in these figures are proportional to the logarithm of the final position estimate error. We can see in Figure 7.10(a) that the ALMS approach offers a large region of convergence as well as very low final error. The region of convergence for a fixed large-scale classification window and no distance-based weighting scheme shown in Figure 7.10(b) is roughly the same size as in (a), but the final error is almost an order of magnitude larger. For the fixed, small-scale classification window and no distance-based weighting shown in Figure 7.10(c), the smallest final error is as good as that found with the multiscale approach; however, the region near the true position for which an initial position estimate converges to this value is far smaller than that of either of the other approaches. The use of a multiple-scale method, however, implies an increase in computational overhead over fixed-scale methods.

This illustrates the trade-off involved in choosing a scale size: a large scale offers a large region of convergence with limited accuracy in the final solution, whereas smaller scales can provide better accuracy but only for initial position estimates already sufficiently close to the true solution. This is not a surprising result, for a large scale will include more outliers whose contribution to the final result will limit the accuracy, and a small scale will

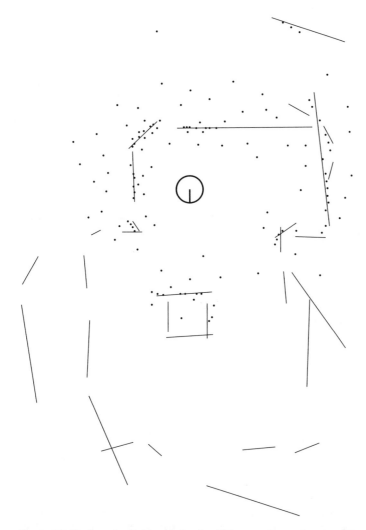

Figure 7.9. Environment with added noise. This map represents sonar data and inferred line segments from an actual environment except that only data points seen from the shown robot position were used. In addition, random range points were added, many valid points were removed, and some of the line segment models were shifted slightly.

effectively ignore outliers but may also weight valid data points too low if the position error is greater than the scale size.

Quality measures For sufficiently poor initial position estimates, it is possible that the estimate produced using position calibration is not the correct position of the robot. To protect a real system from the serious repercussions of such an error, one would like to be assured that not only is the position estimate a local minimum of the estimator but that this estimate represents a "good" solution; that is, that the observed measurements are consistent in absolute terms. We would also like to be able to compare multiple solutions in terms of how well they explain the observed sensor data.

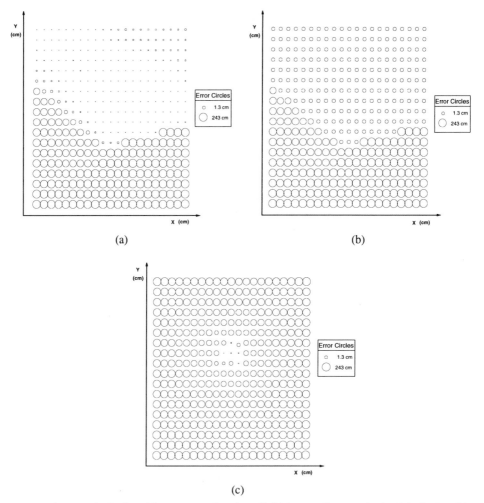

Figure 7.10. Final position error as a function of initial error. The magnitude of the final position error for alternative initial position estimates is shown for three different algorithms in (a)–(c). The circles are centered on alternative initial position estimates, and their radii (i.e., sizes) are proportional to the *logarithm* of the error in the final position estimate. In all cases, the true position of the robot is the center of the region. In (a), the variable-scale weighting scheme was used for which the minimum final error was 1.3 cm, and the region of convergence to this good estimate was large. In (b), a single large-scale was used, and the minimum final error was 10.0 cm. The minimum final error in (c), where a single small scale was used, was also 1.3 cm, but this error only occurred in the immediate region of the true solution.

This suggests two conceptually different types of error estimate that can be used to quantify performance. The first of these is the residual error between observed and expected models most readily captured by a mean-squared error measure. The second type of estimate that is relevant is the number of known models actually employed in the final pose estimate. In the following, we will refer to this as the *classification factor*. The trade-off between the number of models used and the quality or complexity of the individual models is related to the notion of minimal length encoding.

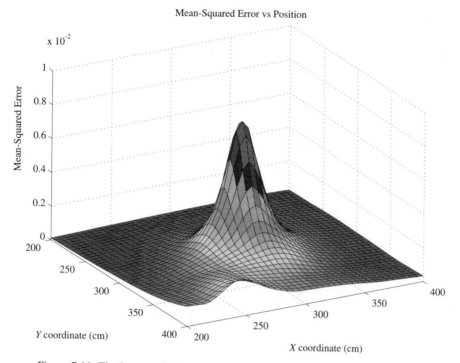

Figure 7.11. The inverse of E_{mse} versus position. With the robot again at (300, 300), we can see the global maximum at this point.

In our example, the mean-squared error measure is straightforward:

$$E_{\mathrm{mse}} = \frac{1}{n} \sum_{i=1}^{n} \| p_i - \ell_i \|^2, \qquad (7.2)$$

where p_i is ith of n range data points, ℓ_i is p_i's target line segment model, and $\| p_i - \ell_i \|$ is the distance from a point p to the closest point on the line segment ℓ. It measures the average discrepancy between data and models.

This function has a global minimum that occurs at the true pose of the robot (this is akin to not providing false negatives). At this pose, it is assumed that all, or at least the vast majority, of the range data points are very close to their target models, thus yielding a small value associated with a correct solution. Figure 7.11 shows the inverse of E_{mse}, which has a global maximum at the true pose of the robot.

There is a difficulty with this function used alone: It is susceptible to outliers, and these will certainly effect the results even if the pose estimate is very accurate. Because it is not known how many outliers exist in the sensor data set, the possible range of values that this function can take on is very broad, and this makes deciding whether a single pose is valid very difficult based solely on this function. However, as we will show, it can be useful when used to compare two alternative solutions.

The classification factor E_{cf} is a quantity based on the fraction of all data points that are *well explained*. This is obtained by computing the fraction of all data points that are within some fixed distance threshold x of their associated model. Under the assumption that models occupy only a small fraction of the environment, a close association between a measurement will occur only randomly and infrequently. Under this assumption, E_{cf} can indicate the quality of a pose estimate. The only time that E_{cf} approaches unity is when either (1) the pose estimate is very close to the actual one, or (2) a very similar but incorrect location exists within the environment. Neglecting the latter, the E_{cf} measure should give a value close to unity when the position estimate is very close to the true position and near zero when the error of the estimate is large.

As with a gating function, using an abrupt, step-like neighborhood threshold has several shortcomings – in particular unstable behavior as errors exceed the threshold value. To address this, a "soft" sigmoid nonlinearity can be exploited once more as a threshold to assure graceful degradation of the solution as a function of the input error. The *classification factor* is thus defined as (see Figure 7.12)

$$E_{cf} = \frac{1}{n} \sum_{i=1}^{n} \left(1 - \frac{d^m}{d^m + c^m} \right)$$

where: $d = \sqrt{\|p_i - \ell_i\|}$, distance from p_i to ℓ_i,
         that is, between measurement and model
       c = neighborhood size
       m = sigmoid steepness

The neighborhood should not be too small to accommodate inaccuracies in the models and should depend on sensor error (in practice, we use a value of between 2 and 5 cm with sonar data.). Figure 7.12 illustrates E_{cf} in the same environment as the previous figures.

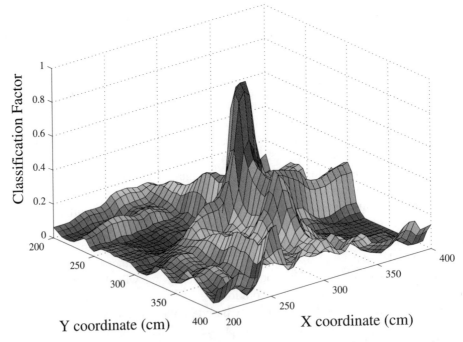

Figure 7.12. The classification factor E_{cf}.

7.5   Nongeometric Methods: Perceptual Structure

One of the most difficult aspects of model-based localization is selecting robust suitable generic models. There are three main difficulties: defining a modeling space (i.e., a set of primitives) general enough to express the set of objects of interest with sufficient accuracy, being able to invert the sensor data so as to make geometric inferences, and fitting the models to the data in a manner that is stable and efficient.

In an attempt to avoid these problems with geometric modeling, methods that directly relate appearance or perceptual structure to pose can be formulated. The premise is that a mapping between sensor data and pose can be constructed *directly* without any intermediate representation based explicitly on 2-D or 3-D scene geometry (this is illustrated in Figure 7.13).

One way to achieve this is to record the sensor data associated with certain positions. This is sometimes referred to as the *signature* of a position. By comparing the currently observed signature with the set of known remembered signatures, a robot can determine when it has returned to a previously visited location. This is the essence of perceptual servoing (see Section 7.3). As we have seen, servo control suffers from several difficulties, including the fact that it does not explicitly attempt to recover a quantitative position estimate. In practice, the particular abstraction used to record signatures and to match signatures is a potentially difficult problem. Furthermore, signatures may not be unique, and some approach to the resolution of such ambiguities is needed.

Methods that avoid full reconstruction have also been used to estimate the position of a mobile robot from laser range data [88]. In that work, the raw data were rerepresented more reliably by projecting them into a lower dimensional subspace computed using a principal components analysis. By matching the subspace projections of current observations to that of past data reliable localization could be obtained, provided the environment is fairly simple, static, and contains no locations that share a common appearance. Other work has dealt with exploiting the geometric characteristics of landmarks for homing tasks [32].

Interpolation between sample images has been used successfully for pose estimation and trajectory following, again using a principal components encoding of the input data [261].

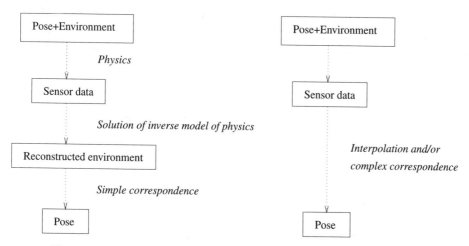

Figure 7.13. Pose estimation using geometric models (left) and perceptual structure (right).

In this work, it is assumed that a one-to-one mapping between visual input images and robot pose exists for a six-degree-of-freedom robot arm in a small workspace. By creating a direct mapping for a low-dimensional subspace of the input images to robot joint angles, the robot can use vision to track a prerecorded trajectory. The low-dimensional description of the input images is obtained by computing a principal components analysis on the input images (eigenvector and eigenvalue analysis) and discarding all eigenvectors except those with the largest eigenvalue. The eigenvectors with the largest eigenvalue are those that account for most of the variance in the input images and that thus best encode the input (in terms of minimizing squared error). In similar work, Thrun derives a probabilistic approach to obtain a pose estimate using a neural net [356].

Other work has achieved accurate pose estimate without an input estimate by using sample images from either sonar or vision that sample the environment of interest [99]. Images are first encoded as edge maps (see Section 4.4) to reduce the effects of illumination variations and shading. These edge images are then described by vectors of roughly 20 statistical descriptors each: the moments of the edge distribution, the orientation of the edge distribution, and so forth, over the entire image and over four subwindows in the four quadrants of the image. These input vectors are then used to train a neural network that maps between input images and output pose estimates. A final processing stage is used to eliminate an otherwise disastrous sensitivity to different locations with roughly the same appearance. An assumption is made that dead reckoning can be used to compute an estimated separation between nearby sample locations. If the estimate pose from such a pair of locations disagrees seriously with the estimate from dead reckoning, the pose estimate is discarded in the hope that a more consistent pair of locations will be observed.

7.5.1   Eigenlandmarks

One approach to generic pose estimation with assuming either scene reconstruction or special-purpose landmarks is to attempt to *learn* suitable landmarks for a given environment.

One approach to landmark learning is to train a system to recognize small subimages with recognizable characteristics [334]. This can be accomplished using principal components (eigenfunction) learning to generate robust landmarks that can be used for interpolation between sample positions; this gives rise to the term eigenlandmark. The environment is first surveyed in an "off-line" phase, and a set of images is extracted from sample locations. The landmarks that are extracted are *image-domain* features as opposed to geometric structures in the environment. During the landmark learning phase, *candidate landmarks* are extracted. These are regions that are statistically distinct with respect to the input images visible.

The on-line phase is performed as often as a position estimate is required and consists of matching candidate landmarks in the input image to the learned tracked landmarks followed by position estimation using an appearance-based linear combination of views. An outline of the method is as follows:

- Off-line "map" construction:
    1. Training images are collected sampling a range of poses in the environment.
    2. *Landmark candidates* are extracted from each image using a model of visual attention.

3. *Tracked landmarks* are extracted as sets of candidate landmarks over the configuration space (the vector space of possible configurations, or poses, of the robot). Tracked landmarks are each represented by a characteristic prototype obtained by encoding an initial set of candidate landmarks by their principal components decomposition. For each image, a local search is performed in the neighborhood of the candidate landmarks in the image to locate optimal matches to the templates.

4. The set of tracked landmarks is stored for future retrieval.

- On-line localization.

1. When a position estimate is required, a single image is acquired from the camera.

2. Candidate landmarks are extracted from the input image using the same model used in the off-line phase.

3. The candidate landmarks are matched to the learned templates employing the same method used for tracking in the off-line phase.

4. A position estimate is obtained for *each* matched candidate landmark. This is achieved by computing a reconstruction of the candidate based on the decomposition of the tracked candidates and their known poses in the tracked landmark. The result is a position estimate obtained as a linear combination of the positions of the views of the tracked candidates in the tracked landmarks.

5. A final position estimate is computed as the robust average of the individual estimates of the individual tracked candidates.

PCA-based landmark extraction   Recognition using principal components analysis (PCA) is based on computing a small set of basis vectors that can be linearly combined to produce an "optimal" approximation to one of a much larger set of training examples. Optimality, in this case, implies that no other equally small set of basis vectors could do any better at approximating the training data, as expressed by squared error. For training data in the form of images, the images are simply encoded as a very long vector (listing the rows sequentially). Each training example is thus expressed as a vector v, and the entire set of these vectors is assembled into a (large) matrix A. The eigenvectors of A are computed using singular values decomposition, producing an orthonormal basis set.* Each vector in the basis set can be represented as an image, and these are sometimes referred to as *eigenfaces* or *eigenpictures* owing to their successful application in face recognition [363].

Consider how PCA-based landmark extraction can be used to allow recognition or interpolation between the subimages to be used as image-domain landmarks. As described by Sim and Dudek [334], consider a set T of m landmark prototypes $t_1, t_2, \ldots, t_m$. For each prototype t_i, we build a column vector v_i by scanning the local intensity distribution in row-wise order and normalizing the magnitude of v_i to one. Note that if the intensity image consists of $s \times t$ pixels, then it follows that v_i is of dimensionality $n = st$. Our goal is to construct a discriminatory using the set of vectors defined by T. This is accomplished by constructing an $n \times m$ matrix A, whose columns consist of the vectors v_i, and expressing

---

* An alternative method is to compute the principal components of $A^T A$, the covariance of A.

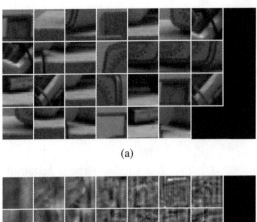

(a)

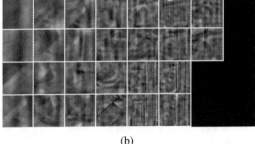

(b)

Figure 7.14. Landmark images and corresponding eigenlandmarks. (a) Landmark images. (b) Eigenlandmarks.
(Figure appears courtesy of R. Sim.)

A in terms of its singular value decomposition by

$$\mathbf{A} = [\mathbf{v_1} \cdots \mathbf{v_m}],$$
$$= \mathbf{UWV^T}$$

where **U** is an $n \times m$ column-orthogonal matrix whose columns represent the principal directions of the range defined by **A** (i.e., **U** gives the eigenvectors of A), **W** is an $m \times m$ diagonal matrix whose elements correspond to the singular values (or eigenvalues) of **A**, and **V** is an $m \times m$ column-orthogonal matrix whose rows represent the projections of the columns of **A** into the subspace defined by **U** (weighted appropriately by the inverses of the eigenvalues). Note that the columns of **U** define a linear subspace of dimensionality m, which can be* much smaller than n. In addition, the principal axes of the subspace are arranged so as to maximize the Euclidean distance between the projections of the prototypes t_i into the subspace, which optimizes the discriminability of the prototypes. Figure 7.14 shows a set of landmark prototypes on the top, and the corresponding eigenvectors, or eigenlandmarks, constructed from the prototypes on the bottom.

Once the subspace is constructed, it can be used for classifying landmark candidates. Given a landmark candidate c, we construct a vector c from the local intensity distribution

---

* In practice, the dimensionality may even be smaller than m; some of the diagonal values of **W** may be zero or small enough to be affected by limited machine precision. In this case, the corresponding eigenvectors are removed.

of c normalized to unit magnitude.* The subspace projection c' of c is obtained using

$$c' = \mathbf{U}^T c,$$

and then c can be matched to the prototype $\hat{t}$ whose subspace projection is closest (in the Euclidean sense) to c' in the subspace. If the subspace projection of prototype t_i is defined using the Euclidean metric,

$$t_i' = \mathbf{U}^T t_i, \tag{7.3}$$

where t_i is obtained from the prototype image in the same fashion as was used to obtain c, then the optimal match $\hat{t}$ is defined as

$$\hat{t} = \min_i \langle t_i, c \rangle$$

The key step is the recovery of the pose estimates using the subspace encoding of the image data. The *tracked landmarks* are image subwindows that have been detected reliably from a series of positions: Their variation in position and appearance is used to recover robot pose. Let us define the *encoding* k_l of a landmark candidate l as the projection of the intensity distribution in the image subwindow represented by l into the subspace defined by the principal components decomposition of the set of all tracked landmark prototypes. The projection is computed using

$$k_l = \mathbf{U}^T l, \tag{7.4}$$

where l is the local intensity distribution of l normalized to unit magnitude, and $\mathbf{U}$ is the set of principal directions of the space defined by the tracked landmark prototypes.

Let us now define a *feature vector f* associated with a landmark candidate l as the principal components encoding k concatenated with two vector quantities, the image position p of the landmark and the camera position c from which the landmark was observed:

$$f = |k \ p \ c|, \tag{7.5}$$

where, in this particular instance alone, the notation $|a \ b|$ represents the concatenation of the vectors a and b.

Given the associated feature vector f_i for each landmark l_i in the tracked landmark $T = \{l_1, l_2, \ldots, l_m\}$, we construct a matrix $\mathbf{F}$ as the composite matrix of all f_i arranged in columnwise fashion and then take the singular value decomposition (SVD) of $\mathbf{F}$,

$$\mathbf{F} = [f_1 \cdots f_n],$$
$$= \mathbf{U_F W V}^T$$

to obtain $\mathbf{U_F}$ representing the set of eigenvectors of the tracked landmark T arranged in columnwise fashion. Note that because c_i is a component of each f_i, $\mathbf{U_F}$ encodes camera position along with appearance. Now consider the feature vector f_l associated with l, the

---

* We normalize the input vectors to have unit magnitude in order to counter the effects of lighting variation.

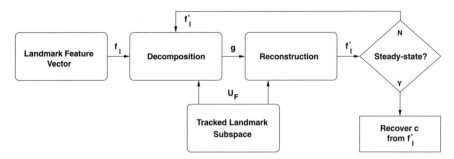

Figure 7.15. The recovery operation. The unknown camera position c associated with a landmark l is recovered by repeatedly reconstructing the landmark feature vector in the subspace defined by the matching tracked landmark.

observed landmark for which we have no pose information – that is, the c component of f_l is undetermined. If we project f_l into the subspace defined by $\mathbf{U_F}$ to obtain

$$\mathbf{g} = \mathbf{U_F^T} f_l$$

and then reconstruct f_l from $\mathbf{g}$ to obtain the feature vector

$$f_l' = \mathbf{U_F g},$$

then the resulting reconstruction f_l' is augmented by a camera pose estimate that interpolates between the nearest eigenvectors in $\mathbf{U_F}$. In practice, the initial value of the undetermined camera pose c in f_l will play a role in the resulting estimate, and so we substitute the new value of c back into f_l and repeat the operation, reconstructing f_l' until the estimate converges to a steady state. This repeated operation, which constitutes the recovery of the unknown c, is summarized in Figure 7.15.

Formally,

$$f_l' = \mathbf{U_F U_F^T f} = \mathbf{W_{opt}} f_l,$$

where $\mathbf{W_{opt}}$ is the optimizing scatter matrix of the feature vectors in T, and hence f_l' corresponds to the least-squares approximation of f in the subspace defined by the feature vectors of the tracked landmark T. Convergence is guaranteed because $\mathbf{U_F}$ is column-orthonormal, and hence $\mathbf{W_{opt}}$ is symmetric and positive-definite. An overview of the eigenlandmark mechanism is provided in Figure 7.16.

7.6 Correlation-Based Localization

One limitation of feature-based methods for localization is that they depend on a process by which geometric features are inferred from sensor measurements. For range sensors, it is possible to exploit the distribution of spatial occupancy directly. We can model a range sensor as a device that returns a probability that specific locations z in space are occupied or unoccupied based on the measurement(s) s observed: $P(z \mid s)$. Localization then entails finding the maximum correlation between the observed spatial occupancy probabilities and the known map subject to constraints from a priori knowledge regarding the robot pose.

Images sampling pose space from different positions

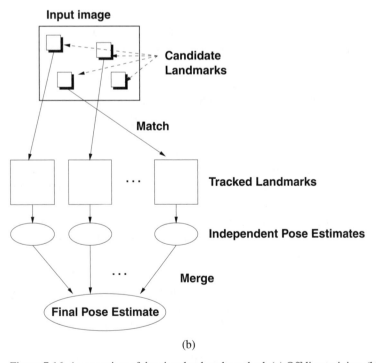

Figure 7.16. An overview of the eigenlandmark method. (a) Off-line training. (b) On-line pose estimation.

In practice, this is often accomplished using a map in the form of a spatial occupancy representation (see Section 5.1.1). Space is represented using a fixed-resolution grid such that each cell in the grid describes the likelihood that a cell is nonempty. The measurement being used is also described using an occupancy grid, and the observed grid is matched to the existing map by simply computing the sum of the squared differences between the observation grid and the map.

7.7   Global Localization

Several methods can be used to refine an erroneous but almost correct pose estimate. This type of problem arises in practice when, for example, the robot is restarted or when it has been determined that the ongoing localization estimate process has failed. Although most practitioners would prefer to assume their robots are robust, most real systems need to "reinitialize" themselves occasionally.

Most existing solutions to position estimation consider performing localization from either one or a few possible vantage points without taking into account the possibility that self-similarity in the environment may make the resulting position estimate ambiguous (e.g., the individual offices in a building or ravines in an outdoor environment may not be readily distinguishable). In principle it may not be possible to obtain an unique solution to the global localization problem from an observation if the environment is sufficiently self-similar. Using multiple measurements from different positions and a known orientation permits the problem to be solved, but at least in certain cases the problem of localization with minimum travel is NP-complete [109] (i.e., no polynomial time algorithm is known to exist).

Some consideration has been given to strategies that collect information from multiple locations in the environment (for example [33, 196, 102]). One approach is to compute a certainty distribution incrementally for the robot's position as a function of the extent to which its current observations can be associated with different parts of the environment. Such an approach, based on "Markov localization," was used by, and is discussed in, the context of incremental mapping in Section 8.1.2. In the following, we examine some of the theoretical limits to localization. In order to simplify the task we consider the use of an idealized range sensor and the difficulty of global localization in the context of a two-dimensional polygon world in which global orientation is known.

In this context, the data returned to the robot by the idealized range sensor can be described as a *visibility polygon V* seen from the position of the robot in the environment: This describes the subregion of the environment that is directly visible from the robot's current position (see Figure 7.17). Because this visible region must fit somewhere within the actual environment, the first step in localization can be framed as the task of embedding this visibility polygon within the map.

Global localization by embedding was addressed by Guibas, Motwani, and Raghavan [138]. Given a polygonal environment map P defined by n vertices and a visibility polygon V seen by the robot, Guibas et al. gave an algorithm to compute the set H of "hypothetical locations" in P whose visible portion of P matches V; that is, the set of regions consistent with the observed sensor data. They show that there can be up to $O(n)$ consistent regions. These alternative ambiguous locations can be "looked up" in $O(mn)$ time, where m is the number of vertices of the visibility polygon V. Guibas et al. also show that, with sufficient preprocessing, the lookup can be achieved even more efficiently.

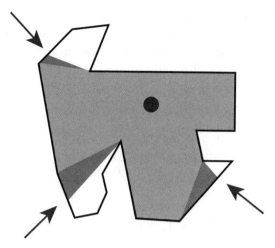

Figure 7.17. A robot shown as a circle in an irregular polygonal environment. The visibility polygon is shaded and the visibility skeleton is the lighter region within the visibility polygon. Arrows indicate the vertices of the visibility polygon that do not correspond to vertices of the environment.

The global localization problem then entails reducing this set of possible locations to a single one by moving about the environment. If the view from the initial position of the robot matches several possible locations in the environment (i.e., if the visibility polygon from this position can be placed in more than one location in the map polygon), then the robot must travel to other positions and make more observations to distinguish between these various possibilities. In the case of idealized sensing, their algorithm could provide the initial input for the strategy summarized below [108, 109].

Kleinberg has also considered the global localization problem using a model of sensing based on determining the relative position and degree of various nodes in a geometric tree [187]. These are trees embedded such that each node corresponds to a specific location in space.

Global localization using visibility polygons involves starting with a visibility polygon measured by our idealized range sensor, computing the set of ambiguous hypothetical locations, and moving about to rule out all but one. More formally, given P and V, determine the set of all points $p \in P$ such that the visibility polygon of p is exactly V (i.e., $V(p) = V$), and if this set H contains more than one point, then travel in P and take further probes until only one location in P is consistent with all of the visibility polygons seen previously. To discretize the problem in this model, P is partitioned into a set of visibility cells. Each cell is associated with a single observation reference point q_i and the set of these is denoted by Q.

A *visibility cell* C of a polygon P is a maximally connected subset of P with the property that any two points in C see the same subset of vertices of P ([48, 138]). That is, each cell C is a neighborhood over which exactly the same set of vertices of the environment can be observed. A *visibility cell decomposition* of P is simply a subdivision of a polygon P into a set of visibility cells. The visibility cell decomposition can be computed in $O(n^3 \log n)$ time [48].

The global localization can be naturally cast in terms of a decision tree: At each place where a new observation can be collected (i.e., each visibility cell) a decision can be made as to where to move to collect additional data. This decision tree can, in principle, be fully precomputed from the known map. The branches of the tree can be weighted to reflect the distance between observation points. We can naturally define the decision problem robot localizing decision tree (RLDT) as that of finding the minimum height tree that assures us that we know where we are.

To perform localization using visibility cells, we construct an *overlay arrangement* A that combines the k translates P_j that correspond to the hypothetical locations together with their visibility cell decompositions. By translate P_j we mean P translated so that the jth hypothetical location p_j in H moves to the origin ($1 \leq j \leq k$). To show the hardness of the global robot localization problem RLDT, we assume that we are given a simple polygon P and a star-shaped polygon V (the subregion visible), both with a common reference orientation, and the set H of all possible initial locations $p_i \in P$ such that $V(p_i) = V$.

Theorem 1 *RLDT is NP-hard.*

Proof sketch: The problem of constructing a minimum height decision tree to localize a robot can be formulated as a decision problem by asking if there exists a decision tree of height $\leq h$ to localize a robot in a polygon P whose initial visibility region is V.

This can be shown to be NP-hard using a reduction from the Abstract Decision Tree (ADT) problem, which was proven to be NP-complete by Hyafil and Rivest [165]. An instance of the abstract decision tree problem consists of a cost h, a set $X = \{x_1, \ldots, x_m\}$ of objects, and a set $T = \{T_1, \ldots, T_n\}$ of subsets of X, each of which represents a binary test, where test T_j is positive on object x_i if $x_i \in T_j$ and is negative otherwise. The problem is to determine, given X, T, and h, whether a binary decision tree of height less than or equal to h can be constructed to identify the objects in X. To identify an unknown object, the test at the root is performed on the object, and if it is positive, the right branch is taken; otherwise, the left branch is taken.

Given an instance of ADT, we create an instance of the localization problem as follows. We construct P to be a staircase-shaped simple closed C^0 continuous curve (i.e., a polygon) with a stair for each object $x_i \in X$ (see Figure 7.18). For each stair we construct $n = |T|$ protrusions, one for each test in T (see Figure 7.19). The structure of each protrusion encodes the result of the corresponding test. $\square$

Consider a robot that is initially located at the shaded circle shown in Figure 7.19 on one of the m stairs. The visibility region V at this point has $O(n)$ vertices and is the same on any stair.

In order for the robot to localize itself, it must either travel to one of the "ends" of P (either the top or the bottom stair) to discover on which stair it was located initially, or it must examine a sufficient number of the n protrusions on the stair where it is located to distinguish that stair from all the others. However, the vertical distance between stairs is very much greater than the lengths of the protrusions or the distance between the first and the last. For this construction, we can show that any procedure for optimal localization can also be used for the ADT problem via this construction. Complete details of the proof are given in [108].

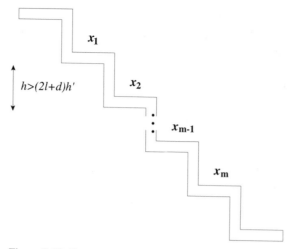

Figure 7.18. Construction showing localization is NP-hard.

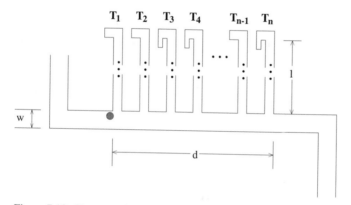

Figure 7.19. Close-up of a stair in NP-hard construction.

Strategy MDL directs the robot to travel along paths from the origin to points in the overlay arrangement A. Suppose that p_j is the true initial location of the robot. We will prove in the next subsection that Strategy MDL only directs the robot to follow paths that are contained in translate P_j. Note that a path from the origin that is contained in P_j is analogous to a path in P from location p_j.

From the initial H and Q, an initial $path(q*)$ can be selected. The strategy directs the robot to travel along this path and to make a probe at its endpoint. The robot then uses the information gained at the probe position to update H and Q and to determine a new $q*$ and a new $path(q*)$ from the origin. The strategy then directs the robot to retrace its previous path back to the origin and then to follow the new path to its endpoint, which is the next probe location. This process stops when the size of H shrinks to 1. At this point the initial location of the robot is determined, and the robot can, if desired, be directed to return to its initial location by retracing its last path.

7.7.1 A Performance Guarantee for Strategy MDL

The following theorems show that Strategy MDL directs the robot along a path whose length compares favorably with the minimum verification length d. First we show that Strategy MDL never directs the robot to pass through a wall. Then we show that Strategy MDL eliminates all hypothetical locations except the valid one, and we establish an upper bound on the length of the path produced by Strategy MDL. A corollary of Theorem 3 is that the localizing decision tree associated with Strategy MDL has a weighted height that is at most $2(k-1)$ times the height of an optimal localizing decision tree.

Theorem 2 *Strategy MDL never directs the robot to pass through a wall en route to another location.*

Proof sketch: Attempting to pass through a wall would imply an attempt to visit a point *farther* than the wall w involved in the collision. Such a wall w would contain a reference point, however, and the strategy always visits the closest reference points first. □

Theorem 3 *Strategy MDL localizes the robot by directing it along a path whose length is at most $(k-1)d$, where $k = |H|$ and d is the length of an optimal verification tour for the robot's initial position.*

Proof sketch: Let p_t denote the true initial location of the robot. We can show that Strategy MDL eliminates all hypothetical initial locations in H except p_t (a similar theorem using different input cells is proven in [109]).

Next we establish the upper bound on the length of the path determined by Strategy MDL. Because the strategy never directs the robot to a sensing site that does not eliminate one or more elements from H, it requires the robot to make a trip from its initial location to some sensing point and back at most $k-1$ times.

We claim that each round trip has length at most d. To see this, we first consider how a robot traveling along an optimal verification tour L would rule out an arbitrary incorrect hypothetical location p_b. Then we consider how Strategy MDL would rule out p_b.

Consider a robot traveling along tour L that eliminates each invalid hypothetical location at the first point x on L where the signature of x relative to the invalid hypothetical location differs from the signature of x relative to P_t. Let w be the point on L where the robot rules out p_b. The point w must lie on the boundary of some cell C in the arrangement A that distinguishes p_b from p_t. Cell C generates a reference point $q_{C,t} \in Q$, which is the closest point of C to the origin, where distance is measured inside P_t, and thus $d_t(q_{C,t}) \leq d_t(w)$. Because p_t is the true initial location of the robot, the distance $d_t(w)$ is equal to or less than the distance along L of w from the origin as well as the distance along L from w back to the origin. Putting these inequalities together, we deduce that the distance $d_t(q_{C,t})$ is equal to or less than half the length of L.

Because p_t is the true initial location of the robot, it remains active throughout the entire execution of the strategy. In particular, it is active at the moment Strategy MDL directs the robot to move from the origin to the sensing site, where it eliminates p_b. Because p_b is about to be ruled out, it is also still active. That means that the reference point $q_{C,t}$ considered in the previous paragraph is still active, for it distinguishes p_b from p_t.

At this time Strategy MDL directs the robot to travel along $path_*(q*) = path_j(q)$. By design, the length $d_*(q*) = d_j(q)$ of this path, which is the distance the robot will travel from the origin to the next sensing position, is the minimum over all $d_i(q)$ for active $p_i \in H$ and $q \in Q$. In particular, because point $q_{C,t}$ is still active, $d_*(q*)$ is equal to or less than $d_t(q_{C,t})$. But as we have already seen, this latter distance is equal to or less than half the length of L. Therefore, Strategy MDL directs the robot to travel along a loop from the origin to some sensing position where the robot eliminates p_b and back, and the length of this loop is at most d. ☐

We can define a *k-competitive robot* localization strategy as one that localizes a robot by traveling a distance no more than k times the length of an optimal verification tour. By this definition Strategy MDL is $(k-1)$-competitive, where $k = |H|$. Note that if a verifying path is not required to return to its starting point, the bound for Theorem 3 becomes $2(k-1)d$.

Corollary 4 *The weighted height of the localizing decision tree constructed by Strategy MDL is at most $2(k-1)$ times the weighted height of an optimal localizing decision tree for the same problem.*

7.7.2 Practical One-Shot Global Localization

In some environments where sufficient local variability is present, the global localization problem may be solvable without having to resort to moving the robot. For example, the ALMS local pose estimator (Section 7.4.1) can be extended to obtain a global estimation without an initial pose estimate. This is accomplished in a manner similar to that by which position calibration was incorporated into orientation calibration: by optimizing the desired parameter using a constrained search and interpolation process (see Section 7.4.1).

The set of possible poses of the robot within the environment can be considered as the domain of a quality function $E'_{cqm}(x, y, \theta)$. Provided that sufficient local variability exists, the true pose of the robot can be computed from a single sensor reading by testing the sensor data against each possible pose value via the function $E_{cqm}(\cdot)$. The space of possible poses is, in general, too large to permit this, and so MacKenzie and Dudek [219] developed a method based on local gradient descent to compute the pose without a prior estimate. This method is based on sampling the space of possible poses and performing a refinement of the pose estimate at each sample point. Sampling is necessary because $E_{cqm}(\cdot)$ is globally nonconvex. In the following, we describe the parallel computation of the multiple local optima, although a multiple restart gradient descent method would be a natural alternative.

Each potential sampled pose $\mathbf{q} = (x, y, \theta)$ within the map region is considered as an initial pose estimate of the robot, and E'_{cqm} is the comparative quality measure of the *converged* pose following local pose localization. More explicitly,

$$E'_{cqm}(x, y, \theta) = E_{cqm}(x_c, y_c, \theta_c),$$

where (x_c, y_c, θ_c) is the pose found by local localization given the *initial* pose estimate (x, y, θ). From this, one obtains a global quality function that describes the quality of localization when applied to a particular location, and the pose for which E'_{cqm} is a global maximum is the true pose of the robot. This results in a highly nonconvex function (although convex local to the global maximum) because any estimate that converges closely to the true pose will have a high quality, and any that do not will have a much lower (often orders of magnitude lower) quality. Therefore, local gradient information in the lower-valued regions may not assist in the search for the global maximum over the domain of the entire environment but only in the convex regions. Once a pose estimate E'_{cqm} of sufficient quality has been found, gradient ascent can be used to refine the estimate.

Sampling in this context is accomplished by applying the localization algorithm to selected poses in (x, y, θ) space and checking the value of E'_{cqm}. With any application of sampling a proper selection of sampling size is critical. Using the methodology presented in the previous section we can make estimates of the region of convergence of the localization algorithm in the selected environment using the selected sensors. If the candidate locations for global localization can be determined in advance, the appropriate regions of convergence can be computed. These, in turn, indicate the sampling interval need for global localization because any sample within the region of convergence of the true pose will provide a good pose estimate with E'_{cqm}.

In the absence of prior information on the loci for localization, selecting the appropriate sampling of the map is more difficult. The sizes of the regions of convergence are not constant over the environment, nor can they be easily computed analytically, although they can be estimated in simulation (assuming the sensor properties can be accurately modeled). This suggests that the correct sample points can be computed on the basis of estimated regions of convergence determined using the map. In general, estimates computed from samples that reside in regions with large areas are more likely to contain the robot, and thus the sampling can be prioritized to maximize efficiency.

This idea can be exploited even without precomputation in a context reminiscent of a scale space. The approach is a "coarse-to-fine" strategy: Initially, the environment is coarsely sampled (samples are placed far apart). If no satisfactory results are found from these samples, the environment is resampled more finely, and the results are again evaluated. This process can continue with smaller and smaller sampling sizes until the true pose has been found.

A final strategy is attractive if the robot is permitted to move about to select the location (with unknown coordinates) for sampling. Using only local information, the robot can move into a comparatively free region of its enclosing space. This will reduce the local clutter, which, in turn, will put the robot into a region associated with a larger region of convergence.

In contrast to localization methods based on Kalman filtering, this approach allows a robot's position to be estimated from a single (noisy) sonar scan. In practice, the estimate from this method may also be combined with data from other sensors, including odometry.

7.8   Further Reading

7.8.1   General Survey
There is a large literature on global pose estimation (the drop-off problem) and local pose estimation, although very few reviews exist. Talluri and Aggarwal [349] provide a general survey of vision-based techniques.

7.8.2   Triangulation-Based Systems
Talluri and Aggarwal [350] describes a vision-based system that relies on rooftop models in urban environments.

7.9   Problems

1. Derive the pose of a robot given a sensor set that computes the robot's position from two-point landmarks by using triangulation under the following assumptions:
   (a) The distance to each landmark can be directly observed.
   (b) The absolute orientation to each landmark can be directly observed.

2. Derive the geometric dilution of precision (GDOP) for a robot that computes its position from two-point landmarks using triangulation under the following assumptions:
   (a) The distance to each landmark can be directly observed with an uncertainty that varies linearly with distance.
   (b) The absolute orientation to each landmark can be directly observed.
   (c) The distance to each landmark can be directly observed with an uncertainty independent of distance.

3. Markov localization accommodates the possibility of ambiguous position estimates that may later be resolved by additional measurements. Suggest two examples of how this can arise in practice indoors and outdoors. The method is based on an assumption that sensor error can be modeled with a Gaussian distribution. Suggest two instances in which this assumption is violated.

4. Pose estimation for a point robot in a 2-D world typically involves estimating translation and orientation.
   (a) Show an example polygon illustrating how position within the polygon cannot be uniquely determined using only perfect range data from a known environment if orientation is unknown. Show an example in which translation can be uniquely determined without knowledge of orientation.
   (b) If the environment is modeled by a polygon, can the amount of uncertainty in position be directly related to the number of ambiguous positions? Will this be the case if the environment is a regular polygon or if the environment is merely a star-shaped polygon?

5. Describe a procedure for determining the pose of a robot in a 2-D world by using only "wall following" and assuming that a perfect map is available and that the absolute orientation of the robot can be determined at any time.

6. Can the procedure described in Problem 5 above be used in a 3-D polygonal environment?

8

Maps and related tasks

Maps are "an inexhaustible fund of interest for any man with eyes to see or with two pence worth of imagination to understand with."[*]

"Here there be dragons."[†]

For autonomous robots, the ability to create maps of the environment autonomously may not, at first glance, seem like a requirement for many tasks. That is, it is sometimes assumed that a robot should be able to take for granted the a priori availability of a map. Unfortunately, this is rarely the case. Not only do architectural blueprints or related types of maps fail to be consistently reliable (for even during construction they are not always updated to reflect necessary alternations)[‡] but, furthermore, numerous aspects of an environment are not likely to appear on a map such as tables, chairs, and other transitory objects.

Perhaps equally important, maps usually represent structural elements in some abstract domain (perhaps with semantic labels), whereas a mobile robot must be able to relate its current location directly to its own perceptions regarding its environment. Maps made for people often depend upon the interpretative skills of the person using the map and on his or her ability to make functional inferences – abilities often absent in computational systems. Further, the sensory characteristics of objects, if annotated at all in maps, will be those of relevance to a human observer.

Actually constructing a map for a robot by hand is an incredibly difficult and tedious job. Although measuring the inside of a single room may be straightforward, reconstructing an accurate metric map of a large indoor environment is difficult to manage because a clear line of sight may not be available between salient environmental features.

The sensory or functional characteristics of relevance to a human may not be of similar relevance to a robot and vice versa. This suggests that an appropriate map for an autonomous robot should relate to the types of sensor data the robot is likely to observe. Thus, it may be appropriate to indicate locations associated with spurious sonar echos, regions with large amounts of radio interference, and so forth, rather than the location of washrooms. In general, these factors imply that the ability to perform some degree of autonomous map construction, update, and validation is of primary importance.

Maps can take many forms. Two specific representational extremes are particularly relevant to mobile robotics: *metric maps*, which are based on an absolute reference frame and numerical estimates of where objects are in space, and *topological maps* (also known

---

[*] R. L. Stevenson, *Treasure Island*.
[†] Label placed by ancient mapmakers for unexplored regions of a map.
[‡] Indeed, one valid robotic application is the construction of "as built" maps of the environment.

as *relational maps*) that only explicitly represent connectivity information, typically in the form of a graph. Each of these categories of representation admits various specific descriptions. Further, many real representations have both a topological and a metric component. For example, metric maps representing the explicit occupancy of space or *geometric maps* representing specific labeled objects often include connectivity information. Metric maps appear to be the most intuitive: a tourist's scale map of a city is a metric map. In terms of mobile robots, perhaps the most explicit form of map is a metric map in configuration space (see Section 5.2.1) in which all possible motions (except those ruled out by non-holonomic constraints) are given explicitly. Recall that obstacles, when transformed into configuration space in the form of C-space obstacles, can take on more complex shapes than in actual space. For example, in the configuration space defined by 2-D translation and rotation, polygonal obstacles become ruled surfaces.

Topological maps, in contrast to metric maps, naturally capture qualitative and relational information while deemphasizing what may be irrelevant or confusing details. As a result, topological maps have a very explicit connection to tasks and the semantics of a problem. A typical subway map, or the typical navigation instructions used by humans over substantial regions of space are examples of topological representations. Several authors have suggested that purely metric maps are not well suited for representing large-scale space.

In order to exploit the advantages of metric and topological representations, it is often appropriate to consider the construction of one representation using observations from another less abstract representation. In addition, it is natural to consider local descriptions before large-scale interrelationships. This leads naturally to a hierarchical layering of successive representations of map data such as the following five layers [99]:

1. **Sensorial.** Raw data signals or signal-domain transformations of these signals.
2. **Geometric.** Two-or three-dimensional objects inferred from sensor data.
3. **Local relational.** Functional, structural, or semantic relations between geometric objects that are near one another (i.e., at individual locations).
4. **Topological.** The large-scale relational links that connect objects and *locations* across the environment as a whole.
5. **Semantic.** Functional labels associated with the constituents of the map.

Giralt et al. [135] were among the first to describe a set of map descriptions that derived a topological representation of the environment from a metric one. In contrast, Kuipers and Levitt [198] have considered the inference of metric data from an essentially topological representation. Their exploration methods, discussed later, consider the use of low-level topological landmarks as the most basic primitive observation from which metric inference can be derived.

A second dichotomy relates to the type of data represented on a map. Most conventional maps depict the occupancy of space in either two or three dimensions. A distinctly different class of map of particular relevance to robots is perceptual maps that directly relate observed sensor measurements to spatial position without resorting to an intermediate description in terms of physical objects. This type of representation is readily imagined in the context of olfaction but is equally applicable to other sensing modalities. Such maps were discussed in the context of visual servoing (Section 7.3) and perceptual structure (Section 7.5).

Map generation is a requirement for many realistic mobile robotics applications. Not only are existing maps of most environments inaccurate, but almost every environment occupied by humans undergoes ongoing change. As a result, mobile robot systems must be able to accommodate change in their environments. If they are to maintain maps, they must be able to update them.

8.1   Sensorial Maps

Maps based on direct sensor readings offer the possibility of coupling the environmental representation as directly as possible with the sensors that the robot uses to perceive the environment. The basic idea is to make sensor measurements coupled with odometry information and to then use a technique such as servo control (Section 7.3) or to identify features in the sensor responses in order to navigate with respect to the map.

8.1.1   Image-Based Mapping

As a robot moves through its environment it can collect sensor readings. If we assume perfect odometry, after some period we will have collected a set of measurements

$$[I_i(x_i, y_i, \theta_i)].$$

If we collect sufficient I_i, such that we can compute a continuous approximation to I_i, say $I(x, y, \theta)$, then one could use servo-control-like methods to navigate with respect to $I(x, y, \theta)$. The difficulty with this approach is that one must know how to sample the set of possible measurements and how to construct the continuous I from the measurements $[I_i(x_i, y_i, \theta_i)]$.

Rather than using I to build a direct mapping from sensor readings to pose, the date I_i can be used as the primary measurements represented in the map. For example, Li et al. [209] describe a system for the construction of 2-D maps of street environments. The robot eventually constructs a graph-like representation of space in which the edges of the graph correspond to streets, whereas the nodes of the graph correspond to intersections. The representation is based upon constructing a visual panorama of the left and right sides of the street as the robot moves. The robot explores by constructing closed loops in the environment (by taking the left-hand street at each intersection) and then identifies closed loops by determining that the current 2-D panorama matches a previously identified panorama. Panoramas can also be exploited in a less well constrained environment. For example, Bourque and others [49, 50] describe a system in which quick-time-VR panoramas are generated at different locations in an indoor environment that become nodes in a graph representing the space. The nodes in this case are defined by an attention operator inspired by models of human visual attention, and the nodes are thus chosen over those that might be most interesting to humans, at least at a presemantic level. In that work, a technique referred to as *alpha-backtracking* (parameterized by the variable α) is used to trade-off additional travel by the exploring robot against the optimality of the sample locations chosen for the topological representation.

8.1.2   Spatial Occupancy Representations

Although most people typically think in terms of representing space by explicitly representing individual objects, one of the simplest classes of maps is based in a representation of space itself without considering the identities or existence of each object.

As we have seen, a major class of such representations is *spatial occupancy representations* (see Section 5.1.1). Recall that the idea is simply to sample 2-D or 3-D space and to store occupancy of each sampling location individually. The simplest manner of accomplishing this is to sample space along a grid in 2-D or 3-D. In the case of a 2-D representation, the map can be regarded as a bitmap or pixmap; this can be viewed as an image, and hence the cells are sometimes referred to as pixels. In 3-D, the cells of the sampling grid are three-dimensional rectanguloids (or cubes in the symmetric case), and they are referred to as *voxels* or volume elements. The number of cells required to represent an environment using a uniform spatial occupancy grid is $O(n^d)$, where n is the number of cells used along each dimension.

A common spatial occupancy technique is to store values in an occupancy grid that reflect the degree of occupancy for each cell: one for a fully occupied cell, and zero for an empty cell. A slightly more refined alternative is to store in each cell a *certainty* $P_{occupied}$ that it is occupied. A third variation is to store the extent to which a cell is occupied: full, partly full, or completely empty.

The use of occupancy grids in mobile robot mapping was pioneered by Elfes and by Moravec [248, 111] (see also [192]). The basic idea is to construct an occupancy grid based on sensor measurements as the robot moves through the environment. Some implementations involved two complementary representations: one for certainty that a cell is empty, a second for the degree of certainty that a cell is full. The maintenance and use of occupancy representations is typically carried out using a Bayesian probability update scheme. To do this, a probabilistic model of the sensor is required that relates different possible measurements to the configurations of the environment that might give rise to them. Ideally, to use a sensor at all, we need to know how different measurements can most likely be explained in terms of the environment.

Consider, for example, the case of a line-of-sight range sensor such as an idealized laser. We wish to measure distance along the line of sight, but when the sensor returns a particular distance reading r it may not accurately reflect the true distance z owing to corruption by electrical noise, optical noise, or other causes. What we need is the probability $P(r\,|\,z)$ of a given range reading r for an actual distance z to the nearest obstacle. Now using Bayes's rule we can compute

$$P(z\,|\,r) = \frac{P(z)P(r\,|\,z)}{P(r)},$$

where the most likely value of z for a given reading r is the one that maximizes this a posteriori estimate. The normalization term $P(r)$ can be computed using

$$P(r) = \int_{z\_\min}^{z\_\max} P(x)P(r\,|\,z)\,dx.$$

An occupancy grid is used to describe regions of the world as occupying one of a discrete set of possible states, each with a fixed probability, computed using the observed sensor data and any prior beliefs:

$$P(W\,|\,R),$$

where W is the world state and R is the set of observations used.

A "split" representation makes the combination of old and new evidence using Bayes's rule somewhat simpler. Each of the two (or more) partial representations can be used to accumulate specific types of evidence (i.e., evidence of emptiness and evidence that a cell is occupied). Before the map is used, the certainties from the two partial maps can be to produce a single "probability" of occupancy, for example;

$$\frac{1}{2}[P_{\text{occupied}} + (1 - P_{\text{empty}})].$$

In the context of map acquisition in an unknown environment, the occupancy grid is initially set to reflect no knowledge of the occupancy of the world. As the robot acquires measurements, elements of the grid are updated using Bayes's rule:

$$P(W \,|\, R) = \frac{P(R \,|\, W)P(W)}{P(R)},$$

which provides the posterior distribution. $P(R \,|\, W)$ describes the behavior of the sensor: how likely it is to return a given measurement for a given state of the world. $P(W)$ describes the *prior* beliefs regarding how likely particular configurations of the world are. $P(R)$ reflects the likelihood of a particular sensor measurement across all possible configurations of the world again computed using

$$P(R_i) = \Sigma_j P(R_i \,|\, W_j)P(W_j).$$

The world model W that maximizes this posterior distribution is then, with respect to Bayesian decision theory, the most "reasonable" description of the environment. This is referred to as a *maximum a posteriori* (or **MAP**) estimate.

The absence of model-specific assumptions makes the technique very general. Occupancy grids provide a uniform framework for combining data from multiple sensors. This advantage, however, is qualified by the need for accurate probabilistic models of sensor performance. In addition, the spatial quantization inherent in the occupancy representation can make it either inefficient in terms of memory utilization or limit the fidelity of the map obtained. A further issue is that, because the spatiotemporal origin of individual measurement is discarded in the mapping process, it can be difficult to construct an accurate geometric model from an occupancy representation. This difficulty is compounded by the need to keep the individual cell size limited.

Once an occupancy representation has been computed, it can be used to localize the robot by correlating the existing grid with a (partial) grid obtained from recent sensor data (see Sections 7.5 and 7.6).

Of course ideal distance sensors and probabilistic representations are not the only possible mechanisms for exploiting occupancy grids in the construction of environmental maps. For example, [252] describes a system that uses trinocular stereo vision and a more ad hoc probability combination rule to build an occupancy grid of the environment.

Accumulated positional errors over time can corrupt the occupancy grid as it is being constructed. Correcting incremental position errors to avoid this while the map is being constructed is difficult because the map still has low certainty. The key to solving this problem is the maintenance of an accurate estimate of the robot's position. One technique for dealing with this problem is to recompute the map and position estimate iteratively, refining the accuracy of each with each iteration. This type of recomputation has been employed to produce large-scale maps of a large environment [356].

A final issue in exploring an occupancy grid representation is how to go about doing the exploration. A common approach involves moving through the known free space towards environmental regions that are the most "unknown." Because the sensors are located on the robot, moving towards unknown regions makes them known, hence extending the known environmental region. Another approach is to use some sort of random-walklike algorithm in which the robot makes straight-line motions until it meets an obstacle, at which point it chooses a new random direction.

Markov models If we wish either to compute the position of obstacles in the environment, or compute the pose of the robot, a particularly general approach is to model the cell occupancies as well as the robot pose and the result of any actions as probability *distributions*. In this case, the choice of how to collect data, or more generally how to behave in a particular state can be referred to as a *policy*. The desirability of a given state (which comprises the occupancy of the environment as well as the robot pose) is expressed by a *utility function*, which is a scalar value associated with a state.

If the transition probabilities and utilities that describe the robot's action depend only on the current state and *not the past history*, then the system has the *Markov property*. The problem of selecting the optimal policy (for some specific objective) in such a context is referred to as a *Markov decision problem (MDP)*. In the case that the instantaneous observations are insufficient to determine the state uniquely in some cases, the system is referred to as *partially observable*, and the problem of finding an (optimal) plan or *policy* is referred to as a *partially observable Markov decision problem (POMDP)*. Selecting what to do then involves considering the distribution of probabilities for the *current state* of the environment (including the pose of the robot) and the probability distribution associated with each possible action of the robot. This framework is similar in spirit to the approach used for Kalman filtering. Rather than assuming that states can be described by Gaussian probability distributions and linear state transition matrices, one can describe a much wider range of functions using the formulation. The disadvantage, of course, is that the computational requirements can be vastly larger.

By integrating over the desirability of the outcome for each action, the best action for the current state can be determined. This can be accomplished using *value iteration*, which iteratively computes the utility for each possible state in the system. One way to do this in the absence of uncertainty is to compute the optimal action for a state with unknown utility by examining how it can lead to a state with known utility. Often this implies *backward chaining*, or reasoning backwards from the goal state(s) we wish to find. In the case of *additive* utility functions, the most natural class of utility functions, value iteration leads to *dynamic programming* (see Section 5.3). Additive utility functions are those through which the utility of a state can be expressed as the sum of the utilities of its predecessor states.

Consider, for example, the case in which the robot pose is given in a 2-D environment by $q = \langle x, y, \theta \rangle$, where x and y specify orientation and θ specifies orientation of the robot. The likelihood (or *belief*) that the robot has a particular pose can be modeled with a three-dimensional grid $Bel(q)$. An action α has a range of possible outcomes $P_\alpha(q)$ even if we know exactly what state q we are in, for there may be a variety of errors or uncertainties. Thus, after an action the grid is updated using

$$Bel(q) \leftarrow \int P_\alpha(q \mid q') Bel(q') \, dq',$$

where $P_\alpha(q \mid q')$ describes the probability of an action α taking us from state q' to state q.

Likewise, an observation s from our sensors can be interpreted in the context of the state we might have been in using a simple application of Bayes's rule,

$$\mathcal{B}el(q) \leftarrow \frac{P(s|q)\mathcal{B}el(q)}{P(s)},$$

where $P(s|q)$ is the probability of read s occurring in state q and $P(s)$ is the intrinsic probability of reading s.

Thrun et al. have applied such a representation to the problem of robot localization by allowing the robot to estimate locally the next action that will increase its certainty regarding its pose [356]. A good pose estimate is associated with a sharp peak in the pose distribution $\mathcal{B}el(q)$, and this can be expressed by computing its entropy as follows:

$$\mathcal{H} = -\int \mathcal{B}el(q) \log \mathcal{B}el(q)\, dq$$

Sensing and acting can then be selected to minimize the *expected* future entropy:

$$E_\alpha[\mathcal{H}] = E\left\{\int \mathcal{B}el_{\alpha,s}(q) \log \mathcal{B}el_{\alpha,s}(q)\, dq\right\}$$

$$= -\int \left[\int \mathcal{B}el_{\alpha,s}(q) \log \mathcal{B}el_{\alpha,s}(q)\, dq\right] P(s)\, ds$$

$$= -\int \int P(s|q)\mathcal{B}el_\alpha(q) \log[P(s|q)\mathcal{B}el_\alpha(q)P(s)^{-1}]\, dq\, ds$$

A similar approach is also used to estimate the map, described by an occupancy grid, that explains sensor data collected from a predetermined trajectory [129]. In this case, a set of measurements d taken along a trajectory are provided a priori, along with a function $P(o|q, m)$ that expresses the probability of the robot observing o while having pose q with map m. This can be reformulated as

$$P(q|o, m) = \frac{P(o|q, m)P(q|m)}{\int P(o|q', m)P(q'|m)\, dq'} = \eta P(o|q, m)P(q|m)$$

The aim is to maximize the probability of the map, given the observed data from a set of poses at times $t = 1 \ldots T$:

$$P(m|d) = \int \cdots \int P(m|q^{(1)}, \ldots, q^{(T)}, d)$$

$$P(q^{(1)}, \ldots, q^{(T)}|d)\, dq^{(1)} \ldots dq^{(T)}$$

$$P(m|d) = \int \cdots \int \frac{1}{P(d|q^{(1)}, \ldots, q^{(T)})} \prod_{t=1}^{T} P(o^{(t)}|m, q^{(t)})$$

$$P(m) \prod_{t=1}^{T-1} P(q^{(t+1)}|u^{(t)}, q^{(t)})$$

$$dq^{(1)} \ldots dq^{(T)}$$

This is accomplished by iteratively computing the pose of the robot given the map and then reestimating the map given the updated estimate of the robot pose. This type of procedure was used by Fox and others to estimate the position of a tour-guide robot [129, 128] (see Fig. 8.1). Estimating the robot's pose with an angular resolution of 2° this makes a three-dimensional state space of 16 million states. More sophisticated representations can also be used to reduce this cost, such as those based on sampling the belief distribution.

8.2 Geometric Maps

Geometric maps (see Section 5.1.2) can be an efficient description of the environment, if one assumes that the sensor provides suitable data, and that the environment to be described is well suited to the geometric modeling primitives to be used.

The exploration of an unknown environment, the construction of a geometric map from that exploration, and other related problems have been studied extensively in the field of computational geometry. Exploration relates to a variety of related capabilities. These include searching for a specific objective or goal position, searching for a route with specific properties, covering free space, and learning about the occupancy of space (i.e., mapping).

A broad class of problems deal with search in unknown or partially known environments. Such problems are of interest not only in their own right but also because they are closely related to environmental exploration in general (where the goal being sought is additional geometric knowledge).

Several algorithms have been developed for navigation in an uncertain environment. These algorithms discover the position of the goal, or of obstacles in the environment, in the course of navigation and hence are naturally classified as a form of exploration algorithm. The Bug algorithm, seen already in Section 5.3.3, provides one such example.

Papadimitriou and Yannakakis [280] considered the task of moving between a known starting position and a known goal in an a priori unknown environment occupied by nonintersecting rectilinear obstacles (i.e., rectangular obstacles aligned with the world coordinate system). These authors describe an elegant and intuitive algorithm similar to Bug that continually moves the robot towards the straight line connecting the starting location and the goal when faced with an obstruction (or in an arbitrary direction at other times). Significantly, they demonstrate that this algorithm is optimal in certain simple cases and that in more general environments no bound is possible.

Different geometric representations can result in very different exploration and search algorithms. For example, a *street* is a polygon such that a start S and goal T on the boundary of the polygon partition the edges into two groups (left and right) and every edge on the left is visible from some point on the right (i.e., they are mutually weakly visible). These polygons can be divided, in essence, into a "right" and "left" side defined by partitioning the polygon into two chains divided at the starting and goal locations. This is illustrated in Figure 8.2. Several researchers have considered the problem of moving from S to T without an a priori map of the polygon. The robot is assumed to be able to observe the side label (*left* or *right*) that any given segment of the wall belongs to. Kleinberg has developed an algorithm with a competitive ratio of $2\sqrt{2}$, improving an earlier result by Klein (see [186]). Using this algorithm, it is possible to find the *optimal L_1-shortest path* in a rectilinear street.

An *LR-chord* is defined as a line connecting a point from the left chain to a point from the right chain. A *generalized street* (or G-Street) is a polygon such that every point on the boundary is visible from some point on some LR-chord; this is a larger class of polygons

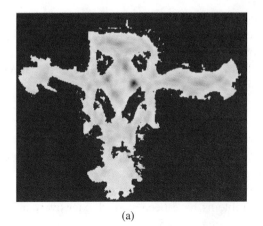

(a)

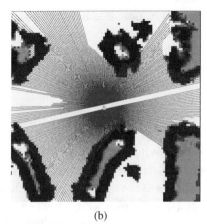

(b)

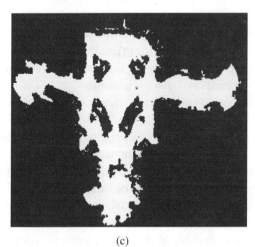

(c)

Figure 8.1. Global localization in the National Museum of American History. The certainty expressed as darkness in the cells of an occupancy grid is shown. The size of the environment is 53×67 m, and each grid cell is 20 cm^2. (a) The belief state after incorporating only a single laser rangefinder data set (the solid exterior is the map). (b) The laser scan projected on the correct position of the robot. (c) The certainty distribution after incorporating a second scan with the positon unambiguous. (Figure courtesy of D. Fox.)

than the streets. It can readily be demonstrated that an optimal path from S to T must move from one LR-chord to another. With only horizontal motions, it is possible to travel anywhere through the polygon, and this, in turn, motivates the use of an L_1 norm as a distance metric. By carefully orchestrating motions and using spiral search to find turning

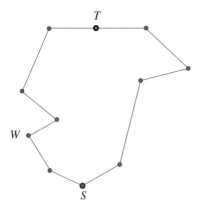

Figure 8.2. A *street* defined by vertices S and T. Note that the pair of vertices S and W do not define a street, because there are points on the clockwise (right) chain that cannot see any point on the other (left) chain.

points so that the robot stays between the appropria e "sides" of the polygon, the algorithm produces a path whose length from S to T is optimal as measured by the L_1 metric.

Datta and Icking [90] and Klein [186] have developed a navigation technique for moving from a starting location to an unknown goal location within a class of polygons known as rectilinear *generalized streets* (G-streets), a broader class of objects than streets.

The task of automatically constructing a geometric map has also been considered as a practical task (see [385]). This system uses the COPIS sensor (see Section 4.7.5) to construct a geometric representation of the free space around the robot. Assuming perfect odometry, the robot constructs a polygonal object that represents the free space around itself. Each time the robot moves, visible vertical lines are tracked, and their positions are recomputed using triangulation. Vertical lines that cannot be associated with a previously viewed environmental structure are postulated as a new structure and are added to the map (it takes two different views of a new feature to obtain a position estimate). All map items are connected in a radial fashion to build up a representation of free space. It is assumed that the space within the polygon formed by linking the edges in a radial fashion is empty.

Figure 8.3 illustrates the process of exploration. Dotted lines connect the robot (depicted as a dark square) with sensed structure, and the free-space polygon is drawn in solid lines. As the robot moves, more sensor measurements are made and a larger region is explored.

This particular approach has a number of limitations. It is difficult to know if all of space has been explored, the system cannot describe very complex open spaces, and the exploration process is driven by an external operator; the system does not decide where or when to explore.

8.2.1 Spiral Search

Spiral search is a key technique in geometric exploration [25]. In essence, spiral search is an optimal search strategy for an object whose position is unknown. It successively examines the set of all points with geometrically increasing distance from some starting location. This approach is closely related to iteratively deepening search, which is employed to examine a state space in traditional artificial intelligence problems.

The term spiral search in fact relates to a family of similar problems based on searching for an object on a line, or on a set of rays joined at a common root, or on a grid. Spiral search algorithms ensure that if an object being sought is a distance d from the initial position, it will be found after traversing a distance that is no more than a small constant

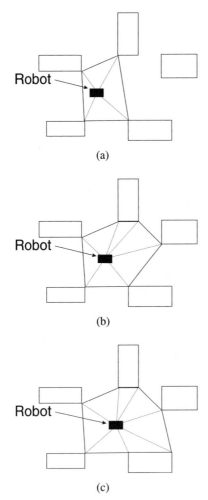

(a)

(b)

Figure 8.3. Three snapshots in the exploration of space using the algorithm described in [385]. Under external control the robot moves and builds a geometric model of free space. (a) Step I. (b) Step II. (c) Step III.

(c)

multiple of d. In the specific case of an obstacle-free 2-D environment, the search pattern is a logarithmic spiral and has an asymptotic performance bound, or *competitive ratio*, of $9d$.

The simplest instance of spiral search for a goal with no information concerning its position is search for a goal on a (one-dimensional) line. From a starting position, the goal could be in one of two possible directions. Moving in only one direction obviously fails to find the goal with 50-percent probability. If we know a priori that the goal is distance d from the starting location, then we can move in one direction a distance d, and, if we do not find the goal, we move in the opposite direction a distance $2d$, at which point we must encounter the goal. This assures we will find the goal with a worst-case travel distance of $3d$ (i.e., competitive ratio of 3) and an average case performance of $\frac{3}{2}d$. Without such advance knowledge of the distance to the goal, the optimal strategy, if one assumes a uniform probability of finding the goal at any specific location, resembles this back-and-forth methodology.

The problem can naturally be formalized in terms of the integer distance $f(i)$ traveled outward from the origin between successive reversals in direction indexed by the "trip number" i. Thus, on trip i the robot moves distance $f(i)$ to the left and then returns to the origin. On trip $i + 1$ the robot moves a distance $f(i + 1)$ to the *right* and then returns to the origin (if it does not find the goal). In order to perform useful work on every trip, the robot must explore new territory on each trip, and thus each trip in a given direction must take it farther than the last:

$$\forall i \geq 1 \quad f(i) > f(i - 2) \tag{8.1}$$

and $f(0) = f(-1) = 0$. When the a priori probability of finding the goal at any specific point is uniform, then an appropriate search strategy is given by a linear spiral search, where $f()$ is given by

$$\forall i \geq 1 \quad f(i) = 2^i.$$

Thus, given that the goal is distance n from the starting location, the total distance traveled is a combination of a series of too-short trips of size 2^i, where $2^i < n$ followed by a final trip of length n that reaches the goal. This total length is given by

$$2 \sum_{i=1}^{\lfloor \log n \rfloor + 1} 2^i + n,$$

which is bounded by $9n$. The effectiveness of this strategy is given below.

Theorem 5 *Given a goal with an unknown position from the origin of a line, linear spiral search finds that goal after traveling a distance of $9d$, where d is that distance from the origin to the goal. This distance is optimal up to lower-order terms [25].*

Surprisingly, for most reasonable symmetric nonuniform probability distributions that have increased probability mass near the center, the number of turns for the average-case optimal solution is infinite (one simple such example is a triangular probability distribution).

A simple generalization to the problem involves searching for a goal along a set of m rays emanating from the origin. We assume that the robot can only walk along the rays, so that search entails going back and forth along the rays. In this case, if what is known is the distance d along some ray to the goal, but the specific ray is unknown, then the robot must move out a distance d along each successive ray, giving an optimal worst-case distance traveled of $(2m - 1)n$, and an average-case distance of half that. If the distance to the goal is not known a priori, then progressive search of the rays becomes necessary. In this case, the generalization of Equation 8.1 is

$$\forall i \geq 1 \quad f(i) \geq f(i - m),$$

with $f(i) = 0$ for all $i \leq 0$. This leads naturally to generalized linear spiral search, where

$$f(i) = \left(\frac{m}{m - 1} \right)^i,$$

which provides an optimal strategy (up to low-order terms) and has a competitive ratio of

$$1 + 2 \frac{m^m}{(m - 1)^{m - 1}}.$$

The spiral search framework has been extended to obstacle-free lattices. In this case, the objective is to find a specific point on a grid. In this case, we have

Theorem 6 *Any algorithm that can find a point at an arbitrary point at a finite distance d in a lattice requires at least $2n^2 + 4n + 1$ grid motions in the worst case [25].*

Proof sketch: This can be shown by using an adversary argument where the adversary places the point at the last point searched by the algorithm that satisfies the distance constraint. Thus, the issue becomes one of how efficiently an algorithm can examine all points with distance no more than d. There are $2(n-1)^2 + 2(n-1) + 1$ points of interest, and a complete visit (on a discrete grid) entails visiting some points more than once.   □

8.3   Topological Maps

To avoid the obvious difficulties in maintaining a long-term metric map of an environment, an alternative class of representations that has been used is based on graphs (see Section 5.1.3). Topological representations avoid the potentially massive storage costs associated with metric representations. In addition, they have appealing apparent analogies with human spatial perception. Purely topological representations, without any distance information, represent a worst-case scenario for position-sensing schemes.

Topological maps describe the environment as a graph that connects specific locations in the world, represented by vertices, with edges that embody their accessibility. Thus, a graph-based map is given by

$$G = (V, E),$$

with set of N vertices V and set of M edges E. The vertices are denoted by

$$V = \{v_1, \ldots, v_N\}$$

and the edges by

$$E = \{e_1, \ldots, e_M\},$$

and edge e_{ij} is given by

$$e_{ij} = \{v_i, v_j\}.$$

If the ordering of v_i and v_j is significant, as it is in some models that presuppose that paths are unidirectional, then we have a *directed graph*. Note that $M < N(N-1)$ for graphs without transitive edges (edges between a node and itself), whereas for *planar graphs* (graphs without any crossing edges) we have a bound on the number of edges $M < 3N - 1$.

Many schemes for determining a topological environment representation from an actual environment have been proposed, often based on restrictive assumptions regarding the types of actual environments that are admissible. The canonical example is the use of a topological model to represent the hallways and junctions of an idealized office environment. Although retraction methods can be used to derive a topological representation of a metric environment, not all topological representations are retractions.

In practice, a topological representation can be defined for a continuous environment based on landmarks or other features. One possible definition of a graph vertex is based on a local distinctiveness measure [197]. In this case, some set of sensor-based functions for the local environment is postulated. For example, the radius of the smallest circle that can be inscribed within a set of observed range measurements can be used to define a node in the topological representation. These nodes of the graph are those locations that, for example, maximize the value of one or more of these functions.

To relate the graph more closely to a map of actual space, the definition of an edge can be extended slightly to allow for the explicit specification of the order of edges incident upon each vertex of the graph. This constrains the embedding of the graph, that is, its possible layout on a surface (e.g., on a plane). This ordering is obtained by enumerating the edges in a systematic (e.g., clockwise) manner from some standard starting direction. An edge $E_{i,j}$ incident upon v_i, and v_j is assigned labels n and m, one for each of v_i and v_j, respectively, where n represents the ordering of the edge $E_{i,j}$ with respect to some consistent enumeration of edges at v_i and m represents the ordering of the edge $E_{i,j}$ with respect to the consistent enumeration of the edges at v_j. The labels m and n can be considered as general directions (e.g., from vertex v_i the nth exit takes edge $E_{i,j}$ to vertex v_j).

Many environments of current interest in land-based mobile robotics may be characterized as unstructured 2-D environments identified by landmarks, but these landmarks and, in fact, the characterization of any specific location, may not by unique. The term *signature* is used to refer to the specific observable characteristics associated with a location (in this case a node). If these signatures are sufficiently distinctive, either because the appearance of the node is distinctive or because appearance coupled with odometry measurements make the signatures unique, then nodes can be well defined, and an embedded graph representation can be constructed autonomously. For example, the TOTO robot [230] creates a topological map (a graph) as it explores its world. As landmarks are detected, they become nodes in the graph along with their qualitative properties, that is, type (left wall, right wall, corridor) and associated compass bearing. A clever "truth maintenance" protocol is invoked to ensure that the same landmark does not become multiple nodes in the graph. This approach illustrates several important components of topological mapping and involves substantial domain-dependent processing.

8.3.1 Marker-Based Exploration

In the worst case, a local disambiguating signature may not be available. The exploration of an arbitrary unlabeled graph without metric information or unique signatures precludes developing a unique map for each environment. That is, it cannot be established when a node has been visited more than once, and hence it is not possible to disambiguate between alternative possible maps. If the robot is equipped with some mechanism for disambiguating nodes, then it may be possible to explore the environment. For example, if the robot is equipped with a can of spray paint or an infinitely long string that the robot can pay out as it moves through the environment, then the robot can mark each location as it is passed and this can be used to provide each node with a unique signature.

Perhaps the simplest such marking mechanism (described in [106, 101]) involves augmenting the robot with one or more unique pebbles or markers that the robot can drop, pick up, or recognize if they are at the robot's current location. (See also [42], which describes a finite state automation that can explore a maze in log-space time using two

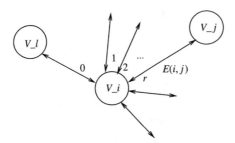

Figure 8.4. Edge ordering.

pebbles and a compass.) The exploration algorithm described in [106, 101] operates by building up a known subgraph of the world and exploring unknown edges incident on the known subgraph, thus incrementally adding to it. The algorithm requires the robot to make $O(N^3)$ moves between locations in the worst case, where N is the number of distinguished locations in its environment. These locations correspond to vertices in the graphlike map that is produced, whereas the moves correspond to the edge traversals.

This exploration algorithm operates on an augmented graphlike representation of the world. The world is defined as an embedding of an undirected graph G. The graph embedding is accomplished by extending the definition of a node to allow for the explicit specification of the order of edges incident upon each vertex of the graph embedding. This ordering is obtained by enumerating the edges in a systematic, manner (e.g., clockwise for a planar map). In keeping with the minimalist representation of the environment, it is also assumed that the robot has very limited sensing and mobility options: The robot can move from one vertex to another by traversing an edge (a *move*), it can pick up a marker that is located at the current vertex, and it can put down a marker it holds at the current vertex (a *marker operation*). The robot in general has K markers at its disposal.

Assume the robot is at a single vertex v_i, having entered the vertex through edge $E_{i,l}$. In a single move, it leaves vertex v_i for vertex v_j by traversing the edge $E_{i,j}$, which is located r edges after $E_{i,l}$ according to the edge order at vertex v_i (see Figure 8.4). This is given by the transition function

$$\delta(v_i, E_{i,l}, r) = v_j$$

The following property is assumed concerning the transition function:

$$\text{If } \delta(v_i, E_{i,l}, r) = v_j \quad \text{and} \quad \delta(v_j, E_{i,j}, s) = v_k, \quad \text{then } \delta(v_j, E_{j,k}, -s) = v_i.$$

This implies that a sequence of moves is invertible and can be retraced. It is also assumed that there does not exist a $t \neq -s$ such that $\delta(v_j, E_{j,k}, t) = v_i$ and that there does not exist a t such that $\delta(v_j, E_{j,k}, t) = v_j$; that is, there are no redundant or degenerate paths.

A single move is thus specified by the order r of the edge along which the robot exits the current vertex, where r is defined with respect to the edge along which the robot entered such vertex. Note that in the special case of a planar embedding of a graph, enumeration of edges in a clockwise fashion satisfies the above assumption.

A marker operation is fully specified by indicating for each of the K markers whether it is being picked up, put down, or not operated upon. This is specified by a K-tuple

$\Omega^K = (op_1, op_2, \ldots, op_K)$, where the element op_k has a value from the set {*pickup*, *putdown*, *null*} according to the operation performed on marker k.

A simple action a is defined as a marker operation accompanied by a move; therefore, $a = (b, \delta)$, where $b \in \Omega^K$. The robot performs some action on the markers in the current vertex and then moves to a new location. A path $A \in a^+$ is a nonempty sequence of actions.

The robot's perception is of two kinds: marker-related and edge-related.

Marker-related perception Assume that the robot is at vertex v_i, having arrived via edge $E_{i,j}$. The marker-related perception of the robot is a K-tuple $B_s = (bs_1, bs_2, \ldots, bs_K)$, where bs_k has a value from the set {*present*, *not-present*} according to whether marker k is present at vertex v_i.

Edge-related perception The robot can determine the relative positions of edges incident on the vertex v_i in a consistent manner (e.g., by a clockwise enumeration starting with $E_{i,j}$). As a result, the robot can assign an integer label to each edge incident on v_i, representing the order of that edge with respect to the edge enumeration at v_i. The label 0 is assigned arbitrarily to the edge $E_{i,j}$ through which the robot entered vertex v_i. The ordering is local because it depends on the edge $E_{i,j}$. Entering the same vertex from two different edges will lead to two local orderings, one of which is a permutation of the other. Note that if the graph is planar and a spatially consistent (e.g., clockwise) enumeration of edges is used, then two permutations will be simple circular translations of each other.

The sensory information that the robot acquires while at vertex v_i is the pair consisting of the marker-related perception at that vertex and the order of edges incident on that vertex with respect to the edge along which the robot entered the vertex. If the robot visits the same vertex twice, it must relate the two different local orderings produced and unify them into a single global ordering, for example, by finding the label of the 0th edge of the second ordering with respect to the first ordering. Determining when the same vertex has been visited twice and generating a global ordering for each vertex is part of the task of the following algorithms.

The exploration algorithm maintains an explored subgraph S and a set of unexplored edges U that emanate from vertices of the explored subgraph. A step of the algorithm consists of selecting a set E of k unexplored edges from U and "validating" the vertex v_2 at the unexplored end of each edge $e = (v_1, v_2)$ in the set E. Validating a vertex v_2 means making sure that it is not identical to any other vertex in the explored subgraph. This is carried out by placing one of the k markers at v_2 and visiting all vertices of the known subgraph S along edges of S, looking for the marker (and each of the other $k - 1$ markers dropped at this step). Note that the other vertex v_1 incident upon e is already in the subgraph S.

If the marker is found at vertex v_i of the explored subgraph S, then vertex v_2 (where the marker was dropped) is identical to the already known v_i (where the marker was found). In this case, edge $e = (v_1, v_2)$ must be assigned an index with respect to the edge ordering of vertex v_2. To determine this, the robot drops the marker at v_1 and goes back to v_2 along the shortest path in the explored graph S. At v_2, the robot tries going out of the vertex along each of its incident edges. One of them will take the robot back to v_1, which the robot will immediately recognize by the existence of the marker. Note that the index of e with respect to the edge ordering of v_1 is known by construction. Edge e is then added to the subgraph S and removed from U.

If the marker is not found at one of the vertices of S, then vertex v_2 is not in the subgraph S and therefore must be added to it. The unexplored edge e is also added to S, which has now been augmented by one edge and one vertex. Adding the vertex v_2 to the subgraph causes all edges incident upon it to be assigned an index with respect to the edge e by which the robot entered the vertex (edge e is assigned index 0), and the new edges are added to the set of unexplored edges U. Note that no other edge of the new vertex v_2 has previously been added to the subgraph; otherwise, v_2 would have already been in the explored subgraph. This index assignment establishes the edge ordering local to v_2.

The algorithm terminates when the set of unexplored edges U is empty. A formal proof of the correctness of the algorithm is presented in [106].

A different way of using the available k markers is to employ two distinct markers in the exploration of a single unexplored edge $e = (v_1, v_2)$. Then the validation and ordering steps can be combined by placing the markers at v_1 and v_2. If v_2 is found in S, then ordering of e with respect to v_2 is accomplished by going out of v_2 along each of its incident edges without having to drop the marker at v_1 and to return to v_2 along the shortest path in S. This variation resulted in poorer performance in our test cases, with asymptotic worst-case complexity that differs only by a constant factor. There is a trade-off between easier vertex validation, with the modified algorithm, and fewer edges added per marker drop.

Figure 8.5 shows two snapshots of the exploration process when applied to a very simple graph. The graph is sketched in thin lines, and the explored portion of the graph (S) is drawn in thicker lines. Nodes in S are filled in, whereas nodes in U are unfilled. The current location of the marker is shown by a diamond, and the current location of the robot is shown by a square. The entire graph is explored in 53 steps (where a step is counted as an edge traversal). Graph exploration can be a very costly process when only a single marker is available.

8.4   Multiple Robots

In principle, tasks such as mapping, which can be achieved with a single mobile robot, can be also be accomplished by a team or collection of robots – potentially with several advantages. In particular, multirobot implementations of search, exploration, or delivery tasks can potentially provide the following generic advantages over a single-robot system:

- **Improved robustness.** A multirobot system can, in principle, keep functioning even if one of the individual robots fails completely. This could be important in tasks ranging from minesweeping to nuclear waste cleanup.
- **Improved efficiency.** Under appropriate conditions, it should also be possible for a group of robots to accomplish a search or exploration task more quickly than an equivalent single robot.
- **Alternative algorithms.** For some tasks, the availability of multiple robots allows feasible or guaranteed algorithms to be implemented when no such algorithm is available for a single robot system. A simple example problem is that of catching

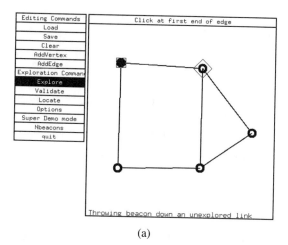

(a)

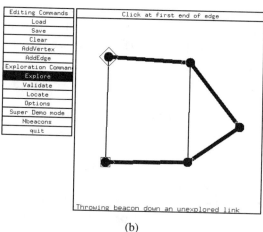

(b)

Figure 8.5. Stages in exploring a graph. (a) Shows the graph at an initial stage with only one vertex explored. The robot (the square outline) has "dropped" the marker (the diamond outline) down at the end of one of the edges to ensure that that node is distinct from the nodes in the explored subgraph. At this point the explored subgraph consists of the node the robot starts at with two edges extending into the unexplored subgraph. (b) Shows the exploration algorithm at a later stage. The marker has just been "dropped" down an edge that has already been visited, and the robot will now return to the starting node through the known subgraph to determine if the location containing the marker is in the known subgraph.

an elusive object in a graph. If the graph is not acyclic, the pursing robot can never cut off the escape route of the object being sought, whereas a sufficiently large team of robots can always accomplish the task by cutting off the escape routes.

In practice, realizing the advantages of a multirobot system over a single robot is not a trivial issue – especially when the additional cost is taken into account. Thus, a team of N fixed-cost robots should be compared, in terms of efficiency per unit cost, with a single robot that costs N times as much as a member of the team (neglecting fixed overhead costs that may be needed to coordinate the team).

In the specific context of multirobot exploration, search, or mapping, a team of robots must contend with several issues such as the following:

1. **Where are the other robots?** This may involve executing a rendezvous with other members of the team.
2. **Partitioning the work.** How the search or exploration tasks is partitioned between members of the team is critical to realizing the potential advantages of a multirobot system but is usually highly task dependent.
3. **Multi-robot planning.** The planned trajectory of each robot should preclude collision with the other robots. This is typically not difficult in itself and is dealt with in Section 5.4.
4. **Merging the data from the individual team members.** This can be accomplished while exploration is being carried out, or, in the more realistic case of limited communication, when team members are sufficiently close to one another. In the most complex cases, this entails solving a full-blown sensor fusion problem.

8.4.1   Rendezvous

Rendezvous refers to having two or more agents (traditionally people, but in this context robots) meet at an appointed place and time. In the simplest cases of multirobot exploration, the robots can all start at the same location, and hence an initial rendezvous can be taken for granted. Even so, there may be issues related to when and if the robots should meet while accomplishing the search task. Rendzevous is proposed typically as a requirement for robots to communicate – the robotic agents are only able to communicate when they are in close proximity – but it may also be required to transfer an object physically from one robot to another.

At the other extreme, if robots start exploring from random positions in an a priori unknown environment, rendezvous can be a serious problem. Rendezvous has been examined in the context of operations research and is similar to games with mobile hiders, referred to as *princess and monster games* [9]. Theoretical variants of the problem include cases with collaborating and noncollaborating agents and with environments that either do or do not have specific locations at which a rendezvous should take place. Purely theoretical variations of the rendezvous problem include variations with discriminable [10] and nondistinguishable agents [12]. In most work in the operations research context, the assumption is made that the environment is completely known in advance. In contrast, mobile robots problems often entail the need to carry out rendezvous while discovering the layout of the map. In most cases, rendezvous is carried out as an implicit part of a more comprehensive search or exploration task.

When robots attempt to solve a problem collaboratively yet robustly without a priori knowledge on one another's position, they need to rendezvous while continuing task execution. Clearly, if they do not rendezvous, they cannot readily benefit from one another's experience. Here we assume rendezvous is necessary for communication. On the other hand, if the robots devote too much energy to rendezvous, they may compromise the robustness and efficiency of the task at hand. The rendezvous problem in the face of noise is parameterized by [324] as follows:

1. The extent to which the two robots agree on their perceptions of the environment. This can, with full generality, be expressed as the extent to which one robot's perceptions differ from those of another.
2. The degree of synchronization that the robots can attain expressed as the likelihood that an appointed rendezvous at a common location will fail owing to a failure to arrive at the same time.
3. The extent of the commonality between the region of space the robots have explored.

Several alternative rendezvous algorithms are possible and are divided broadly into plan-based and stochastic algorithms. For different parts of the problem space, as defined by the noise parameters, alternative algorithms produce the most rapid rendezvous. Representative examples of the types of algorithms that are effective are to have one robot remain stationary while the other seeks (for well-behaved environments where coverage is assured) or to have both robots randomly visit possible rendezvous points selected with a probability that depends on the liklihood of the other robot also finding that location interesting.

8.4.2   Map Fusion

If a group of two or more robots is to profit from their joint efforts, they must be able to share the fruits of their labors. In some cases, this may be implicit. For example, if the problem involves foraging or search using stochastic motion, then little explicit map merging will be needed (because no long-term map is stored). In most cases where a long-term spatial map is needed, an explicit process will be needed to fuse the partial maps produced by the individual robots in the course of their travels. Ishioka et al. developed and implemented a team of heterogeneous robots that act to explore an unknown environment and then fuse their respective maps [166].

In general, the complexity of the map-merging task depends on the extent of the odometry error accumulated in the course of exploration, the fidelity of the sensing used to acquire map data, and the richness of the environment. In the case of accurate sensing and little progressive odometry error, merging can be accomplished using simple global cross-correlation.

8.4.3   Fusion by Correlation

Fusing maps using cross-correlation depends on the assumption that the individual maps are known to overlap "sufficiently" (typically 30- to 50-percent overlap is required, depending on the map content and on the correlation or matching technique used). The problem can be framed as that of matching the map $M_i(x, y)$ acquired by each successive robot to the map belonging to the first robot $M_0(x, y)$ by finding a set of translations T_i and rotations R_i to apply to the successive maps (we consider two-dimensional maps here, but the situation is identical for three-dimensional maps, although more computationally costly).

Let us assume that the map data are stored in homogeneous coordinates, so that rotation and translation can be expressed as matrix multiplication. Then, for each map M_i we need to find the translation and rotation giving $(\delta x, \delta y, \delta \theta)_i$ that minimizes

$$\int \int [M_0(x, y) - R_i T_i M_i(x, y)]^2 \, dx \, dy, \tag{8.2}$$

where we assume that the integral is evaluated only over points that are inside both maps. This type of approach has been used with some success to align laser scans [214, 213] and was discussed in Chapter 3.

8.4.4   Exploration with Multiple Robots

The graph-based algorithm for topological exploration with a single robot described in Section 8.3 has been generalized to operate with multiple robots (see [105]). In this work, the robots are only allowed to communicate when they are in the same node. The basic concept is to have the robots partition the work and to have each robot go and explore its part of the environment. From time to time the robots rendezvous, harmonize their map representations into a single consistent representation, and then redivide the work and continue to explore. In point form, the algorithm can be summarized as follows.

0. Start at an arbitrary "root" node in the mutually known subgraph S^m.
1. Plan partition of work and rendezvous schedule.
   – Agreeing which outgoing edges of the root each robot should depart from.
   – After how many edge traversals they should meet and where.
2. Each robot explores using the single-robot algorithm.
   This allows each to each define its own (evolving) known subgraph S^i.
   These known subgraphs each contain the mutually known subgraph $S^m \subset S^i$.
3. At the predetermined time, the robots return to the agreed point in S^m.
4. Harmonization begins.
   Each robot identifies the perimeter of its known subgraph $P^i = \partial S^i$.
   These are all nodes with an (unexplored) edge leading *out* of the known subgraph.
5. Perimeters of robots' known subgraphs are harmonized without moving.
6. For each boundary node u of each explored subgraph S^i that has not yet been harmonized, harmonize it by physically moving a robot using the single-robot exploration algorithm.
7. Once the perimeters have been harmonized (and thus contained in S^m), the interiors of these regions can be harmonized without moving the robots.
8. If unexplored edges remain in the single harmonized map, continue the algorithm starting with step 0.

8.5   Problems

1. Implement a wall-following algorithm using an idealized (perfect) range sensor.
2. (a) How would an idealized wall follower (as implemented for Problem 1) have to be modified to accommodate a real sonar sensor? (b) Implement your solution on a robot.
3. Using the simulation developed in Chapter 2 and an idealized range sensor, implement Elfes' occupancy-grid-based exploration alogrithm. How did you decide where the robot should move next?
4. Compare and contrast the following methods for representing 2-D spatial occupancy: occupancy grids, sets of line segments, sums of Gaussians probability functions. Suggest a context that is best suited to each representation.

9

Practical mobile robot tasks

Although many mobile robot systems are experimental, systems devoted to specific practical applications are now under development. In this chapter we examine some of the tasks for which prototype mobile robotic systems are beginning to appear and describe several existing experimental and production systems that have been developed. As noted in Chapter 1, tasks for which practical mobile robot systems exist are usually characterized by one or more of the following properties:

- The environment is inhospitable, and sending a human is either very costly or very dangerous such as nuclear, chemical, underwater, battlefield, and outer-space environments.
- The environment is remote, and thus sending a human operator into it is too difficult or takes too long. An extreme instance of this are those environments that are completely inaccessible to humans such as microscopic environments. Many other environments, including mining, outer space, and forestry exhibit these properties.
- The task has a very demanding duty cycle or a very high fatigue factor.
- The task is highly disagreeable to humans.

In addition, domains where the use of a robot may improve efficiency, robustness, or safety are candidates for the development of experimental systems that may subsequently become practical.

Fundamentally, the decision to implement a robotic solution to a given task often comes down to a question of economics. If it is cheaper, more efficient, or simpler to use a person to accomplish a task, then economically it does not make much sense to design and use a robot. Nevertheless, niche applications do exist for autonomous robots, and, as the costs associated with robotic systems decrease and their capabilities improve, more markets are likely to develop.

9.1   Delivery

Many industrial, commercial, and medical applications require the transportation and delivery of material between spatially distributed locations. If the environment can be custom-built or customized to simplify the delivery task, very simple automation systems, such as an assembly line, can be applied to the problem. For some application domains, such as hospitals, this is not the case.

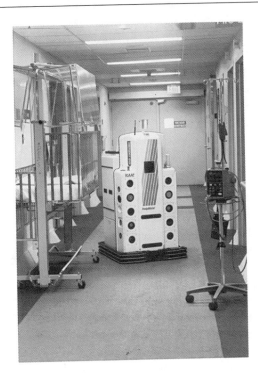

Figure 9.1. HelpMate robot. (Appears with the kind permission of HelpMate Robotics, Inc.)

The hospital domain is characterized by the need to move a number of objects from central locations such as food, linen, documents, and medicine to a number of distributed locations (e.g., the patients in their beds). Currently these tasks are performed by staff, and the efficient utilization of the delivery staff is very difficult.

A mobile robot solution to the problem of delivery in a hospital setting poses several difficult technical problems. The hospital environment cannot be completely modeled: People move about through the environment in unpredictable ways, and there are doors and elevators that have to be navigated. In spite of these technical difficulties, a number of experimental and production robotic systems have been developed to address the delivery problem in hospitals. Perhaps the best-known robotic system for this type of environment is the Helpmate robot [185] (see Figure 9.1).

The Helpmate robot uses a metric map of the environment to plan paths through the hospital and relies on sonar and video sensors to avoid obstacles as it moves. A wireless communications channel permits the robot to operate doors and elevators.

The FIRST robot [327, 310] (Friendly Interactive Robot for Service Tasks) is designed to address similar tasks. It relies on strategically placed laser-scannable targets to solve the global positioning task and uses a gyroscope plus odometry information to deal with local positioning. The environment is modeled topologically, with the targets defining the nodes of the graph, and paths between nodes are defined during a teleoperational training phase.

Delivery robots are not limited to the transportation of small objects in hospital or office environments. For example, the AGV for cargo handling applications [110] is designed to move standard cargo containers in shipping ports. The vehicle is designed to fit under a standard cargo container and uses two steerable wheel assemblies, one at the front and the other at the back, to move cargo containers within a storage area. The vehicle relies on radar sensors and prepositioned radar beacons to perform point-to-point navigation in this known environment.

An especially large-scale application of mobile robots, specifically multiple mobile robots, took place in the context of a project named MARTHA (Multiple Autonomous Robots for Transport and Handling Applications) [4] and was funded under the auspices of a large European research collaboration (under the ESPRIT program). One of the objectives of the project was to develop a system that allows a set of autonomous robots to perform coordinated material transport tasks.

In addition to development work on research vehicles such as the Hilare series of robots, the project involved the use of large vehicles to move cargo shipping containers. These large existing vehicles were retrofitted to make them suitable for robotic control and included the Commutor robot operated by SNCF at Trappes, France, and the Indumat robot at Frankfurt Airport, Germany. Each robot was equipped with local processing as well as a communications device allowing it to communicate reliably with any other robot or to send a broadcast message to robots in its immediate vicinity.

The project involved the integration of a centralized planner (referred to as a central station) with distributed plan execution modules that reside in each robot. The global planner deals with long-term goal satisfaction based on a topological representation of the environment, whereas the distributed local planners deal with plan execution at a metric level, including collision avoidance, conflict resolution (for example with other robots), and error disclosure.

In order to reconcile the resource requirements (including free space) of a large group of robots, a plan-merging paradigm was developed that involves validating and merging new plans with the plans of other robots in the system. This operates using a graph-based planning protocol that exploits temporal precedence constraints to resolve conflicts. Localization is performed using prespecified visual landmarks.

9.2   Robotic Assembly and Manufacturing

Although manipulators and general industrial robotic technology have found wide acceptance in industrial automation, except in limited applications such as materials transport, mobile systems have not penetrated the industrial manufacturing environment. Various research projects, such as one at Daimler-Benz [276], are investigating the introduction of mobile robots onto the shop floor to assist with general assembly and other industrial tasks. The major advantage associated with introducing mobile robot technology over more classical industrial automation is the ability to introduce the technology without requiring a major modification of existing manufacturing processes. At Daimler-Benz, an automobile subassembly function is being examined as a potential task for mobile robot industrial automation.

9.3   Intelligent Vehicles

Automobiles are omnipresent in Western society. They form the transportation backbone of many economies, and a considerable financial investment has been made worldwide to provide the road infrastructure necessary to carry personal, military, and commercial traffic. As a direct result of the importance of the automobile, roads and highways are often congested and inefficiently used. This can be attributed, in part, to the fact that individual drivers often act in their own interest at the expense of overall efficiency and, worse yet, may make decisions that are not even in their own best long-term interest. Further, the modes of communication (and hence the quality of shared information) between drivers are inefficient and highly error prone. Finally, individual driving skill shows considerable variability compounded by the tendency of driving to be tiring and to lead to fatigue and inattention. For all these reasons, road systems rarely approach their theoretically attainable traffic throughput before they become congested. There is considerable demand for the improvement of highway systems and automobiles to provide increased throughput, and because the cost of adding additional bandwidth (lanes) is very high, various groups are investigating the application of mobile robot technology to provide increased traffic throughput.

Aside from merely increasing traffic capacity, intelligent vehicles may offer substantial promise for risk reduction. The performance of a given vehicle is a function of the driver; human error leads to numerous accidents and deaths each year. It is quite conceivable that an autonomous vehicle might provide much greater safety than a human operator.

Other aspects of the transport of people and material over roads may also lead to robotic solutions. Roads are designed for a standard-sized vehicle, and thus the transportation of large quantities of goods (e.g., those required by the military) can require large convoys of vehicles, each with its own driver. Considerable savings could be realized if fewer drivers were required.

Numerous applications of mobile robot technology have been proposed to address these concerns. Although a continuum of approaches has been proposed, several representative classes of methodology have emerged as follows:

- **Driving Assistants.** Provide additional information and sensors to the driver to enhance the human drivers performance in terms of safety and efficiency.
- **Convoy Systems.** Propose to develop automated delivery convoys (lines of vehicles, typically in single file) in which the lead vehicle is driven by a human operator but in which the subsequent vehicles in the convoy navigate autonomously.
- **Autonomous Driving Systems.** Propose to completely take the operator out of the loop and have the individual vehicle drive itself automatically.
- **Autonomous Highway Systems.** Propose to treat the entire highway as a system and control groups of vehicles autonomously.
- **Autonomous Urban Systems.** Propose to address problems related to urban transit through the application of autonomous vehicle technologies.

In fact, the distinction between these individual levels of performance, detailed below, is not precise. The first autonomous driving systems will probably emerge from driving assistants (like cruise control) that take over completely in particular circumstances.

9.3.1 Driving Assistants

Automobile manufacturers wish to develop safer, more sophisticated automobiles. The general direction of this development is typified by the work of Volvo (see [279]). The goal of Volvo's Autonomous Intelligent Cruise Control (AICC) project is to develop an intelligent "driver assistant" that takes the driver's desired speed, the state of upcoming traffic signals, and the speed and relative location of other automobiles on the road into account in order to suggest an appropriate speed to the driver.

The European PROMETHEUS project investigated the development of a driver's warning assistant [114]. This project examined a number of different strategies to provide more information to the driver of a car without requiring modifications to the environment itself. A major thrust of this work has been the development of systems that identify road signs at a distance (e.g., [307, 167]) and can then either signal the driver or influence the car directly.

9.3.2 Convoy Systems

Convoy systems have civilian and military applications. In highway maintenance, a lead vehicle is often followed by a shadow vehicle used to protect the passengers in the lead vehicle from accidents caused by traffic that fails to avoid the service vehicle in time. Obviously, the driver of the shadow vehicle is also at risk, and thus mechanisms to take the shadow driver out of the vehicle improve overall system safety. The Minnesota Department of Transportation currently uses a radio-controlled shadow vehicle remotely operated by a walker who walks just off the highway beside the shadow vehicle. This limits the operational speed of the entire convoy. To overcome this limitation, the Minnesota Department of Transportation is developing and evaluating an autonomous shadow vehicle [147].

The autonomous shadow vehicle operates on a line-of-sight principle, using vision to track a specialized target on the lead vehicle, and integrates this information with the detection of a directed radio beam emitted by the lead vehicle and differential GPS in which the lead vehicle is used as a mobile base station. A neural net integrates these three cues to the lead vehicle's motion, and the shadow vehicle follows the leader. The system is currently undergoing evaluation on a closed test track.

9.3.3 Autonomous Driving Systems

An alternative to just providing information to the driver is for the robot to drive the automobile directly. Such devices have been of interest to the military for some time, and the Autonomous Land Vehicle (ALV) project of the 1980s was responsible for much early research in vision and mobile robotics. The development of vehicles that can navigate themselves has more recently become of interest to civilian organizations. Perhaps the best known of these projects is the Carnegie Mellon University NAVLAB project [355], which developed a series of vehicles that drive autonomously, but other autonomous driving vehicles exist (e.g., [391, 67]). See Figure 9.2.

Although many different problems must be addressed to develop an autonomous driving vehicle, the actual problem of following the road has probably received the most attention. The basic task here is to identify the road surface so that the car can drive down it. One approach to this problem is to identify the structure of the lane markings on the road (cf. [200]). Once the lane markings have been identified, the appropriate steering correction can be computed. An alternative approach is to determine the appropriate steering correction directly from the car's view. This is the approach taken by ALVINN [301, 174] (see Section 6.4). ALVINN is a neural network that takes a reduced 30×32 pixel view of the world and maps this directly to a steering orientation. ALVINN was used to drive Navlab 1 and 2. ALVINN is trained on a single road type such as a single lane road. Higher-level control systems such as the MANIAC neural-network-based system combine multiple ALVINN systems to deal with multiple road types [174].

(a)   (b)

(c)

Figure 9.2. The early Navlab project robot family. (a) Navlab 1. (b) Navlab 2. (c) Navlab 5. Navlab 1 was built in the late 1980s and is built on a Chevy panel van. Navlab 2 was built in 1990 on a modified HMMWV. Navlab 5 is based on the 1990 Pontiac Trans Sport. (Pictures courtesy of Charles Thorpe, Carnegie Mellon University.)

Given a solution to determining where the road is and a mechanism for steering the car along the road, a remaining problem is the task of avoiding other users of the road. As is the case with the road follower, obstacle detection must be quick and accurate, and it also must be integrated within the road follower so that avoiding an obstacle does not lead to the automobile's leaving the road. Solutions typically utilize special-purpose hardware and sensors to address these requirements.

The Navlab project at CMU has constructed a number of autonomous highway vehicles. Navlab 5 (see Figure 9.2) has driven over 6,000 autonomous steering miles on highways in the United States at highway speeds. Although various technologies have been used to control earlier versions of the Navlab, Navlab 5 relies on a differential GPS and a fiber-optic rate gyroscope for gross navigation and on a vision-based line tracker to keep the robot on the highway [69].

In August 1997, Navlabs 6–10 (see Figure 9.3) were involved in extensive on-road testing as part of ongoing development and evaluation of autonomous vehicles [353]. As is

Figure 9.3. The current (1998) generation of Navlab robots. (Picture appears courtesy of Charles Thorpe, Carnegie Mellon University.)

clear from Figure 9.3, autonomous highway vehicles at first glance seem indistinguishable from their human-driven counterparts.

9.3.4 Automated Highway Systems

Rather than dealing with an individual automobile, an alternative approach is to consider the needs of the entire highway system and work towards automating that. In the mid- to late-1990s, the U.S. government pursued a multiyear project to address these critical highway needs. The Intelligent Vehicle Highway System (IVHS) investigated several different approaches to applying robotics to vehicles. These efforts explored the development of systems that range from providing smart sensors to the driver to taking over complete control of the vehicle.

Given the cost of adding and maintaining additional road lanes, the approach of using robotics to increase automotive highway density is very attractive, if somewhat unnerving in practice. For example, in the California Partners for Advanced Transit and Highways (PATH) program, cars are expected to travel autonomously in platoons of 10–20 vehicles separated by 1 m with 100 m between platoons. At present, the obstacles to autonomous highway driving seem to be primarily political and sociological rather than technological. The technology for some form of automated highway is already available, but the issues of liability, user confidence, and cost attribution may prevent its delivery for some time.

9.3.5 Autonomous Urban Systems

In North America work on intelligent vehicles has for the most part concentrated on rural and highway driving, whereas in Europe, urban traffic congestion has become a focus. The driving concept for an autonomous urban system is to remove private automobiles from the central core of urban areas and provide a fleet of "human-controlled" but publically available vehicles instead [210]. The vehicles would be designed for ease of control, environmental friendliness, and limited autonomous action. This last characteristic would assist in collecting the vehicles from where they are left and returning them to central depots.

9.4   Robots for Survey and Inspection

There are many types of industrial operations and environments for which mobile robots can be used to reduce human exposure hazards or increase productivity. Examples include inspection for spills, leaks, or other unusual events in large industrial facilities; materials handling in computer integrated manufacturing environments; the execution of inspections; and the cleaning up of spills. One particular application that has received substantial attention is the execution of repairs and monitoring in the radioactive areas of nuclear power plants with the objective of increased safety by reducing the potential radioactive exposure to workers. Consider the Stored Waste Autonomous Mobile Inspector (SWAMI) robot from the University of Southern California. Based on the Helpmate robot, it is being evaluated at the Savannah River Technology Center with the aim of making the job of inspecting drums of radioactive material safer and more efficient. The robot examines storage drums and returns photos of the drums augmented with barcode readouts from the drums to identify the drums and their contents.

Industrial environments are significantly different from the office environments for which many mobile robots are designed. The ARK project [263] examined the production of a self-contained mobile robot with sensor-based navigation capabilities specifically designed for operation in a real industrial setting (see Figure 9.4). For example, ARK's test environment, the engineering laboratory at the Atomic Energy of Canada Limited (AECL) CANDU in Mississauga, Ontario, covers approximately 50,000 ft^2 of space and accommodates 150 employees. Such an environment presents many difficulties, including the lack of vertical flat walls; the presence of large open spaces (the main aisle is 400 ft long)

Figure 9.4. ARK 2 Robot in the AECL industrial bay.

as well as small cramped spaces; high ceilings (50 ft); large windows near the ceiling resulting in time dependent and weather dependent lighting conditions; a large variation in light intensity as well as highlights and glare; many temporary and semipermanent structures; many (some very large) metallic structures; people and forklifts moving about; oil and water spills on the floor; floor drains (which could be uncovered); hoses and piping on the floor; chains hanging down from above; protruding structures and other transient obstacles to the safe motion of the robot.

Large distances, often encountered in the industrial environment, require sensors that can operate at such ranges. The number of visual features (lines, corners, and regions) is very high, and techniques for focusing attention on specific, task-dependent features are required. Most mobile robotic projects assume the existence of a flat ground plane over which the robot is to navigate. In the industrial environment this ground plane is generally flat, but regions of the floor are marked with drainage ditches, pipes, and other unexpected low-lying obstacles to movement. In order to operate in such an environment a robot must be equipped with sensors that can reliably detect such obstacles.

The ARK robot's onboard sensor system consists of sonars, one or more ARK robotic heads (see Section 4.7.4), and a floor anomaly detector (see Section 4.5.4). The head consists of a color camera and a spot laser range finder mounted on a pan-tilt unit [169]. The pan, tilt, camera zoom, camera focus, and laser distance reading of the ARK robotic head are computer controlled. The ARK project investigated different technologies for Floor Anomaly Detection (FAD) to detect objects on the floor that cannot be detected by the sonar system and are too large for ARK to traverse. One technology that was developed was a laser-based system built around the NRC BIRIS laser head [39] (see Section 4.5.4). An alternative approach is to use stereo vision to localize potential floor anomalies.

The ARK robot navigates through its environment autonomously and cannot rely on modifications to its environment such as the addition of radio beacons, magnetic strips beneath the floors, or the use of visual symbols added to the existing environment. In order to do this, the ARK robot uses naturally occurring objects selected by a human operator as landmarks. The robot relies on vision as its main sensor for global navigation, using a map of permanent structures in the environment (walls, pillars) to plan its path. While following the planned path, the robot locates known landmarks in its environment. Positions and salient descriptions of the landmarks are known in advance and are stored in the map. The robot uses the measured position of the detected landmarks to update its position with respect to the map.

9.5 Mining Automation

Almost every country with a sizable mining industry has a research program in mining automation. In addition, equipment manufacturers, such as Caterpillar and Komatsu, have research programs that investigate the potential of autonomous or tele-robotic mining operations. Corke et al. [80] identify three potential advantages to the introduction of mining automation:

1. Increased safety of the workers.
2. Higher productivity of the mine.
3. Lower equipment maintenance costs.

In general, mining takes place in one of two modes: open pit and underground. Open pit mining is characterized by large, heavy, expensive equipment such as a dragline. Draglines are large, cranelike devices (the boom on a dragline can exceed 100 m) that are used to collect overburden and deposit it in a specified position. These machines require considerable skill to control, and the distances involved make visual control by an operator very difficult (see [79]).

Underground mining is characterized by the requirement to perform dangerous tasks is a constricted environment. Many underground tasks involve the positioning of a tool with respect to some object or structure in the environment. Placing of explosive charges, identifying and removing rocks, and drilling and inserting roof-support bolts are dangerous operations for which autonomous or telerobotic systems have been proposed. Owing to the potential hazard of rockfall, remote underground mining is common in modern mines. In many operations, the operator does not operate the vehicle directly but rather stands some distance away from the vehicle and operates it remotely. One short-term goal of mining technology is the development of teleoperational systems that would permit the operator to move farther from the vehicle [26]. Related problems include the task of actually determining where the vehicles are in the mine and establishing a reliable, high-bandwidth communication network within the mine to support teleoperation.

A longer-term goal in mining automation is the development of fully automated operations. In Canada, Noranda has developed an automated underground load haul dump (LHD) vehicle [298] (see also [163]). This LHD is capable of sensing the forces acting on the LHD's bucket in order to provide automatic "muck pile" loading. An Automatic Guidance System (AGS) capable of operating LHDs and trucks autonomously in underground drifts has also been developed. This system uses two video cameras mounted on the LHD to sense a robust retroreflective tape fixed to the roof of the drift. This "optical guide" is analyzed to command steering, throttle, transmission, and brakes. The prototype system can deal with branching corridors and turns within the drift.

9.6   Space Robotics

Outer space is an almost ideal operational environment to motivate the use of robots. It is expensive and dangerous to project a manned presence on the moon much less on more distant planetary bodies. Given a desire to explore even our closest planetary neighbors, it is quite reasonable to propose to send automated systems rather than humans. When proposing an autonomous or semiautonomous system for interplanetary exploration, it is important to realize that robotic systems do not offer the same level of flexibility as a manned mission. They do, however, offer the possibility of continuing exploration with reduced political and financial support.

9.6.1   NASA and JPL

Under National Aeronautics and Space Administration (NASA) and Jet Propulsion Laboratory (JPL) programs, the United States has engaged in a long-term series of unmanned robotic interplanetary probes. The early Ranger series of the 1960s crash landed on the moon and was not able to interact with the environment. The Surveyor systems of the mid-to-late 1960s performed soft landings on the moon. The Surveyor Robots did not move; they used a robot arm to collect samples. A similar Viking project was deployed to Mars in 1975.

Figure 9.5. Sojourner Rover Vehicle. (Photograph in public domain.)

The Mars Pathfinder project was launched in 1996. This project landed an instrument package on Mars in 1997, including a Microrover Flight Experiment (MFEX). Known as the Sojourner Rover, the vehicle is 630 mm long by 480 mm wide and is driven by each of its six wheels. The front and rear wheels are steerable. Figure 9.5 shows a view of the lander. Essentially, the vehicle was operated in a telerobotic manner using dense way points selected manually at an Earth-based control center. The demands on the human operators who carried out navigation were, apparently, severe and exhausting. This was exacerbated by the resilience of the robot, which permitted it to be used more extensively than had been originally anticipated.

Future missions are expected to include a long-range Mars rover that will move several kilometers from its touchdown site. This robot will almost certainly have to operate highly autonomously because communications delays will become unacceptable and the demands of continuous human operation infeasible. An even more ambitious possibility is a "sample return" mission that would involve collecting samples (perhaps selected automatically) and bringing them back to a launch site for eventual return to Earth.

9.6.2 Soviet

The Former Soviet Union launched two Lunokhod (moon walker) robots in the late 1960s and early 1970s [146]. These eight-wheeled automatic vehicles were the first vehicles to drive on the moon. Teleoperated from Earth, Lunokhod 1 ran from November 1970 to October 1971 and traveled over 10 km. Lunokhod 2 ran from February 1973 to June 1973 and traveled over 37 km.

9.6.3 LunaCorp

LunaCorp is a company that is planning a private venture to the moon in the near future. LunaCorp plans to send two robots to the moon and to have them land near the Apollo 11 landing site. The current robot design is based around a four-wheeled vehicle utilizing solar power for daytime travel and RHU cells for warmth at night. After landing and visiting the Apollo 11 landing site, it is planned that these robots would then visit a number of manned and unmanned landing sites on the moon as part of a theme park operating back on Earth. Customers of the park would have the opportunity to "experience" the motion of the robots on the moon in a virtual reality environment by using immersive "bubbles" providing 360° video combined with a motion platform. Teleoperational systems for an Earth-based simulation of the robots on the moon as well as limited teleoperational control of the moon-based robots are also planned.

9.7   Autonomous Aircraft

Although the development of autonomous aerial vehicles currently places emphasis on a set of issues somewhat different from ground vehicles, it is worth considering briefly. Teleoperated aircraft were first developed in the 1940s in the form of crude wire-guided bombs. Since then, simple autonomous flying vehicles have been developed for use as military drones for reconnaissance as well as missiles (e.g., cruise missiles that can travel hundreds of miles using terrain registration).

More recently there have been several efforts to develop highly capable autonomous aircraft that can even take off and land without human assistance, either vertically or in a traditional manner. This includes autonomous helicopters, which present particular control problems, as well as autonomous fighter aircraft, and even a project to develop an autonomous stealth (B-12) airplane (known as "Dark Star"). Although position estimation methods are relevant to such applications, the key issues are the stable and robust control of complex nonlinear systems. Because many complex systems of this type must alternate between automatic and manual control, the graceful handoff of system control between human and machine operators is a serious issue.

The Sikorsky Cypher Unmanned Aerial Vehicle (see Figure 9.6) is perhaps one of the most well-developed autonomous aircraft systems. The Cypher has sophisticated autonomous capabilities in that it can automatically take off, hover, perform point-to-point

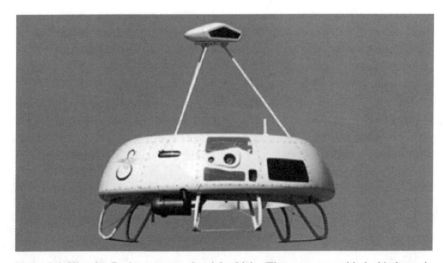

Figure 9.6. Sikorsky Cypher unmanned aerial vehicle. (Figure appears with the kind permission of Sikorsky.)

locomotion, and land. The Cypher is intended for remote survey and inspection tasks for the modern battlefield.

9.8   Military Reconnaissance

The *Tactical Mobile Robot* (TMR) project being funded by the U.S. military examines the use of portable mobile robots for military applications. In particular, the use of small robots for building reconnaissance is being evaluated. The objective is to develop one or more systems with a substantial degree of autonomy that could be operated by persons with limited technical training. A tracked vehicle developed by IS Robotics for this project is sufficiently robust that it can be thrown from a second-floor window and continue operating.

9.9   Bomb and Mine Disposal

Bomb or mine disposal is an almost ideal application for mobile robots. The task is dangerous and repetitive and is often conducted in inhospitable environments. More technically known as *Explosives Ordinance Disposal* (EOD), it entails detecting and disposing of explosive munitions or making them harmless. Typical weapons that require disposal include undetonated air-dropped bombs, mines, rockets, artillery shells, grenades, mortars, and bullets. There are currently two significantly different domains for EOD applications. The first of these is the identification, detection, and elimination of infrequently occurring devices in otherwise safe but unpredictable environments, as is the case with terrorist bomb disposal. The second domain is the detection and disposal of weapons, typically mines, that have been deposited as part of a military operation. In the case of terrorist bombs the emphasis is on highly dexterous systems that can be remotely operated. The sporadic and highly calculated nature of the individual weapon makes the amount of effort and cost available per event substantial. In contrast, in a context such as mine disposal, a large territory must often be covered. Sadly, there is often a paucity of trained operators, and the permissible budget per mine disposed of is frequently exceptionally small. Further, the rugged, ongoing, and low-budget nature of demining operations means that the vehicle must be highly physically robust yet also extremely simple to operate and maintain.

EOD is inherently dangerous. It is a considerable investment to train people to locate, identify, and disable mines, and any mechanism that allows the task to be accomplished remotely contributes to solving the problem. The military problem is severe. Millions of landmines are manufactured each year, and 500–800 deaths and 2,000 maimings due to landmines are reported each month [265].

Mine-clearing robots are designed to either be light enough not to set off the mine while searching for it (e.g., [266]) or are armored so as to be able to withstand small explosions (e.g., [372]). An experimental underwater system has also been developed by Rockwell International and IS Robotics that uses Legged Underwater Vehicles (ALUV) to find mines on a beach. These small (22 in. long, 22 lb) robots are constructed so as to explode on command and hence destroy the mines. Mine-clearing robots currently operate teleoperationally, but experimental systems are being developed to clear larger regions autonomously. An additional task in this case is the development of sufficiently

Figure 9.7. Andros bomb disposal robot. (Figure appears with the kind permission of ROBOTECH.)

good position estimation to enable the robots to clear all of the mines in an area. The UXO (UneXploded Ordinance) Gathering System (BUGS) uses various localization strategies such as GPS and beacons to ensure complete mine clearance.

Systems for the disposal of terrorist bombs are typically more expensive, and the amount of time and money available per EOD incident is larger than in the demining context. Robots are teleoperated, and commercial systems are available from a number of companies. These robots use treads or wheels with skid steering and have special-purpose actuators either to pick up a suspicious package or disarm it (see Figure 9.7). Brute-force devices for disarming a bomb operate by destroying the detonator, or its connection to the main explosive, before the bomb can go off. Typical approaches involve shooting it with a robot-mounted shotgun or with a jet of extremely high-pressure water.

9.10 Underwater Inspection

The inspection of underwater, and in particular deep-sea, structures poses many difficulties for humans. Inspections can be costly and dangerous, and the structure may also pose a hazard. For example, one underwater inspection task involves the inspection of water intake and outflow pipes for power generation stations. These pipes can be quite long and thus present a considerable danger to human inspectors. Many commercial remotely operated vehicles designed to survey underwater structures exist. For example, the Jason, Medea, and ARGO-II vehicles of the Wood's Hole Oceanographic Institute are designed for open water inspection. Jason and Medea are designed to operate in a tethered manner to a depth of 6 km. These devices are maneuvered via the tow line to a mother ship and are equipped with video, still camera, and sonar sensors. The ARGO-II uses thrusters for navigation and is also linked to a mother ship via a tow line. The position of the device is maintained via GPS (to localize the ship) and from transponder arrays.

9.11   Agriculture and Forestry

Autonomous systems in agriculture and forestry must meet specific operational constraints that are different from those found in industrial or office environments. The terrain is rugged, potentially lacking either flat ground surfaces or even a well-defined ground plane. The environment is not easily modeled and evolves (grows) as it is maintained. Nor is the climate well-suited to machines. On the other hand, the tasks involved in agriculture are onerous and can be quite dangerous.

9.11.1 Forestry Maintenance

To obtain a high yield from commercial forests, it is necessary to perform weeding and thinning operations. This involves visiting the forest some number of years after the initial planting and removing competing plants from around the intended commercial trees. This is a very expensive operation because the forests tend to be remote, and it can be dangerous, for some of the tools required to thin the forests (e.g., brush saws) are quite powerful.

In 1993–94, the Canadian Forest Service (Petawawa National Forest Institute) constructed a series of robots to investigate the application of autonomous robots to tree stand maintenance. The JACOB walking robot was the most complete of these prototypes. Based on the Martin Marietta/JPL/NASA rover beam-walker, the robot was built from industrial aluminum ladders with legs that move vertically. At 600 pounds, and with dimensions of 2.1 × 2.3 m, the robot stood 2 m high and was powered by an onboard gasoline generator. The robot was designed essentially to walk over the small trees and to thin between them using a large saw mounted onboard.

9.11.2 Greenhouse Robot

Greenhouses are used for intensive agriculture tasks such as growing seedlings and decorative plants. A typical industrial greenhouse is a rectangular structure of 100 × 20 m. Within a greenhouse, plants are arranged in rows, and narrow corridors provide access. The favorable growth conditions within a greenhouse lead to pests and other undesirable organisms. Pesticides, fungicides, and other chemical products are commonly used to keep these undesirable organisms under control. Coupled with the closed environment, these chemicals lead to a potentially dangerous environment for the human gardener. Thus, mechanisms to reduce human exposure within a greenhouse, especially during spraying, become necessary.

Current mechanisms for automation are typically based on fixed gantry structures, although autonomous systems are beginning to be developed. For example, the AURORA [222] robot is an unmanned robot that navigates along greenhouse corridors using low-cost sensor systems. It uses sonar sensing to follow the corridors, although it sometimes gets stuck and requires external operator intervention.

9.11.3 Lawn-Mowing Robots

Although effective domestic lawn-mowing robots are still the stuff of fiction, lawn-mowing robots have been developed for larger, more structured areas such as football fields and golf courses. A lawn-mowing robot based on a ridable mower is described by Miyake [243]. This vehicle employs GPS, a gyroscope, and dead reckoning to mow a lawn using a preplanned mowing sequence. The vehicle lacks sensors to detect and avoid obstacles and is thus unsuitable for domestic lawns, although it appears to be effective in constrained environments.

9.11.4 Harvesting Robots

Harvesting is one of the most labor-intensive activities in agriculture. Often the material to be harvested can be bruised or damaged by inappropriate handling, and considerable time and money is spent in harvesting fruits and vegetables. Fruits in particular pose a problem because they are often located in high trees requiring the use of a ladder to collect them. Michelini et al. [240] describe some initial research into the construction of a mobile robot system for citrus fruit harvesting. Key to the system described in [240] is the development of sensing mechanisms and special-purpose end effects to manipulate the fruit.

9.12   Aids for the Disabled

Perhaps the largest potential application for mobile robotics is in providing aids for the disabled or for the elderly (eldercare). Deployed systems to date have concentrated primarily on the application of robotic techniques to power wheelchairs. Two general approaches have emerged. The first is to incorporate local robotic assists in a wheelchair to provide safety and fine dexterous motion. For example, the robotic wheelchair robots Tin Man (I and II) [242] perform limited autonomous tasks; they go through doorways, follow hallways, and perform limited navigation using dead reckoning. These are essentially powered wheelchairs outfitted with simple sensors and special-purpose controls for specific applications. Of particular importance in these general-purpose "fine grain" systems is the need to provide a robust user interface. The Wheelesley robot [386], for example, provides a graphical user interface that replaces the joystick with a set of buttons that describe the set of primitive actions the robot understands: move forward, turn right, dock to desk, and so forth.

A second approach is to develop a full-blown robotic system that carries the operator around with it. For example [296] uses a global map to define the environment, and the robot can be commanded to move relative to the map. Such systems often require considerable environmental modification. For example, [373] describes a system that requires the installation of magnetic marker lanes for navigation, and [272] discusses a wheelchair system that uses sonar to identify and follow walls in the environment. The issue of operator–chair interaction is addressed by [336] in which the operator provides instructions to the chair via voice commands.

An extreme approach is to develop a robotic companion for the disabled. This is the approach suggested by the Playbot project [362]. Playbot proposes to build a robot that acts as an extension of a disabled child and allows the child to interact with objects in its environment.

9.13   Entertainment

Mechatronics has long been a staple of amusement parks. More recently, fully autonomous systems have begun to appear. Perhaps the most sophisticated of these is the

GO-2 system currently in development for deployment at Scienceworks in Spotswood, Australia [168].

The GO-2 system is a complete mobile robot system designed to operate with minimal professional interaction under ongoing public scrutiny. Fundamentally a device to demonstrate to the public a mobile robot in action, the system must be robust within its display environment. This environment is highly structured but contains a number of unknown obstacles around which it must navigate under the control of visitors to the center. In addition to a purely robotic control mode, simulated and teleoperational modes are also available to the public.

The GO-2 is built from a modified electric wheelchair. It uses a Denning scanning sensor for localization. Barcodes are placed at known locations in the environment, and the sensor obtains the distance to visible barcode beacons. Bumpers and a scanning time-of-flight laser provide local obstacle detection. The environment is modeled as an occupancy grid, and laser distance information is used to provide updates to the grid. A distance transform path planner is used to provide point-to-point navigation.

A recent addition to the field of entertainment robots has been the formation of an international robot soccer league [184]. In this competition, robot teams – there are three to five robots per team and different-sized robots compete in different classes – play off against each other. Various manufacturers provide robots that meet the requirements for different categories of the competition. For the smallest class, an entire team can be purchased for about 5,000 U.S. dollars. The game is played much like a real soccer game with an appropriate-sized playing field. From a technical point of view, the tasks of sensing the locations of the ball and players and planning the appropriate moves are challenging. Sony has introduced a fully autonomous walking robot dog for home entertainment use. Teams of these robot pets have also competed in a special league of the robot soccer league.

9.14   Cleaning Robots

Although domestic robots are still the fare of science fiction, cleaning robots exist for a number of commercial and industrial applications. Companies such as Cyberworks, Electrolux and Robosoft manufacture several different cleaning robots for applications such as floor scrubbing, street sweeping, and vacuuming. Although these robots could be deployed in general environments, the cost trade-off typically limits their application to Special-purpose environments such as "clean rooms" in which it is not cost-effective to use a human cleaner. The Robosoft Autonomous Vacuum Cleaner, for instance is designed to be used as a remotely controlled device. Relying on a differential drive for locomotion, the AutoVac is driven by teaching the robot the path to follow and then relying on onboard ultrasonic sensors to detect unknown obstacles.

9.15   Problems

1. Take a task for which mobile robots are often proposed (e.g., carpet vacuuming). Estimate the financial cost associated with having the task performed by a human for a 5-year period. Estimate the cost associated with developing and supporting a robotic

solution for this task. (Note that many platform companies have the retail prices of their hardware on the Web.) Does it make economic sense to build an autonomous robot for this task? What assumptions would have to change in order for the robotic system (or the human system) to be more cost-effective?

2. Investigate an industrial robotic system currently in production. What task is the system designed to perform? What limitations does the system place on its operational environment? What level of human operator interaction is required?

10

The future of mobile robotics

"The Encyclopedia Galactica defines a robot as a mechanical apparatus designed to do the work of a man. The marketing division of the Sirius Cybernetics Corporation defines a robot as 'Your Plastic Pal Who's Fun To Be With'."*

The research problems and solutions discussed in this book leave several issues unresolved. Given the current state of mobile robotics, what can be considered essentially solved and what tasks remain? It is clear that for restrictive environments and for limited tasks, autonomous systems can be readily developed. Tasks such as parts delivery in a warehouse, materials transport in hospitals, limited autonomous driving, and so forth, can all be "solved" for tight definitions of the task provided that restrictive assumptions can be made concerning the environment. If the environment can be populated with unique markers, or if a guidewire can be buried in the floor and dynamic features (including people) can be removed, most of the problems involved in point-to-point navigation can be completely solved.

Unfortunately, systems that require such engineering of the environment are fragile and prone to failure if the key landmarks fail or are somehow obscured. Perhaps more important, the inflexibility inherent in constraining the environment makes the use of robot systems less appealing for financial and logistic reasons. In addition to imposing environmental constraints, the use of existing robot systems implies a restricted and well-defined task specification. Existing systems are typically not general purpose but are designed for specific, one-off tasks.

It is clear that open problems exist across the entire spectrum of mobile robotics research. Several key requirements constrain mobile robots from being more widely and generally applied. Dividing the area broadly into locomotion, sensing, and control, several important problems can be identified.

10.1   Locomotion

10.1.1 Smooth Terrain

The vast majority of autonomous systems for ground-contact locomotion are based on simple wheels. Most systems are nonholonomic and have rather limited kinematics and dynamics; thus, they can only execute a restricted class of motions. Not only

---

* Adams [1], p. 73. Used with permission.

does this make path planning more complex, but it limits the robot's applicability and makes accurate modeling of the robot's actual behavior difficult. The use of compound wheels may help alleviate the limitations on the kinematic properties of wheeled robots, although it further complicates issues of accurate odometry (and cost). To date, a number of holonomic robots have been built, but their use is not widespread, and the research on these vehicles has, to date, concentrated primarily on the kinematics of the wheels rather than on evaluating the usefulness of the robots, which rely on the more complex wheel design.

As we have seen, legged walking robots may provide solutions to some of these difficulties. They certainly provide a technology to overcome the need for a continuous floor surface between start and goal positions. At present, however, few walking robots have been constructed, and almost none have been used to carry out significant tasks in real environments. Although the technology appears very promising, problems associated with controlling devices with many degrees of freedom and making them energy efficient, robust, and economical remain to be addressed. In practice, the use of complex gaits or feedback rules to maintain dynamic stability in a partially known environment makes serious demands on the sensing system of the robot. How can sensors be designed and positioned so that the ground upon which the feet might fall is sensed, and how can it be ensured that the ground will be able to hold the weight of the robot as it moves?

10.1.2 Flying and Swimming

Although most of the Earth's surface is covered by water, few submersible robotic systems exist. The design of systems for the actuation and control of underwater robots is fraught with unresolved issues. The use of underwater robots is limited by a combination of factors that hinder command and control: reasoning systems for fully autonomous behavior have not been sufficiently well developed, sensing for underwater applications is difficult, and communications with underwater robots is restricted. Together, these problems make the use of underwater robots difficult, but the partial resolution of problems with either autonomy or teleoperation would make such devices practical.

Flying robots are, to a large extent, constrained by problems of size, weight, and energy efficiency. Although lightweight computer systems are now available, the batteries needed to operate them as well as propulsion systems are a major difficulty for extended flight. As dynamically stable limbed robots, flying robots other than floaters (i.e., aerobots) must also meet very strict real-time constraints. Although a dynamic limbed robot may exhibit instabilities or potentially fall over when the real-time sensing and reasoning constraints are not met, jet-powered or helicopter-based flying robots literally fall out of the sky unless reliable real-time sensing and computational constraints can be met. Thus, the problems of computation and sensing that plague ground-plane robots are multiplied for flying vehicles.

These problems are compounded by the fact that if a flying robot is actually to accomplish a nonpassive task, it must also be equipped with effectors of some sort. One notable innovation in this regard is several types of experimental insect robots currently under development. In this context we should also mention nanorobots. Several teams are attempting to develop robots at a very small scale either for assembly tasks or biological applications such as diagnosis or therapy delivery. In a reversal of their operating scales, the problems faced by nanorobots dwarf those that constrain progress by either conventional flying or swimming mobile robots.

10.2   Sensors

Many key problems, not only for mobile robotics, but for intelligent systems as a whole, depend on sensing technologies. Even gait planning can be greatly simplified if the perception system of a robot is sophisticated enough to select appropriate foot placements.

Although vision and related sensing tasks often appear simple, many apparently simple sensing problems are still extremely challenging.

Perhaps the most fundamental statement that can be made concerning the development of sensors for mobile robots is that if the robot cannot sense an unexpected event, it cannot react to it. Most existing sensing technologies suffer from incomplete reporting of the data of interest (i.e., they fail to see some things) as well as the presence spurious measurements. Thus, it is not surprising that modern mobile robots typically use a number of different sensors designed to provide reasonably complete coverage of the entire space about the robot and to fuse the sensor readings to compensate for the shortcomings in any single sensing methodology. Weaknesses in one class of sensor can be addressed by providing different classes of sensors covering the same region about the robot. Establishing which sensors are correct (if any) and how to establish when the environment is suited to a particular sensor thus emerge as serious issues. This is the problem of sensor fusion: combining data from each of the sensors to establish a coherent environmental representation.

10.2.1 Nonvisual Sensors

The last few years have seen a considerable increase in our understanding of the performance and capabilities of various nonvisual sensors. Sonar, IR, radar, and inertial sensors have all been studied extensively, and their capabilities and limitations are reasonably well understood. Although the capabilities of individual sensors may be well understood, it is not always the case that existing algorithms exploit the known properties or live within the known restrictions of existing sensor classes. For example, errors in sonar measurements are not well approximated by a Gaussian error process, but many algorithms use this approximation as a first-order model.

10.2.2 Vision-Based Sensors

Vision is complicated by the vast quantities of data that are recovered and the problems inherent in understanding a three-dimensional world from the two-dimensional projection that is available from the video image. Vision systems that combine vision with other technologies such as BIRIS or LaserEye attempt to overcome some of the limitations of vision while retaining the advantages of really "seeing" the environment. On the other hand, there is a consensus that vision is a key technology for most mobile robotics applications.

10.3   Control

Because most robots are being built to solve specific tasks, the highest level of control that is typically built into working systems is at a task-specific level. Research into more general reasoning systems proposes to generate robots that can be programmed in a high-level, declarative language as opposed to the procedural language paradigm that is used in most systems. As the capabilities of the underlying robotic system become more robust and better understood and modeled, it may be that these capabilities can be expressed formally in higher-task-level control systems. This expression of performance and capabilities could then be exploited at the task level. Thus, one major advance that can be expected in terms of high-level robotic control is that knowledge of the robot's low-level performance can be integrated into higher levels of control. More generally, the construction of control systems that accommodate liveness, multiple spatial and temporal scales, and evolving task constraints is an important yet unrealized objective.

At lower abstraction levels, existing robotic systems typically rely on various real-time architectures to provide time-critical safety control of the robot. Many systems are manually tuned with no formal guarantee of safety or correctness. Advances in real-time control theory can be expected to transform these low-level controllers into systems with known performance bounds and known limits on their capabilities.

10.3.1 User Interface

As robots become truly useful, the design of effective user interfaces becomes even more essential. The classic floor-plan view with a point-and-click user interface that is common to many mobile robot projects may be well suited for point-to-point navigation but is inadequate for task-based control. At this very high "task level," considerable research is required into the design of effective user interfaces. A warehouse-cleaning robot should not be controlled by requiring the user to define specific paths throughout the warehouse, but at the same time more control is required than just some high-level function such as "clean" – a lower level of control may be required in certain situations but at a level higher than "go from (x_1, y_1) to (x_2, y_2)."

10.3.2 Shared Control

An even more complex user interface problem occurs when the goal is to provide *shared control*; that is, to keep the user in the control loop at an appropriate level of discourse. The problem is how to let the operator control different aspects of system behavior at different abstraction levels without interfering with other control systems that may be working on other goals.

10.4   System Integration

Although readily underestimated, the integration of disparate subsystems for control and sensing at a hardware and software level is a formidable challenge – one that is still as much an art as a science. A mobile robot system must combine a number of special-purpose pieces of hardware, deal with inputs from a variety of sensors with different time scales, and respond to external events in real time while attempting to meet various external goals. This is a daunting task in terms of software development with only these limitations, but in addition the system should run with minimum power consumption, use light- and shock-insensitive hardware, be relatively insensitive to unmodeled or unexpected environmental events, and exhibit intelligent recovery in the event of failure.

Software tools to support the development of autonomous systems are relatively rare, and tools for more static systems are not always readily applicable to the autonomous case. Thus, one fundamental hurdle to the development of robotic systems is the development of tools and techniques to support the development and integration of autonomous hardware and software systems.

Robots in science fiction seem empowered with performance characteristics far beyond what is possible with today's technology. Even partially anthropomorphic robots such as Cog [59] and others (e.g., [323]) have very little in common with the robots of science fiction. The problems of power, locomotion, processors, and so forth are formidable indeed, and static ground-based artificial intelligence systems are nowhere near the level of performance exhibited by even the most trivial robot of science fiction.

10.5   Future Directions

Given that the robots of science fiction are far beyond what is possible in the near future, what directions are likely for mobile robots in the near future? Although advances in the hardware mechanisms that underlie mobile robots are to be expected, it is the computational and sensing abilities of current mobile robots that impose the strongest constraints on current robot performance. Thus, for robots to move out of the laboratory and into the general environment, improvements in computation and sensing are essential. Research into sensing, representing, and manipulating space and planning within this space are essential to build more general-purpose autonomous robot systems.

Despite these intimidating obstacles, mobile robotic systems can be applied today to many real tasks. Mobile robotics also provides the leveraging technology for much of the rest of artificial intelligence and robotics: truly practical systems will have to be mobile. In addition, as a research domain, mobile robotics provides a context for truly legitimate system validation because few real issues can be ignored or dismissed, and interaction must occur in the real world and in real time (even when experiments are carried out in a research laboratory).

Although it may be several years before robots can be commanded to carry out arbitrary tasks with nonspecialized vocabulary, as our understanding of computational principles that underlie mobile robotics improves, we may one day be able to construct autonomous systems that respond appropriately to general commands:

> "Gort, Klaatu Barada Nikto."

10.6   Problems

1. Suggest what you believe is the most important single technical obstacle to the success of mobile robotics. Describe how you think this problem may eventually be resolved, assuming that it will be. What do you think the time line will be for this progress?
2. Suggest what you believe is the greatest non-technical obstacle to the widespread adoption of mobile robotics technologies. Discuss the issues involved and how you expect things to unfold.
3. Suggest an unexploited application domain for mobile robots. Propose an approach.

Bibliography

[1] D. Adams. *The Hitchhiker's Guide to the Galaxy*. Pan Books, London, 1979.

[2] P. E. Agre and D. Chapman. Pengi: An implementation of a theory of activity. In *Proc. 6th National Conference on AI*, vol. 1, pp. 268–272. Morgan Kaufman, 1987.

[3] L. Aguilar, R. Alami, S. Fleury, M. Herrb, F. Ingrand, and F. Robert. Ten autonomous mobile robots (and even more) in a route-networklike environment. In *Proc. IEEE/RSJ IROS*, vol. 2, pp. 260–267, Pittsburgh, PA, 1995.

[4] R. Alami, S. Fleury, M. Herrb, F. Ingrand, and F. Robert. Multi-robot cooperation in the MARTHA project. *IEEE Robotics & Automation Magazine*, 5(1):36–47, 1998.

[5] J. S. Albus, R. Quintero, and R. Lumia. An overview of NASREM: The NASA/NBS Standard Reference Model for Telerobot Control System Architecture. NIST Technical Report 5412, National Inst. of Standards and Technology, Gaithersburg, MD, April 1994.

[6] J. C. Alexander and J. H. Maddocks. On the kinematics of wheeled mobile robots. *Int. J. Robotics Res.*, 1990. Reprinted in *Autonomous Robot Vehicles*, I. J. Cox and G. T. Wilfong (eds.), Springer-Verlag, New York, pp. 5–24, 1990.

[7] J. Y. Alloimonos, L. Weiss, and A. Bandyopadhyay. Active vision. In *Proc. 1st ICCV*, IEEE Press, London, UK, pp. 35–54, 1987.

[8] J. Y. Aloimonos. Perspective approximations. *Image and Vision Computing*, 8(3):179–192, 1990.

[9] S. Alpern. The rendezvous search problem. *SAIM J. Control and Optimization*, 33(3):673–683, May 1995.

[10] S. Alpern and G. Shmuel. Rendezvous search on the line with distinguishable players. *SIAM J. Control and Optimization*, 33(4):1270–1276, 1995.

[11] N. M. Amosov, E. M. Kussul, and V. D. Fomenko. Transport robot with network control system. In *Proc. 4th IJCAI*, Tbilisi, Georgia, 1975.

[12] R. J. Anderson. SMART: A modular control architecture for telerobotics. *IEEE Robotics & Automation Magazine*, 2(3):10–18, September 1995.

[13] R. Arkin and R. Murphy. Autonomous navigation in a manufacturing environment. *IEEE Trans. Robotics and Automation*, 6(4):445–454, 1990.

[14] R. C. Arkin. Motor schema based navigation for a mobile robot: An approach to programming by behavior. In *Proc. IEEE Conference on Robotics and Automation*, pp. 264–271, Raleigh, NC, 1987. (Reprinted in *Autonomous Mobile Robots*, vol. 2, S. S. Iyengar and A. Elfes (eds.), IEEE Computer Society Press, 1991.)

[15] R. C. Arkin. Motor-schema-based mobile robot navigation. *Int. J. Robot. Res.*, 8(4):92–112, 1989.

[16] R. C. Arkin. Integrating behavioral, perceptual and world knowledge in reactive navigation. In P. Maes (ed.), *Designing Autonomous Agents*, pp. 105–122. MIT Press, Cambridge, MA, 1990.

[17] R. C. Arkin and J. D. Hobbs. Dimensions of communication and social organization in multi-agent robotics systems. *Proc. 2nd Int. Conf. on Simulation of Adaptive Behavior*, J.-A. Meyer, Rovitblat and S. Wilson (eds.), A Brandferd Book, 1992.

[18] B. Ash (ed.). *The Visual Encyclopedia of Science Fiction*. Harmondy Books, New York, 1977.

[19] I. Asimov. *Runaround*. In M. Greenberg (ed.), *The Asimov Chronicles, Volume I*. Ace Books, New York, 1990.

[20] N. Aucoin, O. Sandbekkhaug, and M. Jenkin. An immersive 3D user interface for mobile robot control. In *IASTED Int. Conf. on Applications of Control and Robotics*, pp. 1–4, Orlando, FL, 1996.

[21] D. Avis and H. Imai. Locating a robot with angle measurements. *J. Symbolic Computation*, 10:311–326, 1990.

[22] N. Ayache. *Artificial Vision for Mobile Robots: Stereo Vision and Multisensory Perception*. MIT Press, Cambridge, MA, 1991.

[23] N. Ayache and O. D. Faugeras. Maintaining representations of the environment of a mobile robot. *IEEE Trans. Robotics and Automation*, 5(6):804–819, 1989.

[24] K. Azarm and G. Schmidt. Conflict-free motion of multiple mobile robots based on decentralized motion planning and negotiation. In *Proc. IEEE Int. Conf. on Robotics and Automation*, pp. 3526–3533, Albuquerque, NM, 1997.

[25] R. A. Baeza-Yates, J. C. Culberson, and G. J. E. Rawlins. Searching in the plane. *Information and Computation*, 106:234–252, 1993.

[26] G. R. Baiden. Future robotic mining at INCO Limited – The next 25 years. *CIM Bulletin*, 89:36–40, 1996.

[27] R. Bajcsy and D. A. Rosenthal. Visual and conceptual focus of attention. In S. Tanimoto and A. Klinger (eds.), *Structured Computer Vision*. Academic Press, 1980.

[28] N. C. Baker, D. C. MacKenzie, and S. A. Ingalls. Development of an autonomous aerial vehicle: A case study. *Applied Intelligence*, 2(3):271–298, 1992.

[29] D. Ballard and C. Brown. *Computer Vision*. Prentice-Hall Inc., Englewood Cliffs, NJ, 1982.

[30] A. H. Barr. Superquadrics and angle-perserving transformations. *IEEE Comp. Graphics and Applications*, 1:11–23, 1981.

[31] J. Barraquand and J.-C. Latombe. Robot motion planning: A distributed representation approach. *Int. J. Robot. Res.*, 10:628–649, 1991.

[32] R. Basri and E. Rivlin. Homing using combinations of model views. In *Proc. Int. Joint Conf. of Artificial Intelligence*, pp. 1656–1591, Morgan Kaufman Publishers, Chambery, France, August 1993.

[33] K. Basye and T. Dean. Map learning with indistinguishable locations. In M. Henrion, L. N. Kanal, J. F. Lemmer (eds.), *Uncertainty in Artificial Intelligence 5*, pp. 331–340. Elsevier Science Publishers, 1990.

[34] M. Bayouth, I. Nourbakhsh, and C. Thorpe. A hybrid human-computer autonomous vehicle architecture. In *Proc. 3rd. ECPD*, pp. 137–143, Bremen, Germany, 1997.

[35] S. S. Beauchemin and J. L. Barron. The computation of optical flow. *ACM Computing Surveys*, 27(3):433–4666, 1995.

[36] G. A. Bekey. Biologically inspired control of autonomous robots. *Robotics and Autonomous Systems*, 18:21–31, 1996.

[37] G. Beni and J. Wang. Swarm intelligence in cellular robotic systems. In *Proc. NATO Advanced Workshop on Robotics and Biological Systems*, Il Ciocco, Tuscany, Italy, 1989.

[38] M. Betke and L. Gurvits. Mobile robot localization using landmarks. *IEEE Trans. Robotics and Automation*, 13(2):251–263, 1997.

[39] F. Blais, M. Rioux, and J. Domey. Compact three-dimensional camera for robot and vehicle guidance. *Opt. Lasers Eng.*, 10:227–239, 1989.

[40] A. Blake and A. Yuille (eds.). *Active Vision*. MIT Press, Cambridge, MA, 1992.

[41] R. P. Blakemore and R. B. Frankel. Magnetic navigation in bacteria. *Scientific American*, 245, 1981.

[42] M. Blum and D. Kozen. On the power of the compass (or why mazes are easier to search than graphs). In *19th Ann. Symp. Foundations of Computer Sci.*, pp. 132–142, October 1978.

[43] B. Bogert, J. Healy, and J. Tukey. The quefrequency analysis of time series for echoes: Cepstrum, pseudo-autocovariance, cross-cepstrum and saphe cracking. In M. Rosenblat (ed.), *Proc. Symp. on Time Series Analysis*, pp. 209–243. Wiley, New York, NY, 1963.

[44] M. Bolduc and M. D. Levine. A foveated retina system for robotic vision. In *Proc. VI'94*, Banff, Canada, 1994.

[45] D. L. Boley, E. S. Steinmetz, and K. Sutherland. Robot localization from landmarks using recursive total least squares. In *Proc. IEEE Int. Conf. on Robotics and Automation*, pp. 1381–1386, Minneapolis MN, April 1996.

[46] J. Borenstein and Y. Koren. Real-time obstacle avoidance for fast mobile robots. *IEEE Trans. Systems, Man, and Cybernetics*, 19(5):1179–1187, 1989.

[47] J. Borenstein and Y. Koren. The Vector Field Histogram – Fast obstacle avoidance for mobile robots. *IEEE Trans. Robotics and Automation*, 7(3):278–288, 1991.

[48] P. K. Bose. Visibility in Simple Polygons. Master's thesis, University of Waterloo, Waterloo, Ontario, Canada, December 1991.

[49] E. Bourque and G. Dudek. Automated image-based mapping. In *Workshop on Perception for Mobile Agents*, pp. 61–70. IEEE/CVPR, Santa Barbara, CA, 1998.

[50] E. Bourque, G. Dudek, and P. Ciaravola. Robotic sightseeing – A method for automatically creating virtual environments. In *Proc. IEEE Int. Conf. on Robotics and Automation*, Leuven, Belgium, 1998.

[51] S. M. Bozic. *Digital and Kalman Filtering*. Halsted Press, 1979.

[52] A. M. Bradley and D. R. Yoerger. Design and testing of the autonomous benthic explorer. In *Proc. AUVS-93 20th Ann. Technical Symposium and Exhibition*, p. 1044, Washington, DC, 1993.

[53] M. Briot and A. R. de Saint-Vincent. Three dimensional perceptory systems for autonomous mobile robots. In *Proc. 6th Int. Conf. on Robot Vision and Sensory Controls*, pp. 127–137, Paris, France, 1986.

[54] M. Briot, J. C. Talou, and G. Bauzil. Le systeme de perception du robot mobile HILARE. In *2eme Congres AFCET/IRIA*, Toulouse, France, 1979.

[55] R. A. Brooks. Solving the find-path problem by a good representation of free space. *IEEE Trans. Systems, Man, and Cybernetics*, 13(3):190–197, 1983.

[56] R. A. Brooks. A robust layered control system for a mobile robot. *IEEE J. of Robotics and Automation*, 2:14–23, 1986.

[57] R. A. Brooks. A robot that walks: Emergent behaviors from a carefully evolved network. In P. H. Winston and S. A. Shellard (eds.), *Artificial Intelligence at MIT Expanding Frontiers*, vol. 2, pp. 29–39. MIT Press, Boston, MA, 1990.

[58] R. A. Brooks. A robust layered control system for a mobile robot. In P. H. Winston and S. A. Shellard (eds.), *Artificial Intelligence at MIT Expanding Frontiers*, vol. 2, pp. 3–27. MIT Press, Boston, MA, 1990.

[59] R. A. Brooks and L. A. Stein. Building brains for bodies. Technical report, MIT, August, 1993.

[60] B. Brumitt and A. Stentz. Dynamic mission planning for multiple mobile robots. In *Proc. IEEE Int. Conf. on Robotics and Automation*, pp. 2396–2401, Minneapolis, MN, April 1996.

[61] B. Brummit. Dynamic mission planning for multiple mobile robots. In *Proc. IEEE Int. Conf. on Robotics and Automation*, Minneapolis, MN, 1996.

[62] B. Brummit and M. Hebert. Experiments in autonomous driving with concurrent goals and multiple vechicles. In *Proc. IEEE Int. Conf. on Robotics and Automation*, Leuven, Belgium, 1998.

[63] P. Burt, P. Anandan, K. Hanna, G. van der Wal, and R. Bassman. A front-end vision processor for vehicle navigation. In *IAS-3*, pp. 653–662, Pittsburgh, PA, 1993.

[64] G. Campion, G. Bastin, and B. D'Andrea-Novel. Structural properties and classification of kinematic and dynamic models of wheeled mobile robots. *IEEE Trans. Robotics and Automation*, 12(1):47–62, 1996.

[65] J. Canny. A computational approach to edge detection. *IEEE Trans. Pattern Analysis and Machine Intelligence*, 8(6):679–698, 1986.

[66] Y. U. Cao, A. S. Fukunaga, A. B. Kahng, and F. Meng. Cooperative mobile robotics: Antecedents and directions. In *Proc. IEEE/RSJ IROS*, vol. 1, pp. 226–234, Pittsburgh, PA, 1995.

[67] A. Chang. The intelligent vehicle on an automated highways system: ADVANCE-F. In *Proc. IAS-3*, pp. 225–229, Pittsburgh, PA, 1993.

[68] R. Chatila and J. Laumond. Position referencing and consistent world modelling for mobile robots. In *Proc. IEEE Int. Conf. on Robotics and Automation*, pp. 138–170, 1985.

[69] M. Chen, T. M. Jochem, and D. A. Pomerleau. AURORA: A vision-based roadway departure warning system. In *Proc. IEEE/RSJ IROS*, vol. 1, Pittsburgh, PA, 1995.

[70] M. Cheney. *Tesla, Man Out of Time*. Prentice Hall, Englewood Cliffs, NJ, 1981.

[71] S. K. Choi. Design of advanced underwater robotic vehicle and graphic workstation. In *Proc. IEEE Int. Conf. on Robotics and Automation*, vol. 2, pp. 99–105, Atlanta, GA, 1993.

[72] S. K. Choi, J. Yuh, and G. Y. Takashige. Development of the omnidirectional intelligent navigator. *IEEE Robotics & Automation Magazine*, 2(1):44–51, 1995.

[73] W. W. Chow, J. Geo-Banacloche, L. M. Pedrotti, V. E. Sanders, W. Schleich, and M. O. Scully. The Ring Laser Gyro. *Reviews of Modern Physics*, 57(1):61–104, 1985.

[74] J. Clark and N. Ferrier. Attentive visual servoing. In *Active Vision*, pp. 137–154. MIT Press, Cambridge, MA, 1992.

[75] A. C. Clarke. *2001: A Space Odyssey*. Hutchinson/Star, London, 1968. A novel based on the original screenplay by Stanley Kubrick and Arthur C. Clarke.

[76] L. S. Coles, A. M. Robb, P. L. Sinclair, M. H. Smith, and R. B. Sobek. Decision analysis for an experimental robot with unreliable sensors. In *Proc. 4th IJCAI*, 1975.

[77] C. Connolly. Harmonic functions and collision probabilities. In *Proc. Int. Conf. on Robotics and Automation*, pp. 3015–3019, San Diego, CA, 1994.

[78] C. Connolly and R. Grupen. On the applications of harmonic functions to robotics. *J. Robotic Systems*, 10(7):931–946, 1993.

[79] P. I. Corke, D. Hainsworth, G. Winstanley, Y. Li, and H. Gurgenci. Automated control of a dragline using machine vision. In *Proc. Electrical Engineering Congress*, pp. 597–600, Sydney, Australia, 1994.

[80] P. I. Corke, G. J. Winstanley, J. M. Roberts, and Z.-D. Li. Applications of robotics and robot vision to mining automation. In *Proc. Workshop on Robotics and Robot Vision*, pp. 56–61, Gold Coast, Australia, 1996. Held in conjunction with the 4th Int. Symp. on Signal Processing and Applications.

[81] R. Courant and D. Hilbert. *Methods of Mathematical Physics*, vol. 1. Interscience Publishers, New York, 1937.

[82] I. J. Cox. Blanche – An experiment in guidance and navigation of an autonomous robot vehicle. *IEEE Trans. Robotics and Automation*, 7(2):193–204, April 1991.

[83] I. J. Cox and G. T. Wilfong (eds.). *Autonomous Robot Vehicles*. Springer-Verlag, New York, 1990.

[84] J. C. Craig. *Introduction to Robots*. Addison-Wesley, Don Mills, Canada, 1986.

[85] J. L. Crowley, P. Bobet, and M. Mesrabi. Layered control of a binocular head. In *SPIE Conf. on AI X: Machine vision and robotics*, pp. 47–61, Orlando, FL, 1992.

[86] J. L. Crowley and H. I. Christensen (eds.). *Vision as Process*. Springer-Verlag, Berlin, Germany, 1995.

[87] J. L. Crowley and A. Parker. Transfer function analysis of picture processing operators. In R. M. Haralick and J. C. Simon (eds.), *Issues in Digital Signal Processing*, pp. 3–30. Sitjhoff and Hoordhoff, Germantown, MD, 1980.

[88] J. L. Crowley, F. Wallner, and B. Schiele. Position estimation using principal components of range data. In *Proc. IEEE Conf. on Robotics and Automation*, pp. 3131–3128, Leuven, Belgium, 1998.

[89] Cyclovision Technologies, Inc. *The ParaCamera System*. Undated product sheet.

[90] A. Datta and C. Icking. Competitive searching in a generalized street. In *Proc. 10th Ann. Symp. Computational Geometry*, pp. 175–182, Stony Brook, NY, June 6–8, 1994. ACM Press.

[91] J. G. Daugman. Six formal properties of two-dimensional anisotropic visual filters: Structural principles and frequency/orientation selectivity. *IEEE Trans. Sys. Man. Cyb.*, 13:882–887, 1983.

[92] X. Deng and A. Mirzaian. Competitive robot mapping with homogeneous markers. *IEEE Trans. Robotics and Automation*, 12(4):532–542, August 1996.

[93] Modular Research Vehicle MRV-1: Heavy duty mobile robot. Undated product sheet, Denning Mobile Robots Inc.

[94] R. Deriche. Using Canny's criteria to derive an optimal edge detector recursively implemented. *IJCV*, 2:167–187, 1987.

[95] A. Desrochers (ed.). *Intelligent Robotic Systems for Space Exploration*. Kluwer Academic Publishers, Boston, MA, 1992.

[96] P. K. Dick. *Blade Runner (Do Androids Dream of Electric Sheep?)*. Ballantine Books, New York, 1982.

[97] B. R. Donald. A search algorithm for motion planning with six degrees of freedom. *Artificial Intelligence*, 31(3):295–353, 1987.

[98] S. Dubowsky and E. Papadopoulos. The kinematics, dynamics and control of free-flying and free-floating space robotic systems. *Special Issue on Space Robotics of the IEEE Transactions on Robotics and Automation*, 9(5):531–543, 1993. (Invited paper).

[99] G. Dudek. Environment mapping using multiple abstraction levels. *Proc. IEEE*, 84(11):375–397, 1996.

[100] G. Dudek and M. Jenkin. A multi-level development environment for mobile robotics. In *IAS-3*, pp. 542–550, Pittsburgh, PA, 1993.

[101] G. Dudek, M. Jenkin, E. Milios, and D. Wilkes. Robotic exploration as graph construction. Technical Report RBCV-TR-88-23, Research in Biological and Computational Vision, Department of Computer Science, University of Toronto, 1988.

[102] G. Dudek, M. Jenkin, E. Milios, and D. Wilkes. Map validation and self-location in a graph-like world. In *Proc. 13th Int. Conf. Artificial Intelligence*, pp. 1648–1653, Chambery, France, August 1993.

[103] G. Dudek, M. Jenkin, E. Milios, and D. Wilkes. On the utility of multi-agent autonomous robot systems. In *Proc. IJCAI-93 Workshop on Dynamically Interacting Robots*, Chambery, France, pp. 101–108, 1993.

[104] G. Dudek, M. Jenkin, E. Milios, and D. Wilkes. A taxonomy for swarm robotics. In *Proc. IEEE/RSJ IROS*, pp. 441–447, Yokohama, Japan, 1993.

[105] G. Dudek, M. Jenkin, E. Milios, and D. Wilkes. Topological exploration of unknown environments with multiple robots. In *ISORA'98*, Anchorage, AL, 1998. Proceedings on CDROM.

[106] G. Dudek, M. Jenkin, E. Milios, and David Wilkes. Robotic exploration as graph construction. *IEEE Trans. Robotics and Automation*, 7(6):859–864, 1991.

[107] G. Dudek, M. R. M. Jenkin, E. Milios, and D. Wilkes. A taxonomy for multi-agent robotics. *Autonomous Robots*, 3:375–397, 1996.

[108] G. Dudek, K. Romanik, and S. Whitesides. Localizing a robot with minimum travel. Technical Report SOCS-94.5, School of Computer Science, McGill University, August 1994.

[109] G. Dudek, K. Romanik, and S. Whitesides. Localizing a robot with minimum travel. In *Proc. 6th ACM-SIAM Symp. Discrete Algorithms*, San Francisco, CA, January 1995.

[110] L. Durrant-Whyte. An automated guided vehicle for cargo handling applications. *Int. J. Rob. Res.*, 15(5):407–440, 1996.

[111] A. Elfes. Sonar-based real-world mapping and navigation. *IEEE J. Robotics and Automation*, 3(3):249–265, June 1987.

[112] R. Ellepola and P. Kovesi. Mobile robot navigation in a semi-structured environment. In *Proc. ICARCV*, vol. 2, pp. 914–918, Singapore, 1996.

[113] S. P. Engelson and D. V. McDermott. Image signatures for place recognition and map construction. In *SPIE Proc. Sensor Fusion IV: Control Paradigms and Data Structures*, pp. 282–293, 1991.

[114] W. Enkelmann, G. Nirschl, V. Gengenbach, W. Krüger, S. Rössle, and W. Tölle. Realization of a driver's warning assistant for intersections. In *Proc. Intelligent Vehicles '93*, pp. 72–76, 1993.

[115] M. Erdmann and T. Lozano-Perez. On multiple moving objects. *Algorithmica*, 2(4):477–521, 1987.

[116] H. R. Everett. *Sensors for Mobile Robots: Theory and Applications*. A. K. Peters, Wellesley, MA, 1995.

[117] G. Farin. *NURB Curves and Surfaces from Projective Geometry to Practical Use*. A. K. Peters, Wellesley, MA, 1995.

[118] O. Faugeras. *Three-Dimensional Computer Vision: A Geometric Viewpoint*. MIT Press, Cambridge, MA, 1993.

[119] N. J. Ferrier and J. J. Clark. The Harvard binocular head. In *Active Robot Vision: Camera Heads, Model Based Navigation and Reactive Control*, pp. 9–32. World Scientific Press, Singapore, 1993.

[120] L. Ferrière, B. Raucent, and J.-C. Semin. ROLLMOBS, a new omnidirectional robot. In *IEEE/RSJ IROS*, pp. 913–918, Grenoble, France, 1997.

[121] J. Feruson and A. Pope. THESEUS: Multipurpose Canadian AUV. *Sea Technology Magazine*, 1995.

[122] R. E. Fikes and N. J. Nilsson. STRIPS: A new approach to the application of theorem proving to problem solving. *Artif. Intell.*, 2:189–208, 1971.

[123] R. J. Firby. Task networks for controlling continuous processes. In *Proc. 2nd Int. Conf. on AI planning Systems*, Chicago, IL, 1994.

[124] M. Fischler and O. Firschein, (eds.). *Readings in Computer Vision: Issues, Problems, Principles, and Paradigms*. Morgan Kaufmann, Los Altos, CA, 1987.

[125] D. Fleet and A. D. Jepson. A cascaded filter approach to the construction of velocity sensitive mechanisms. Technical report, Research in Biological and Computational Vision, RBCV-TR-84-6, University of Toronto, 1984.

[126] S. Fleury, P. Souères, J.-P. Laumond, and R. Chatila. Primitives for smoothing mobile robot trajectories. *IEEE Trans. Robotics and Automation*, 11(3):441–448, 1995.

[127] J. Forsberg, U. Larsson, P. Ahman, and A. Wernersson. Navigation in cluttered rooms using a range measuring laser and the Hough transform. In *Proc. IAS-3*, pp. 248–257, Pittsburgh, PA, 1993.

[128] D. Fox, W. Burgard, and S. Thrun. Estimating the absolute position of a mobile robot using position probability grids. In *Proc. 13th National Conf. Artificial Intelligence (AAAI'96)*, pp. 896–901, Portland, OR, 1996.

[129] D. Fox, W. Burgard, S. Thrun, and A.B. Cremers. Position estimation for mobile robots in dynamic environments. In *Proc. 15th National Conf. on Artificial Intelligence (AAAI'98)*, Madison, WI, 1998.

[130] J. A. Freeman and D. M. Skapura. *Neural Networks: Algorithms, Applications, and Programming Techniques*. Addison-Wesley, Reading, MA, 1991.

[131] L. Fu. *Neural Networks in Computer Intelligence*. McGraw-Hill, New York, 1994.

[132] T. Fuji, U. Tamaki, and Y. Kuroda. Mission execution experiments with a newly developed AUV 'The Twin-Burger'. In *Proc. 8th Int. Symp. Unmanned Untethered Submersible Technology*, pp. 92–105, Durham, NC, 1939.

[133] A. Gelb. *Applied Optimal Estimation*. MIT Press, Cambridge, MA, 1974.

[134] R. Gershon, A. D. Jepson, and J. K. Tsotsos. Highlight identification using chromatic information. In *Proc. Int. Conf. Computer Vision*, pp. 161–170, 1987.

[135] G. Giralt, R. Chatila, and M. Vaisset. An integrated navigation and motion control system for autonomous multisensory mobile robots. In M. Brady and R. Paul (eds.), *1st Int. Symp. Robotics Research*, pp. 191–214. MIT Press, Cambridge, MA, 1984.

[136] T. Gomi and P. Volpe. Collision avoidance using behavioral-based AI techniques. In *Proc. Intelligent Vehicles*, pp. 141–145, Tokyo, 1993.

[137] E. Grimson. *From Images to Surfaces*. MIT Press, Cambridge, MA, 1981.

[138] L. J. Guibas, R. Motwani, and P. Raghavan. The Robot Localization Problem in Two Dimensions. In *Proc. 3rd Ann. ACM-SIAM Symp. on Discrete Algorithms*, pp. 259–268, Orlando, FL, January 27–29 1992.

[139] S. Hackwood and G. Beni. Self-organization of sensors for swarm intelligence. In *IEEE Trans. Robotics and Automation*, pp. 819–829, 1992.

[140] K. Z. Haigh. Situation-Dependent Learning for Interleaved Planning and Robot Execution. Ph.D. thesis, Computer Science Department, Carnegie Mellon University, Pittsburgh, PA, February 1998.

[141] K. Z. Haigh and M. M. Veloso. Planning, execution and learning in a robotic agent. In R. Simmons, M. Veloso, and S. Smith (eds.), *Proc. AI Planning Systems '98*, pp. 120–127, Pittsburgh, PA, 1998.

[142] R. Hanley. *Is Data Human: The Metaphysics of Star Trek.* Basic Books, New York, 1997.

[143] K. R. Harinarayan and V. Lumelsky. Sensor-based motion planning for multiple mobile robots in an uncertain environment. In *IEEE/RSJ IROS, Int. Conf. Intelligent Robots and Systems.*, vol. 3, pp. 1485–1492, Munich, Germany, 1994.

[144] S. Y. Harmon. The ground surveillance robot (GSR): An autonomous vehicle designed to transit unknown terrain. *IEEE Trans. Robotics and Automation*, 3(3), 1987.

[145] L. Harris and M. Jenkin, (eds.) *Vision and Action.* Cambridge University Press, New York, 1998.

[146] B. Harvey. *The New Russian Space Program: From Competition to Collaboration.* John Wiley and Sons, Chichester, UK, 1996.

[147] M. Heller, J.-P. R. Bayard, and M. Kress. An autonomous shadow vehicle using microwave, vision and GPS technology. In *Proc. ICARCV*, vol. 2, pp. 883–887, Singapore, 1996.

[148] J. Hertz, A. Krobh, and R. Pamer. *Introduction to the Theory of Neural Computation.* Addison–Wesley, Reading, MA, 1991.

[149] M. Hildebrand. Symmetrical gaits of horses. *Science*, 150:701–708, 1967.

[150] K. Hirai, M. Hirose, Y. Haikawa, and T. Takenaka. The development of Honda humanoid robot. In *Proc. IEEE Conf. Robotics and Automation*, pp. 1321–1326, 1998.

[151] J. Hodgins and M. H. Raibert. Planar robot goes head over heels. *ASME Winter Annual Meeting*, Boston, MA, 1987.

[152] J. K. Hodgins and M. H. Raibert. Biped gymnastics. In P. H. Winston and S. A. Shellard (eds.), *Artificial Intelligence at MIT Expanding Frontiers*, pp. 180–205. MIT Press, Cambridge, MA, 1990.

[153] W. D. Holcombe, S. L. Dickerson, J. W. Larsen, and R. A. Bohlander. Advances in guidance systems for industrial automated guided vehicles. In *Proc. SPIE Mobile Robots III*, Cambridge, MA, 1988.

[154] A. A. Holenstein, M. A. Müller, and E. Badreddin. Mobile robot localization in a structured environment cluttered with obstacles. In *IEEE Int. Conf. Robotics and Automation*, pp. 2576–2581, Nice, France, May 1992.

[155] B. Hölldobler. Colony-specific territorial pheremone in the African weaver ant *oecophylla lognioda (latreille).* In *Proc. National Academy of Science of the USA*, vol. 74, pp. 2072–2075, 1977.

[156] B. Hölldobler, R. C. Stanton, and H. Markl. Recruitment and food-retrieving behavior in *novomesor (formicidae, hymenoptera)* i. chemical signals. *Behav. Ecol. Sociobiol.*, 4:163, 1978.

[157] B. Horn. *Robot Vision.* MIT Press, Cambridge, MA, 1986.

[158] B. K. P. Horn and B. G. Schunk. Determining optical flow. *Artif. Intell.*, 17:185–204, 1981.

[159] I. Howard. *Human Visual Orientation.* John Wiley and Sons Ltd., Chichester, NY, 1982.

[160] I. Howard and B. Rodgers. *Binocular Vision and Stereopsis.* Oxford University Press, Oxford, 1995.

[161] H. Hu. Sensor-based control architecture. In S. Cameron and P. Probert (eds.), *Advanced Guided Vehicles: Aspects of the Oxford AGV Project*, pp. 17–36. World Scientific Press, Singapore, 1994.

[162] H. Hu and M. Brady. A parallel processing architecture for sensor-based control of intelligent mobile robots. *Robotics and Autonomous Systems*, 17:235–257, 1996.

[163] R. Hurteau, M. St-Amant, Y. Laperriere, and G. Chevrette. Optical guidance system for underground mine vehicles. In *Proc. IEEE Int. Conf. on Robotics and Automation*, vol. 1, pp. 639–644, Nice, France, 1992.

[164] Y. K. Hwang and H. Ahuja. A potential field approach to path planning. *IEEE Trans. Robotics and Automation*, 8(1):23–32, 1992.

[165] L. Hyafil and R. L. Rivest. Constructing Optimal Binary Decision Trees is NP-Complete. *Information Processing Letters*, 5(1):15–17, May 1976.

[166] K. Ishioka, K. Hiraki, and Y. Anzai. Cooperative map generation by heterogeneous autonomous mobile robots. In *Proc. of the Workshop on Dynamically Interacting Robots*, pp. 58–67, Chambery, France, 1993.

[167] R. Janssen, W. Ritter, F. Stein, and S. Ott. Hybrid approach for traffic sign recognition. In *Proc. Intelligent Vehciles '93*, pp. 390–395, 1993.

[168] R. Jarvis and A. Lipton. GO-2: An autonomous mobile robot for a science museum. In *Proc. ICARCV*, vol. 1, pp. 260–266, Singapore, 1996.

[169] P. Jasiobedzki, M. Jenkin, E. Milios, B. Down, J. Tsotsos, and T. Campbell. Laser eye – A new 3d sensor for active vision. In *SPIE Intelligent Robotics and Computer Vision: Sensor Fusion VI*, pp. 316–321, Boston, MA, 1993.

[170] M. Jenkin and A. Jepson. Detecting floor anomalies. In *Proc. BMVC*, pp. 731–740, York, U.K., 1994.

[171] M. Jenkin, A. Jepson, and J. K. Tsotsos. Techniques for disparity measurement. *CVGIP: IU*, 53(1):14–30, 1991.

[172] A. Jepson and M. J. Black. Mixture models for optical flow computation. In *Proc. IEEE Conf. Computer Vision and Pattern Recognition (CVPR)*, pp. 760–761, New York, June 1993.

[173] A. D. Jepson, D. Fleet, and M. R. M. Jenkin. Improving phase-based disparity measurements. *CVGIP: IU*, 53(2):198–210, 1991.

[174] T. M. Jochem, D. A. Pomerleau, and C. E. Thorpe. MANIAC a next generation neurally based autonomous road follower. In *Proc. IAS-3*, pp. 592–599, Pittsburgh, PA, 1993.

[175] D. G. Jones and J. Malik. A computational framework for determining stereo correspondence from a set of linear spatial filters. In *ECCV'92*, pp. 395–410, Santa Margherita Ligure, Italy, 1992.

[176] J. Jones and A. Flynn. *Mobile Robots: Inspiration to Implementation*. A. K. Peters, Wellesley, MA, 1993.

[177] L. P. Kaelbling. *Learning in Embedded Systems*. MIT Press, Cambridge, MA, 1993.

[178] R. E. Kalman. A new approach to linear filtering and prediction problems, *Trans. ASME J. of Basic Engineering*, 35–45, 1960.

[179] I. Kamon and E. Rivlin. Sensory based motion planning with global proofs. In *Proc. IEEE/RSJ IROS*, vol. 2, pp. 435–440, Minneapolis, MN, 1995. IEEE Press.

[180] K. Kant and S. W. Zucker. Towards efficient trajectory planning: The path-velocity decomposition. *Int. J. Robot. Res.*, 5(3):72–89, 1986.

[181] L. Kavraki, P. Svestka, J.-C. Latombe, and M. H. Overmars. Probabilistic roadmaps for path planning in high-dimensional configuration spaces. *IEEE Trans. Robotics and Automation*, 12(4):566–580, 1996.

[182] O. Khatib. Real-time obstacle avoidance for manipulators and mobile robots. *Int. J. Robotics Res.*, 5(1):90–98, 1986.

[183] Khepera: The miniature mobile robot. Undated product sheet, Khepera Support Team.

[184] J.-H. Kim, H.-S. Shim, H.-S. Kim, M.-J. Jung, and P. Vadakkepat. Micro-robot soccer system: Action selection mechanism and strategies. In *Proc. 3rd. ECPD*, pp. 151–156, Bremen, Germany, 1997.

[185] S. J. King and C. F. R. Weiman. HelpMate autonomous mobile robot navigation system. In *Proc. SPIE Mobile Robots V*, pp. 190–198, Cambridge, MA, 1990.

[186] R. Klein. Walking an Unknown Street with Bounded Detour. *Computational Geometry: Theory and Applications*, 1:325–351, 1992.

[187] J. M. Kleinberg. The localization problem for mobile robots. In *Proc. 35th IEEE Conf. Foundations of Computer Science*, Santa Fe, NM, Nov. 1994. IEEE Computer Society Press.

[188] D. E. Koditschek. Robot planning and control via potential functions. In O. Khatib, J. J. Craig, and T. Lozano-Perez (eds.), *The Robotics Review 1*. MIT Press, Cambridge, MA, 1989.

[189] J. J. Koenderink. The structure of images. *Biol. Cyber.*, 50:363–370, 1984.

[190] S. Koenig and R. G. Simmons. Unsupervised learning of probabilistic models for robot navigation. In *Proc. IEEE Int. Conf. Robotics and Automation*, pp. 2301–2308, 1996.

[191] A. B. Kogan. The effect of a constant magnetic field on the movement of paramecia. *Biofizika*, 10:292, 1965.

[192] K. Konolige. Improved occupancy grids for map. *Autonomous Robots*, 4:351–367, 1997.

[193] A. Kosaka and J. Pan. Perdue experiments in model-based vision for hallway navigation. In *Proc. IEEE Workshop on Vision for Robots*, pp. 87–96, Pittsburgh, PA, 1995.

[194] E. Krotkov, R. Simmons, and W. Whittaker. Autonomous walking results with the ambler hexapod planetary rover. In *Proc. IAS-3*, pp. 46–53, Pittsburgh, PA, 1993.

[195] R. Kuc and M. W. Siegel. Physically based simulation model for acoustic sensor robot navigation. *IEEE Trans. Pattern Analysis and Machine Intelligence*, 9(6):766–768, 1987.

[196] B. J. Kuipers and Y.-T. Byun. A qualitative approach to robot exploration and map-learning. In *Proc. IEEE Workshop Spatial Reasoning and Multi-Sensor Fusion*, pp. 390–404, Los Altos, CA, 1987.

[197] B. J. Kuipers and Y.-T. Byun. A robot exploration and mapping strategy based on a semantic hierachy of spatial representations. *Robotics and Autonomous Systems*, 8:46–63, 1991.

[198] B. J. Kuipers and T. Levitt. Navigation and mapping in large-scale space. *AI Magazine*, pp. 25–43, summer 1988.

[199] S. Lacroix and G. Dudek. On the identification of sonar features. In *Proc. IEEE/RSJ IROS*, Grenoble, France, September 1997.

[200] C. Lailler, J.-P. Deparis, and J.-G. Postaire. Adaptive white line detection and modelisation for autonomous visual navigation of a road following vehicle for real-time obstacle detection in road traffic. In *Proc. IAS-3*, pp. 116–124, Pittsburgh, PA, 1993.

[201] S. Lange, L. Korba, and A. Wong. Characterizing and modelling a sonar ring. In *Proc. SPIE Mobile Robotics IV*, pp. 291–304, Philadelphia, 1989.

[202] J.-C. Latombe. *Robot Motion Planning*. Kluwer, Norwell, MA, 1991.

[203] D. T. Lee and R. L. Drysdale III. Generalized Voronoi diagrams in the plain. *SIAM J. Comput*, 10(1):73–87, 1981.

[204] J. J. Leonard and H. F. Durrant-Whyte. Mobile robot localization by tracking geometric beacons. *IEEE Trans. Robotics and Automation*, 7(3):376–382, 1991.

[205] J. J. Leonard and H. F. Durrant-Whyte. *Directed Sonar Sensing for Mobile Robot Navigation*. Kluwer Academic Publishers, Boston, MA, 1992.

[206] J. J. Leonard, H. F. Durrant-Whyte, and I. J. Cox. Dynamic map building for an autonomous mobile robot. *Int. J. Robotics Research*, 11(4):286–298, August 1992.

[207] H. J. Levesque, R. Reiter, Yves Lesperance, F. Lin, and R. B. Scherl. Golog: A logic programming language for dynamic domains. *J. of Logic Programming. Special Issue on Reasoning About Action and Change*, 1997.

[208] M. A. Lewis, A. H. Fagg, and G. A. Bekey. The USC autonomous flying vehicle: An experiment in real-time behavior-based control. *Proc. IEEE/RSJ IROS*, Yokohama, Japan, 1993.

[209] S. Li, A. Ochi, Y. Yagi, and M. Yachida. Making 2d map of environments by observing scenes both along routes and at intersections. In *Workshop on Perception for Mobile Agents*, pp. 71–78. IEEE/CVPR, Santa Barbara, CA, 1998.

[210] L. Lisowski and G. Baille. Specifications of a small electric vehicle: Modular and distributed approach. In *Proc. IEEE/RSJ IROS*, pp. 919–924, Grenoble, France, 1997.

[211] R. A. Liston and R. S. Mosher. A versatile walking truck. In *Proc. 1968 Transportation Engineering Conference ASME-NYAS*, Washington, DC, 1968.

[212] J. Loeb. *Forced Movements, Tropisms, and Animal Conduct*. Philadelphia, London, 1918, Lippincott, Philadelphia, PA.

[213] F. Lu and E. Milios. Globally consistent range scan alignment for environment mapping. *Autonomous Robots*, 4(4):333–349, 1997.

[214] F. Lu and E. Milios. Robot pose estimation in unknown environments by matching 2d range scans. *J. Intelligent and Robotic Systems*, 18:249–275, 1997.

[215] V. Lumelsky, S. Mukhopadhyay, and K. Sun. Sensor-based terrain acquisition: The "sightseer" strategy. In *Proc. IEEE Conf. on Decision and Control Including the Symposium on Adaptive Processes*, vol. 2, pp. 1157–1161, IEEE Service Center, Piscataway, NJ, USA, 1989.

[216] V. Lumelsky and A. Stepanov. Path-planning strategies for a point mobile automaton moving amidst unknown obstacles of arbitrary shape. *Algorithmica*, 2(4):403–440, 1987.

[217] V. J. Lumelsky, S. Mukhopadhyay, and K. Sun. Dynamic path planning in sensor-based terrain acquisition. *IEEE Trans. Robotics and Automation*, 6(4):462–472, 1990.

[218] W. S. MacDonald. Design and implementation of a multilegged walking robot. Senior Honours Thesis, 1994.

[219] P. MacKenzie and G. Dudek. Precise positioning using model-based maps. In *Proc. Int. Conf. Robotics and Automation*, pp. 1615–1621, San Diego, CA, 1994.

[220] N. Maitland and C. Harris. A video based tracker for use in computer surgery. In *Proc. BMVC*, vol. 2, pp. 609–615, 1994.

[221] R. Malik and E. T. Polkowski. Robot location densities. In *Proc. SPIE Mobile Robotics V*, pp. 280–290, Boston, 1990.

[222] A. Mandow, J. M. Gomez de Gabriel, J. L. Martinez, V F. Munoz, A. Ollero, and A. Garcia-Cerezo. The autonomous mobile robot AURORA for greenhouse operation. *IEEE Robotics & Automation Magazine*, pp. 18–28, 1996.

[223] D. J. Manko. *A General Model of Legged Locomotion on Natural Terrain*. Kluwer Academic Publishers, Norwell, MA, 1992.

[224] I. Mantegh, M. R. M. Jenkin, and A. A. Goldenberg. Reformulating the potential field method for goal-attaining, real-time path planning. In *3rd ECPD Int. Conf. Advanced Robotics, Intelligent Automation and Active Systems*, pp. 132–144, Bremen, Germany, 1997.

[225] D. B. Marco, A. J. Healey, and R. B. McGhee. Autonomous underwater vehicles: Hybrid control of mission and motion. *Autonomous Robots*, 3:169–186, 1996.

[226] D. Marr. *Vision*. W. H. Freeman and Co., New York, 1982.

[227] D. Marr and E. Hildreth. Theory of edge detection. *Proc. Roy. Soc. (Lond.) B*, 207:187–217, 1980.

[228] A. B. Martinez, J. Climent, R. M. Planas, and J. M. Asensio. Vision-base compass for mobile robot orientation. In *Proc. Intelligent Vehicles*, pp. 293–296, Tokyo, 1993.

[229] P. Masani (ed.). *Norbert Wiener: Collected Works with Commentaries, Vol. IV*. MIT Press, Cambridge, MA, 1985.

[230] M. J. Mataric. Environmental learning using a distributed representation. In *IEEE Int. Conf. Robotics and Automation*, vol. 1, pp. 402–406, 1990.

[231] M. J. Mataric. Minimizing complexity in controlling a mobile robot population. In *IEEE Trans. Robotics and Automation*, pp. 830–835, 1992.

[232] M. J. Mataric, M. Nilsson, and K. T. Simsarian. Cooperative multi-robot box-pushing. In *Proc. IEEE/RSJ IROS*, vol. 3, pp. 556–561, Pittsburgh, PA, 1995.

[233] J. Mayhew, J. Frisby, and P. Gale. Psychophysical and computational studies towards a theory of human stereopsis. *Art. Intel.*, 17:349–385, 1981.

[234] J. McCarthy and P. J. Hayes. Some philosophical problems from the standpoint of artificial intelligence. *Mach. Intell.*, 4:295–324, 1969.

[235] J. McClelland and D. Rumelhart. *Parallel Distributed Processing Vols. I and II*. MIT Press, Cambridge, MA, 1986.

[236] D. McDermott. A reactive plan language. Technical Report YALEU/CSD/RR 864, Yale University Department of Computer Science, 1991.

[237] R. B. McGhee. Some finite state aspects of legged locomotion. *Mathematical Biosciences*, 2:67–84, 1968.

[238] C. D. McGillem and G. R. Cooper. *Continuous and Discrete Signal and System Analysis*. Holt, Rinehart, and Winston, 1974.

[239] F. Steinand and G. Medioni. Map-based localization using the panoramic horizon. *IEEE Trans. Robotics and Automation*, 11(6):892–896, 1995.

[240] R. C. Michelini, G. M. Acaccia, M. Callegari, R. M. Molfino, and R. P. Razzoli. Robot harvesting of citrus fruits. In *Proc. 3rd. ECPD*, pp. 447–452, Bremen, Germany, 1997.

[241] E. Milios, M. Jenkin, and J. Tsotsos. Design and performance of TRISH, a binocular robot head with torsional eye movements. In *Active Robot Vision: Camera Heads, Model-Based Navigation and Reactive Control*, pp. 51–68. World Scientific Press, Singapore, 1993.

[242] D. Miller and M. Slack. Design and testing of a low-cost robotic wheelchair. *Autonomous Robots*, 2:77–88, 1995.

[243] N. Miyake, T. Aona, K. Fujii, Y. Matsuda, and S. Hatsumoto. Position estimation and path control of an autonomous land vehicle. In *Proc. IEEE/RSJ IROS*, vol. 2, pp. 690–696, Grenoble, France, 1997.

[244] H. P. Moravec. Towards automatic visual obstacle avoidance. In *Proc. 5th International Joint Conf. on Artificial Intelligence (IJCAI)*, p. 584, Cambridge, MA, 1977, AAAI Press, Menlo Park, CA.

[245] H. P. Moravec. *Obstacle avoidance and navigation in the real world by a seeing robot rover*.

Ph.D. thesis, Stanford University, 1980. published as *Robot Rover Visual Navigation*, Ann Arbor, MI: UMI Research Press, 1981.

[246] H. P. Moravec. The Stanford Cart and the CMU Rover. *IEEE*, 71(7):872–884, 1983.

[247] H. P. Moravec. Three degrees for a mobile robot. In *Proc. ASME on Advanced Automation: 1984 and Beyond*, vol. 1, pp. 274–278, 1984.

[248] H. P. Moravec and A. Elfis. High-resolution maps from wide angle sonar. In *Proc. IEEE Int. Conf. on Robotics and Automation*, pp. 116–121, 1985.

[249] R. S. Mosher. Test and evaluation of a versatile walking truck. In *Proc. of the Off-Road Mobility Res. Symp. Int. Soc. Terrain Vehicle Systems*, pp. 359–379, Washington, DC, 1968.

[250] D. W. Murphy and J. P. Bott. The air mobile ground security and surveillance system (AMGSSS). In *Unmanned Systems*, 1995.

[251] D. Murray, F. Du, P. McLauchlan, I. Reed, P. Sharkey, and M. Brady. Design of stereo heads. In A. Blake and A. Yuille (eds.), *Active Vision*, pp. 155–174. MIT Press, Cambridge, MA, 1992.

[252] D. Murray and J. Little. Using real-time stereo vision for mobile robot navigation. In *Workshop on Perception for Mobile Agents*, pp. 19–27. IEEE/CVPR, Santa Barbara, CA, 1998.

[253] D. J. Musliner, E. H. Durfee, and K. G. Shin. CIRA: A cooperative intelligent real-time control architecture. *IEEE Trans. on SMC*, 23(6), 1993.

[254] E. Muybridge. *The Human Figure in Motion*. Dover Publications, Inc., New York, 1955 (first published in 1901).

[255] E. Muybridge. *Animals in Motion*. Dover Publications, Inc., New York, 1957 (first published in 1899).

[256] H.-H. Nagel. Displacement vectors derived from second-order intensity variations in image sequences. Technical Report 97, Department of Computer Science, University of Hamburg, Germany, 1982.

[257] R. Nakajima, T. Tsubouchi, S. Yuta, and E. Koyanagi. A development of a new mechanism of an autonomous unicycle. In *IEEE/RSJ IROS*, vol. 2, pp. 906–912, Grenoble, France, 1997.

[258] Y. Nakamura and R. Mukherjee. Nonholonomic path planning of space robots via bi-directional approach. In *IEEE Trans. Robotics and Automation*, vol 7. No. 4, pp. 500–514, 1991.

[259] V. S. Nalwa. *A Guided Tour of Computer Vision*. Addison–Wesley, Reading, MA, 1993.

[260] F. Nashashibi and M. Devy. 3d incremental modeling and robot localization in a structured environment using a laser range finder. In *Proc. IEEE International Conf. on Robotics and Automation*, pp. 20–27, Atlanta GA, May 1993. IEEE Computer Society Press.

[261] S. K. Nayar, H. Murase, and S. A. Nene. Learning, positioning, and tracking visual appearance. In E. Straub and R. S. Sipple (eds.), *Proc. Int. Conf. Robotics and Automation. Volume 4*, pp. 3237–3244, Los Alamitos, CA, 1994.

[262] B. Nickerson, P. Jasiobedzki, D. Wilkes, M. Jenkin, E. Milios, J. Tsotsos, A. Jepson, and O. N. Bains. Autonomous robots for known industrial environments. *Robotics and Autonomous Systems*, vol. 25, 83–104, 1998.

[263] B. Nickerson, M. Jenkin, E. Milios, B. Down, P. Jasiobedzki, J. Tsotsos, N. Bains, and K. Tran. ARK - autonomous navigation of a mobile robot in a known environment. In *Proc. Int. Conf. Intelligent Autonomous Systems: IAS-3*, pp. 288–296, Pittsburgh, PA, 1993.

[264] S. B. Nickerson, M. Jenkin, E. Milios, B. Down, P. Jasiobedzki, A. Jepson, D. Terzopoulos, J. Tsotsos, D. Wilkes, N. Bains, and K. Tran. Design of ARK, a sensor-based mobile robot for industrial environments. In *Proc. Intelligent Vehicles 1993*, pp. 252–257, Tokyo, 1993.

[265] J. Nicoud. Mines Advisory Group. Report to the UN Int. Meeting on Mines Clearance, 1995.

[266] J. D. Nicoud and P. Mächler. Pemex-B: A low-cost robot for searching anti-personnel mines. In *Workshop on anti-personnel mine detection and removal (WAPM)*, Swiss Federal Institute of Technology Microprocessors and Interfaces Laboratory, Switzerland, 1995.

[267] N. Nilsson. A mobile automaton: An application of artificial intelligence techniques. In *Proc. IJCAI, 1969*. Reprinted in *Autonomous Mobile Robots: Control, Planning and Architecture*. vol. 2, 233-239.

[268] N. J. Nilsson. *Principles of Artificial Intelligence*. Tioga Publishing Co., Palo Alto, CA, 1980.

[269] E. Nitz and R. C. Arkin. Communication of behavioral state in multiagent retrieval tasks. In *IEEE Trans. Robotics and Automation*, Atlanta, GA, 1993.

[270] The NOMAD 200: Merging mind and motion. Undated product sheet, Nomadic Technologies.

[271] C. Ó'Dúnlaing and C. K. Yap. A retraction method for planning the motion of a disc. *J. Algorithms*, 6:104–111, 1982. Reprinted in J. T. Schwartz, M. Sharir, and J. Hopcroft (eds.), *Algorithmic and Geometric Aspects of Robotics*, pp. 187–192, Lawrence Erlbaum Associates, Hillsdale, NJ, 1987.

[272] T. Öfer. Routemark-based navigation of a wheelchair. In *Proc. 3rd ECPD*, pp. 333–338, Bremen, Germany, 1997.

[273] A. V. Oppenheim and R. Schafer. *Digital Signal Processing*. Prentice-Hall Inc., Englewood Cliffs, NJ, 1975.

[274] Oto Melara: R.2.5.robotized system. Undated product sheet, OTOBREDA.

[275] M. Otte and H.-H. Nagel. Optical flow estimation: Advances and comparisons. In *Proc. ECCV*, vol. 1, pp. 51–60, Stockholm, 1994.

[276] W. Paetsch and E. Schmidt. ASR: Advanced Servicing Robot Project. In *Proc. 3rd ECPD*, pp. 460–466, Bremen, Germany, 1997.

[277] K. Pahlavan and J.-O. Eklundh. Heads, eyes and head-eye systems. In *Active Robot Vision: Camera Heads, Model Based Navigation and Reactive Control*, pp. 33–50. World Scientific Press, Singapore, 1993.

[278] P. K. Pal and A. Kar. Mobile robot navigation using a neural net. In *Proc. IEEE Conf. Robotics and Automation*, pp. 1503–1508, Nagoya, Japan, 1995.

[279] U. Palmquist. Intelligent cruise control: A key component towards improved traffic flow control. In *Proc. Intelligent Vehicles '93*, pp. 56–59, 1993.

[280] C. Papadimitriou and M. Yannakakis. Shortest paths without a map. *Theoretical Computer Science*, 84:127–150, 1991.

[281] E. Papadopoulos. Nonholonomic behaviour in free-floating space manipulators and its utilization. In Z. Li and J. F. Canny (eds.), *Nonholonomic Motion Planning*, pp. 423–445. Kluwer Academic Publishers, Boston, MA, 1993.

[282] E. Papadopoulos and S. Dubowsky. Failure recovery control for space robotic systems. In *Proc. American Control Conf.*, pp. 1485–1490, Boston, MA, 1991.

[283] E. Papadopoulos and S. Dubowsky. Dynamic singularities in the control of free-floating space manipulators. *ASME J. Dynamic Systems, Measurement and Control*, 115(1):44–52, 1993.

[284] E. Papadopoulos and S. A. A. Moosavian. Dynamics and control of space free-flyers with multiple manipulators. *J. Advanced Robotics, Robotics Society of Japan*, 9(6):603–624, 1995. Special Issue on Space Robotics.

[285] F. Pardo and E. Martinuzzi. Hardware environment for a retinal CCD visual sensor. In *EU-HCM SMART Workshop: Semi-autonomous Monitoring and Robotics Technologies*, Ispra, Italy, 1994.

[286] I. Park and J. R. Kender. Topological direction-giving and visual navigation in large environments. *Artificial Intelligence*, 78(1–2):355–395, 1995.

[287] J. R. Parker. *Algorithms for Image Processing and Computer Vision*. John Wiley and Sons, New York, 1997.

[288] L. E. Parker. Designing control laws for cooperative agent teams. In *IEEE Trans. Robotics and Automation*, vol. 3, pp. 582–587, Atlanta, GA, 1993.

[289] L. E. Parker. The effect of action recognition and robot awareness in cooperative robotic teams. In *Proc. IEEE/RSJ IROS*, vol. 1, pp. 212–219, Pittsburgh, PA, 1995.

[290] L. E. Parker. ALLIANCE: An architecture for fault tolerant multirobot cooperation. *IEEE Trans. Robotics and Automation*, 14(2):220–240, 1998.

[291] T. Pavlidis. *Structural Pattern Recognition*. Springer-Verlag, New York, 1977.

[292] D. Payton. An architecture for reflective autonomous vehicle control. In *IEEE Trans. Robotics and Automation*, pp. 1838–1845, 1986.

[293] D. W. Payton, K. Rosenblatt, and D. M. Keirsey. Plan guided reaction. *IEEE Trans. Sys. Man and Cyber.*, pp. 1370–1382, 1990.

[294] J. Peng and S. Cameron. Task planning. In S. Cameron and P. Probert, (eds.), *Advanced Guided Vehicles*, pp. 205–225. World Scientific Press, Singapore, 1994.

[295] A. Pentland. Perceptual organization and the representation of natural form. *Artificial Intelligence*, 28:293–331, 1986.

[296] M. A. Perkowski and K. Stanton. Robotics for the handicapped. *Northcon Conference Record*, pp. 278–284, 1991.

[297] W. Pfeffer. Lokomotorische Richtungsbewegungen durch chemische Reize. Leipzig, 1881–1888.

[298] A. Piché and P. Gaultier. Mining automation technology – The first frontier. *CIM Bulletin*, 89:51–54, 1996.

[299] K. K. Pingle. Visual perception by a computer. In A. Grasselli, (ed.), *Automatic Interpretation and Classification of Images*. Academic Press, New York, 1969.

[300] T. Poggio, V. Torre, and C. Koch. Computational vision regularization theory. *Nature*, 317:314–319, 1985. Reprinted in M. Fischler and O. Firschein (eds.), *Readings in Computer Vision: Issues, Problems, Principles and Paradigms*, Morgan Kaufmann, Los Altos, CA, 1987.

[301] D. A. Pomerleau. *Neural Network Perception for Mobile Robot Guidance.* Ph.D. thesis, Carnegie Mellon University, 1992.

[302] D. A. Pomerleau. Neural networks for intelligent vehicles. In *Proc. Intelligent Vehicles*, pp. 19–24, Tokyo, 1993.

[303] D. Poussart, M. Tremblay, and A. Djemouiaia. VLSI implementation of focal plane processing for smart vision sensing. In R. Plamondon and H. Cheng (eds.), *Pattern Recognition: Architectures, Algorithms and Applications*, pp. 5–23, World Scientific Publishing Co., Singapore 1991.

[304] W. H. Press, S. A. Teukolsky, and W. T. Vetterling. *Numerical Recipes in C. 2nd ed.* Cambridge University Press, New York, 1993.

[305] J. M. S. Prewitt. Object enhancement and extraction. In B. S. Lipkin and A. Rosenfeld (eds.), *Picture Processing and Psychopictorics*. Academic Press, New York, 1970.

[306] A: Price. *Pictorial History of the Luftwaffe: 1939-1945*. ARCO Publishing, New York, 1969.

[307] L. Priese, V. Rehrmann, R. Schian, R. Lakmann, and L. Bilderkennen. Traffic sign recognition based on color image evaluation. In *Proc. Intelligent Vehicles '93*, pp. 95–100, 1993.

[308] D. Pugh, E. Ribble, V. Vohnout, T. Bihari, T. Walliser, M. Patterson, and K. Waldron. Technical description of the adaptive suspension vehicle. *Int. J. Robotics Research*, 9(2):24–42, 1990.

[309] T. P. Quinn. Evidence for celestial and magnetic compass orientation in lake migrating sockeye salmon fry. *J. Comp. Physiol.*, 137, 1981.

[310] C. Rafflin and A. Fournier. Learning with a friendly interactive robot for service tasks in hospital environments. *Autonomous Robots*, 3:399–414, 1996.

[311] M. H. Raibert. Running with symmetry. *Int. J. Robotics Research*, 5(4), 1986. Reprinted in I. Cox and G. Wilfong (eds.), *Autonomous Robot Vehicles*, pp. 45–61, Springer-Verlag, New York, 1990.

[312] M. H. Raibert. Legged robots. In P. H. Winston and S. A. Shellard (eds.), *Artificial Intelligence at MIT Expanding Frontiers*, pp. 149–179. MIT Press, Cambridge, MA, 1990.

[313] M. H. Raibert, H. B. Brown, Jr., and M. Chepponis. Experiments in balance with a 3D one-legged hopping machine. *Int. J. Robotics Res.*, 3:75–92, 1984.

[314] M. H. Raibert, M. Chepponis, and H. B. Brown, Jr. Running on four legs as though they were one. *IEEE Trans. Robotics and Automation*, 2:70–82, 1986.

[315] RWI B12, Interfacing your ideas with the real world. Undated RWI B12 product sheet, Real World Interface, Inc.

[316] D. B. Reister. A new wheel control system for the omnidirectional Hermies III robot. In *Proc. IEEE Int. Conf. Robotics and Automation*, pp. 2322–2327, Sacramento, CA, 1991.

[317] REMOTEC ANDROS MARK V-A. Undated product sheet, REMOTEC, Inc.

[318] E. Rimon and D. E. Koditschek. Exact robot navigation using artificial potential functions. *IEEE Trans. Robotics and Automation*, 8(5):501–518, 1992.

[319] L. G. Roberts. Machine perception of three-dimensional solids. In J. T. Tippett, D. A. Berkowitz, L. Clapp, C. J. Koester, and A. Vanderburgh, Jr. (eds.), *Optical and Electro-Optical Information Processing*. MIT Press, Cambridge, MA, 1965.

[320] M. Robinson and M. Jenkin. Reactive control of a mobile robot. In C. Archibald and P. Kwok (eds.), *Research in Computer and Robot Vision*, pp. 55–70. World Scientific Press, Singapore, 1995.

[321] Mobile Robots Robotized Vehicles. Undated product sheet, Robotsoft.

[322] B. Rochwerger, C. L. Fennema, B. Draper, A. R. Hanson, and E. M. Riseman. Executing reactive behavior for autonomous navigator. Technical Report CMPSCI TR94-05, Department of Computer Science, University of Massachusetts at Amherst, 1994.

[323] M. E. Rosheim. In the footsteps of Leonardo. *IEEE Robotics & Automation Magazine*, 4(2):12–14, 1997.

[324] N. Roy and G. Dudek. Learning to rendezvous during multi-agent exploration. In *Proc. 6th European Workshop on Learning Robots*, Brighton, England, 1997.

[325] D. Rus, B. Donald, and J. Jennings. Moving furniture with teams of autonomous robots. In *Proc. IEEE/RSJ IROS*, vol. 1, pp. 235–242, Pittsburgh, PA, 1995.

[326] H. Samet. Region representation: Quadtrees from boundary codes. *Comm. ACM*, 23(2):163–170, 1980.

[327] F. Sandt and L. H. Pampagnin. Distributed planning and hierarchical control for a service mobile robot. In *Int. Symp. Intelligent Robotic Systems (IRS'94)*, Grenoble, France, 1994.

[328] T. D. Sanger. Stereo disparity computation using Gabor filters. *Biol. Cybern.*, 59:405–418, 1988.

[329] A. Scheuer and Th. Fraichard. Continuous-curvature path planning for car-like vehicles. In *IEEE/RSJ IROS*, vol. 2, pp. 997–1003, Grenoble, France, 1997.

[330] K. Schilling and J. de Lafonatine. Autonomy capabilities of European deep space probes. *Autonomous Robots*, 3:19–30, 1996.

[331] J. T. Schwartz and M. Sharir. On the piano movers problem. II General techniques for computing topological properties of real algebraic manifolds. *Advances in Applied Mathematics*, 4:298–351, 1983.

[332] L. S. Shapiro. *Affine Analysis of Image Sequences*. Cambridge University Press, Cambridge, UK, 1995.

[333] J. Shen and S. Castan. An optimal linear operator step edge detection. *CVGIP: GU*, 54(2):112–133, 1992.

[334] R. Sim and G. Dudek. Position estimation using principal components of range data. In *Proc. IEEE/RSJ IROS*, Victoria, BC, Canada, 3:1060–1065, 1998.

[335] R. Simmons, R. Goodwin, C. Fedor, and J. Basista. *Task Control Architecture*. Carnegie Mellon University, School of Computer Science/Robotics Institute, 1997. Programmer's Guide to Version 8.0.

[336] R. C. Simpson and S. P. Levine. Adaptive shared control of a smart wheelchair operated by voice commands. In *Proc. IEEE/RSJ IROS*, vol. 2, pp. 622–626, Grenoble, France, 1997.

[337] S.-M. Song and K. J. Waldron. *Machines that Walk: The Adaptive Suspension Vehicle*. MIT Press, Cambridge, MA, 1989.

[338] H. Sorenson. Least squares estimation: From Gauss to Kalman. *IEEE Spectrum*, pp. 63–68, June 1970.

[339] B. Stanley and L. McKerrow. Measuring range and bearing with a binaural ultrasonic sensor. In *Proc. IEEE/RSJ IROS*, vol. 2, pp. 565–571, Grenoble, France, 1997.

[340] B. Steckemetz, F. Spuida, and H. Michalik. Autonomous gliding parachute landing system. In *ECPD Int. Conf. Advanced Robotics, Intelligent Automation and Active Systems*, p. 429, Bremen, Germany, 1997. Paper is not available in the proceedings.

[341] B. Steer, J. Kloske, P. Garner, L. LeBlanc, and S. Schock. Towards sonar based perception and modelling for unmanned untethered underwater vehicles. In *Proc. IEEE Int. Conf. Robotics and Automation*, vol. 2, pp. 112–116, Atlanta, GA, 1993.

[342] D. G. Stork (ed.). *HAL's Legacy: 2001's Computer as Dream and Reality*. MIT Press, Cambridge, MA, 1997.

[343] K. Sugihara. Some location properties for robot navigation using a single camera. *Computer Vision, Graphics and Image Processing*, 42:112–129, 1988.

[344] K. T. Sutherland and W. B. Thompson. Inexact navigation. *Proc. 1993 IEEE Int. Conf. Robotics and Automation*, vol. 1, pp. 1–7, Atlanta, GA, 1993.

[345] K. T. Sutherland and W. B. Thompson. Pursuing projections: Keeping a robot on path. *Proc. Int. Conf. Robotics and Automation*, vol. 4, pp. 3355–3361, Los Alamitos, CA, 1994.

[346] M. J. Swain and D. H. Ballard. Color indexing. *Int. J. Comp. Vis.*, 7(1):11–32, 1991.

[347] R. Taggert. *Marine Principles and Evolution*. Gulf Publishing Co., 1969.

[348] O. Takahashi and R. J. Schillinger. Motion planning in a plane using generalized Voronoi diagrams. *IEEE Trans. Robotics Automation*, 5(2):143–150, 1989.

[349] R. Talluri and J. K. Aggarwal. Position estimation techniques for an autonomous mobile robot – A review. In C. H. Chen, L. F. Pau, and P. Wong, (eds.), *The Handbook of Pattern Recognition and Computer Vision*, pp. 769–801. World Scientific Press, Singapore, 1993.

[350] R. Talluri and J. K. Aggarwal. Mobile robot self-location using model-image feature correspondence. *IEEE Trans. Robotics and Automation*, 12(1):63–77, 1996.

[351] K. Tam, J. Lloyd, Y. Lespérance, H. Levesque, F. Lin, D. Marcu, R. Reiter, and M. Jenkin. Controlling autonomous robots with Golog. Submitted for publication, 1999.

[352] A. M. Thompson. The navigation system of the JPL robot. In *Proc. 5th IJCAI*, 1977, AAAI Press, Menlo Park, CA.

[353] C. Thorpe. Mixed traffic and automated highways. In *Proc. IEEE/RSJ IROS*, pp. 1011–1017, Grenoble, France, 1997.

[354] C. E. Thorpe. An analysis of interest operators for FIDO. In *Proc. Workshop on Computer Vision: Representation and Control*, Annapolis, MD, 1984.

[355] Charles E. Thorpe (ed.) *Vision and Navigation: The Carnegie Mellon Navlab*. Kluwer Academic Publisher, Boston, MA, 1990.

[356] N. Thrun. Finding landmarks for mobile robot navigation. In *Proc. IEEE Int. Conf. Robotics and Automation*, pp. 958–963, Leuven, Belgium, May 1998.

[357] A. N. Tikhonov and V. Y. Arsenin. *Solutions of Ill-Posed Problems*. Winston, Washington, DC, 1977.

[358] N. Tinbergen. *The Study of Instinct*. Oxford University Press, Oxford, 1951. Reprinted in 1989.

[359] A. Torige, S. Yagi, H. Makino, T. Yegami, and N. I. Wa. Centipede type walking robot (CWR-2). In *IEEE/RSJ IROS*, pp. 402–407, Grenoble, France, 1997.

[360] TRC LABMATE: Autonomous Mobile Robot Base. Undated product sheet, Transitions Research Corporation.

[361] J. K. Tsotsos. Intelligent control for perceptually attentive agents: The S* proposal. *Robotics and Autonomous Systems*, 21:5–21, 1997.

[362] J. K. Tsotsos, S. Dickinson, M. Jenkin, E. Milios, A. Jepson, B. Down, E. Amdur, S. Stevenson, M. Black, D. Metaxas, J. Cooperstock, S. Culhane, F. Nuflo, G. Verghese, W. Wai, D. Wilkes, and Y. Ye. The playbot project. In *Proc. IJCAI Workshop on AI Applications for Disabled People*, Montreal, 1995.

[363] M. Turk and A. Pentland. Eigenfaces for recognition. *J. Cognitive Neuroscience*, 3(1):71–86, 1991.

[364] M. A. Turk, D. G. Morgenthaler, K. D. Gremban, and M. Marra. VITS – A vision system for autonomous land vehicle navigation. *IEEE Trans. Pattern Analysis and Machine Intelligence*, 10(3):342–361, 1988.

[365] C. W. Tyler. The horoptor and binocular fusion. In D. Regan (ed.), *Binocular Vision*, pp. 19–37. CRC Press, Boca Raton, FL, 1991.

[366] T. Ueyama, T. Fukuda, and F. Arai. Configuration of communication structure for distributed intelligent robot system. In *IEEE Trans. Robotics and Automation*, pp. 807–812, 1992.

[367] S. Ullman. *The Interpretation of Visual Motion*. MIT Press, Cambridge, MA, 1979.

[368] I. Ulrich and J. Borenstein. VFH+: Reliable Obstacle Avoidance for Fast Mobile Robots. In *Proc. IEEE Conf. Robotics and Automation*, pp. 1572–1577, Leuven, Belgium, 1998.

[369] S. E. Umbaugh. *Computer Vision and Image Processing: A practical approach Using CVIPtools*. Prentice-Hall, Inc., Upper Saddle River, NJ, 1998.

[370] J. van der Spiegel, G. Kreider, C. Claeys, I. Debusschere, G. Sandini, P. Dario, F. Fantini, P. Belluti, and G. Soncini. A foveated retina-like sensor using CCD technology. In C. Mead and M. Ismail (eds.), *Analog VLSI Implementation of Neural Systems*, pp. 189–212. Kluwer Academic Publishers, Boston, MA, 1989. Proceedings of the Workshop on Analog Integrated Neural Systems.

[371] P. van Turennout, G. Honderd, and L. J. van Schelven. Wall-following control of a mobile

robot. In *Proc. IEEE Int. Conf. on Robotics and Automation*, vol. 1, pp. 280–285, Nice, France, 1992.

[372] G. Velez and H. Thomas. Requirements for robotics in explosive ordinance disposal operations in tropical and desert areas. In *Workshop on Anti-Personnel Mine Detection and Removal (WAPM)*, Swiss Federal Institute of Technology Microprocessors and Interfaces Laboratory, Switzerland, 1995.

[373] H. Wakaumi, K. Nakamura, and T. Matsumura. Development of an Automated Wheelchair Guided by a Magnetic Ferrite Marker Lane. *J. Rehab. Res. Dev.*, 29:27–34, 1992.

[374] W. G. Walter. *The Living Brain*. Duckworth, London, 1953.

[375] J. Wang and W. J. Wilson. 3D relative position and orientation estimation using Kalman filter for robot control. In *IEEE Int. Conf. on Robotics and Automation*, pp. 2638–2645, Nice, France, 1992.

[376] L.-B. Wee, M. Walker, and N. H. McClamroch. An articulated-body model for a free-flying robot and its use for adapative motion control. *IEEE Trans. Robotics and Automation*, 13(2):264–277, 1997.

[377] P. Werbos. *Beyond Regression: New Tools for Prediction and Analysis in the Behavioral Sciences*. Ph.D. thesis, Harvard, Cambridge, MA, 1974.

[378] D. Wettergreen, H. Pangels, and J. Bares. Behavior-based gait execution for the Dante II walking robot. In *Proc. IEEE/RSJ IROS*, vol. 3, pp. 274–279, 1995.

[379] D. Wettergreen, C. Thorpe, and W. Whittaker. *Exploring Mount Erebus by walking robot*. In *Proc. IAS-3*, pp. 72–81, Pittsburgh, PA, 1993.

[380] D. Wilkes, G. Dudek, M. Jenkin, and E. Milios. Modelling sonar range sensors. In C. Archibald and E. Petriu (eds.), *Advances in Machine Vision: Strategies and Applications*, pp. 361–370. World Scientific Press, Singapore, 1992.

[381] P. H. Winston. *Artificial Intelligence, 2nd ed.* Addison-Wesley, Reading, MA, 1984.

[382] A. Witkin, D. Terzopoulos, and M. Kass. Signal matching through scale space. In *Proc. 5th Nat. Conf. Artif. Intel.*, pp. 714–719, Philadelphia, PA, 1986.

[383] A. P. Witkin. Scale-space filtering. In *Proc. IJCAI-83*, pp. 1019–1022, Karlsruhe, Germany, 1983.

[384] Y. Yagi, S. Kawato, and S. Tsuji. Real-time omnidirectional image sensor (COPIS) for vision-guided navigation. *IEEE Trans. Robotics Automation*, 10:1–12, 1994.

[385] Y. Yagi, Y. Nishizawa, and M. Yachida. Map-based navigation for a mobile robot with omni-directional image sensor COPIS. *IEEE Trans. Robotics Automation*, 11:634–648, 1995.

[386] H. Yanco, A. Hazel, A. Peacock, S. Smith, and H. Wintermute. Initial report on Wheelesley: A robotic wheelchair system. In *IJCAI Workshop on Developing AI Applications for the Disabled*, Montreal, Canada, 1995.

[387] D. R. Yoerger, A. M. Bradley, and B. Walden. System testing of the autonomous benthic explorer. In *Mobile Robots for Subsea Environments*, pp. 2–6, Monterey, CA, 1994.

[388] A. L. Yuille and T. A. Poggio. Scaling theorems for zero crossings. *IEEE Trans. Pattern Analysis and Machine Intelligence*, pp. 15–25, 1986.

[389] S. Yuta and S. Premvuti. Coordinating autonomous and centralized decision making to achieve cooperative behaviors between multiple mobile robots. In *Proc. IEEE/RSJ IROS*, pp. 1566–1574, Raleigh, NC, 1992.

[390] A. Zelinsky and S. Yuta. Reactive planning for mobile robots using numeric potential fields. In *Proc. IAS-3*, pp. 84–93, Pittsburgh, PA, 1993.

[391] G.-W. Zhao and S. Yuta. Obstacle detection by vision system for an autonomous vehicle. In *Proc. IAS-3*, pp. 31–36, Pittsburgh, PA, 1993.

[392] S. Zilberstein. Resource-bounded sensing and planning in autonomous systems. *Autonomous Robots*, 3(4):31–48, 1996.

[393] J. Zurada. *Introduction to Artificial Neural Systems*. West Publishing Company, New York, 1992.

Index